Jesus as Torah in John 1–12

Jesus as Torah in John 1–12

Dan Lioy

WIPF & STOCK · Eugene, Oregon

JESUS AS TORAH IN JOHN 1–12

Copyright © 2007 Dan Lioy. All rights reserved. Except for brief quotations in critical publications or reviews, no part of this book may be reproduced in any manner without prior written permission from the publisher. Write: Permissions, Wipf and Stock, 199 W. 8th Ave., Eugene, OR 97401.

ISBN 13: 978-1-55635-475-5

Manufactured in the U.S.A.

Unless otherwise noted, Scripture quotations are taken from the Holy Bible, Today's New International Version™ TNIV®. Copyright © 2001, 2005 by International Bible Society®. All rights reserved worldwide. Used by permission.

Scripture quotations marked KJV are taken from the King James Version. Copyright © 2000, by Holman Bible Publishers. Used by permission. All rights reserved.

Scripture quotations marked NAB are taken from the New American Bible. Copyright © 1995, by Confraternity of Christian Doctrine (CCD), Washington, D.C. Used by permission. All rights reserved.

Scripture quotations marked NET are taken from the New English Translation. Copyright © 1996–2005, by Biblical Studies Press. Used by permission. All rights reserved.

Scripture quotations marked NKJV are taken from the New King James Version. Copyright © 1979, 1980, 1982, by Thomas Nelson, Inc. Used by permission. All rights reserved.

Scripture quotations marked NLT are taken from the Holy Bible, New Living Translation, copyright © 1996, 2004. Used by permission of Tyndale House Publishers, Inc., Wheaton, Illinois 60189. All rights reserved.

Scripture quotations marked NRSV are taken from the New Revised Standard Version Bible, copyright © 1989, by the Division of Christian Education of the National Council of the Churches of Christ in the United States of America. Used by permission. All rights reserved.

Chapter 2 of this work is a modified and augmented form of a journal article by the same title appearing in *Conspectus* (Vol. 3, March 2007) and is reprinted with permission of the South African Theological Seminary. All rights reserved worldwide.

Portions of chapter 4 of this work are a modified and augmented form of a journal article, "Jesus as Torah in John 2:1–22," which appears in *Conspectus* (Vol. 4, September 2007) and is reprinted with permission of the South African Theological Seminary. All rights reserved worldwide.

To my dear wife, Marcia, for her love and companionship; and to my precious son, Joshua, for his affection and playfulness.

Contents

Preface | ix

1 The Framework and Intent of This Study / 1

2 The Moral Law in Christ-Centered Perspective / 19

3 Jesus as Torah in John 1 / 49

4 Jesus as Torah in John 2–4 / 75

5 Jesus as Torah in John 5–6 / 109

6 Jesus as Torah in John 7–9 / 137

7 Jesus as Torah in John 10–12 / 173

8 Affirming the Truth of Jesus as Torah / 209

Appendix: Making Sense of Reality:
A God-Centered and Christ-Centered View / 247

Bibliography | 257

Subject Index | 271

References Index | 277

Preface

A VARIETY of people have read portions of this book and offered kind and intelligent critique, most notably, Dr. Kevin Smith (the Vice-Principal of South African Theological Seminary), Dr. Lars Kierspel (the Chair of the Biblical Studies at Trinity Theological Seminary), and Rev. Stephen Lewis (the senior pastor of Evergreen Presbyterian Church). Others have attentively listened while I expounded on this idea or that theory related to the investigations undertaken in this study. I wish to express my thanks for their careful reading and comments both perceptive and constructive. Others, friends and travelers, have shared stimulating conversation over aspects of the concepts and arguments, and in ways unknown to themselves given encouragement and direction.

I especially want to express my love for and appreciation to my wife, Marcia. Without her encouragement, affection, and companionship, the long hours of writing would not have been possible. My son, Joshua, likewise remained patient and understanding during the manuscripting process. Finally, I am indebted to my other family members and friends for their prayers and support during this venture.

Dan Lioy
Salem, Oregon
June 2007

1

The Framework and Intent of This Study

Identifying Two Different Worldly Cultures

SPECIALISTS ACROSS a variety of disciplines have noted the prevalence in today's society of two different cultures. Entitlement characterizes the first, while merit is the credo of the second. According to Anderson, a culture of entitlement maintains that people "do not have to earn what they get."[1] Instead, they automatically "deserve what they get" and receive "what they want."[2] The foundation for this claim is the inherent worth of the person(s) or group, not what they have accomplished. There is an obsession with putting one's own needs first, feeling good about oneself, and being happy.[3] People also tend to devalue what they have and demand more things (for instance, possessions, privileges, and so on). Olson notes, "Personal desires and aspirations seem to trump any concern for the greater good."[4]

This mindset is exemplified in the contemporary prosperity gospel movement; and Joel Osteen is perhaps its best known spokesperson today within American evangelicalism. Jason Byassee points out that Osteen's message is a continuation of what others before him have taught (such as Russell Conwell, Norman Vincent Peale, and Bruce Wilkinson): "just improve your attitude, keep your chin up, and God's blessings will rain down on you."[5] Osteen urges people to "enlarge their vision" about the "good things" God supposedly wants to do for them and "expect people to go out of their way" to offer help. Osteen asserts that when people think "upbeat, self-confident" thoughts about themselves and "speak words of victory" over dire situations, happiness and abundance will result. In

1. Anderson, "Changing a culture of entitlement."
2. Cf. Irvine, "Young workers"; Salerno, *Sham*, 4.
3. Twenge, *Generation me*, 10.
4. Olson, "The importance of protocol."
5. Byassee, "Be happy," 20–23; cf. Salerno, *Sham*, 8.

short, this message is a "pagan gospel of acquisition," "self-help," and "self-improvement."

A culture of merit takes an entirely different approach to life. Those among the "talented" are "chosen and moved ahead on the basis of their achievement."[6] Expressed differently, social positions of prestige and responsibility have to be earned, and competence is demonstrated against the backdrop of fierce competition. Individuals, in their "relentless pursuit of perfection," strive "to chart their own courses," "master their destinies," and "make themselves over."[7] Anderson notes that in a predominantly merit-based culture, those who are "strongest" are "fully supported," while those deemed to be the "weakest" are "weeded out."[8] The basis for such a determination is whether people succeed or fail to "meet performance standards." There is peer pressure to "produce results" and hostility toward "mediocrity."

This mindset pervades spiritual traditions that consider "rituals, sacraments, and liturgical prayers" as a means of salvation and sanctification.[9] One example of this from the past would be the religious elite of the first century AD. They believed that righteousness (or living in conformity to God's perfect ethical standard)[10] was attained by meticulously heeding the Mosaic law (cf. Rom 9:31).[11] Despite their enthusiasm for God, their zeal was misdirected, being based on human merit rather than divine grace (cf. 10:2–3). Paul, before his conversion, exemplified this way of life. Like the most admired of his peers, his credentials were laudatory. He was a pure-blooded Hebrew, a member of the Pharisees (undoubtedly, the most pious religious group of the day), an ardent observer of the law, and even a persecutor of Jesus' followers (Phil 3:5–6). Paul and other members of the religious elite were so smug about their ability to earn God's favor that they disdained those who failed to achieve their self-imposed benchmarks of piety (cf. Luke 18:9–14). Those entrapped by this arrogant outlook publicly performed such good deeds as charitable giving, praying, and fasting to win the admiration of others (cf. Matt 6:1–18).

---

6. Mish, "Meritocracy."

7. McGee, *Self-help*, 12, 145.

8. Anderson, "Changing a culture of entitlement."

9. Blunt, "Marginalized again."

10. Cf. chapter 2 of this study for a discussion of the paradigm known as the "new perspective" on Paul (or NPP), especially as it relates to the issue of righteousness.

11. Stern (*Jewish New Testament commentary*, 168) clarifies that the Torah "opposes legalism and the mere performance of acts and routines without true, spiritual involvement."

The Framework and Intent of This Study

Embracing an Attitude of Humility

Both a culture of entitlement ("it's all about me") and a culture of merit ("you only get what you earn") embody a religion of self in which people believe they are the measure of all things. Like other forms of humanism, it is an "attitude or way of life centered on human interests or values."[12] When people insist they are complete within themselves, it leads to a rejection of virtually every truth-claim about God and His existence.[13] A God-centered ethical norm is jettisoned for a man-centered, materialistic one. Also, rather than look to Scripture for moral guidance, ethical standards are determined by one's own feelings and experience.[14]

Society might regard those who advocate these views as being worldly wise (or "street smart"); but when people make themselves, rather than God, the center of their existence, they remain ignorant of the true nature of the divine kingdom. Their lives propagate such vices as bitterness, envy, and selfish ambition. The trail of deceit and strife they leave behind is nothing to boast about; in fact, their bragging and lying are used to cover up the truth (cf. Jas 3:14). Verse 15 spotlights the real source of worldly wisdom. The jealousy and selfishness it spawns originate from below, not "from heaven."[15] Verse 16 explains that where envy and selfish ambition are present, the natural result is confusion and a variety of immoral behaviors.

The solution is to replace all pagan doctrines of mind and behavior with an attitude of humility. In 1 Corinthians 1:26–30, Paul urged believers to consider the Lord Jesus to be the center of God's wisdom and power. With respect to the apostle's original readers, few if any of them were intellectually impressive or touted stellar educational credentials, at least according to the sophisticated society of the day; yet God had entrusted to the "foolish," the "weak," the "lowly," and the "despised" the most valuable message the world has ever known. The presence in the church of those who had no rank or standing completely negated what the world thought was important. In a brief but simple phrase, Paul explained God's purpose in allowing the foolish to understand and accept His message: "so

12. Mish, "Humanism."

13. Cf. the appendix of this study for a discussion of a God-centered and Christ-centered view of making sense of reality. Also, cf. Adler, "The new naysayers"; Tolson, "The new unbelievers"; Van Biema, "God vs. science."

14. Kinnaman, "A new generation"; cf. McGee, *Self-help*, 19–21; Salerno, *Sham*, 33–34; Twenge, *Generation me*, 160–61, 179.

15. Unless otherwise noted, all Scripture quotations are taken from *Today's New International Version* (hereafter abbreviated, TNIV).

that no one may boast before him" (v. 29). Through the message of the cross of Calvary, the Father showed conclusively that human beings can do nothing to earn salvation. All forms of entitlement and merit in the world could not result in anyone's deliverance. Righteousness, holiness, and redemption only come through faith in the Son (v. 30). Thus, no one has any right to boast about how he or she has earned God's favor (v. 31; cf. Jer 9:24).

Living in Humble Submission to the Lord

Both the Old and New Testaments lift up for consideration the lives of those who humbly made the Lord, not themselves, the sum total of their lives. Abraham is one noteworthy example. According to Isaiah 41:8, God considered the patriarch to be His friend. The discussion that went on between the two concerning the impending judgment of Sodom and Gomorrah confirms the closeness of their relationship (cf. Gen 18:16–33). God told Abraham what He was planning to do; and the patriarch interceded on behalf of the people of the plain. At one point in the exchange, Abraham noted how bold he had been to "speak to the Lord" (v. 27) and humbly referred to himself as being "nothing but dust and ashes" (cf. Job 30:19; 42:6). While such a view might be objectionable to modern sensibilities, it reflects a profound theological truth, namely, that God is the exalted Lord and sovereign Judge, while people exist as a humble part of His creation (cf. Gen 2:7).

Paul is another person of faith who exemplified an attitude of humility toward God. In 2 Corinthians 12:11, Paul claimed to be in no way inferior to a group of so-called "super-apostles." These individuals were nothing more than false messengers of the Lord Jesus who had infiltrated the church at Corinth. Though Paul defended his rights as an apostle, he also referred to himself as "nothing." By doing so, he might have been citing one of his rivals' charges against him. If so, he used it to affirm that his apostolic calling and empowerment came from God. Paul was neither entitled to nor merited such an appointment to ministry. Indeed, compared to the all-glorious Lord, the apostle (along with the rest of humanity) was nothing. Appropriately, then, God's grace to Paul meant everything.

The statements John the Baptizer made about himself disclose a similar attitude of humility (cf. John 3:22–35). Sometime after Jesus' conversation with Nicodemus, the Savior continued His ministry in the countryside of Judea. John was still baptizing people at Aenon near Salim, which suggests there was an overlap between the two ministries until Herod the

The Framework and Intent of This Study

Great imprisoned John. Some of John's disciples approached him about an argument that arose between them and a Jewish inquirer over the issue of ceremonial purification. Nothing is said about their views, but the subject of baptism apparently had bothered John's disciples.

Not only were Jesus' disciples baptizing people as John's were, but people were leaving John's ministry and flocking to Jesus. Evidently, John's disciples were upset by the fact that their teacher was being upstaged by Jesus. The Baptizer could have easily expressed jealousy, hurt, and betrayal, especially as he saw his influence diminish and that of Jesus increase; but John knew his purpose, and he understood that this turn of events was the will of God. Even the concern of John's disciples did not shake his humility. In John 1:19–28, the Baptizer had already declared that he was not the Messiah, but the person whom God had sent ahead to testify to the Lord Jesus as the Redeemer.[16]

Once again at Aenon near Salim, John reaffirmed his subordinate position. He used the example of a bridegroom and an attendant to illustrate his relationship to Jesus. The Savior was the bridegroom and John was the best man (cf. 1 Macc 9:39). The bride—that is, God's people—belonged to the Messiah and not to the Baptizer. Indeed, John was overjoyed to know that many people were going to Jesus, just as the best man at a wedding was thrilled to see the bride when she appeared at the back of the sanctuary. In the Jewish culture of the day, the best man supervised many details of the wedding and was responsible for bringing the bridegroom and the bride together for the ceremony. In an analogous way, John had completed this task by preparing the hearts of the people, including those of his disciples, to meet and trust in the Lord Jesus.

John 1:30 records the same attitude of humility verbalized by Abraham and Paul. John declared it was of divine necessity that he had to become less important, while at the same time the Messiah had to increase in importance. The *New Living Translation* captures the essence of John's statement in this way: "[Jesus] must become greater and greater, and I must become less and less." The idea is that on the stage of life, there is only one person who has the lead role—the Messiah. All other characters play subordinate parts. Likewise, their place on the stage is entirely due to divine grace, not because they are entitled to be there or have earned the right to enjoy such a privilege.

At this point it is difficult to determine whether the words recorded in verses 31–36 are a continuance of the Baptizer's remarks to his disciples, a transposition of an earlier speech by Jesus, or another reflection by

16. Cf. chapter 3 of this study for a discussion of John 1:19–28.

John the apostle. In any case, this passage proclaims the supremacy of the Messiah by noting that Jesus' origin was from heaven. He was far superior to anyone on earth, including the Baptizer. Since Jesus was from heaven, He could testify firsthand to the truths He imparted, for He personally experienced these truths.

Regrettably, some refused to accept Jesus' testimony. In contrast, others demonstrated, by accepting the Messiah's witness, their conviction that what the Father declared about the Son was true. Accordingly, trusting in the Son is the same as believing that the Father is truthful. In this regard, the Son is not merely from heaven, but the one whom the Father sent to earth. Moreover, the Son is not merely one of many inspired messengers speaking what the Father declared. Instead, the Son is the divine, incarnate Torah, the very enfleshment of the Father's truth to the world (cf. 1:1, 14, 17–18; 5:45–47; 6:45–51; 7:16–19; 8:14–17, 31–32, 54–58; 10:25–30, 34–38; 14:6–7, 9–11).[17]

Though the three persons of the Godhead have their distinct functions, there is unity among them. John 3:34 makes this point when it says that the Father gives the Holy Spirit to the Son without measure. There were no restrictions upon the Son as He revealed the truth of God to the world, for the Son operated in the fullness of the Spirit. This extraordinary level of intimacy and affection has always characterized the relationship between the Father, Son, and Spirit. Indeed, the trust between the various persons of the Godhead is so great that the Father has placed everything into the hands of His Son.

The Lord Jesus has authority over all things in the same way that God reigns over all creation (v. 35). Appropriately, then, those who put their faith in the Messiah have eternal life. This is not something that begins in heaven, but rather it is given at the moment of conversion. With so much of everlasting importance centered in the Redeemer, it is understandable that those who reject the Son must constantly bear the weight of the Father's wrath (v. 36). Here we see a dividing line drawn between belief and unbelief, with the former being the only eternally viable option.

Recognizing Jesus as Torah in the Fourth Gospel

In the previous section, the Lord Jesus was referred to as the divine, incarnate Torah. Casselli helps establish the rationale for this designation[18] by

---

17. Cf. the following section for more information about the central importance of this meta-theme in the Fourth Gospel.

18. Presumably, some readers might decide against embracing the point of view put

noting that in the Fourth Gospel, the Evangelist presented the Messiah "in a way that is consistent with the Judaisms[19] of his day." The depiction one encounters is "profoundly Torah centered."[20] Furthermore, in keeping

---

forward here. That said, it is beyond the scope of the study to replicate the efforts of others—such as the specialists formally cited in this section—who have offered a detailed and rigorous explanation for the plausibility of the working hypothesis being adopted (in particular, cf. Beyler, *Torah*; Casselli, "Jesus as eschatological Torah"; Keener, *John*; Reed, "How Semitic was John"; Ratzinger, *Jesus of Nazareth*; Schoneveld, "A new reading"). Instead, the aim is to let the underlying notion of Jesus as Torah in the Fourth Gospel establish a philosophical frame of reference that guides the examination and analysis of the biblical text.

19. Beyler (*Torah*, 3) clarifies that the term "Judaism" denotes the "religion of the Jews after the fall of the kingdom of Judah in 586 BC." Hoppe ("Judaism," 501) adds that practitioners of Judaism "worshiped Yahweh, the national God of ancient Israel" and patterned their "behavior according to the Torah, which they believed to be the revelation of Yahweh's will for them." DeSilva (*Introduction*, 479) explains that the Jews adopted the term *Judaism* "in opposition to Hellenism." Put differently, the former "represents the Jewish way of life" that contrasts sharply with the "way of life of the Greeks." Devout adherents of the Torah maintained that the beliefs, practices, and institutions connected with their religion were being threatened by "Hellenizing Jewish elites," who imposed their pagan customs and values "on Jerusalem and Judea" (cf. 2 Macc 2:21; 4:13; 8:1; 14:38).

20. Casselli, "Jesus as eschatological Torah," 16. Admittedly, as Neusner (*Rabbinic literature*, 7–8, 10–11) explains, the references to the Torah in Jewish literature come from a variety of sources spanning a period of time that precedes, overlaps, and extends beyond the first century AD. Nonetheless, with respect to the later-occurring sources, some of these likely represented Jewish traditions that prevailed in the intertestamental period and during the lifetime of Jesus (cf. Beyler, *Torah*, 6–7). For example, Evans (*Word and glory*) states "there are instances where targumic readings, as well as interpretive traditions, have their roots in older traditions" (25). Also, "at several points Johannine biblical interpretation coheres with the exegesis preserved in the midrashim and the targumim" (113). Moreover, all "these bodies of writings are mutually illuminating at many points" (114). Evans thinks the "rabbinic and targumic sources" that postdate the Fourth Gospel "can be used, but careful qualification is required" (18). He puts forward the following criteria for consideration (italics are his): (1) "Is there external (as opposed to internal) evidence that the later source reflects traditions that probably existed in one form or another in the first century or earlier?" (i.e. "*antecedent documentation*"); (2) "Are there indications that the later source has been influenced by the New Testament (or the Fourth Gospel) itself? (i.e. "*contamination*"); (3) "Is it likely that the later document contains traditions that were part of the milieu of the New Testament writer or the traditions he utilized?" (i.e. "*provenance*"); and (4) "Is the parallel merely formal, perhaps even coincidental, or does it point to a genuine and meaningful relationship of language and conceptuality?" (i.e. "*coherence*"; 19). Evans maintains that when "the traditions contained in the rabbinic compendia" are "sifted and analyzed," a portion of the documents "can be shown to derive from the first century," while "much of it cannot" (20). Accordingly, taking the pertinent references to the Torah into consideration can help to establish the "cultural and religious context, at least broadly speaking, against which the Fourth Gospel should be understood" (113). Also, cf. Borchert, *John 1–11*, 63–64; Ridderbos, *John*, 112.

with the Evangelist's end-time theological perspective, he portrayed the Son as the "eschatological Torah." Put another way, Jesus of Nazareth is the "final realization of the Torah itself." In point of fact, the entire "scope of Jewish theology" is re-read "through the lens" of the Savior's "death, resurrection, and ascension."[21] Likewise, the "interpretive traditions" that form the historical and cultural backdrop of the Fourth Gospel must be viewed through the Torah-fulfillment prism of Jesus' redemptive mission.[22]

According to Keener, Jesus as the perfection of the gift of the Torah is a recurrent theme first introduced in John 1:1–18 and reiterated throughout the Fourth Gospel.[23] While there are other conceptions of God—including

---

21. Casselli, "Jesus as eschatological Torah," 17. Schoneveld ("A new reading," 80) adopts the broad meaning that the Torah refers to what God "revealed to Moses on Mount Sinai." Even so, Meir ("The historical Jesus," 55) clarifies that the "very concept of Torah, even the written Torah of Moses, was still in flux at the time of Jesus." In fact, during the first century of the Christian era, the "list of books accepted as Jewish Scripture was not yet definitively fixed and closed." Perhaps the presence of textual variants in the wording of the Torah was due in part to the efforts of the "Rabbinic sages" (Nuesner, *The perfect Torah*, xi) to produce "the most perfect of all possible Torahs" (xii). This "medium through which the one, unique God makes himself known" (ix) was regarded as being flawless with respect to its "legal system," its "theological structure," and its "media of expression and analysis" (xii). An examination of the Fourth Gospel indicates that Jesus of Nazareth is the one in whom all these aspects of the written and oral Torah are fully and finally realized (cf. Beyler, *Torah*, 199).

22. Casselli, "Jesus as eschatological Torah," 18. Based on Casselli's examination of the historical data, he postulates that there exists, "at least on the surface," an "early tradition in the Christian church that understood Jesus as *nomos* [Torah] in some sense" (23; cf. 1 Cor 9:21; Gal 6:2).

23. Keener, *John*, 1:278. He explains that the "prologue presents Jesus as Torah, greater than Moses" (1:51). Also, the role the Son plays in the Fourth Gospel mirrors that of the Torah "in contemporary Judaism" (1:361). With respect to the latter, Jaffee ("Torah," 13:9231) states that "in Judaism," the word *tôrâ* was "the quintessential symbol." In like manner, Sanders ("Torah and Christ," 381) notes that by the first century of the common era, the "Torah was . . . the symbol par excellence, incomparable, indestructible and incorruptible, of Judaism." Indeed, the Torah "meant Judaism's identity and way of life" (cf. Sir 45:5; John 5:39; Rom 7:10; Gal 3:21). Marshall ("Johannine theology," 2:1085) adds that "rabbinic Judaism" spoke of the Torah "in personal terms," declared it to be "preexistent and an agent in creation," and referred to the Torah as "the giver of light and life" to humanity. In the view of Davies (*Torah*, 93), the Fourth Gospel epitomizes Jesus as "the personalized Torah" of Judaism.

those of Wisdom[24] and the Word[25]—none of these eclipses that of Torah to convey the "thought of one who was divine yet distinct from the Father."[26]

24. Reed ("How Semitic was John"), based on his study of the Old Testament Apocrypha, concludes that an "amalgamation evolved between the Greek *sophia* (wisdom) and the Greek *logos* (word)" in which the two terms were viewed as "synonymous" (716; cf. Wis 9:1–2; 2 Enoch 3:8). Over time, "the rabbis parted with wisdom and settled for Torah, or law" (719). Correspondingly, Glasson's examination of the rabbinic writings from the Second Temple period of Judaism suggests that Wisdom was believed to have its source in the Torah (cf. Sir 15:1; 19:20; 39:1). In addition, Wisdom was so identified with the Torah that there was a transference to the Torah of what had been ascribed to Wisdom (*Moses*, 87–88; cf. Bar 3:29—4:1; Gen Rab. 17:5; 31:5; 44:17; Lev Rab. 11:3; 19:1; 4 Macc 1:16–17; Sir 24:1, 23–34; 34:8; Wis 18:15). Carson (*John*, 115–16) postulates that "the lack of Wisdom *terminology* in John's Gospel suggests that parallels between Wisdom and John's *Logos* may stem less from direct dependence than from common dependence on Old Testament uses of 'word' and *Torah*, from which both have been borrowed" (italics are his). Moreover, Keener (*John*, 1:354) proposes that the Evangelist favored "Logos because 'Word' had broader OT connotations more apt to conjure up the image of Torah," yet "without excluding the common nuances his readers would have associated with Wisdom." Also, cf. Beyler, *Torah*, 127–30; Coloe, *God dwells with us*, 62, 214; Epp, "Wisdom, Torah, Word," 132–33, 135; Evans, *Word and glory*, 130; Heschel, *Heavenly Torah*, 681–82; Lincoln, *John*, 96; McGrath, *John's apologetic Christology*, 151–52, 154, 177; Sidebottom, *The Christ of the Fourth Gospel*, 34; Thompson, *God of the Gospel of John*, 130–133; Whitacre, *John*.

25. Reed ("How Semitic was John") points out that "several times the LXX uses *logos* (word) to refer to the Torah either literally or in an abstract form" (cf. Exod 35:1; Deut 1:1; Ps 119:105). He suggests that "some Jewish writers and translators had no qualms about replacing *logos* with *nomos*." In effect, the "two terms became synonymous in Jewish thought" (718). In like manner, Casselli ("Jesus as eschatological Torah") argues that when the Evangelist employed the Greek noun *logos* (cf. John 1:1, 14), he was thinking of the Old Testament phrase rendered "the word of the Lord" (25). In light of the connections between the Fourth Gospel and the "Pentateuchal tradition," it is quite probable the Evangelist considered *logos* to be "basically interchangeable with Torah" (26). This supposition is confirmed by the Septuagint reference to the Ten Commandments (which the Lord gave to Moses on Mount Sinai) as *tous deka logous* or the "ten words" (Exod 34:28; Deut 10:4; cf. Exod 24:3; Deut 32:47). Further confirmation is found when the Septuagint version of the following Old Testament verses are considered: Isaiah 1:10, in which *logon kyriou* ("word of the Lord") and *nomon theou* ("law of God") are used in synonymous parallelism; Isaiah 2:3 and Micah 4:2, in which *nomos* ("law") and *logos kyriou* ("word of the Lord") are used in synonymous parallelism; Isaiah 5:24, in which *nomon kyriou* ("law of the Lord") and *logion* ("word") are used in synonymous parallelism; and Jeremiah 6:19, in which *logon* ("words") and *nomon* ("law") are used in synonymous parallelism; cf. Beyler, *Torah*, 121–22. There is enough precedent to conclude that both *logos* and *nomos* denote the "independent personified expression of God" (Danker, *Greek-English lexicon*, 601).

26. Keener, *John*, 1:281. He proposes that the Evangelist addressed a "community of predominantly Jewish Christians" who, due to their "faith in Jesus," had been "rejected by most of their non-Christian Jewish communities." One can imagine the religious elite of the day making the following claims: (1) Judaism is a "religion of Torah"; and (2) the "prophetic, messianic Jesus movement has departed from proper observance of God's

With the advent of the Son, the Father did not just break His "prophetic silence" and speak again. More importantly, the incarnation of the divine Torah "means that all that God had already spoken was contained in Jesus, the ultimate embodiment of all God's Word."[27] In short, Jesus as Torah functions as a dominant leitmotif (together with Logos)[28] to conceptualize the totality of the person and work of the Son.[29] Moreover, it is a powerful Christological symbol that illumines all the other major themes appearing in the Fourth Gospel. Jesus as Torah is the center from which the divine plan of redemption, as conveyed in John's Gospel, is fulfilled.[30]

Word (particularly from orthodox monotheism)" (1:364). The Evangelist responded in the Fourth Gospel with these counterclaims: (1) the Messiah is the "full embodiment of Torah" and completes "what was partial (but actually present) in Torah"; (2) the Son "embodies the hope of Judaism" (1:417); (3) the decision to become a follower of the Savior "entails true observance of Torah"; and (4) because "Jesus himself is God's Word," no person is able to "genuinely observe Torah without following Jesus" (1:364). Keener's proposal helps to explain why, as Whitacre (*Johannine polemic*, 29) observes, "every explicit dispute in John makes reference to Moses and/or the Law" (cf. 1:17, 45; 2:22; 5:39, 45–47; 6:32; 7:19, 22–28; 8:17; 9:28–29; 10:34–35; 12:34; 13:18; 15:25; 17:12; 19:24, 28, 36–37; 20:9). Also, cf. Ellis, *Genius of John*, 4–6; Evans, *Word and glory*, 184–186; Lincoln, *John*, 77–78; Whitacre, *Johannine polemic*, 1–2, 5–6, 10–11.

27. Keener, *John*, 1:361. Schoneveld ("A new reading"), based on his conclusion that "Logos equals Torah" (79), claims that Jesus of Nazareth is the "embodiment of the Torah" (92). Kysar ("John," 3:923) likewise asserts that the Son is the "revealed, public side of the divine being" who communicates openly and directly with humanity.

28. Cahill ("Johannine Logos as center") postulates that the "Johannine usage of *logos* in the prologue" (54) establishes it as the symbolic center of the Fourth Gospel (55–56). As such, it functions as the "revelation of the sacred *par excellence*" (58). There is a "joining of eternity and time, immaterial and material, divine . . . and human, sacred and profane" (65). Be that as it may, Schoneveld ("A new reading," 80) cites John 5:38–39, 10:35, and 15:25 to support an amalgamation of "Logos and Torah" (80). In like manner, Reed ("How Semitic was John") draws attention to the concatenation between *logos* and *tora* when he proposes that John 1:1 be rendered as follows: "In the beginning was the Torah, and the Torah was toward God, and Godlike was the Torah" (721). Similarly, he observes that the "written Torah became the living Torah—the Incarnation, Jesus" (726). This one-to-one correspondence between *logos* and *tora* is also seen in Schoneveld's rendering of 1:14, "And the Torah emerged as flesh and tabernacled among us" ("A new reading," 81).

29. Keener (*John*) suggests two reasons why in the Prologue to the Fourth Gospel, the Evangelist calls "Jesus the Logos" instead of "the *Nomos*, that is, Torah" (1:361): (1) a "neutral term like Logos could draw on associations with personified Wisdom already offered in Hellenistic Judaism," yet "without compromising its bridge to the Torah, which was also recognized as God's Word," especially "in Pharisaic circles"; and (2) the Evangelist possibly considered "the narrower nuances of *nomos* as too potentially misleading to his readers to employ throughout his prologue" (1:362).

30. According to Wucherpfennig ("Torah," 213–14), the Prologue to the Fourth Gospel not only "presumes that the center of the scripture remains the Torah," but also

The Framework and Intent of This Study

As Beasley-Murray notes, there is no single term or phrase that can "represent all that the man Jesus is set forth" to be in the Fourth Gospel. Regardless of whether one is focusing on Logos, Wisdom, Torah, and so on, as the conceptual nexus for the Gospel of John, it "needs to be complemented with all" that is signified by the "other titles attributed to Jesus in this Gospel."[31] A representative list would include the following: the Word (1:1, 14); the one and only Son (1:18; 3:16, 18); God's Chosen One (1:34); Son of God (1:49; 10:36; 11:27); the Son (3:17, 36; 5:19–27); Son of Man (1:51); Rabbi (1:49; cf. 20:16); a teacher who has come from God (3:2); a prophet (4:19; 9:17); the Prophet who is to come into the world (6:14; cf. 7:40); the one whom the Father sent into the world (3:16–17, 34; 5:30; 7:16–18; 10:36); he who comes in the name of the Lord (12:13); the Messiah (1:41; 4:29; 11:27); the king of Israel (1:49; cf. 6:15; 12:13; 18:33–37); the King of the Jews (19:19–22); the Holy One of God (6:69); the Lamb of God (1:29, 36); the man (19:5); I am (8:24, 28, 58; cf. the corresponding predicates: the Bread of Life, chapter 6; the Good Shepherd, chapter 10; the Resurrection and the Life, 11:25; the Way, the Truth, and the Life, 14:6; and the true Vine, 15:1–10); an Advocate (14:16); the Lord (20:18; 21:7; cf. 6:68); my Lord and my God (20:28; cf. 1:1).[32]

Jesus, as the final expression of God's Tanakh,[33] created all things and is the source of light and life (1:1–13). The children of the light are those who put their trust in the Messiah (12:35–36) and receive eternal life (3:36). They enjoy a growing relationship with the triune God that lasts for time and eternity (17:3). The Fourth Gospel reveals that Jesus, as the eternal, living "Word" (1:1, 14), is infinitely greater than the angels (1:51), Abraham (8:56–58), Jacob (4:11–14), Moses (1:17; 6:49–51), the Mosaic law (1:17; 8:1–11), the Sabbath (5:8; 7:21–23; 9:14–33), and

---

that "in Jesus Christ the Torah is revealed in a unique and singular way." Casselli ("Jesus as eschatological Torah," 25) builds on this thought by maintaining that the Evangelist "finds in Jesus the eschatological realization of the Exodus" and "the Torah"; cf. Lincoln, *John*, 77; Westcott, *John*, vii.

31. Beasley-Murray, *John*, lxxxiii.

32. For an examination of prominent Christological titles appearing in the Fourth Gospel, cf. Carson, *John*, 95–97; Kim, *Seven sign-miracles*, 107–25; Kümmel, *Theology*, 266–87; Schnackenburg, *John*, 1:507–514.

33. Neusner ("Rabbinic Judaism," 11:7583) explains that the word "Tanakh" is "an acronym" identifying the entire Hebrew Bible, which includes the "Torah (Law), Nevi'im (Prophets), and Ketuvim (Writings)." Throughout this study, the words "Torah" and "Tanakh" will be used interchangeably in reference to the Messiah. This approach is based on the fact that now and then in the Fourth Gospel, the corpus of Hebrew sacred writings is referred to as the "Law" (cf. John 10:34; 12:34; 15:25).

the Jerusalem temple—along with its associated rites, rituals, and festivals (2:18–21). Philip told Nathanael that Jesus is the person about whom Moses and the prophets wrote (1:45; cf. 3:14). Accordingly, those who claimed to be disciples of the great lawgiver (7:19; 9:28–29) but rejected what he said about the Messiah, placed themselves under God's judgment (5:45–47; 12:48).

During his lifetime, Moses beheld God's glory, especially in the giving of the law at Sinai. The Messiah's followers see an even greater manifestation of God's glory in Jesus as Torah (1:14). Beginning with John the Baptizer, they bear witness to the Son in a way that mirrors the testimony Moses gave to the law (1:6–8, 15). As the Savior's disciples, believers never walk in spiritual darkness, for they have the life-giving light of the world (8:12; 9:5; 12:46). In the Old Testament era, true members of the covenant community accepted and obeyed God's disclosure in the Mosaic law. Similarly, in the New Testament era, those who truly belong to God's family receive and heed His revelation through the Logos (1:12–13; cf. 5:38). Umoh noted that "what the Torah as a whole symbolized for Israel is now to be identified" in the Son, whom the Father "sent into the world."[34] Jesus, as "God's Wisdom come in the flesh," discloses the character of the triune God, and in so doing, gathers a "community of the faithful from both Jews and Greeks."[35]

Establishing the Reference Points for This Study

The preceding sections of this chapter have presented two diametrically opposed approaches to life. In the first orientation, life revolves around the individual. This self-centered path adheres to a worldly wise, "street smart" philosophy. It is characterized by either a culture of entitlement or merit (or possibly a mixture of both) and leads to arrogance, envy, and immorality. In the second option, all of existence is centered in the Lord Jesus. This redeemer-centered approach embraces the wisdom of Scripture. It is characterized by humble submission to the Lord, operates according to His grace, and acknowledges the Son to be the divine, incarnate Tanakh.

These truths are evident in the Fourth Gospel and serve as useful reference points for examining it afresh. In order to keep the size and scope of the present study manageable and feasible, the first 12 chapters of John's Gospel are the primary focus. Special emphasis is given in chapters three through seven to Jesus as Torah in John 1–12; but before this is done, the

---

34. Umoh, *The plot to kill Jesus,* 191; cf. Bock, *Jesus,* 411–12.
35. Witherington, *John's wisdom,* 19.

second chapter provides a broader theological context for understanding the concept of the moral law from a Christ-centered perspective. Finally, in chapter 8, general observations made throughout the body of the present study are reiterated. This is followed by a discussion of selected portions of chapters 13–21 in light of the recurrent theme of Jesus as Torah. The observations are put forward in a concise, non-technical manner to round out the preceding discussion.

Throughout this study, a canonical and integrative approach is used to interpret the Gospel of John in its literary, historical, and theological context.[36] Also, because this work treats the text of the Fourth Gospel in its present form, such matters as source, form, and redaction criticism receive little comment. For a discussion of those issues, one should consult the major commentaries on the Gospel of John (such as those listed in the bibliography and formally cited throughout this study). My intent is to explore the Fourth Gospel's portrait of Jesus as the fulfillment of the Mosaic law. Connected with this purpose statement is the central thesis that the Messiah appears in John's Gospel as the realization of all the law's redemptive-historical types, prophecies, and expectations. A corresponding major claim is that those who trust in Jesus for eternal life and heed His teaching, fully satisfy the requirements of the moral law recorded in Scripture.

The former statements reflect the predominately evangelical interpretive approach taken in this work. The term *evangelical* refers to those from across a spectrum of "denominational and confessional boundaries" who affirm the tenets of historic, biblical Christianity.[37] With the "gospel of Christ" as the center of their "thinking and living," they endeavor to "unfold the implications of salvation through the cross" and "live by them."[38] Evangelicals also affirm the "centrality of the conversion . . . experience" and regard the Bible as God's reliable and authoritative "revelation

---

36. Regarding the term "canonical," this study affirms the view put forward by Burge (*John*, 34) that it refers to the "received literary form" of the sacred text "accepted in the church." Furthermore, this study shares the same aim as "canonical exegesis" (Ratzinger, *Jesus of Nazareth*), namely, to "read individual texts within the totality of the one Scripture." In turn, this theological hermeneutic "sheds new light on all the individual texts." One underlying premise is that to "understand the Scripture in the spirit in which it is written," one has to "attend to the content and to the unity of Scripture as a whole" (xviii). A second corresponding premise regards the Lord Jesus as "the key . . . to understand the Bible as a unity" (xix). For an overview of the integrative approach to the interpretation of Scripture, especially with respect to the Fourth Gospel, cf. Ng, *Water symbolism in John*, 44–45.

37. Pierard and Elwell, "Evangelicalism," 405; cf. Webber, *Younger evangelicals*, 14–15.

38. Morris, "What do we mean by 'evangelical'?"

to humankind.[39] Together the Old and New Testaments are taken to be the divinely inspired word of God and inerrant in the originals. As such, they are also understood to be the foremost "epistemological foundation" for "faith, theology, and practice."[40] Admittedly, while other ecclesiastical sources of authority cannot be ignored, they neither supplant nor eclipse the supreme authority of Scripture.[41]

With respect to the literary and exegetical analysis of John's Gospel that appears in this study, certain operating presuppositions are at work.[42] No attempt is made to substantiate their validity, especially given the lack of scholarly consensus on such matters.[43] This includes the absence of any agreement concerning the literary structure of the Fourth Gospel.[44] For the purposes of this study, the working assumption is that there are four principal divisions.[45] In this arrangement, the Gospel's Christocentric orientation is emphasized,[46] especially its focus on Jesus as Torah:

I. The Prologue: Revealing Jesus as Torah (1:1–18)

II. The Signs Performed by Jesus as Torah (1:19—12:50)

III. The Salvation Provided by Jesus as Torah (13:1—20:31)

IV. The Epilogue: Recognizing Jesus as Torah (21:1–25)

---

39. Balmer, *Encyclopedia of evangelicalism*, 236.

40. Balmer, *Encyclopedia of evangelicalism*, 75.

41. Kellstedt, "Evangelicalism."

42. Cf. Lioy, *Search for ultimate reality*, 17–19.

43. Beasley-Murray, *John*, cxlii; Carson, *John*, 37–38; Hurtado, *Lord Jesus Christ*, 353; Schnelle, *Antidocetic Christology*, 1–2. For a overview of introductory issues connected with the Fourth Gospel, cf. Beasley-Murray, *John*, xxxii–xcii; Blomberg, *Historical reliability*, 17–67; Harris, *John*; Köstenberger, *Studies on John and gender*, 7–47; Morris, *John*, 4–59; Westcott, *John*, v–xcvii.

44. Cf. the detailed survey of views appearing in Mlakuzhyil, *Christocentric literary structure*, 17–85.

45. Cf. Bock, *Jesus*, 39–40; Brown, *John*, cxxxviii–cxxxix; Brown, *Introduction*, 334–35; deSilva, *Introduction*, 405; Köstenberger, *John*, 10–11; Lincoln, *John*, 4–5.

46. Cf. Mlakuzhyil, *Christocentric literary structure*, 238–41, 350.

The Framework and Intent of This Study

It is affirmed that John authored the Fourth Gospel.[47] He was the younger son of Zebedee and Salome and an apostle in the early church.[48] John, of course, never explicitly named himself as the author, perhaps to ensure that the spotlight of attention remained on the one who is the divine, incarnate Tanakh.[49] Nonetheless, the identity of the writer was well known to his contemporaries, as reflected in John's self-identification as the disciple with whom Jesus had a special bond of affection (cf. 13:23; 19:26; 20:2; 21:7, 20). John was also one of the three disciples of Jesus who belonged to His inner circle (the other two being Peter and James, the brother of John).

These last two statements put John in a unique position to write an accurate and true historical record of what Jesus said and did during His earthly ministry (cf. John 19:35; 21:24; 1 John 1:1–4).[50] The writer

---

47. Contra such commentators as O'Day ("John," 9:475), who maintains that the identity of the author is "no longer recoverable for contemporary readers." Keener (*John*, 1:139) concludes his discussion of the authorship of the Fourth Gospel by affirming the likelihood that "John son of Zebedee authored the substance of the finished Gospel, and as more plausible than usually recognized that both John and Revelation could share a common authorship." Harris (*John*) points out that while the Synoptic Gospels were penned from a first person viewpoint (in other words, "as if the author had personally observed all the events"), the Fourth Gospel reflects a third person, post-resurrection perspective (in other words, as if the author is "removed from the events" he related). On the one hand, the Evangelist was both an "eyewitness of the life" of the Lord Jesus and a "participant in the events" connected with His earthly ministry. On the other hand, the Evangelist "looks back upon" all he experienced. As a result, readers of his treatise benefit from his years of reflecting upon and making sense of the theological ramifications of his encounter with the Messiah (cf. 2:17, 22; 12:16; 20:9).

48. For a extensive study of the biblical and extra-biblical traditions associated with John, cf. Culpepper, *John, the son of Zebedee*.

49. Cf. Ridderbos, *John*, 83.

50. The conclusions reached by Blomberg (*Historical reliability*, 283–294) call into question the view of such commentators as Lindars (*John*, 54), who advocates a "degree of skepticism concerning the value of the Fourth Gospel as an historical document." Keener (*John*) observed that the "usual skepticism toward the contents of the Fourth Gospel, which has sometimes proved almost thoroughgoing, seems to be more influenced by scholars' presuppositions than by any demand of historical-critical methodology itself" (1:45). He maintains that the Fourth Gospel (along with the Synoptic Gospels) should be "placed among the most, rather than the least, reliable of ancient biographies" (1:25). Likewise, Thomas ("Fourth Gospel," 181–82) says that, based on his research, the Gospel of John accurately reflects the "practices and thought of Pharisaism and/or emerging rabbinic Judaism." Similarly, the analysis conducted by Lea ("Reliability of history," 388) on the "historical material in the fourth gospel" led him to conclude that it is "reliable, trustworthy, deserving our confidence, and inviting to our faith." In a similar vein, Morris (*John*, 35) admits that while the Fourth Gospel is an "interpretative document," this "does not necessarily mean distortion of the facts." Furthermore, the "absence of interpretation

adopted a narrative-discourse form of expression in which the plot of the Fourth Gospel is developed through a series of interconnected episodes.[51] The period covered is approximately AD 26–30.[52] The narrative begins around the time when Jesus of Nazareth was baptized and ends with His reinstatement of Peter after the Savior's resurrection from the dead. John probably authored his account in the latter half of the first century AD, which would have been approximately two generations after Jesus' crucifixion and decades after the writing of the Synoptic Gospels.

According to early church tradition, John wrote the Fourth Gospel from Ephesus, where he served as an elder (cf. 2 John 1; 3 John 1). This ancient city had a large Christian community, and the apostle undoubtedly had an active ministry among the believers living there as well as in the environs of Ephesus. There is no record that when John penned his treatise, anyone contested his rendition of Jesus' words and works. This includes the absence of dissenting voices from the first and second generation of believers, along with other eyewitnesses and those closely affiliated with them. In fact, members of the early church used the truths about the Messiah found in the Fourth Gospel to shape the orthodoxy of the Christian community in the second through fourth centuries AD.

The Logos-Torah theology of the Prologue (John 1:1–18) strongly suggests that the Fourth Gospel was intended to rebut unorthodox views about the Redeemer. This implies that the locus of the danger to the early church was the menace of heretical teachings concerning the person and

---

may sometimes mean distortion." Admittedly, "if one does not agree with John's view of Jesus much may be disputed"; however, if the Evangelist is correct regarding the divine, incarnate Torah, then "this interpretative document is of the utmost importance for those who want the fullest light on the facts." Thompson ("John," 375) notes that "simply because information is found only in John is no reason to discard it as of no historical value." For instance, contemporary scholarship affirms the plausibility that "Jesus' ministry lasted two or three years (as John implies), that he was in and out of Jerusalem (as the other Gospels hint—e.g. Luke 13:34), that some of the disciples of Jesus were first disciples of John the Baptist (John 1:35–37), and that Jesus and his disciples conducted a ministry of baptism (3:22)."

51. According to Harris (*John*), while the "long discourses" recorded in the Fourth Gospel "do not necessarily represent Jesus' exact words (*ipsissima verba*)," they still "give a faithful summary and interpretive paraphrase (*ipsissima vox*) of what he actually said." Also, Keener (*John*, 1:74) states that "accuracy in reporting the substance does not suggest anything in the nature of a verbatim transcript"; cf. Ng, *Water symbolism in John*, 58; O'Day, "John," 9:493; Tenney, "John," 9:12; Wright, *Jesus*, 52–54.

52. The dates for the life of Christ used in this study are based on the timeline appearing in the *Zondervan TNIV Study Bible* (1656–658), which states in its disclaimer that "all dates are approximate."

work of the Savior. This circumstance called for a fresh, more theologically distinctive presentation of Jesus as the Messiah, yet one that remained as authentic and authoritative as that found in the Synoptic Gospels. By portraying Jesus as Tanakh in the Fourth Gospel, John enabled the believers of his day to resist the temptation to compromise their apostolic beliefs concerning the Redeemer. Furthermore, by affirming Him to be "the Messiah, the Son of God" (20:31), they would remain secure in their faith.[53]

---

53. Cf. Lioy, *Search for ultimate reality,* 9–11.

2

The Moral Law in Christ-Centered Perspective

A Canonical and Integrative Approach[1]

Introduction

THE INTENT of this chapter is to examine the nature of the moral law from a Christ-centered perspective and to do so in a canonical and integrative manner. It builds on the findings, arguments, and conclusions presented in my monograph dealing with the relationship between the Decalogue and the Sermon on the Mount. In that study, I maintained that God's universal ethical absolutes were applicable for the church today. In the final chapter of the monograph, I noted some areas for further research. This included how Matthew 5:17–20 interlaced with other pivotal texts (for instance, Romans 10:4 and the book of Hebrews) regarding the continuing applicability of the moral law. The latter part of the present chapter investigates these matters further, along with exploring other relevant portions of the New Testament; but before that is done, a foundation of understanding is laid regarding the biblical concept of the law and the relationship of Jesus and His followers to the law.

The Biblical Concept of the Law

Foundational to this study is the biblical concept of the law, an issue I have previously discussed at length.[2] This includes understanding various legal terms used in the Old Testament, the primary one of which is the Hebrew noun *tora*. Depending on the context in which the word is used, it can mean "direction," "instruction," or "law." *Tora* appears not only in legal

---

1. This chapter is a modified version of my journal article by the same title appearing in *Conspectus* (Vol. 3, March 2007) and is reprinted with permission.
2. Lioy, *Decalogue in the Sermon on the Mount*, 13–34.

texts, but also in narratives, speeches, poems, and genealogies. An examination of Scripture indicates that for the ancient Hebrews, morality was not an abstract concept disconnected from the present; rather, it signified ethical imperatives concerning how people of faith should live.

A similar mindset is found in the New Testament, especially in connection with the Greek noun *nomos*. The focus of this term is on ethical standards and rules of conduct, as established by tradition. Such synonyms as "custom," "principle," and "norm" help to convey the lexical range of meanings found in *nomos*. The term is also used to denote what people should do, with such terms as "ordinance," "rule," and "command" helping to capture this sense of the noun. Depending on the context, *nomos* is used to refer to the Pentateuch, guidelines for ethical behavior, and the promise of God. The noun denotes ethical instruction that is divine in origin and concerns the way of life characterized by righteousness and blessing. While in the New Testament, *nomos* does not refer to the teaching tradition of Israel's religious leaders, an awareness of the oral Torah can help one to better understand and appreciate the New Testament concept of the law.

Clarifying the biblical concept of the law includes a discussion of its nature, various categories, and interrelated purposes. With respect to its nature, the law reflects the holiness of God and His will for humankind. Also, by means of His law, God evaluates how closely people live up to His flawless moral standard (cf. Rom 3:20). While there is an essential unity to the law, it would be incorrect to view it as a judicial monolith, for its various ordinances deal with civil, ceremonial, and ethical matters. While the administrative and ritual aspects of the Mosaic legal code are no longer binding on Christians, the moral aspects of God's law remain authoritative for the church (cf. John 14:15; 1 Cor 9:21; Gal 5:13–14; 6:2; 1 John 5:2–3). Admittedly, Scripture does not explicitly map out these particular distinctions; nonetheless, they represent a valid and useful demarcation of the three main types of law appearing in Scripture.

The three main categories of biblical law served distinct, though related, purposes. Because ancient Israel was a theocracy (in which the people recognized God as their King), the civil codes and religious ordinances were limited in their application to that nation during the period of the Old Testament. The moral law, however, transcends the time and culture of ancient Israel and has enduring applicability for the household of faith today. Two premier examples of the ethical aspect of God's law would be the Ten Commandments (recorded in Exod 20:1–17 and Deut 5:6–21) and the Sermon on the Mount (recorded in Matt 5–7). Because these portions of Scripture represent the epitome of God's will for humankind, they also serve as useful starting points for recognizing His universal moral absolutes.

Just as there are various categories of biblical law, there are also several interrelated purposes. The first of these is to increase the cognizance people have of their sin (cf. Rom 3:20; 4:15; 5:13; 7:7–11). They recognize that they have violated God's will and fall short of His glorious moral standard (3:23). Second, the law spotlights the transgressors' need for a Redeemer, that is, salvation through faith in the Son (Gal 3:19–24). Third, the law helps to restrain evil by specifying the kinds of acts that are wicked. In this way, it assists governing authorities to maintain civil order, protect the innocent, and penalize the unjust. Fourth, the law helps God's people to recognize and live uprightly by giving them an ethical frame of reference. They are able to do so, for they are indwelt by the Spirit and energized by the Father's love.

The Relationship of the Messiah to the Law

In any discussion concerning the relevancy of the law for believers, it is important to clarify the nature of the relationship between the Messiah and the law. Throughout His time on earth, Jesus remained subject to the law (Gal 4:4), and as a righteous Jew, acted in accordance with its stipulations (Luke 2:21–23; 4:16). Jesus also upheld the truth that the moral law continued to be relevant and binding (Matt 5:17–18). Furthermore, as Israel's greatest teacher (cf. Matt 7:28–29; John 13:13–14), He expounded on the meaning of the law and clarified its significance for God's people (e.g. Matt 5:21–48). In particular, Jesus stated that love for God and all people were the foremost commandments of Scripture (Matt 22:37–40; cf. Lev 19:18; Deut 6:5).

In His teaching ministry, Jesus disclosed the true meaning and intent of the law. He also affirmed the divine authority of the Hebrew sacred writings. This included condemning the extra-biblical traditions added to the Mosaic code (cf. Matt 15:1–9; 23:1–36) and censuring rigid, inaccurate views of the law (cf. 5:20, 38). He sought neither to invalidate God's commands nor add new edicts to what already existed; instead, He strove to undo humanly imposed notions of right and wrong that ran counter to the divine intent of the law (cf. Mark 7:1–23).

When Adam and Eve violated God's command (Gen 3:1–7), sin entered the world and brought death along with it (Rom 5:12). The law of God was within its rightful authority to condemn all people, for all of

Adam's descendants had violated what the Lord decreed (3:23). Through Jesus' atoning sacrifice at Calvary, the fundamental relationship between regenerate sinners and the law was radically altered. To be specific, the Messiah, through His work on the cross, rendered powerless the law's ability to condemn those trusting in Him. As a result of their spiritual union with Christ (6:1–7), they were pardoned (or acquitted) of sin and delivered from eternal damnation (8:1).

In addition, Jesus' death and resurrection put an end to the need for the ritualistic elements of the Mosaic code. As the sacrificial Lamb of God, Jesus satisfied the demands of the law completely and for all time (cf. John 1:29; Heb 7:26–28; 9:1, 9–10, 23–27). In this way, the Savior brought to pass the spiritual reality foreshadowed by the ceremonial laws, thus rendering them obsolete and outdated (Heb 8:13). The consequence is that neither the civil nor ceremonial aspects of the Mosaic legal code remain binding for believers today; nonetheless, these aspects of the law continue to have educational value for believers, especially as they seek to understand and adhere to God's moral law.

The Relationship of Believers to the Law

Jesus, through His atoning death at Calvary, frees believers from the condemnation of the law, but not from living in accordance with its timeless moral precepts and injunctions. After all, the "law is holy" (Rom 7:12); likewise, its commandments are "holy, righteous and good." The implication is that God's universal moral absolutes are eternal in nature, unchanging, and perfect. As such, they transcend historical eras and societal constructs, having applicability for Christians down through the centuries.

The New Testament affirms the abiding validity of the ethical precepts of the Mosaic legal code. Paul noted that when we "live . . . according to the Spirit," the "righteous requirement of the law" is "fully met in us" (Rom 8:4). Similarly, John exhorted the believers in his day to "keep yourselves from idols" (1 John 5:21). This injunction brings to mind the second commandment of the Decalogue prohibiting idolatry (Exod 20:4; Deut 5:8). Clearly, the holy God revealed in the Old Testament is the same Lord disclosed in the New Testament.

Some might argue that biblical concepts of God have changed between the time of Abraham and Moses in the Old Testament and Jesus and the disciples in the New Testament. This notion, however, is undercut by the indistinguishable theological orientation found throughout the Judeo-Christian Scriptures, especially as seen in their moral directives. As a matter of fact, legal imperatives are an inseparable part of the Lord's covenant relationship with His people. In short, the covenant and law go hand in hand to create a unified and holy community of the redeemed down through the ages (cf. Heb 12:18–29). Not surprisingly, then, the ethical instruction given by Jesus and His apostles reflects an affirmation of the Mosaic legal code and its reapplication to believers this side of Calvary.

The Messiah's Fulfillment of the Law (Matt 5:17–20)

I have previously discussed the way in which the Messiah fulfilled the moral law, and a review of that information is in order here.[3] The key biblical text is Matthew 5:17–20, with verses 21–48 forming a broader pertinent scriptural context. A pivotal interpretative issue concerns whether Jesus was taking umbrage with the Mosaic law recorded in the Old Testament or the Pharisaic interpretation of the same. In this discussion, I am siding with the latter premise; in other words, the Messiah was challenging the Halakha—the collective body of Jewish religious law, including talmudic and rabbinic ordinances, customs, and traditions.

In verse 17, Jesus' collectively referred to the Hebrew sacred writings as "the Law" and "the Prophets," which mirrors how religious experts of the day would have talked about the entire Old Testament. Some think the Messiah wanted to abrogate, supersede, or replace the Mosaic legal code. Others conjecture that He radicalized the demands of the law and intensified its requirements, and in the process nullified some longstanding injunctions. Still others maintain that Jesus introduced demands that go beyond and in different directions from those found in the law.[4]

None of these options are acceptable, for they contradict Jesus' statement that He did not "come to abolish the Law and the Prophets." "Abolish" renders the Greek verb *katalyo*, which means "to put an end to the effect or validity of something." The idea is that during the Savior's first advent, He did not seek to annul, repeal, do away with, or make invalid

---

3. Lioy, *Decalogue in the Sermon on the Mount*, 104–106, 136–144.
4. Cf. Banks, *Jesus and the law*, 210, 229–30, 235; Barth, "Matthew's understanding of the law," 153–59; Davies *Christian origins*, 33–34, 39; Geisler, *Christian ethics*, 204–7; Guthrie, *New Testament theology*, 676–77; Fanning, "Theology of Hebrews," 431; Jeremias, *New Testament theology*, 206; Lowery, "Theology of Matthew," 47–48; Marshall, *New Testament theology*, 118–19; Menninger, *Israel and the church*, 104–8; Moo, "Law," 450, 454–56; Moo, "Law of Christ," 350–53; Pate, *Reverse of the curse*, 350–51; Sanders, *Jesus and Judaism*, 260; Sanders, *Jewish law*, 93–94; Thielman, *Theology of the New Testament*, 87, 89–90.

the Mosaic legal code. Instead, His primary concern was to dismantle incorrect views about the law, especially faulty interpretations promulgated by the religious specialists of the day. This included a works-based form of righteousness in which strict adherence to the law would gain people their salvation (cf. Rom 9:30–33).

Rather than tear down all that the law stood for and represented, Jesus came to "fulfill" (Matt 5:17) the same. The Greek verb *plēroō* has three interrelated meanings,[5] each of which apply to what Jesus said about Himself. The Messiah fulfilled the law by carrying out its ethical injunctions, showing forth its true spiritual meaning, and bringing all that it stood for prophetically to completion.[6] The idea is that Jesus obeyed the law perfectly, thoroughly, and absolutely. He is the realization of its types and prophecies and the exclusive inspired interpreter of its teachings. Furthermore, He alone fully satisfied the payment for sin required by the law. Thus, He is more than an ideal example of how God's people should act. The Son is the object of the believers' faith, enabling them to be declared righteous in the Father's sight. Jesus also leads them beyond a surface-level compliance with the law to an inward adherence to its moral expectations.

There is no dichotomy, then, between Jesus and the Mosaic legal code. What He taught and did stood in continuity with the Old Testament, while at the same time made a break with the prevalent legalistic traditions of the day. Jesus endeavored to clarify what God originally revealed in the law, truths that had been obscured by some religious experts in the intertestamental period. The Savior made it clear that erroneous views about the law were separate from it and worthy of being rejected. Accordingly, His goal was to abrogate unscriptural notions by replacing them with the truth.

The moral law forms the backdrop of Jesus' declaration recorded in verse 18. This is due in part to the fact that during His earthly ministry, He began to nullify the ceremonial aspect of the Mosaic legal code (cf. Mark 7:19; Acts 10:15; 1 Tim 4:4). Indeed, because of Jesus' high priestly ministry, the ceremonies and sacrifices connected with the Levitical priest-

---

5. Cf. Barth, "Matthew's understanding of the law," 67–68; Branscomb, *Jesus and the law of Moses*, 226–29; Jeremias, *New Testament theology*, 84–85; Meier, *Law and history*, 73–75; Motyer, *Look to the Rock*, 61; Sanders, *Paul*, 261; Suggs, *Wisdom*, 115–19.

6. Cf. Bock, *Jesus*, 132; Bolton, *True bounds*, 61–62; Henry, *Christian personal ethics*, 318–19; Ladd, *Theology of the New Testament*, 122–23; Loader, *Jesus' attitude*, 167–68; McQuilkin, *Biblical ethics*, 46–49; Murray, *Principles of conduct*, 150; Sprinkle, *Biblical law*, 27; VanGemeren, "Law as the perfection of righteousness," 38–39.

hood ceased to be valid (Heb 8:13). While the administrative and liturgical functions of the law were no longer in force, God's universal moral absolutes remained in effect. This is made clear when Jesus solemnly assured His listeners that "the smallest letter" (Matt 5:18) and "the least stroke of a pen" found in the law would never "disappear" from it until everything recorded in it was achieved. Not even "heaven and earth" would vanish before God had "accomplished" all that He declared would come to pass.

Ginomai is the Greek verb rendered "accomplished" and it refers to attaining to or arriving at something. From a Christ-centered standpoint, Jesus satisfied all the demands of the Torah, fulfilled their prophetic announcements, and flawlessly elucidated their divinely inspired teaching. These interrelated purposes find their fullest and most ultimate expression in the Savior's atoning sacrifice on the cross. Through His death and resurrection, He makes it possible for believers to live in accordance with the ethical standards of the law. Likewise, all the hopes and dreams for saved humanity, as expressed in the law, reach their consummation and closure as a result of the Son's redemptive work.

Behind Jesus' statements in verse 19 is His refusal to countenance any misinterpretations and misapplications of the law. The religionists of the day ignored the least commandment by using the Mosaic legal code to win acceptance with God; and they encouraged others to disregard the law by perpetuating the incorrect notion that a mere outward compliance with rules and regulations ensured that one's relationship with God remained intact. In the end, the meticulous observance of human traditions and opinions is an inadequate substitute for the moral law. Those who so depreciated the ordinances of Scripture would be considered least in the kingdom of the Lawgiver. In contrast, those who affirmed the moral law—from the least to the greatest of its injunctions—would correspondingly be "called great in the kingdom of heaven."

The ethical demands of the kingdom exceed what anyone can humanly achieve on their own. Indeed, no matter how closely religionists might try to abide by the technicalities of the law, their sinful nature undermines their best efforts (cf. Rom 7:7–25). Even the smallest infraction makes one guilty of breaking all of God's commands (cf. Jas 2:10). This was just as true for such pious leaders as "the Pharisees and the teachers of the law" (Matt 5:20). Because they remained entrenched in their legalism and hypocrisy, they failed to secure redemption for themselves. Only those who relied on God—completely and exclusively—were admitted to the divine kingdom.

The Messiah as the Divine, Incarnate Torah (John 1:1, 14, 16–18)

I have elsewhere explored the Johannine view of Jesus' relationship to the Mosaic law, information that is germane to this chapter.[7] Foundational is the apostle's presentation of Jesus as the eternally preexistent, divine Word. John 1:1 uses the Greek noun *logos* to refer to the Messiah as "the independent personified expression of God" to the world.[8] *Logos* represents a fusion of the religious-philosophical outlook of ancient Greece and the monotheistic orientation of biblical Judaism. The resulting emphasis is on Jesus being the Creator, Sustainer, Ruler, and Judge of the universe. In short, He is the divine, incarnate Torah, the one who embodies God's wisdom, revelation, and command.

The opening verse of John's Gospel uses the Greek term *archē* (translated "beginning") in connection with the Messiah. At the dawn of time, when the material universe came into being, the Logos already existed. Every aspect of life, whether temporal or eternal, originated from and was consummated in the Logos. Also, because He is Torah, the Logos is the source of whatever is considered right and true. With the enfleshment of the Word, God has entered the scene of human history to usher in a new age of redemption. The climax of this cosmic drama is the Son's atoning sacrifice at Calvary, which proves to be the success, not failure, of His divinely foreordained mission. In this way, the Logos reveals the heart of the Father and enables believing sinners to become His spiritual children (cf. v. 12).

John 1:1 states that the divine, incarnate Tanakh was with the Father from all eternity. Their relationship is intimate, personal, and (in a manner of speaking) face-to-face.[9] The apostle, by using the Greek noun *theos* in reference to Jesus, emphasized that the Logos is truly God, just as are the Father and the Holy Spirit. Indeed, the fullness of the Godhead resides in all three Persons of the Trinity, implying that they each fully share the same divine nature (cf. John 5:18; 8:58; 10:30; 17:11; Rom 9:5; Phil 2:6; Col 2:9; Heb 1:3; 2 Pet 1:1). Also, because the Son is uncreated, He is not dependent on anyone or anything; instead, every entity throughout the universe exists because of Him and for Him.

---

7. Lioy, *Search for ultimate reality*, 66–71, 80–87.
8. Danker, *Greek-English lexicon*, 601.
9. Ratzinger (*Jesus of Nazareth*, xiv) explains that the "true center of [Jesus'] personality" is most clearly understood and appreciated "in light of his communion with the Father."

Logos is again used in John 1:14 in connection with the divine Torah of eternity becoming a human being (literally, "flesh") and taking up residence among humankind. Jesus, without giving up any of His attributes as God (cf. Phil 2:6–8), took upon Himself a full and genuine human nature. Thus, within the person of the Messiah was the complete and perfect union of His divine and human natures (Col 1:19; 2:9; Heb 1:3). In becoming incarnate, the Word remained untainted by and free from sin (cf. Rom 8:3; Heb 4:5; 7:26). These truths are not a theological abstraction, but rather signify the literal enfleshment of the Creator in space and time.

"Made his dwelling" translates the Greek verb *skēnoō*, which is more literally rendered "tabernacled." This serves as a reminder of the shrine in the wilderness wherein the Lord displayed His glory among the Israelites (cf. Exod 25:8; 40:34–35; 1 Kgs 8:10–11).[10] The grandeur and splendor of God were also present in the Messiah, whose "glory" (John 1:14) the disciples noted.[11] In one sense, the luminescent perfection of God shining forth from Jesus is implied by the Greek term *doxa* (cf. the account of the Transfiguration recorded in Matt 17:1–13; Mark 9:2–13; Luke 9:28–36); but the most profound way in which Jesus' followers witnessed His glory was through His death on the cross, followed by His resurrection and ascension (cf. John 7:39; 12:23, 28; 13:31–32; 17:1, 4–5).

This is none other than the glory of Jesus as Tanakh, whom John 1:14 refers to as "the one and only Son." The phrase renders the Greek word *monogenēs*, a term that points to something distinctively unique, special,

---

10. The word "glory," when applied to God in Scripture, refers to the luminous manifestation of His being. In other words, it is the brilliant revelation of Himself to humanity. This definition is borne out by the many ways the word is used in the Bible. For example, brilliant light consistently went with manifestations of God (Matt 17:2; 1 Tim 6:16; Rev 1:16). Moreover, the word "glory" is often linked with verbs of seeing (Exod 16:7; 33:18; Isa 40:5) and of appearing (Exod 16:10; Deut 5:24), both of which emphasize the visible nature of God's glory; cf. Davies, "Glory," 2:401–2; Harrison, "Glory," 2:478–79; Huttar, "Glory," 288.

11. The rabbis later described the glory of the Lord abiding with Israel as *shekinah*, from the Hebrew word for "dwelling." God's *shekinah* dwelt with the Israelites in the wilderness period, came to Solomon's temple when it was built, and then departed when the temple was destroyed. One tradition of the rabbis says that God's glory returned to heaven, while another says that some of the *shekinah* remains even today in the Western (or Wailing) Wall in Jerusalem, the last remnant of Herod's temple (cf. Kohler and Blau, "Shekinah"; Unterman, "Shekhinah," 18:440–1). The Evangelist in the Fourth Gospel depicts Jesus as God's *shekinah* returned to earth (John 1:14). In a similar vein, Paul said it was possible to see God's glory in Jesus when He was on earth and that believers have the promise of sharing in that glory (Rom 5:2). The latter will occur at the resurrection, when the bodies of believers are transformed into the same kind of glorified body that Jesus had after His resurrection (1 Cor 15:35–57; Phil 3:20–21).

or one-of-a-kind. With respect to the Logos, He alone is the eternal Son of God, the extraordinary object of the Father's love, and equal to the Father and the Spirit as God. Just as important is the apostle's statement about the Logos being "full of grace and truth." *Charis* (literally, "grace") denotes God's enduring love (*hesed* in Hebrew), while *alētheia* (literally, "truth") refers to God's faithfulness (*'emet* in Hebrew). In the Old Testament, the Lord made His mercy and compassion known through an intermediary such as Moses (cf. Exod 33:18–19; 34:6–7). Now, with the advent of the Messiah, grace and truth from God have reached their full and final expression (cf. John 14:6; Eph 2:8).

The eternal preexistence of the divine, incarnate Torah was the basis for John the Baptizer declaring that the Messiah far outranked him (John 1:15). The same preeminent, incarnate Lord inundated His disciples with the fullness of His presence. The apostle referred to it as *charin anti charito*, which is literally rendered "grace upon grace" (v. 16). Admittedly, God's unmerited favor was already present throughout the Old Testament era; yet John, without diminishing this truth, noted that the enfleshment of the Logos resulted in even more of an inexhaustible supply of divine grace being piled on top of grace for the redeemed. Less likely is the view that the grace of God available under the new covenant somehow replaces or displaces what was available under the old covenant.[12] Ultimately, there is a strong correspondence and continuity between the testaments with respect to the compassion and faithfulness of the Lord that He made available to the faith community.

This emphasis on continuity between the testaments also applies to the "law" (*nomos*), which is mentioned in verse 17. After all, it was the triune God who revealed the law to Moses, and he in turn made it known to Israel (cf. Heb 1:1). That same body of teaching pointed to the long awaited Messiah, the very individual about whom Moses wrote (John 5:46). Likewise, Abraham and Isaiah foresaw the advent of the Redeemer (cf. 8:56; 12:41). Admittedly, the perspective of these and other Old Testament saints was limited (cf. 1 Pet 1:10–12); nonetheless, the Spirit enabled them to prophesy about the humiliation and exaltation of the Messiah (cf. Deut 18:15, 18; Ps 2:1–2; 22; 28:16; 118:22; Isa 52:13—53:12; Matt 21:42; Luke 24:25–27, 44–47; Acts 4:11, 25–26; 1 Cor 10:3).

Jesus, as Tanakh, is the ultimate revelation of God (cf. Heb 1:2–3). He is also the one through whom God's "grace and truth" (John 1:17; cf. Exod 33:13) are made available to believers in fullest abundance. While there is an implied contrast between Moses and the Messiah in John 1:17,

---

12. Cf. McQuilkin, *Biblical ethics*, 52; Moo, "Law," 461; Räisänen, *Paul and the law*, 196.

it would be incorrect to conclude that Jesus either displaced and repudiated the law or questioned its abiding validity and authority;[13] instead, the emphasis is on Jesus fulfilling the Mosaic corpus.[14] Jesus is not simply a new Moses. More importantly, the Son utterly transcends Israel's lawgiver as well as all other prominent individuals in the Old Testament (cf. Heb 3:1–7).[15] With the advent of the divine, incarnate Torah, the old era is subsumed by the new one. Indeed, all the redemptive-historical types and prophecies recorded in the sacred Hebrew writings find their consummation in the Son (cf. 10:1).

Although the Mosaic law is holy (cf. Rom 7:12), it could only provide an incomplete understanding of God (cf. Heb 1:1–2).[16] In addition, He who "lives in unapproachable light" (1 Tim. 6:16) has never been seen in the fullness of His glory by human eyes (John 1:18; cf. Exod 33:20; 1 John 4:12). The only exception is Jesus as Tanakh (John 6:46). All that the law anticipated and declared is embodied in the Messiah. He is not only the "one and only son" (1:18; Greek, *monogenēs huios*), but also "God" (*theos*) made in "human likeness" (Phil. 2:6). John 1:18 uses the Greek noun *kolpos* to declare that the Lord Jesus abides in intimate relationship

---

13. Cf. Loader, *Jesus' attitude*, 448–451; Pancaro, *Law in the fourth Gospel*, 539–543; Paroschi, *Incarnation and covenant*, 162–5.

14. Cf. Fernando, *Relationship between law and love*, 70; Ladd, *Theology of the New Testament*, 266–67; Murray, *Principles of conduct*, 123, 150; Motyer, *Look to the Rock*, 61, 134; Sloyan, *Christ*, 118; Sprinkle, *Biblical law*, 31–32, 38–39; VanGemeren, "Law as the perfection of righteousness, 37–38.

15. The absolute supremacy of Jesus over all individuals and institutions of the Old Testament era is brought out in the episode involving the Son's transfiguration on a high mountain (cf. Matt 17:1–8; Mark 9:2–8; Luke 9:28–36). While He was with Peter, James, and John, Jesus' appearance was transformed, so that His face shone with the brightness of the sun, and His clothes turned as white as light. In that moment, Jesus' eternal glory was unveiled. Next, two former heroes of faith—Moses (Israel's famed lawgiver) and Elijah (a legendary prophet)—appeared and began talking with Jesus. The subject of their conversation was the Lamb of God's upcoming death in Jerusalem and return to heaven. The presence of Moses and Elijah was a visual reminder that Jesus fulfilled the Law and the Prophets. Indeed, He is the culmination of the entire Old Testament revelation. This truth is confirmed by the voice originating from the bright cloud (representing the divine presence), in which the Father identified Jesus as His dearly beloved Son, in whom He took great delight. Because Jesus is the eschatological Torah, the disciples were to obey Him. At the end of the incident, only Jesus was left with Peter, James, and John. The implication is that Jesus was not just another hero of faith, but rather the Anointed One of God. He is not only infinitely superior to Moses and Elijah, but also equal with the Father and displayed His glory on the cross; cf. Clowney, *Jesus transformed*, xiv; Ratzinger, *Jesus of Nazareth*, 309–311, 316–17.

16. Guthrie, *New Testament theology*, 684.

with the Father (as well as the Spirit).[17] As the premier soteriological and eschatological revelation of the Torah, the Son has made the Father known to humankind.

With the advent of the Messiah, the Father's revelation to believers is ultimate, complete, and final.[18] This truth is emphasized by the Greek verb *exegeomai*, which means "to expound" or "to set forth in great detail." Interestingly, the English noun "exegesis" is derived from the verb and refers to a critical explanation or interpretation of a text. What the law of Moses could not elucidate about the triune God has now been fully unveiled in Jesus as Tanakh. Only He could reveal the essential being of the Godhead, for the Messiah alone is "the image of the invisible God" (Col 1:15), the "exact representation of [God's] being" (Heb 1:3), and the One in whom "all the fullness of the Deity lives in bodily form" (Col 2:9). We should not be surprised, then, that Jesus said to Philip, "Anyone who has seen me has seen the Father" (John 14:9).

The Messiah as the Culmination of the Law (Rom 3:21, 28, 31; 6:6, 14; 7:5–6; 8:1–4; 9:30–32; 10:3–4; 13:8–10)

The Pauline writings contain a wealth of information about the moral law, and the apostle's letter to the Romans is possibly his most seminal text on the issue. His epistle affirms the truth that there is a fundamental unity and continuity between the testaments, in which the same world view and theological message is consistently maintained.[19] For instance, the gospel Paul declared had its origin in the Hebrew Scriptures and previously was the subject of the prophets' interest (Rom 1:2). In fact, the message of truth had even been proclaimed to Abraham (Gal 3:8); and so the good news Paul heralded was not something novel or deviant, but rather grounded in the revelation of the Old Testament.

This literary and theological coherence between the testaments is reflected in Paul's discussion of the moral law. By way of example, Romans 3:21 states that the entire Hebrew corpus testified to the "righteousness of God." The precise meaning of this phrase is debated, with one option

---

17. Ratzinger (*Jesus of Nazareth*, 6) observes that "what was true of Moses only in fragmentary form has now been fully realized in the person of Jesus." Moreover, the eternal Tanakh "lives before the face of God, not just as friend, but as a Son." Indeed, only the divine-human Logos "lives in the most intimate unity with the Father."

18. Fernando, *Relationship between law and love*, 68.

19. Cf. Lioy, *Search for ultimate reality*, 15.

being that the emphasis is on God's attribute of righteousness. Without denying the general truth of the latter, a more likely exegetical option is that Paul was emphasizing God's justifying activity in conferring an upright status on believers; hence, the verse is referring to righteousness from God, which He imputes to sinners who trust in the Messiah for salvation (cf. 1:17; 3:22).[20]

In 3:31, Paul asked whether his stress on faith in the Son as the basis for imputed righteousness nullifies the law (that is, renders it inoperative). Expressed differently, does an emphasis on faith somehow imply that believers can forget about the law? The apostle's response was an emphatic "not at all!" The basis for this assertion stems from the interrelated purposes of the law, which were mentioned earlier in this chapter. In short, God did not give the law to provide justification but rather to show people their state of sin and their need to be reconciled with Him. Consequently, the faith of those who trust in the Messiah actually upholds the law, especially its continuing authority to condemn those who reject the Son. From what has been said, the Messiah is central to the believers' ongoing relationship with the law.

In 6:14, Paul revealed that sin is no longer the believers' master. Here the apostle metaphorically depicted sin as a powerful foe that enslaves people (cf. Ps 19:13). Sin misuses the law to arouse evil desires within the lost. In turn, these forbidden passions yield a harvest of ungodly deeds, resulting in death (Rom 7:5). The situation is different for believers. Their identification with Jesus' in His death, burial, and resurrection means they have died to the law (6:1–14). Consequently, they are no longer held captive like prisoners under its condemnation. Now that they are "released from the law" (7:6), they can serve God by living in the Spirit.[21]

Paul, in saying that believers are no longer "under the law" (6:14), did not mean they have no obligation to heed God's universal ethical absolutes. In fact, when believers operate "under grace," the Spirit enables them to do all that the moral law enjoins. Put another way, under the disciplinary authority of grace, believers have the freedom to live according to a higher principle—a principle that is rooted in the resurrection life of the Lord Jesus (cf. Titus 2:11–12). He has unshackled them from slavery to sin so that they can become slaves, or willing servants, to righteous living (cf. Rom 6:15–18).

---

20. Cf. Kruse, *Paul*, 170, 188–89; Martin, *Christ*, 126–27; McGrath, "Justification," 520–1; Thielman, *Theology of the New Testament*, 346; VanDrunen, *Report on justification*, 43.

21. Cf. VanDrunen, *Report on justification*, 4.

Jesus' atoning sacrifice on the cross is the basis for God showering believers with His love and grace, rather than giving them the punishment they deserve (cf. 5:1–11). Jesus' redemptive work at Calvary is also the reason why there is no condemnation, or looming eternal punishment, for those who are united to Him by faith (8:1). His followers operate in the power of the Spirit, who is life-giving, rather than the power of sin, which is death-producing. In verse 2, the Greek noun translated "law" (*nomos*) can refer to a controlling principle (cf. 3:27; 7:21–23). Another possibility is that Paul meant the law of God as it functioned within two different contexts. In one circumstance, sin misuses the law and brings about death for sinners. In the contrasting situation, believers operate in the Son, through the Spirit, to obey the moral law, which leads to life.[22]

The viability of this second option is reinforced by the explanation Paul supplied in 8:3. He noted that the sinful nature weakened the Mosaic law by arousing forbidden passions within the lost; and in this crippled state, the law was "powerless" to free them from sin and death. What the law failed to achieve—providing righteousness for humanity—the Father did by sending His Son "in the likeness of sinful humanity." The latter phrase implies that sin never controlled the Messiah; in turn, His human nature remained morally pure and spiritually undefiled. This qualified Him to be God's offering to atone for the sins of the world (cf. John 1:29; 1 John 2:2).

By one righteous act on the cross, the incarnate Messiah "condemned sin in human flesh" (Rom 8:3). Likewise, the believers' "old self" (6:6) was crucified with the Son. "Old self" refers to everything people were before trusting in Jesus for salvation, when they were still enslaved to sin (cf. 3:9), were ungodly (cf. 5:6), and were God's enemies (cf. v. 10). In short, the old self is our state before being born again. The crucifixion of our pre-conversion, unregenerate self is the basis for sin losing its power in our lives and for our post-conversion, regenerate self being enlivened and empowered by the Spirit.

When people trust in the Son, a miraculous exchange occurs. Their guilty status as condemned sinners is transferred to the Messiah on the cross and His perfect righteousness is transferred to them. Through this exchange, the requirements of the law are met in full. Jesus' righteousness operating in believers enables them to consistently live according to the Spirit of God, rather than according to the sinful nature (8:4). Additionally, the Savior makes it possible for the moral law of God to become part of the innermost being of believing sinners and for its ethical injunctions

22. Cf. Bandstra, *Law*, 108–10; Martin, *Christ*, 31; Thielman, "Law," 201–2.

and principles to affect their thoughts, emotions, and decisions (cf. Jer 31:31–4).[23]

These truths have sobering implications. To be specific, those who trust in the Son and operate in the power of the Spirit are declared righteous. Also, they live in such a way that they fully satisfy the requirements of the moral law. In contrast, those who reject the Messiah and operate in the "old way of the written code" (Rom 7:6)—that is, the letter of the Old Testament law—remain eternally condemned sinners (9:30–32). Their unregenerate status will never change as long as they insist on trying to get right with God by scrupulously keeping the law or assert that maintaining their covenant status as God's people depends on them performing a never-ending catalog of meritorious works.[24] The fundamental truth of the gospel is that people receive God's imputed righteousness through faith in the Messiah, not earn it by doing what is commanded in the Mosaic legal code (cf. Acts 15:11; Rom 3:28; 10:3; Gal 2:16).[25]

Recent critical scholarship has largely abandoned the "traditional Reformation understanding" of the doctrine of justification by faith taught in Paul's writings.[26] Indeed, despite the "plethora of new proposals" that specialists have offered, "no consensus has yet emerged."[27] For instance, one current paradigm known as the "new perspective" on Paul (or NPP) is not a "unified, homogeneous group," but rather a "spectrum of viewpoints."[28] Admittedly, supporters of the NPP are right in disapproving any caricature of rabbinicism prevalent during the Second Temple period of Judaism (approximately 515 BC–AD 70).[29] Moreover, adherents are correct in emphasizing the importance of carefully analyzing primary sources written during that time, especially to obtain a clearer, more accurate understanding of the New Testament corpus, including the Pauline epistles.[30]

23. Cf. Ladd, *Theology of the New Testament*, 553–54.
24. Cf. Thielman, "Law," 532, 538; VanDrunen, *Report on justification*, 9–11, 45.
25. Cf. Schreiner, "Works of the law," 975, 978.
26. Hafemann, "Paul and his interpreters," 671.
27. Hafemann, "Paul and his interpreters," 673; cf. Gager, *Reinventing Paul*, 146; Thielman, *Paul and the law*, 45–7.
28. VanDrunen, *Report on justification*, 36; cf. Chancey, "Paul and the law," 21; Farnell, "New perspective," 201–2; Waters, *Justification*, 151.
29. Cf. Chancey, "Paul and the law," 20; Gieschen, "Paul and the law," 121, 144; Lichtenberger, "Understanding of the Torah," 7, 22.
30. Cf. Bird, "When the dust finally settles," 63–64, 68–69; Mattison, "Summary on the new perspective"; Mitchell, "Works righteousness."

Such affirmations notwithstanding, the major tenets of the NPP are undermined by an objective analysis of the biblical and extra-biblical data. According to Carson, the NPP tries to adopt a single, tidy explanation for a diverse array of extra-biblical literature, with the result that the formulation is both "reductionistic" and "misleading."[31] Kim notes that the NPP's sociological and philosophical reconstruction of Second Temple Judaism has attained the "status of a dogma" that "insists on interpreting Paul" only through the distorted lens of that credo.[32] Others have observed that the NPP contradicts far more accurate and nuanced interpretations of the apostle's theology found in conservative, confessional forms of Protestantism.[33]

VanDrunen advances the discussion with the observation that those favoring the "new perspective" put too much "interpretive weight" on the literature found in first-century Judaism (Diaspora, Palestinian, and Qumran writings) and too little on the Judeo-Christian Scriptures (especially the broader historical and theological perspective found in them).[34] They redefine "righteousness" as living in covenant relationship with God and remaining faithful to His covenant promises, over against the more traditional understanding of conforming to God's perfect "moral standard."[35] "Works of the law" is said to refer to "boundary markers identifying Israel as God's covenant people" (in particular, being circumcised, keeping the Sabbath, and observing dietary regulations), not attempts to create one's own upright status before God by doing what the Mosaic law demands. "Justification" refers to the vindication of God's covenant people before the pagan nations, not His unconditional pardoning and acceptance of

---

31. Carson, "Summaries and conclusions," 544; cf. O'Brien, "Paul," 253.

32. Kim, *Paul*, 294–95.

33. Cf. Busenitz, "Reformer's understanding," 258–259; Farnell, "New perspective," 203, 243; Riddlebarger, "Reformed confessionalism"; Trueman, "Man more sinned against"; Venema, "Evaluating the new perspective"; Waters, *Justification*, 151, 191–98; Watson, "Not the new perspective."

34. VanDrunen, *Report on justification*, 54.

35. In the New Testament, the Greek word translated "righteousness" comes from a root term that means "straightness" and refers to that which is in accordance with established moral norms. In a legal sense, righteousness means to be vindicated or treated as just. From a biblical perspective, God's character is the definition and source of righteousness. As a result, the righteousness of human beings is defined in terms of God's holiness. Because the Lord solely provides righteousness, it cannot be produced or obtained by human efforts. God makes His righteousness available to all people without distinction. Just as there is no discrimination with Him in universally condemning all people as sinners, so God does not show partiality by offering righteousness to one particular ethnic group. The Lord freely gives it to all people—regardless of their race or gender—when they trust in the Messiah.

The Moral Law in Christ-Centered Perspective

believing sinners.[36] The basis for justification is shifted from the "finished work" of the Lord Jesus at Calvary to the "Spirit-produced works of the believer." Finally, NPP adherents reject the notion that the sin of the first Adam has been imputed to humanity and that the righteousness of the second (eschatological) Adam has been imputed to believers.[37]

Romans 10:4 explains that the Savior is the *telos* (literally, "end") of the law for all who trust in Him. One implication is that He is the terminus of "using the law to establish one's own righteousness."[38] There are two other interpretive options worth mentioning in connection with this verse. The first is that Jesus somehow brings about the cessation or abolition of the Mosaic law, either historically, existentially, or both.[39] While it is true that the Messiah's death and resurrection put an end to the civil and ceremonial aspects of the law (a point made earlier in this chapter), its universal moral absolutes remain authoritative and applicable for His followers. Also, as previously explained, it is incorrect to suppose that Jesus sought to annul, repeal, or do away with the Mosaic legal code. Accordingly, a second interpretive option is preferred, namely, that *telos* points to Jesus being the culmination (that is, the destination, goal, outcome, and fulfillment) of the law (cf. Matt 5:17).[40] The implication is that all its types and prophe-

---

36. In the New Testament, the Greek word translated "justified" signified, in Paul's day, a court setting, with a judge declaring an individual "not guilty." The idea of justification comes from a judge pronouncing someone to be righteous or innocent of a crime. The word had a technical forensic application of a one-time rendering of a positive judicial verdict. Paul used the term to refer to God's declaration that the believing sinner is righteous because of the atoning work of the Messiah on the cross.

37. Cf. Bird, "When the dust finally settles," 58–63; Das, *Paul*, 5, 273; Gaffin, "Reformed critique"; Gieschen, "Paul and the law," 121–22; Horton, "Déjà vu"; Hughes, "New perspective's view," 275; Johnson, "Defense of the old perspective"; O'Brien, "Paul," 295–96; Seifrid, "Narrative of Scripture," 19–28; Thomas, "Hermeneutics," 315–16; Waters, *Justification*, 151–190; Westerholm, "Justification," 16–25.

38. Schreiner, "Paul's view," 121, 135; cf. Das, *Paul*, 93.

39. Cf. Adeyemi, *New covenant Torah*, 133–36, 206; Kruse, *Paul*, 226–29; Martin, *Christ*, 133–34, 141, 154; Pate, *Reverse of the curse*, 248–49; Räisänen, *Paul*, 54–56, 82, 199–200; Sanders, *Paul*, 38–40; Strickland, "Inauguration," 266–70.

40. Cf. Badenas, *Christ*, 114–15, 117–18, 143, 151; Bandstra, *Law*, 101–6, 183; Bolton, *True bounds*, 61; Das, *Paul*, 249–251; Fairbairn, *Revelation of law*, 443–44; Gager, *Reinventing Paul*, 134–35; Guthrie, *New Theology theology*, 694; Henry, *Christian personal ethics*, 180; Kaiser, "Law," 188; Meyer, *Word in this world*, 86, 89, 92; Moo, "Law of Christ," 358–59; Moo, "Israel and the law," 214–15; Morris, *New Testament theology*, 62; Motyer, *Look to the Rock*, 38, 182; Rhyne, *Faith*, 103–4, 113–14, 118; Rhyne, "Nomos dikaiosynes," 492–3, 498–9; Sloyan, *Christ*, 171; Thielman, *Paul and the law*, 207–8; Wenham, *Paul*, 228; Wright, *Climax of the covenant*, 24–244.

cies are realized in Him, its teachings find their most perfect expression in Him, and its demands are most fully satisfied in Him (cf. Gal 3:24).

The ongoing relevance of the ethical and social aspects of the Mosaic law for believers is evident in Romans 13:8–10, where Paul stressed that Christians are duty-bound to show love to all people (v. 8). This reflects Jesus' teaching in Matthew 22:34–40. He said the greatest commandment is to love God unconditionally and to love others as we love ourselves. There are always opportunities for believers to help others in need (Gal 6:10) and thus "fulfill the law of Christ" (v. 2). The latter phrase refers to "the moral norms" of the Old Testament legal code,[41] especially as interpreted by the Savior.[42] To refuse to assist the disadvantaged would be a denial of God's love for us (cf. 1 John 3:16–18). We must pay the debt of love even to those who do not love us. For this, we must rely on the Spirit for the strength to be kind to the mean and coldhearted (cf. Gal. 5:22).

To unconditionally love others fulfills the moral requirements of the law of Moses (Gal 5:14). Romans 13:9 lists four of the ten commandments that appear in Exodus 20:1–17 (cf. Deut 5:6–21), and these four all concern relationships with other people. The Lord forbids His people from committing adultery, murdering, stealing, and coveting the possessions of others. Paul could have mentioned numerous additional injunctions. This was unnecessary, however, for the command in Leviticus 19:18 sums up every conceivable law: "Love your neighbor as yourself." This directive acknowledges a self-evident truth, namely, that we instinctively love ourselves. When we make every effort to treat others with the sensitivity and compassion of the Messiah, we do what is prescribed in the moral law. In fact, love is the essence of God's universal ethical absolutes (Rom 13:10).

The Messiah as the Realization of the Law's Types, Prophecies, and Expectations (Heb 1:1–4; 8:8–13)

The Book of Hebrews occupies a distinctive place among the New Testament writings for its emphasis on the superiority of the Messiah to leading figures and institutions existing during the Old Testament era. The epistle teaches that because of who Jesus is and what He has done,

---

41. Schreiner, "Law of Christ," 542, 544; cf. Bandstra, *Law*, 111–14; Das, *Paul*, 171–73; Ridderbos, *Paul*, 284–85; Sprinkle, *Biblical law*, 21; contra Adeyemi, *New covenant Torah*, 108–119.

42. Cf. Kim, *Paul*, 267; Ratzinger, *Jesus of Nazareth*, 99–100; Stanton, "Law," 115–16; Stanton, *Jesus*, 113, 116, 122.

He is the realization of the law's types, prophecies, and expectations. This truth harmonizes with what has been said up to this point concerning the Savior's relationship to the Mosaic legal code.

Hebrews 1:1 declares that during the era of the Old Testament, God spoke redemptively to His people through His prophets on a number of occasions. The Lord did so in various portions and in a variety of ways (for example, through visions, dreams, and riddles). The idea is that His revelation was fragmentary and partial, though fully inspired and authoritative. Prophets used a variety of means to convey God's message to people, including oral, dramatic, and written forms. Prophets did not spend all of their time predicting the future. Much of their efforts involved observing what was taking place around them and declaring God's message concerning those situations. The prophets were not speaking on their own behalf or for their personal benefit. Rather, they were God's messengers, whom He authorized to convey vital truths to others.

The basis for God choosing to reveal Himself in progressive stages rests on the fact that He works with us according to the level of our understanding. At first, He revealed Himself only in shadows and symbols; but as people came to know more about Him and the way He works, He became more explicit in His dealings and disclosures. It is important to acknowledge these ancient revelations for what they taught people about God, while simultaneously noting that they pointed to a time when God would reveal Himself more fully and finally in "his Son" (v. 2).

The candid statements appearing in verse 1 were not meant to diminish the value of God's revelation through the Hebrew prophets. The fact that He considered them the transmitters of divine truth is evidence of just how much respect He held for these faithful servants of the Lord; but the same God who had partially revealed Himself in times past, now had disclosed Himself totally and ultimately in His Son. With the advent of the Messiah, everything is centered in Him. Expressed differently, He is the meta-narrative of life, whether temporal or eternal in nature.[43] Likewise, He is the key to understanding human identity, and the sole channel to the knowledge of the triune God. The Son gives full and final expression to all that was previously revealed (cf. Luke 24:44), and He does so in a way that is focused, clear, and relevant.

"In these last days" (Heb 1:2) would carry a special significance for the first readers of the epistle, who probably interpreted the phrase to mean that Jesus, as the Savior, had ushered in the messianic age. He is not

---

43. Cf. the appendix of this study for a discussion of a God-centered and Christ-centered view of making sense of reality.

merely the end of a long line of Old Testament prophets, but more importantly the one for whom the Hebrews had waited for centuries. He is the complete and distinct revelation of God. Even with the coming of the Savior, the inspired nature of God's communication has not changed. The messages He conveyed through the prophets to the community of faith were graced by His power and love; and this remains true now that the Son has unveiled the Father to us. In fact, what the Messiah has disclosed is in harmony with all that appears in the Old Testament, for what the prophets foretold finds its realization in the Messiah (cf. Rom 1:2; 3:21).

Having pointed out Jesus' distinction as the Son of God, the author of Hebrews proceeded to explain ways in which God's revelation through the Savior is better than all other revelations of the Lord. To show this superiority, the writer made a number of statements describing the Son. First, the Father appointed His Son as "heir of all things" (1:2). In Hebrew culture, the firstborn son was the highest ranked of all children. Therefore, he was also the family heir. Jesus is the heir, owner, and Lord of God's creation. Second, it is through the Son that the Father "made the universe." The Greek term rendered "universe" refers to the temporal ages and includes the spatial realm, which exists in those time periods. Before time and matter were created, the Messiah eternally preexisted.

Third, the Son is the "radiance" (v. 3) of the triune God's glory. This does not mean Jesus is merely a reflection of the Lord's majesty. The Messiah is God Himself, for the glory of God is His radiance. In Jesus' incarnation, He unveiled to humankind the majesty of the divine. Fourth, the Son is the "exact representation" of the triune God's being. The Greek word behind this translation originally referred to the die used in minting coins. The term later came to refer to the impression on coins. The writer of Hebrews was saying that who Jesus is corresponds exactly to that of the Godhead. Thus, He alone is the precise image of God's essence. While the Son is one with the Father and the Spirit in terms of their being, there remains a distinction of the divine persons of the Trinity. Fifth, not only did the Son create the universe, but He also holds it together by His powerful word. Through His sustaining royal decree, He prevents the cosmos from destruction. Clearly, the Son has a continued interest in the world and loves it. Thus, He is carrying it toward the fulfillment of His divine plan.

Sixth, at the heart of the divine plan and revelation to humankind is making redemption available for the lost. This is why the Son died to wash us from the stain of our sins. The Greek noun for "purged" is *katharismos*, from which we derive the term *catharsis*, meaning a purging that brings about spiritual renewal. The idea is that through His atoning sacrifice at

Calvary, Jesus accomplished cleansing for humanity's transgressions. The writer expressed his thoughts in the past tense to underscore that the Messiah's redemptive work on our behalf has already been accomplished. Seventh, because Jesus completed the task for which He was sent, He was granted the place of highest honor—to sit at God's right hand in a posture of rest (as opposed to endlessly ministering in a standing position; cf. 10:11). The Lord Jesus did once and for all what the Hebrew priests were required to do on a regular basis. Now, as our great High Priest, the Messiah continually applies to us the purification for sins He obtained at the cross. This enables us to worship in God's presence.

For the various reasons given by the writer of Hebrews, the Son is to be considered superior to every other entity, including the following: the prophets (1:1–3); the angels (1:4–14; 2:5); Moses (3:1–6); Joshua (4:6–11); the Aaronic high priest (5:1–10; 7:26—8:2); the Levitical priests (6:20—7:25); Abraham (7:1–10), the tabernacle ministry (8:3–6; 9:1–28); the old covenant (8:7–13); the temple sacrificial system (10:1–14); and the Mosaic law given at Mount Sinai (12:18–24). As the unique Son of God who made the supreme sacrifice of Himself to the Father, Jesus is described by the writer of Hebrews as the "pioneer of [our] salvation" (2:10), the "perfecter of [our] faith" (12:2), and the "great Shepherd of the sheep" (13:20). Unlike the earthly and external aspects of the Old Testament sanctuary, the Messiah sanctifies believers for the true worship of God, so that they can draw near to heaven itself with clean consciences (9:14; 10:22). In short, the Messiah is the realization of all the types, prophecies, and expectations connected with the Mosaic legal code.

Of particular relevance is the discussion appearing in Hebrews 8 concerning the interrelationship between the old and new covenants.[44] Verses 1–5 indicate that because Jesus' ministry is heavenly and unlimited, it is superior to that of the Levitical priests. The Savior, as the mediator between God and humanity (1 Tim 2:5), has inaugurated a new and better covenant than the old one based on the Mosaic law. The new covenant is superior, precisely because it is "established on better promises" (Heb 8:6). The writer of Hebrews argued that if the first covenant had sufficiently met the needs of people and had adequately provided for their salvation, then there would have been no need for a new covenant to replace it (v. 7); but the old covenant was insufficient and inadequate in bringing people to God, and therefore a new covenant had to be established.

The nexus of the shortfall was not the covenant in and of itself, but those living under it. God had found fault with the Israelites, primarily

---

44. Lioy, "Progressive covenantalism."

because they did not continue in that covenant (v. 8). While God initiated the old covenant with His people, they also willingly agreed to it (cf. Josh 24). Thus, the covenant was a mutual obligation between God and the people. Nonetheless, the people often failed to live up to their part of the obligation (cf. Neh 9; Dan 9:1–19). As a result, human failure rendered the old covenant inoperative (cf. Rom 7:7–25).

The establishment of a new covenant naturally implies that the old covenant—especially its "ceremonies and rituals"[45]—is obsolete, needs to be replaced, and will eventually disappear from the scene altogether (Heb 8:13). It would be incorrect to conclude from the preceding remarks that the writer of Hebrews disparaged or maligned the old covenant, or that he indicated the abrogation of the moral law associated with it.[46] The contrast is not between an evil system (namely, the old covenant) and a good system (namely, the new covenant), but between what is good and what is better. According to Jones, the way in which the administrative and liturgical aspects of the Sinaitic covenant were "rendered nonbinding is by redemptive accomplishment rather than legislative repeal."[47] Furthermore, as Ladd notes, "all that the old order symbolized was fulfilled in the reality of Christ."[48]

The theme of fulfillment is also found in the address Stephen delivered before the Sanhedrin, and signifies a refutation of the three points of reference a first century AD Jew most revered: the land, the law, and the temple. The Jews venerated the promised land, but Stephen argued that while it is important, God's activities in Israel's history often took place outside of Palestine. Also, wherever God is present, that locale is considered holy (Acts 7:2–36). Furthermore, the Jews revered the law and, in turn, the one who gave them the law—Moses; but Stephen reminded his listeners that this legendary figure clearly pointed to a coming Prophet who was greater than he and the law. Likewise, the people rejected Moses and embraced idol worship, just as they spurned Jesus (vv. 37–43). Finally, the Jews looked on the temple as a symbol of God's past workings with the nation of Israel. Tragically, many also seemed to confine God's work to the shrine alone, so that they neither could see Him living among them in the person of Jesus, nor recognize the work of the Holy Spirit. Additionally, rather than listen to the Tanakh of God, they schemed with the civil au-

45. Kaiser, "Law," 186.
46. Cf. Fanning, "Theology of Hebrews," 401–3; Rhee, *Faith in Hebrews*, 144.
47. Jones, *Biblical Christian ethics*, 110.
48. Ladd, *Theology of the New Testament*, 630; cf. Murray, *Principles of conduct*, 150–1; Portalatin, *Temporal oppositions*, 58–60.

thorities to have the Messiah killed, as they had other messengers whom God previously sent (vv. 44–53). Since Stephen had knocked down the three pillars of the Jewish faith and proclaimed that Jesus is the Messiah, the long-awaited "Righteous One" (v. 52), the religious leaders' natural reaction was to brand Stephen as a blasphemer and take him out to be stoned (vv. 54–60).

The Abiding Relevance of the Moral Law for Christians (Jas 1:19–20, 22–27; 2:8–27)

The implications of the moral law, especially its abiding relevance for believers, receives considerable attention in the letter of James. Of particular importance is the biblical concept of righteousness, which is first mentioned in 1:20. In verse 19, James exhorted his readers to be slow to get angry. Human anger is a volatile emotion that can easily get out of control, especially in tense situations. When inappropriate forms of anger erupt, whether toward evildoers or unwanted circumstances, it does not accomplish God's "righteousness" (v. 20). This means the aftermath of human anger falls short of God's righteous moral standard, does not reflect the upright standing He gives believers in the Messiah, does not result in any of the good things God wants done, and is contrary to the equity and justice He will establish in His future eternal kingdom. In short, human anger does not produce the righteousness God desires, regardless of its form.

For many Christians, the concept of righteousness might seem too abstract to understand. This difficulty is decreased as they grow in their appreciation of what it means to live in a holy or morally pure manner. People are considered righteous when their personal behaviors are in harmony with God's will as it is revealed in Scripture. The righteous person voluntarily serves the Lord (Mal 3:18), takes delight in Him (Ps 33:1), and gives thanks to Him for His mercy and love (140:13). The righteous are blessed by God (5:12) and upheld by Him (37:17). The righteous may experience hardships and trials in life, but God promises to help them through the difficulties (34:19).

No matter how severe the believers' afflictions might be, the Lord will never forsake them (37:25) or allow them to fall (55:22). The prospect for the righteous is joy (Prov 10:28) and the way of the Lord is their strength, or refuge (v. 29). The Lord promises to be with them in their darkest moments (11:8) and to be a refuge for them in death (14:32). In summary, James was urging his readers to leave whatever sinful paths they might have been on, and to follow the path of uprightness. Otherwise, they would be sinning by refusing to do what they knew to be "good" (Jas 4:17). Here we see that sins of omission (neglecting to do what is right) are just as inappropriate as sins of commission (opting to do what is wrong).

James told his readers that passively listening to God's Word was not enough to promote spiritual growth. It was just as important for them to obediently act upon what it says (1:22). To hear what the moral law declares without implementing its teachings is nothing but self-deception. Those who hear but do not heed God's Word are like people who observe their reflection in a mirror, walk away, and quickly forget the image they saw (vv. 23–24). James exhorted his readers to look carefully into and fix their attention on the "perfect law that gives freedom" (v. 25). They were to live out, not forget, what the law of liberty taught. The sustained and thoughtful study of God's universal ethical precepts would bring them true liberty, spiritual vitality, and abundant blessing in whatever they undertook.

"Religion" (v. 26) is another important biblical concept in James, especially in terms of the abiding relevance of the moral law for Christians. The Greek word translated "religious" denotes the practice of external rituals and observances of a spiritual tradition, such as attendance at worship, prayer, fasting, and giving to the poor.[49] Merely doing these things does not in itself constitute true religion. Those who are genuinely pious demonstrate their faith by controlling what they say. On the other hand, failure to bridle the tongue betrays the self-deception in those who regard themselves as religious and exposes a form of spirituality that has no eternal value.

Verse 27 shifts the focus from outward observances to service for others, particularly "orphans and widows." In Scripture, widows, orphans, and aliens are usually depicted as the most helpless among people. Often, they had none but God as their patron and protector (cf. Exod 22:22–23; Deut 10:18; Isa 1:17). Moreover, in Bible times, there was no social safety net to catch the dispossessed and homeless when their source of support was suddenly gone. Widows, orphans, and foreigners were frequently reduced to begging, especially if there was no friend, relative, or benefactor to care for them (cf. Gen 38:11; Ruth 1:8).

James 1:27 reflects this biblical perspective by focusing attention on orphans and widows who live in a state of distress. The writer maintained that clean and undefiled religion is demonstrated, not just in rituals and observances, but also in the upright conduct and righteous character as-

---

49. For a discussion of differing approaches to defining the concept of "religion," cf. Blasi, "Religion"; Rule, "Religion."

sociated with God's moral law. Examples of this type of behavior include caring for those in anguish and keeping oneself clean in an ethically polluted world. The writer's intention in this passage was not to give a formal definition of religion. Rather, his aim was to draw a contrast between religion as mere ritualistic observance and faith in action that pleases God. Religion that demonstrates genuine spirituality and Christian maturity is an active faith motivated by love.

A similar emphasis can be found in 2:8, in which the writer focused on the directive recorded in Leviticus 19:18. It is the supreme commandment in terms of defining how people should treat one another. This dictum is also royal, for among all the commandments given by God (who is the sovereign King of the universe), it sums up the entirety of the "moral norms" contained in the Old Testament legal code.[50] James 2:8 builds on this truth by stressing that the royal law will become the guiding principle in the future messianic kingdom. The author observed that believers are doing well when they love others as much as they love themselves. The point is that they cannot heed the most important directive in Scripture and discriminate against others at the same time (cf. vv. 1–7).

As this chapter on the nature of the moral law has maintained, both testaments of Scripture are one unified expression, given by one Lawgiver. This means believers cannot make exceptions or subtract the ethical injunctions of God that they dislike. Against the backdrop of His infinitely perfect moral standard (Rom 3:23), the person who observes every divine law except for one, is still liable for violating them all (Jas 2:10).[51] The sobering reality is that everyone fails to heed the whole law (Rom 3:9–18), which is why people must depend on the imputed righteousness of the Lord Jesus in order to be saved (v. 24).

James set up a clear contrast between treating others the way we would like to be treated and showing favoritism toward somebody for any reason (Jas 2:9). Doing the first pleases God, while doing the second is sin. Accordingly, failing to observe the royal law—the most liberating, relationship-building command God ever gave—makes one a lawbreaker. Perhaps James thought that some among his readers would look upon showing favoritism as more a social convention than as sin. How, they might ask, could such a custom compare to sins like adultery and murder (v. 11)? The answer James provided is clear and direct. If we transgress any part of the moral law, we are guilty of breaking all of it (v. 10).

---

50. Cf. Schreiner, "Law," 645.
51. Cf. VanDrunen, *Report on justification*, 5–6.

To better understand this concept, imagine a balloon with all the commands of God written upon it. Next, imagine trying to cut out one of the commands with a razor blade without affecting the others. James used the weighty sins of adultery and murder to explain that selective obedience to the provisions of God's universal ethical code was absurd. The author would scoff at the popular notion that certain iniquities do not affect our relationship with God because they are less serious than others.

The author seems to have associated obedience to the moral law with fellowship with God, the one who gave the law. From this perspective, heeding the precepts of God's abiding ethical absolutes is a display of faith and springs from love. Disobedience to the moral law, on the other hand, is a breach of faith that disrupts fellowship with God, the Lawgiver. In James 2:12, the author placed an equally strong emphasis on talking and acting as if one is going to be judged by the liberating law of God. In the original language, there is also an emphasis on making this behavior a habit. Because of the wise counsel contained in God's perfect moral law, James could say that it gives spiritual freedom (cf. 1:25)—but only if it is respected and obeyed. Disobedience results in bondage and restricted living (cf. John 8:34).

According to James 2:13, the believer who has been merciful will be shown mercy when his or her character flaws and weaknesses are exposed on the final day. In contrast, those who have shown little mercy to others will receive little themselves. Furthermore, the believer who has demonstrated mercy to others will have nothing to fear at the time of divine assessment, for the mercy shown to him or her will triumph over that judgment (cf. 1 John 4:17). As Jesus' followers strive to become more merciful, there is hope. The liberating power of the Son working within them makes it possible to obey God's moral law more fully and completely.

James 2:14–27 spotlights the relationship of faith to good works. For some, these verses seem difficult to reconcile with Paul's teaching concerning justification by faith;[52] but an objective and balanced study of the New Testament indicates the two men were in agreement and that James was possibly "responding to a misunderstood Pauline teaching."[53] Both writers would affirm that saving faith is a voluntary change in a sinner's mind that results in turning to God with a corresponding turning away from sin. It includes a transformation of one's view, feeling, and purpose in

---

52. Cf. Laato, "Paul's theology," 213–5.

53. Davids, "James and Paul," 458; cf. Guthrie, *New Testament theology,* 598–99; Ladd, *Theology of the New Testament,* 639; Marshall, *New Testament theology,* 692–93; Sloyan, *Christ,* 112.

The Moral Law in Christ-Centered Perspective

life. An exercise of faith involves the whole person—the mind, emotions, and will—and eventually one's behavior. With the mind, one believes in God's existence and in the teaching of Scripture; emotions are connected to personal faith in the Son as the only one who can redeem from sin; and with the will, one surrenders to the Messiah and trusts Him as Lord and Savior. The natural consequence of saving faith is a lifestyle that actively promotes and demonstrates righteousness through doing good works (cf. Eph 2:8–9; Titus 2:11–14).[54]

James used two rhetorical questions to begin his discussion about the nature of genuine, saving faith. To paraphrase, those questions were: (1) What good is faith that is not accompanied by righteous deeds? and (2) How can a faith that is devoid of good works save anybody (Jas 2:14)? The author's point was that faith resulting in eternal life will naturally manifest itself in virtuous acts. The construction of the second question in the Greek shows that "No" was the expected answer. There is no contradiction here with Paul's teaching that salvation cannot be attained through works (cf. Rom 3:28). James was simply saying that true faith will manifest itself in a life of active obedience to God's moral law. The author's rebuke is directed toward a spurious kind of "faith" that is merely an intellectual assent, not a life-changing trust in the Messiah. Because this kind of "faith" is devoid of good works, it is worthless. Expressed differently, belief without action is dead on arrival (Jas 2:16–17).

Verse 18 anticipates an imaginary objector declaring, "You have faith; I have deeds." The idea is that there are two equally valid types of faith—one that simply believes and another that acts on that belief. James challenged the idea that genuine, saving faith has no effect on the way a person acts. In short, trusting in Jesus as Torah is authenticated by doing kind deeds to others. Next, the author commented on the presumed value of merely believing in the existence of God by noting that this by itself does not result in eternal life. After all, even the demons are monotheists, for they affirm that there is only one God and it causes them to tremble with fear (v. 19; cf. Deut 6:4; Mark 12:29). The obvious conclusion is that "faith without deeds is useless," for dead orthodoxy is barren of eternal fruit (Jas 2:20).

To reinforce his point, James presented illustrations from the lives of two prominent Old Testament characters—the patriarch Abraham and the prostitute Rahab. James introduced each example by means of a question with which his readers were expected to give full and hearty agreement. In the case of Abraham, when he was about 85, he believed God's promise

---

54. Cf. McGrath, "Justification," 522; Morris, *New Testament theology,* 314.

concerning a son to be born through Sarah (Gen 15:5). Verse 6 indicates that the patriarch considered the Lord's pledge as being reliable and dependable. Indeed, the patriarch was confident that God was fully capable of bringing about what He had promised. Consequently, Abraham's faith was "credited . . . to him as righteousness." Expressed differently, the Lord considered the patriarch's response of faith as proof of his genuine commitment and evidence of his steadfast loyalty. Paul referred to this verse in Romans 4:3 to stress that an upright standing before God comes through faith, not by means of obedience to the law (cf. Gal 3:6). As Abraham's life illustrated, God forgives the believing sinner on the basis of Jesus' atoning sacrifice (Rom 3:25–26).

Years later, when Abraham was about 116, he submitted to God's test to sacrifice Isaac (Gen 22:1–19). This was an act of faith on the part of the patriarch (Heb 11:17–19) in which he demonstrated that he feared God (Gen 22:12). This meant Abraham followed the Lord in absolute obedience. James 2:21 explains that the patriarch's willingness to sacrifice his son, Isaac, proved that his faith was genuine and that he existed in a right relationship with God. It was not the deed that justified Abraham; rather, he showed himself to be justified through the saving faith that was manifested in his virtuous deed. Verse 22 says that the patriarch's faith and actions worked together, with his actions making his faith complete.

James 2:23 and Romans 4:3 both quote Genesis 15:6 when referring to Abraham's justification. Paul maintained that God counted the patriarch to be righteous because of his faith. James stressed a related truth, namely, that Abraham vindicated the reality of his previously-existing faith and his upright status before God by obeying the Lord.[55] The patriarch showed by his actions that he genuinely was God's friend (cf. 2 Chr 20:7). This indicates that Abraham so pleased God by his life that the Lord showered the patriarch with His favor in a distinctive way.

A superficial reading of James 2:24 seems to teach that people are justified by what they do and not by faith alone. Furthermore, it might be unclear how the author's concept of justification relates to Paul's teaching on the subject (cf. Rom 3:28; Gal 2:16; 3:11); but a careful examination of Scripture indicates there is no contradiction. For Paul, "justification" means to declare a sinner not guilty before the Father by means of faith in the Son and His death in the sinner's place. Because the Messiah died for sin, the repentant sinner can enjoy a standing of righteousness before God. In James, the concept of "justification" is taken one step further to include the validation of one's faith in the sight of God and others. Expressed dif-

---

55. Cf. Fanning, "Theology of James," 429.

ferently, the upright status of believers with God is vindicated by the way they choose to live.

Rahab, the prostitute, is the second example of genuine, saving faith put forward by James. Joshua 2:1–21 records the episode in which Rahab hid the Israelite spies and sent them safely away by a different road. Like Abraham, Rahab was shown to be righteous when her trust in God prompted her to act in a way that met with His approval (Jas 2:25). God was pleased with Rahab's virtuous deed because she operated in faith (cf. Heb 11:6, 31). James 2:26 reveals that the connection between genuine, saving faith and godly deeds is as close as that between body and spirit. When the spirit is separated from the body, the latter dies (cf. Eccl 12:7). Likewise, faith that is barren of any fruit is just as dead. Oppositely, living faith manifests itself in good works advocated by God's moral law.

It is worth noting that John also insisted on the inseparable connection between genuine faith and righteous deeds. He wrote that loving God meant keeping His commands (1 John 5:3). The idea is that love for God has less to do with emotions than with a complete compliance with His universal ethical absolutes. Likewise, our love for other believers is not just something we talk about. It is also demonstrated by truly helping those in need (cf. 3:18). Regrettably, when people who are not Christians think about God's demands, they equate them with the sort of ordinances endorsed by the religious elite of Jesus' day. This maze of regulations and rituals feels irksome and overwhelming (5:3). The new birth, however, changes the perspective of believers and gives them strength through the Spirit to live in accordance with God's moral law. As Jesus Himself declared, His yoke is easy and His burden is light (Matt 11:30).

Conclusion

This chapter has examined the nature of the moral law from a Christ-centered perspective and has done so in a canonical and integrative manner. The discussion began by considering the biblical concept of the law. From the vantage point of the Old Testament, morality concerned how people of faith should live. Similarly, the New Testament regarded ethical instruction as being concerned with a way of life that is characterized by righteousness and blessing. The Mosaic legal code dealt with civil, ceremonial, and ethical issues, of which the administrative and ritual aspects are no longer binding on Christians. In contrast, the universal ethical absolutes of God's law remain authoritative and applicable for Jesus' followers.

Two interrelated purposes of His moral law are helping people recognize their sin and see their need for a Redeemer.

This chapter affirms that the Lord Jesus always remained subject to the law and sought to fulfill it. He did the latter by carrying out its ethical injunctions, showing forth its true spiritual meaning, and bringing to completion all that it stood for prophetically. He also endeavored to dismantle incorrect views about the law, such as the erroneous interpretations put forward by the religious elite of His day. Jesus particularly took issue with the works-based form of righteousness they promulgated, especially its insistence on people earning their salvation by strictly following the law.

As the atoning sacrifice for humankind, the Messiah satisfied the demands of the law completely and for all time. Accordingly, those who trust in Him for eternal life are freed from the condemnation of the law. The natural consequence of saving faith is a lifestyle that actively promotes and demonstrates righteousness through doing good works. In short, the Holy Spirit empowers believers to do what the moral law enjoins.

The implication is that God wants believers to abide by His universal ethical absolutes—not ignore, disregard, or minimize them. The sustained and thoughtful study of the moral law brings them true liberty, spiritual vitality, and abundant blessing in whatever they undertake. Through their new life in Jesus as Torah and the enabling presence of the Spirit, all that the moral law advocates influences the believers' thoughts, emotions, and decisions. The foremost way this is demonstrated is by showing unconditional, Christlike love to others.

3

Jesus as Torah in John 1

Introduction

THE PRECEDING chapter used a canonical and integrative approach to examine the nature of the moral law from a Christ-centered perspective. It was affirmed that the Messiah, as the divine, incarnate Torah (John 1:1, 14, 16–18), fulfilled the law by carrying out its ethical injunctions, showing forth its true spiritual meaning, and bringing to completion all that it stood for prophetically (Matt 5:17). The Redeemer is the culmination (that is, the destination, goal, outcome, and fulfillment) of the law for believers (Rom 10:4) and the realization of the law's types, prophecies, and expectations (Heb 1:1–4; 8:8–13). While His death and resurrection put an end to the administrative and ritual aspects of the law, its universal moral absolutes remain authoritative and applicable for His followers (Jas 1:19–20, 22–27; 2:8–27). The foremost way they heed the moral law is by showing unconditional, Christlike love to others (Rom 13:8–10; Jas 2:8).

The conclusions of chapter two build on the major premise articulated in chapter one, namely, that in the Fourth Gospel, Jesus is portrayed as the perfection of the gift of the Torah. Accordingly, those who trust in the Son for eternal life and heed His teaching fully satisfy the requirements of the moral law recorded in Scripture. These emphases are broached in the opening verses of John's Gospel, in which it is revealed that the divine Word came to earth as a human being and made His dwelling among people. Furthermore, He made the Father known by manifesting His glory, grace, and truth. While many rejected Jesus as the divine, incarnate Tanakh, others turned to Him in faith and became members of God's spiritual family (1:1–14).

The Witness of John the Baptizer to Jesus as Torah (John 1:19–42)

The Baptizer's denial of being the Messiah (John 1:19–28)

John the Baptizer is the person who introduced the Word to the world.[1] In keeping with John's divine commission, he prepared the hearts of his fellow Jews for the coming of the Messiah. (In the Fourth Gospel, the name *John* always refers to the Baptizer.) For the apostle John, it was imperative to establish numerous witnesses to testify that Jesus is the Messiah. John the Baptizer was the first of many to vouch for the Son's authenticity. Because of John's powerful preaching, some had mistakenly identified John as the Messiah. John was not the Light, but had been called by God to attest to it (John 1:6–8).[2]

---

1. The Greek noun rendered "world" (*kosmos*, John 1:9) is an important term in the Fourth Gospel. In its most basic usage, *kosmos* referred to an ornament, such as in 1 Peter 3:3, where it is used to mean the "adornment," namely, the ornamentation of jewelry and clothing. The term can also be used of the universe with its orderly ornamentation of stars and planets. Eventually *kosmos* came to refer to the earth, since (from the human perspective) that is the most important part of the universe, and also people, since they are the most significant inhabitants of the planet. In the Fourth Gospel, "world" most often refers to the majority of people and their temporal pursuits (including their goals, aspirations, values, and priorities). Since most rejected the Messiah, "the world" in this Gospel sometimes denotes humanity in opposition to Him. John's "world" is hostile to the Savior and to His followers because of their association with Him (7:7; 15:18–19); yet despite the world's hatred of God, He still loves it and gave His Son so that its people might receive eternal life (3:16). How ironic it is that even though the world came into being through the Messiah, it remained ignorant of His identity (1:10). Even many of the Jews, God's chosen people, rejected Jesus as the Messiah during His earthly ministry (v. 11).

2. In Scripture, light represents what is good, true, and just, while darkness symbolizes what is wicked, counterfeit, and debased. Transgression and maltreatment are linked to darkness, whereas holiness and purity are associated with light. Both the Old and New Testaments equate light with the truth of the Word. For instance, Psalm 119:105 says that God's word of truth is a lamp to the believers' feet and a light for their path. Also, in 2 Corinthians 4:4, Paul said that the devil had blinded the eyes of unbelievers so that they could not see "the light of the gospel" that displays "the glory of Christ." The early church used the metaphor of light to denote righteousness and the analogy of darkness to refer to despicable behavior. By way of example, in Ephesians 5:9, Paul said that the fruit of Christians, the children of light, consists of "goodness, righteousness and truth." Moreover, believers should have "nothing to do with the fruitless deeds of darkness" (v. 11). An ongoing emphasis in the Fourth Gospel is that the disciples of the Son live in the light, while the followers of Satan abide in the darkness.

Jesus as Torah in John 1

In the Fourth Gospel, a clear distinction is made between John the Baptizer and Jesus as Torah. While John was a great man, he was only a witness to the Light that God sent into the world. Jesus was God and the true Light of the world. John was a person whose mission was to point others to Jesus. The Greek participle *erchomenon* (translated "was coming" in v. 9) could refer to *phōs* (translated "light"), in which case this verse is talking about the Son's incarnation. A second option is that the participle refers to *anthrōpon* (translated "everyone"). The idea then would be that the true light enlightens all those who come into the world. Verse 10, however, speaks of the light being in the world. Accordingly, the first option seems preferable.

Elsewhere in the Fourth Gospel, the Messiah is spoken of as coming into the world (6:14; 9:39; 11:27; 16:28). In fact, in 12:46, Jesus directly referred to Himself as a light that has come into the world so that all those who believed in Him would not remain in darkness. Through His Incarnation, the Son brings the light of divine truth to a sin-cursed world and in so doing discloses the spiritual need all people have for salvation. All who encounter the light can either choose to receive or renounce it (cf. 3:19–21). Only those who believe in Him are enlightened in the truest sense of the word.

The identity of Jesus of Nazareth is closely connected to the Second Temple period of Judaism.[3] The clothes He wore (e.g. the *tzitzit*—tassels attached to the edge of one's garment; and the *tallit*—a prayer shawl), the food He ate (in accordance with the dietary stipulations mandated by the Torah), and the religious customs He observed (e.g. keeping the Sabbath holy) reflected the history and culture of the Jewish people living in first-century Palestine. Like other Jews of the day, Jesus and His first disciples regarded the Torah as being sacred. Also, in the manner of the prophets of the Old Testament era, Jesus spoke candidly and bluntly in order to declare what the Torah taught. A "critically aware, historically informed"

---

3. Burge (*John*) points out that many scholars view the "cultural orientation" of the Fourth Gospel to be "heavily dependent on the Palestinian Judaism of Jesus' day" (24). Indeed, the Evangelist's "frame of reference is primarily indebted to traditional Jewish religious concepts" (54). According to Keener (*John*, 1:171), a "Gospel that structures its chronology around Jerusalem festivals, engages in polemic with a Jewish elite as its main competitor, and exploits a variety of Jewish symbols cannot be understood apart from early Judaism." For a discussion of the historical, cultural, political, and religious backdrop of Galilee in the time of Jesus, cf. Edersheim, *Sketches of Jewish social life*; Edersheim, *Life and times*; Horsley and Hanson, *Bandits, prophets, and messiahs*; Lee, *The Galilean Jewishness of Jesus*; Vermes, *Jesus and the world of Judaism*.

understanding of this setting helps to explain why some people "choose to follow him, others to dismiss him and still others to seek his death."[4]

While many spurned the ever-present, life-giving Word, not all did. The latter are those who received or accepted Him as the Messiah (v. 12). This means they put their faith in His name, which equates to believing that He is the eternal and fully divine Logos. The saving mission of Jesus as the culmination of the Torah included making God known and accessible to humankind.[5] In this case, those who put their faith in the Messiah received the right, or legal entitlement, to become God's children.[6] This new

---

4. Levine, "How the church divorces Jesus from Judaism," 21. Köstenberger (*Studies on John and gender*, 65) maintains that it is imperative to understand Jesus "in terms of his Jewish cultural context." Likewise, O'Day ("John," 9:647) urges the interpreter to "work diligently and carefully to understand the text in its original social and historical context in order to avoid making simplistic and destructive extrapolations to contemporary church settings"; cf. Smith, *John*, 8.

5. For an overview of the way in which God is portrayed in the Fourth Gospel, cf. Thompson, *God of the Gospel of John*, 69–100. Tolmie ("Characterization of God") maintains that God is consistently depicted as "the Father of Jesus" and the "One who initiated and authorized Jesus' mission" (67). This characterization is done "in such a convincing way that there can be no doubt as to the identity of Jesus." The author's intent is to guide the "reader deeper into faith in Jesus Christ, the Son of God" and consequently become a partaker of eternal life (59). Anderson ("The having-sent-me Father") carries the discussion further by noting that the relationship between the Father and the Son in the Fourth Gospel is "rooted in the Prophet-like-Moses typology" of Deuteronomy 18:15–22 (33). The Father sends the Son to earth. In turn, He functions as "the Mosaic prophet, who speaks on the Father's behalf with authentic congruity" (36). This "emissary function is foundational to understanding adequately the Johannine Father-Son relationship" (34). Indeed, the "Father-Son relationship becomes the backbone of the Johannine presentation of Jesus' words and works" (33). In a correspondent fashion, Meyer ("The Father") stresses that the "unity of the Father and Son is continually set before the reader as a total coalescence of the two in the activity of giving life to the world" (260). Also, "Jesus' constancy in doing the Father's will . . . is grounded in, and springs from, the prior unity of Jesus with the Father" (261). In a different vein, Spencer ("Father-ruler," 442) clarifies that the metaphor "father" is not applied to God because He is masculine in gender; rather, in antiquity, "father" was a "helpful metaphor to communicate certain aspects of God's character." Similarly, Lee ("Symbol of divine fatherhood") considers the "term 'Father' as a symbol rather than a literal description of divine essence." She notes that because "biblical language is androcentric, the grammatically masculine gender is used to express not only specific maleness but also that which is universal, cosmic, normative, and therefore gender-neutral'" (177). Moreover, "no human label can adhere to the innermost being of God, including that of gender" (178).

6. In the Fourth Gospel, there is a qualitative difference between the phrases "children of God" and "Son of God." The second title points to Jesus' status as the Messiah and spotlights His divine commission to carry out the work of redemption. Other related emphases are the Son's obedience to the Father, the Son's intimate knowledge of and fellowship with Him, and the Son's experience of the Father's love, mercy, blessings, and protection.

birth was not a human-centered, self-initiated process. It was a spiritual event initiated and accomplished by the will of God (v. 13).

Centuries before the advent of the everlasting Tanakh, Moses[7] made one of the boldest requests ever petitioned before God: "Now show me your glory" (Exod 33:18). Since no human being can see God in His full glory and live, what Moses requested was more than the Lord would grant—for Moses' own good. Nevertheless, God did agree to place Moses in a crevice and then cause His glory to pass by (33:19–23). As a human being, Moses could not stare directly into the glory of God Himself, for to do so would be fatal. Thus, God protected Moses from accidentally viewing His glory by placing His hand (in a manner of speaking) over Moses' face until His glory had passed by. It was only after God's glory had passed by that He removed His protecting hand. At that moment Moses caught a glimpse of God's back. Other passages reveal that God is spirit (John 4:24) and, as such, is invisible (Col 1:15). Also, the Hebrew word translated "back" (Exod 33:23) carries connotations of "aftereffects." Thus, what Moses saw was probably a manifestation of God and His glory; and yet Moses did not see God's glory directly. Nonetheless, once the divine effulgence had gone past Moses, God allowed the lawgiver[8] to view the results—the afterglow—that His glorious presence had produced.[9]

This incident was a vivid reminder to the people of Jesus' day that it was impossible to directly see God and survive. The Messiah's disciples probably shared the same apprehension about seeing God. Thus, when

---

Jesus' divine sonship was unique to Him; that is, it exclusively applied to Him. As the Son of God, Jesus does not just represent the Father, but also manifests His presence in the world (John 1:18). Furthermore, because Jesus is the radiance of God's glory and the exact representation of His essence (Heb. 1:3), the Son can work, speak, and act as the Father's counterpart. People should direct their spiritual longing and need to Jesus because He is the divine, incarnate Word (John 1:1, 14).

7. For a discussion of how the New Testament portrays Moses and Israel, cf. Lierman, *The New Testament Moses*. According to the author, Moses is depicted "as the greatest of Israel's prophets, as Israel's king and redeemer, and as her lawgiver" (293). One is left with the impression that "Moses was a recognized proto-messianic figure, while Jesus in turn was recognized among the first Christians as a Mosaic messiah" (279–80). The author postulates that "it was this lofty appraisal of Moses" that "suited him for his role as the focus of Jewish loyalty and the source of Jewish identity" (293–94).

8. Harstine (*Moses*, 44) observes that in the Fourth Gospel, "Moses is characterized through his relationship to the law." In short, "he stands as the human authority behind the authoritative religious writings of Judaism. He is first and foremost the *noumothetes*, the giver of the law."

9. For differing rabbinic views concerning the nature and extent of God's glory that was revealed to Moses, cf. Heschel, *Heavenly Torah*, 290–92, 305–8.

Philip asked the Son as Torah to show the Father to them, Philip was likely making a request to see God in the same way Moses had. If Jesus could do that for them, they would be satisfied and it would end any doubts they had (John 14:8). The divine, incarnate Tanakh noted that by knowing and seeing Him, they had come to know and see the Father (vv. 7, 9).[10] Later New Testament writers made similar affirmations. For instance, Paul stated that the incarnate Torah was "in very nature God" (Phil. 2:6) as well as the "image of the invisible God" (Col 1:15). Moreover, in the Tanakh of God "all the fullness of the Deity lives in bodily form" (2:9). Also, according to Hebrews 1:3, "the Son is radiance of God's glory and the exact representation of his being."[11]

The Baptizer could personally attest to the glory of the one who came down from heaven (John 1:14–18). Because John was older than Jesus and began his ministry earlier (cf. Luke 1:5–45), many naturally assumed that John was the greater of the two. In fact, people in ancient times gave the older person more respect and honor than the younger; but John reversed that custom by proclaiming that the everlasting Torah far outranked him because, in reality, the Son existed as God for an eternity before He was born (John 1:15). This perspective formed the backdrop of John's witness

---

10. Keener (*John*, 1:51) remarked that "Moses was the greatest prophet because he knew God 'face to face'" (Deut 34:10). In stark contrast, "Jesus himself is God's face" (John 1:18).

11. There are at least four reasons why Jesus had to be fully divine. First, only someone who is the infinite God could bear the full penalty of all the sins of all who would believe in Him. Second, no mere human or creature could ever save people; only God Himself could (cf. Jonah 2:9). Third, only someone who was truly and fully God could be the one mediator between God and human beings (cf. 1 Tim 2:5), both to bring people back to God and to reveal God most fully to people (John 14:9). Fourth, only the Son of God could perfectly obey the Father, and thus be the pure, spotless, and righteous Lamb of God (cf. John 1:29, 36; Heb 7:26; 1 Pet 1:18–19).

to the large crowds of people who came to him from Jerusalem[12] and the whole Judean countryside (Mark 1:5).[13]

The various Gospel accounts of John's life and ministry can be dated around AD 26 when John was about 31 years old. He was known as the Baptizer because that was the most auspicious thing he did (Matt 3:6). John started to preach and baptize in the "wilderness" (Mark 1:4), so called because it did not sustain farming, but only grazing. It is a dry, hilly, barren territory between Jerusalem and the Jordan River, overlooking the Dead Sea. One oasis in the desert is the city of Jericho, which is probably where John preached at first, for two reasons: it was the main center for travelers from all over the East, and it was close to the river.[14] When the people in Jericho heard the Lord's herald, the news spread quickly to Jerusalem.

---

12. Set on a hill some 2,500 feet above sea level, Jerusalem is 33 miles east of the Mediterranean Sea and 14 miles west of the Dead Sea. Because access was difficult and the city lacked natural resources, it at one time enjoyed a relatively protected location; but when a major regional trade route developed through the city, Jerusalem became commercially and strategically desirable to every subsequent political force that came to power. The following are some key facts about the holy city: it appears in the Bible as early as Abraham (Gen 14:18), though the site had probably been inhabited for centuries before; it was captured by David and made the capital of Israel; Jerusalem was the site of Solomon's temple and, in the first century, Herod's temple; the city's estimated population in Jesus' day was probably 50,000 (though during Passover, it possibly grew to 100,000 to 120,000); Jerusalem was besieged and destroyed by the Romans in AD 70; and the city was relatively small geographically, but had a sizable metropolitan area with numerous suburban towns.

13. The land of Israel is located in the Fertile Crescent, which is made up of the Nile and Mesopotamia river basins. A mountainous region is located to the north and the Arabian Desert is situated to the south. On the west side is the Mediterranean Sea. Israel is often called the "Land Between," the "Land Bridge," or the "Point of Balance," because the Mediterranean Sea and the Arabian Desert force traffic through the narrow area of Palestine. The land of Israel is split into four main longitudinal zones, running north to south: (1) the coastal plain: this is a flat, well-watered area along the coast about 8 to 15 miles wide. It provides the easiest and most natural route for travel from the areas of Babylon, Assyria, and Syria to Egypt; (2) the hill country or central mountains: this is a range of mountains that rise over 3,000 feet in elevation in some places. It runs from Galilee in the north to the Negev highlands in the south; (3) the Jordan Rift Valley: this is a deep depression in the earth that stretches about 3,700 miles from southern Turkey into Africa. It is part of what is known as the Syro-African Rift. The Sea of Galilee (6,690 ft.) and the Dead Sea (-690 ft.) as well as the Jordan River are located in this zone; (4) the TransJordan plateau: to the east of the Jordan Rift Valley rise the towering mountains of the TransJordan. This area has steep slopes, is somewhat rugged, and receives quite a bit of rain and even some snow.

14. Jericho is considered one of the oldest cities in the world; some archaeologists date its beginnings back to perhaps 8,000 BC The city is located in the Jordan River valley less than 15 miles east-northeast of Jerusalem. It may have been a major trading center,

There was no mistaking John's message. He summoned people[15] to repent and be baptized. Repentance was necessary because God's kingdom, in the person of Jesus as Tanakh, was near at hand. Repentance meant a change in behavior. John looked for deep and lasting change. Repentant sinners acknowledged that they had broken God's laws and that they deserved His judgment. The baptism people underwent signified that they had turned from their sins and turned to God to be forgiven. This process was the way in which the Father used John to prepare for the Savior's advent, as foretold by Malachi (Mal 3:1) and Isaiah (Isa 40:3). In Bible times there were no superhighways. When an important dignitary was expected to travel through the country, a messenger would go out in advance to tell the people to prepare the way for the dignitary's coming. This meant they had to improve roads by cutting down trees, leveling steep hills, and generally clearing away obstacles. Figuratively speaking, this was the ministry of John. He was a messenger preparing the hearts of people for the coming Messiah.

John was not the kind of person one might expect to get the job of the Messiah's forerunner. As far as we know, John never served as a priest,[16]

---

especially for perfumes and fragrances. Jericho was built near a bountiful freshwater spring, eventually called the fountain of Elisha (2 Kings 2:18–22). Because it was located on the edge of the desert just north of the Dead Sea, water was considered one of its most valuable assets. Its warm winter climate earned Jericho the nickname "the City of Palms" (Deut. 34:3).

15. In the first century of the common era, the Jewish social spectrum was wide and diverse. The upper class consisted of the priestly and lay aristocracies and the scribes. The priestly nobility included the high priest, any retired high priests, and the chief priests who administered temple affairs. The middle class consisted of Jews of pure descent, among whom were found the ordinary priests (who served in the temple), the Levites (who served as temple musicians and servants), merchants, artisans, and farmers. The lower classes embraced all Jews who were not of pure descent as well as Jewish slaves, Jews with slight blemish (proselytes), Jews with a grave racial blemish (eunuchs), and Jews who worked in despised trades. Gentile slaves and Samaritans held the lowest rank in this social order. Jewish men ranked higher than women in all forms of public life. Even within the home, the man was master, and boys ranked higher than girls. For example, only boys received formal schooling. Except for those of nobility, Jewish women took no part in public life. They were to stay indoors and live in retirement; however, where economic necessity dictated, wives helped their husbands with their work. Rules of propriety forbade a man to look at a married woman or to greet her. Also, it was disgraceful for a scholar to speak to a woman in the street. While rural woman had a little more freedom, they did not speak to men they did not know.

16. The priests were descendants of Levi through Aaron. They oversaw the offering of sacrifices at the temple and operated as mediators between God and His people in making atonement for their sins. The Levites assisted the priests by preparing sacrifices, ministering in music at worship gatherings, ensuring the upkeep of the temple, and serving as doorkeepers.

even though he was born into a priestly family (cf. Luke 1:5). Neither did he serve as a scribe,[17] Pharisee,[18] or Sadducee.[19] John avoided cities, taking his message instead to the rugged area near the place where the Jordan River empties into the Dead Sea (Mark 1:5). Furthermore, John was eccentric in his dress and behavior. He wore a garment of camel's hair, which he tied at his waist with a leather strap. His diet included locusts and wild honey (v. 6). All of this was appropriate for a man of the desert, but John's lifestyle also served to denounce greed, self-indulgence, and pride. Moreover, the Baptizer's appearance resembled that of Elijah, the desert prophet of Old Testament times (cf. 2 Kgs 1:8; Mal 4:5–6).[20]

17. The scribes were the keepers and registers of public documents. They studied and interpreted the Mosaic law to people, were considered the highest form of teacher, and were primarily Pharisees.

18. There were about 6,000 Pharisees in the time of Jesus. They would be classed as a conservative, ritualistic party and were more popular with the people because of their anti-foreign attitude and high regard for the Scriptures. In the Sanhedrin (the supreme religious court of justice in that day), the Pharisees held a majority. They believed the oral law with its many interpretations and traditions to be just as binding as the Old Testament. They went to great lengths to perform all the prescribed religious duties and to keep themselves separated from everything that they considered unclean. Hypocrisy was their most notorious and persistent sin. The Pharisees believed in a future state and the resurrection of the dead. They also kept the messianic hope alive, though their concept of the Messiah tended to be erroneous.

19. The Sadducees were the priestly party and were smaller in number than the Pharisees. They were mostly from wealthy influential priestly families. The Sadducees were the rationalists of the day, only believing what they thought was reasonable. They denied the authority of the oral law, the resurrection, future punishment and rewards. It is a paradox that these very same unbelieving priests were the ones who ministered in the temple and offered the sacrifices; yet, as a class, they did not personally believe in the value or necessity of those sacrifices.

20. Elijah's name means "Yahweh is my God," and it summarized well the message of his life. Elijah began prophesying about 875 BC during the 22-year reign of King Ahab. Nothing is known about Elijah's family and little is known about his life before the initial confrontation with Ahab. First Kings 17:1 identifies Elijah as being from Tishbe in Gilead, a region that extended to the upper reaches of the part of Israel east of the Jordan River. The Bible regards Elijah as a rugged and tough wilderness dweller, much like John the Baptizer (2 Kings 1:8). Elijah's unquestioning devotion to God made the prophet a bold and persuasive spokesperson for the Lord. Elijah spent most of his time announcing the dire consequences for the Israelites of breaking their covenant with God; but Elijah's presence and the power of his ministry testified to the concern of the living God, who called His people to return to Him. The New Testament regards Elijah as a hero of faith. He appeared with Jesus during the Transfiguration (Matt 17:3; Mark 9:4; Luke 9:30–31). James 5:17 describes Elijah as being a man with the same human frailties that all people have; yet he also "prayed earnestly" that there would be no rain. Consequently, none fell "on the land for three and a half years" (cf. 1 Kings 17:1; 18:41–46). In the end, God took Elijah

Despite John's peculiarities, he was tremendously popular with the masses. People came from Jerusalem and other parts of Judea to hear him teach. At this time, he was east of the Jordan River near Bethany[21] (John 1:28), an otherwise unidentified village having the same name as the more familiar town located about two miles from Jerusalem (cf. 11:1, 18; 12:1). John's popularity signified that he was doing a genuine work of God. It is rare for people to flock to someone who tells them they need to repent; but these people even complied with John's message about their need for baptism. In those days, non-Jews who wanted to make Judaism their religion were baptized as a symbol of spiritual cleansing; but because Jews already considered themselves to be members of the covenant community, they did not think they needed to be baptized.[22] Besides calling people to repentance and baptism, John pointed them to Jesus, the Messiah of Israel. John did not come to establish a movement or build an institution of his own. Even with all his popularity, John knew the Son was infinitely superior to him in status, rank, and work.

John 1:19—2:11 concerns a week-long period at the start of the Messiah's earthly ministry.[23] The first three days involve the witness the

---

directly to heaven in a chariot of fire (2 Kings 2:11–12).

21. Another less likely textual reading is "Bethabara."

22. The rite John performed was unique in that he called candidates for baptism to repent and be cleansed spiritually. His baptism was for everyone who repented, regardless of whether they were orthodox Jews, ceremonially unclean Jews, or even Gentiles. Pious Gentiles were attracted by Judaism's high ethical standards. They were also disillusioned with the parade of pagan gods common in the first century AD. That led many Gentiles to accept Judaism. More women than men actually embraced the religion of the Jews, for they needed to fulfill only two of the three requirements: (1) be circumcised, (2) be baptized, and (3) offer sacrifice. Those who had not met all the requirements but were close were called "God-fearers." They could worship in the synagogues, and they were devout in their observances of the Jewish laws. They were most receptive to the Gospel, since circumcision was not a condition for salvation.

23. Concerning the possible significance of this week-long period, one theory is that it somehow parallels the "days of creation" in Genesis 1:1—2:3 and that this literary "framework . . . suggests creative activity" on the part of the Messiah at the outset of His redemptive mission (Morris, *John*, 114; cf. Carson, *John*, 167–68; Ellis, *Genius of John*, 41; Köstenberger, *John*, 53). Despite the innovativeness of this hypothesis, not all seven days at the start of the Savior's earthly ministry can be sufficiently accounted for in the opening chapters of the Fourth Gospel. Ridderbos (*John*, 103) asks "whether the Evangelist, if he in fact wanted us to engage in all this 'counting,' could not have furnished us with less ambiguity." In brief, while the theory has a measure of plausibility, in the final analysis it seems like an improbable interpretation; cf. Brown, *John*, 106; Bruce, *John*, 66; Keener, *John*, 1:451, 496–97; Lincoln, *John*, 116, 126; Lindars, *John*, 128; Tenny, "John," 9:37; Whitacre, *John*.

Baptizer gave concerning the Messiah; and verses 19–28 detail John's encounter during the first day with a delegation of priests and Levites sent by the religious leaders in Jerusalem (1:19). Many of the latter were members of the Sanhedrin. This ruling council assumed the responsibility of investigating all reports of insurrectionists and false messiahs who tried to disturb the peace and raise the ire of Rome.[24] Pharisees and Sadducees were also among those who came to hear John (Matt 3:7; John 1:24).

The original recipients of John's Gospel were dealing with false teachers who denied the identity of the Son and failed to appreciate the central role that He served in the Father's plan of redemption. That is why the apostle emphasized the testimony of Jesus Himself along with the witness of others, such as John the Baptizer.[25] One is left with the impression that throughout Jesus' ministry, He was on trial, a situation that mirrors the courtroom language of the Old Testament (see Isa 43–48).[26] Harvey states that in the Fourth Gospel the "case for and against Jesus" is "argued out at length."[27] In accordance with Deuteronomy 17:6 and 19:15, several witnesses are presented in the Fourth Gospel, and each confirmed the truth regarding Jesus as the final expression of God's Torah.[28] By way of example,

---

24. Meeks (*The prophet-king*) states that evidence exists from a "variety of sources that the figure of the false prophet . . . was a subject of concern, speculation, and legislation in divers circles of Judaism around the time the Fourth Gospel was written" (47; cf. Deut 13:1–6; 18:18–22). These sources include such apocalyptic documents as "the Sibylline Oracles, the Qumran texts, and even the Mandaean *Ginza*." Furthermore, "according to Jewish tradition, Jesus was executed as a magician and seducer of the people, that is, a false prophet" (55).

25. Cf. Bultmann, *John*, 87–88.

26. Cf. Asiedu-Peprah, *Johannine sabbath conflicts*, 11–13, 212, 233; Beasley-Murray, *John*, 77–78; Trites, *Witness*, 84, 88, 112.

27. Harvey, *Jesus on trial*, 6. The author notes that this "presentation of the claims of Jesus in the form of an extended 'trial'" is a literary device the author of the Fourth Gospel used to present to his readers the case involving the itinerant rabbi from Nazareth. The Evangelist, in objectively setting forth the historical facts, challenged the readers of his Gospel to "reach their own verdict" concerning the identity of Jesus (17), specifically, that He is "the Messiah, the Son of God" (20:31). For an examination of the lawsuit motif and its influence on shaping the narrative discourse found in the Fourth Gospel, cf. Lincoln, *Truth on trial*, 21–29, 139–158. He states that the "Fourth Gospel is not simply about a trial; it is itself a testimony in the trial" (170).

28. Harstine (*Moses*) observes that "unlike the Synoptics, the Fourth Gospel uses intermediaries as the means of calling people to believe." In this regard, "Moses should be included on the list of witnesses who appear in this trial scene." Like the other witnesses, "Moses functions . . . by testifying to the identity of Jesus" (52). Additionally, throughout the Fourth Gospel, "Moses functions as a historical anchor . . . and an authoritative figure" to validate the messianic claims of Jesus (74).

in John 5:31–47, the Son identified four different but interconnected testimonies that validated the truthfulness of His messianic claims: John the Baptizer, the Son's own miracles, God the Father, and Scripture (in particular, Moses; cf. 8:17–18). The Messiah's trial before Pontius Pilate brings the witness/trial motif to a climax.[29]

In the first century AD, speculations about the Messiah were rampant, and many who flocked to hear John wondered if he might be the Christ (cf. Luke 3:15).[30] *Christ* is a word borrowed from Greek. It means "Anointed One," signifying divine commissioning for a specific task. In Old Testament times, kings and priests were anointed with oil as a sign of their divine appointment. The Hebrew word for the Anointed One is translated *Messiah*. It was used of the promised one who would deliver Israel from oppression. Most Jews thought He would be a political leader. They did not consider that His mission might be to free them from sin.[31]

The delegation sent from Jerusalem was concerned that the law be properly interpreted and taught by authorized representatives; and since John acted as an independent agent, members of the religious establishment scrutinized the Baptizer's activities. When asked if he claimed to be the Messiah, John clearly and emphatically said no (1:20). Next, the

---

29. Cf. Trites, *Witness*, 79–80; Witherington, *John's wisdom*, 135–36.

30. For an examination of references in the Fourth Gospel to Jewish and Samaritan statements about the Messiah, cf. de Jonge, "Jewish expectations," 246–270. His analysis leads him to the following conclusion: "Everything in the Gospel is centered on its consistent and persistent search for the right terms and conceptions to express the truth about Jesus the Son of God, the Son of Man" (266); cf. Wilson, *Our father Abraham*, 57–58.

31. God had chosen David to be the first of many successive kings of Israel (2 Sam 7:8–16); but the dynastic rule was broken when Jehoiakim died and his son, Jehoiachin, was carried away in exile to Babylon (2 Kings 24:15; 25:27–29; Jer 36:30). Later, the prophets said that God would one day restore David's dynasty (Ezek 37:24–25; Amos 9:11). By the second century BC, there began to develop among the Jews a growing expectation for a future anointed leader. The Jewish group that wrote what are known as the Dead Sea Scrolls recorded on some of the scrolls their belief that three prominent figures would come instead of one—the prophet of Deuteronomy 18:15, 18; a priestly figure named the "Messiah of Aaron"; and a kingly Davidic figure called the "Messiah of Israel." In the first century BC, the Jews longed for an anointed, righteous king who would liberate God's people from their unpopular leaders. Some Jewish writings from this period linked this expected heavenly figure with the day of judgment. By the first century of the common era, the Jews wanted freedom from Rome. Expectations ran high that God would raise up a warrior-prince who would throw off the yoke of Gentile rule and usher in a Jewish kingdom of worldwide proportions. John 6:14–15 and Acts 1:6 show traces of this hope among the people. This explains why Jesus was careful not to give false impressions about the exact nature of His messiahship (John 18:33–37). He saw His destiny in terms of service to God and sacrificial suffering (Mark 8:31; 9:31; 10:33–34; Luke 24:45–46).

interlocutors asked the Baptizer if he was Elijah, whom Malachi prophesied would return to proclaim the advent of the Messiah (cf. Mal 4:5–6). Since John's rugged characteristics, ascetic behavior, and fiery personality were similar to the Old Testament description of Elijah, many Jews hoped that John was the old prophet come back to life (cf. Mark 6:14). While the Baptizer operated in the stature, strength, and spirit of Elijah (Matt 11:14; 17:10–13; Luke 1:17; 7:24–28), John denied being that person (John 1:21).

Still dissatisfied with the Baptizer's answers, his interrogators asked whether he was "the Prophet." Based on Deuteronomy 18:15 and 18, the Jews expected a great "Prophet" to appear in connection with the Messiah.[32] Undeniably, it would have been an honor for John to be this expected prophet, but again, perhaps to the dismay of some in the delegation, he answered no.[33] The envoys were at a loss as to what to write in their report. They insisted that John give them an answer they could take back to the authorities in Jerusalem (John 1:22). In response, the Baptizer applied the prophecy of Isaiah 40:3 to his ministry.[34] In a display of humility, John only claimed to be a voice preparing the way for the arrival of the divine, incarnate Logos (John 1:23).

---

32. Cf. Bruce, *John*, 48.

33. From the earliest days of the church, Christian scholars have identified the prophet as the Messiah Himself.

34. Williams ("Isaiah and Johannine christology") cites the "statistical evidence" confirming that "Isaiah was of special interest to the author of the Fourth Gospel." In particular, the Evangelist explicitly quotes from Isaiah four times (cf. John 1:23; 6:45; 12:38, 40). This equates to "nearly a quarter of the quotations in a Gospel that generally favors allusive references combined from more than one scriptural source" (107). In all likelihood, the "Greek Septuagint is the underlying source" for the first three quotations, while the Evangelist possibly "made use of the Hebrew text" in quoting from 12:40 (108). The placement of these quotations in the Fourth Gospel "link together the beginning and end of Jesus' public ministry" (122). The culmination of what the Baptizer announced is the "universal manifestation of God's glory in the death and exaltation of his Servant." Jesus, as "God's Chosen One" (John 1:34; cf. Isa 42:1), concludes "his earthly way in Jerusalem, where he manifests God's glory for all to see through his enthronement on the cross" (123). For a discussion of how the quotations and allusions from the Book of Isaiah factor into the theological argument of the Fourth Gospel, cf. Pond, *Theological dependencies*. The author maintains that the Evangelist "referenced the prophet Isaiah in his Gospel" to "communicate theologies of the presentation of God's grace and of God's rejection of persistent unbelievers unto judgment" (58). In the "theology of presentation" motif, the Evangelist depicts God offering His "divine blessing or grace" to people "even amid judgment." In the "theology of rejection" motif, the Evangelist demonstrates that the "consistent refusal of offered grace results in God's reprobative judgment," that is, His "hardening of the unbeliever's heart" (59).

John had flatly denied being the Messiah, Elijah, or the Prophet. Evidently, some Pharisees who were part of the delegation grew frustrated at John's increasingly laconic responses (v. 24).[35] These strict observers and interpreters of the Mosaic law pressed for more details concerning John's credentials. They questioned his right to baptize, especially since performing this ritual was a claim to authority. The religious leaders believed that the Jews, as God's chosen people, did not need to be cleansed. Some expected a general purification of God's people before the advent of the Messiah. This would have made John's baptizing efforts even more remarkable to his Jewish peers, especially as they looked for the Savior's coming.

John responded to the interrogators' challenge in a manner that exalted the Lord Jesus and diminished the Baptizer's own importance as the Redeemer's messenger. The Synoptic Gospels record John's statement about the baptism of the Holy Spirit (Matt. 3:11; Mark 1:8; Luke 3:16); but in John 1:26, the messenger emphasized the supreme importance of the Messiah. While the forerunner baptized only with water, Jesus, as the embodiment of the Torah, would perform an even greater baptism, one involving the third person of the Trinity. The baptism John performed "anticipates salvific cleansing of the eschatological kingdom."[36] John also stated that the members of the delegation did not recognize the presence of the Savior in their midst (cf. v. 11). The Baptizer's words might suggest that Jesus was in the crowd that day, listening to all that transpired. Such a possibility notwithstanding, verse 33 indicates that John did not immediately know for sure that Jesus of Nazareth was the Messiah until John baptized Him.

The forerunner declared that he was unworthy to stoop down and loosen the thongs of the Redeemer's leather sandals (Matt 3:11; Mark 1:7; Luke 3:16; John 1:27). Those who heard John's comment understood exactly what he meant. During that time, Jewish disciples compensated their teachers by performing menial tasks for them; however, untying the straps of their teacher's footwear was one chore they were not expected to do, for such an act was considered too humiliating. It was reserved for the lowest of slaves, who took off a person's sandals to wash that person's dirty feet (cf. John 13:5). The Baptizer not only demonstrated his humility, but

---

35. Less likely is the translation of John 1:24, "Now they had been sent from the Pharisees," a rendering that regards the verse as a parenthetical note inserted by the author; cf. Hoskyns, *The Fourth Gospel*, 172–73; Lenski, *St. John's Gospel*, 114–15; Lindars, *John*, 105; Schnackenburg, *John*, 1:292.

36. Ng, *Water symbolism in John*, 68. For an overview of the use of water as a symbol throughout the Fourth Gospel, cf. 58–86.

Jesus as Torah in John 1

also indicated by his statement the exalted stature of the one who came after him.

The Baptizer's Affirmation of Jesus as Torah (John 1:29–34)

This passage narrates the second day of the Baptizer's testimony concerning the Messiah. The conceptual backdrop to the messenger's remarks is the Mosaic law, especially its instructions about the sacrificial offering of lambs to atone for the sins of God's people.[37] In ancient Judaism, lambs were sacrificed as guilt offerings (Lev 14:10–25), as part of the Nazarite vow (Num 6:12, 14), and as offerings for Passover (Exod 12:21). When the Baptizer saw Jesus—the divine, incarnate Torah—coming toward him, the forerunner declared Him to be the "Lamb of God" (John 1:29). "Lamb" translates the Greek noun *amnos*, which literally refers to a year-old male sheep.[38] Metaphorically speaking, the Lord Jesus was like an innocent lamb who suffered and died as a sacrifice of atonement to take away "the sin of the world" (cf. 1 John 2:2). Perhaps the Baptizer was with some of his disciples when he made this profound statement about the one who is the realization of the law's types, prophecies, and expectations.

There are four sources worth mentioning that might form the conceptual backdrop for the lamb terminology in the Fourth Gospel: apocalyptic

---

37. For an investigation of the Old Testament quotations appearing in the Fourth Gospel, cf. Freed, *John*. Based on his analysis, he concludes that when the Evangelist quoted a passage from the Old Testament, he was "bound by no rule or fixed text, testimony or other." Regardless of the quote being examined, it "appears to be adapted to its immediate context, to his literary style, and to the whole plan of the composition of his gospel." In short, "theological motives and ideas" were the Evangelist's "primary concern" (129). Barrett ("Old Testament in the Fourth Gospel," 155) observes that the numerous Old Testament allusions found in John's Gospel "govern . . . the whole movement" of its literary and thematic development. Barrett notes that the Evangelist used the Old Testament "in a novel manner, collecting its sense rather than quoting" (156). Indeed, for John, the Old Testament was "itself a comprehensive unity, not a mere quarry from which isolated fragments of useful material might be hewn." Moreover, the entire Hebrew corpus "formed a background, a framework, upon which the new revelation rested" (168; cf. Barrett, *St. John*, 30). According to Beutler ("John," 158), the "impression conveyed is that John is convinced that scripture as a whole bears witness to Jesus." In a more general sense, Whitacre (*Johannine polemic*, 64) thinks the author of the Fourth Gospel evidences a "very positive view of God's revelation within Judaism." Also, Hanson ("John's use of Scripture," 364) maintains the Evangelist used the Old Testament for "halaka, for help in living according to God's law, not merely for haggada, for elaboration and embroidery of events in salvation history in order that we might understand its significance for us."

38. Danker, *Greek-English lexicon*, 54.

lambs, the Akedah (binding of Isaac) in Genesis 22:8, the lambs of Isaiah 53:7 and Jeremiah 11:19, and Passover and sacrificial lambs.[39] With respect to the non-canonical, apocalyptic literature (e.g. Test of Benjamin 3:8; Test of Joseph 19:8–11; 1 Enoch 89:45; 90:6, 9–19, 37–38), the general impression is that an end-time, lamb-like figure would deal with iniquity and injustice by vanquishing its foes and vindicating its flock. The Akedah episode recorded in Genesis 22:8 draws attention to what first-century Palestinian Jews regarded as a pivotal event, namely, Abraham's willingness to offer his son, Isaac, as a sacrifice on Mount Moriah. In response to Isaac's question, Abraham declared that "God himself will provide the lamb for the burnt offering." This promise finds its ultimate fulfillment in the Redeemer's provision of eternal salvation.

Concerning Isaiah 53:7, a lamb-like, messianic figure is led "to the slaughter" to remit the sins of God's people. The suffering Servant does so even while remaining silent "before its shearers." Similarly, Jeremiah 11:19 refers to a "gentle lamb" that is "led to the slaughter" to pay the price for the transgressions of others. With respect to the Passover and sacrificial lambs of ancient Judaism (cf. Exod 12:1–11), evidence from the New Testament suggests that the early church connected the Messiah with the paschal lamb. For instance, Paul referred to the Messiah as "our Passover lamb" who "has been sacrificed" (1 Cor 5:7). Peter equated the "precious blood of Christ" (1 Pet. 1:19) to that of a "lamb without blemish or defect" (cf. Exod 12:5; Lev 22:17–25). The apostle also said that believers have been healed by the Messiah's "wounds" (1 Pet 2:24). Finally, Revelation 5:6 notes John's sight of a "Lamb, looking as if it had been slain." The divine, incarnate Logos triumphed over sin and death so that all who trust in Him would enjoy freedom from and forgiveness of sin (cf. 1:5; 5:9; 7:14; 12:11).

The Father had earlier revealed to John that He would identify His Son through the forerunner's baptizing ministry. Because John and Jesus were related (cf. Luke 1:36), John most likely was already acquainted with Jesus; but it was not until the forerunner baptized Jesus that His messianic status became crystal clear. By the time of the delegation's visit from Jerusalem, John had already baptized Jesus and the devil had tempted Him in the wilderness. In declaring Jesus to be the Lamb of God, John was fulfilling his role as the one who heralds the Redeemer (John 1:29). Because the embodiment of the Torah eternally preexisted before His messenger was ever born, Jesus surpassed John in greatness (v. 30). The Baptizer rec-

---

39. Cf. Lioy, *Revelation*, 119–20.

ognized the amazing privilege God had given him to make the Messiah known to the people of Israel (v. 31).

At the Savior's baptism, John saw the Holy Spirit appear in bodily form as a dove, descend from the sky, and settle on Jesus (John 1:32–33; cf. Matt 3:16; Mark 1:10; Luke 3:22).[40] In that culture, the dove was considered a symbol of reconciliation with God (cf. Gen 8:8, 10). Accordingly, the bird became an emblem of peace. The dove also represented tender affection (cf. Song 1:15; 2:14). An examination of ancient Jewish writings suggests that the Spirit's presence in the form of a dove signaled that Jesus as Torah was inaugurating the promised age of covenant renewal for the people of God.[41] This includes the Messiah's baptism of believers with the Holy Spirit (cf. Jer 31:31–34; Joel 2:28–32; Acts 2:16–21). The New Testament reveals that the permanent, indwelling presence of the Spirit in believers started on the day of Pentecost (cf. Acts 1:5; 2:1–4; 11:15–16) and is now the common experience of all who have repented of their sins and experienced the new birth (cf. Acts 2:38; 1 Cor 12:13; Gal 3:2).

The Spirit's presence as a dove and the Father's pronouncement concerning Jesus (cf. Matt 3:16–17; Mark 1:11; Luke 3:22) confirmed the latter's status as the divine, anointed Son. Accordingly, the Baptizer testified publicly to the people and privately to his disciples that Jesus was "God's Chosen One" (John 1:34; cf. Isa 42:1). Also, with John's blessing, some of his followers eventually became disciples of Jesus. A number of

40. According to Russell ("The Holy Spirit's ministry," 228), the Evangelist speaks "consistently of the Holy Spirit in the terminology of OT eschatology." Also, "the giving of the Spirit inaugurates a new age centered in Messiah." Bennema ("Giving of the Spirit," 195) furthers the discussion by noting that "the Spirit has a salvific role in John's Gospel." For instance, Jesus declared that one must be "born of the Spirit" (3:8) to enter the kingdom of God. Jesus identified the Spirit with the "living water" of salvation (7:37–38; cf. 4:10–14). Jesus clarified that while "the flesh counts for nothing," it is the Spirit who gives eternal life (6:63). The Spirit is "the Advocate" (14:16, 26; 15:26; 16:7) whom Jesus promised to send to His disciples after His resurrection from the dead and ascension into heaven. The third member of the Trinity, as the "Spirit of truth" (14:17), bears witness to Jesus, makes the meaning of His teaching clear to His disciples, and guides them into all the truth (14:26; 15:26; 16:13–14). The Spirit proves "the world to be in the wrong about sin and righteousness and judgment" (16:8). In anticipation of the Spirit's permanent indwelling and empowerment of believers, Jesus gave His disciples an anticipatory endowment of the Spirit on the evening of the first Easter Sunday (20:22). For an analysis of the pneumatology of the Fourth Gospel, cf. Bammel, "Jesus und der Paraklet," 199–217; Barrett, *St. John*, 88–92; Beasley-Murray, *Gospel of life*, 59–84; Beyler, *Torah*, 178–184; Brown, *Johannine pneumatology*, 75–169; Burge, *The anointed community*; Dodd, *Fourth Gospel*, 213–227; Johnston, *The Spirit-Paraclete*, 3–58; Tew, *Pneumatology of John*, 125–147; Thompson, *God of the Gospel of John*, 145–188; Whitacre, *Johannine polemic*, 98–103.

41. Cf. Lioy, "Jesus as the divine Messiah."

Greek manuscripts read "the Son of God," rather than "the Chosen One of God." Admittedly, "Son of God" occurs throughout the Fourth Gospel (cf. 1:49; 3:18; 5:25; 10:36; 11:4, 27; 19:7; 20:31) and the majority of textual evidence supports this reading. Nonetheless, because "Chosen One of God" occurs in the earliest manuscripts and is considered the more difficult textual reading, it most likely reflects what was in the original version of John 1:34.[42]

The Baptizer's disciples encountering Jesus as Torah (John 1:35–42)

This passage narrates the third day of the Baptizer's testimony concerning the Messiah. Perhaps the Baptizer was still on the east of the Jordan River near Bethany as he stood with two of his disciples (John 1:35; cf. v. 28). Verse 40 identifies one of them as Andrew, the brother of Simon Peter. The pair were from Bethsaida (v. 44), a town located northwest of the Sea of Galilee[43] (cf. 12:21). They made their living on this body of water as fishermen (Matt. 4:18; Mark 1:16–18). Though the biblical text is silent on the identity of the second disciple of the Baptizer who was with Andrew, tradition has it that this man was the apostle John.[44] This would have made him an eyewitness to the unfolding episode, which is not narrated in the Synoptic Gospels.

Though the Baptizer was prominent in his own right (cf. Matt 11:11), he did not hesitate to step back so that the Messiah could take center stage. Indeed, as the Baptizer saw Jesus walking by, the forerunner declared Him to be the Lamb of God (John 1:36). This statement encouraged the Baptizer's two disciples to immediately begin to follow Jesus (v. 37).[45] We

---

42. Cf. Brown, *John*, 57.

43. The Sea of Galilee is located in what was northern Palestine during the first century of the common era. The Sea of Galilee was known by at least three other names: the Sea of Kinnereth (Josh 11:2), the Lake of Gennesaret (Luke 5:1), and the Sea of Tiberias (John 6:1). At its farthest distances, the lake is 13 miles long and 7.5 miles wide. In places it reaches a depth of 160 feet. The lowness of the lake surface, 685 feet below sea level, contributes to the almost tropical character of the weather. The steep hills that surround most of the lake's shoreline were prime locations for villages in the time of Jesus. Despite its relatively small size and unpredictable, often violent weather, the Sea of Galilee was vital to the economy of the local villages.

44. Cf. Ellis, *Genius of John*, 35; Haenchen, *John 1*, 158; Sanders and Mastin, *John*, 99; Tenney, "John," 9:40.

45. According to Ratzinger (*Jesus of Nazareth*, 169), the Savior called His disciples to live in "communion with [him], who is himself God's living Torah." The Gospels reveal that being a true follower of the Messiah was demanding. Jesus' disciples agreed not only

can only imagine how intrigued Andrew and his peer were concerning what the Baptizer had said about Jesus. As the Messiah walked ahead, He spotted the two men coming up from behind. Perhaps as Jesus turned around, He noticed their friendly and earnest demeanor.[46] The Greek of verse 38 is literally rendered, "What are you seeking?" More generally, by asking the question, Jesus gave Andrew and John the opportunity to state their motives.

The narrative suggests that Jesus already knew the intent of the two and welcomed their company. In addressing Jesus as "Rabbi," the pair signaled their regard for Him as an esteemed religious teacher of Judaism. Throughout the Fourth Gospel, His "contemporaries perceived and addressed Jesus" chiefly in this way (cf. 1:49; 3:2; 4:31; 6:25; 9:2; 11:8; 20:16).[47] "Rabbi" is a Hebrew word that literally means "My great one" or simply "Master." It is easy to imagine the two searching for words until they finally asked where Jesus was staying; and perhaps with an inviting gesture, the Messiah signaled for them to come with Him and see for themselves (v. 39).[48]

This was a life-changing encounter Andrew and John had with Jesus. It was so impressionable for John that he remembered the approximate time in which the episode occurred, namely 4:00 P.M. (literally, "about the tenth hour," which reflects Jewish reckoning). Because of the relative lateness of the day, the two probably lodged with Jesus that night. If so, it would have been early the following morning when Andrew went to his brother, Simon Peter, and announced that the Messiah had been found (v. 41). Like most Jews at that time, Andrew probably had a yearning expectation for a national deliverer, and Jesus seemed to be that person. Of course,

---

to obey Him in all He said, but also to order their priorities for His sake. They sought to serve Him as a slave would serve a master. The followers of Jesus sought to be like Him in their thoughts and actions. Furthermore, their desire was to abide in His words and heed His commands. The disciples of Jesus did not merely perpetuate His teachings, transmit His sayings, or imitate His life. They also bore witness in their own words and actions that their Lord dwelt within them. Thus, Jesus was much more than a mere teacher or guru to His followers; for them He was the embodiment and fulfillment of the Tanakh.

46. Cf. Goldsmith, *Gospel of John*.

47. Köstenberger, *Studies on John and gender*, 68. For an examination of the changing perceptions of Jesus' role as a Jewish rabbi and teacher, cf. Pelikan, "Jesus as Rabbi." Schoneveld ("A new reading") maintains that in the Fourth Gospel, the Evangelist presents the Son as the Rabbi *par excellence*. In short, the "Torah is embodied in Jesus Christ as its authoritative Teacher" (85) and "Interpreter" (89).

48. Keener (*John*, 1:470) suggests that "like most first-century Jewish teachers, Jesus had no formal schoolhouse for his academy except his own home or that of a disciple."

Andrew's initial understanding of Jesus' as the Anointed One would have been limited. In time, though, Jesus' followers would come to more fully appreciate the nature of His messiahship.

Peter's whereabouts at this time are not stated. Perhaps Andrew found his brother preparing a boat and nets for fishing on the Sea of Galilee. If so, he would have been preoccupied with getting ready for the day's work; but Andrew was sufficiently persuasive to get his brother to set aside his chores and meet Jesus (v. 42). The loss of a day's wages earned from fishing would be more than compensated by seeing such a remarkable person as the Messiah. Jesus might have been seated under a shady tree when He looked intently at Peter.[49] Immediately, Andrew's brother was struck by Jesus' omniscience, which He displayed by telling Peter not only his name ("Simon"), but also that of his father ("John"; cf. "Jonah" in Matt 16:17). Even more remarkable was Jesus' declaration that the fisherman would be called "Cephas" (John 1:42). The nicknames *Cephas* (from the Aramaic) and *Peter* (from the Greek) both mean "rock."[50] In ancient Jewish culture, a person's name epitomized his or her character. Despite Peter's volatile and impulsive personality, after Jesus' resurrection, Peter would be known for his strength of character and stable leadership to a fledgling church.

The Witness of Others to Jesus as Torah (John 1:43–51)

John 1:43–51 narrates the following day's events involving Jesus. The divine, incarnate Torah set out for Galilee, most likely to attend an upcoming wedding in Cana (cf. 2:1). It would have taken a day or two to reach this village, which was located northeast of Nazareth, the Redeemer's hometown. Jesus deliberately sought and found a man named Philip, who like Andrew and Peter, was from Bethsaida (1:44). In all likelihood, Andrew and Peter had told Philip about Jesus. Thus, when the Savior found Philip, He invited the young man to become one of His disciples (v. 43). Like Andrew, Philip was immediately convinced of Jesus' messiahship. This prompted Philip to make his way quickly through town and tell the good news to a friend named Nathaniel (v. 45), who originally was from Cana (cf. 21:2). Because Nathaniel is not listed among the Twelve in the Synoptic Gospels (cf. Matt 10:2–4; Mark 3:1–19; Luke 6:14–16; Acts

---

49. Cf. Goldsmith, *Gospel of John*.

50. In all likelihood, Jesus was trilingual, being conversant in Hebrew, Aramaic, and Hellenistic Greek. His ability to speak fluently in these languages enabled Him to minister effectively to the general populace living in Palestine during His first advent.

1:13), some think he may have been Bartholomew, who is consistently paired with Philip in the other accounts.[51]

There must have been a tone of excitement in Philip's voice as he told Nathaniel about Jesus of Nazareth. Philip related that the famed lawgiver, Moses,[52] had written about Jesus in the Torah.[53] In fact, Philip stated that the Old Testament prophets had written about "the son of Joseph" (1:45). In short, the entire Hebrew corpus anticipates the advent and redemptive

---

51. Cf. Harris, *John*; Ridderbos, *John*, 87–88.

52. For an overview of how Moses functions as a character in the Jewish narratives penned during the Second Temple period of Judaism, cf. Harstine, *Moses*, 96–129. Based on his analysis of numerous texts, he concludes that "Moses is characterized as the lawgiver, as the founder of the cult, as a philosopher, and as a historical figure" (117). In these roles, Moses has "four main functions: to authorize the law, to authenticate religious activity, to serve as an exemplar for piety, and to stand as the prophet *par excellence*" (126). For an examination of how rabbinic Judaism and early Christianity influenced the nature of the belief in the end-time prophet like Moses, cf. Teeple, *Mosaic eschatological prophet*, 29–122. Glasson (*Moses,* 20) remarks that during the Second Temple period of Judaism, "the figure of Moses" foreshadowed "the Messiah himself." In point of fact, "ample evidence" can be found "in Rabbinic writings that Moses was called the first deliverer and the Messiah the second deliverer." Admittedly, "this evidence is mostly later than New Testament times as far as its written character is concerned." Nonetheless, "there can be little doubt that this particular form of Messianic hope originated in the pre-Christian period" (cf. Evans, *Word and glory*, 97–99). Meeks (*The prophet-king*) furthers the discussion by noting that, based on his "exploration of Moses' legends and midrash of very diverse provenance," there is substantial evidence that "Moses was frequently described by . . . a combination of royal and prophetic images." Furthermore, "in some circles of both Judaism and Samaritanism Moses was regarded as the prototypal king and prophet of Israel." The basis for his "prophetic-royal mission . . . was his enthronement in heaven (the Sinai theophany), where he received the Torah and, with or within it, all truth." From then on, Moses became "God's emissary or agent . . . and his vice-regent on earth." Most likely, sectarian groups cultivated these legends in an effort to exalt "Moses as the center of their religious concerns, as the intermediary, in some sense, between them and God" (286). Meeks concludes that the "Moses traditions" provide "an adequate background for the prophetic-royal christology of John" (287; cf. Meeks, "Moses as God and King," 370–371). In a similar vein, Lierman ("Mosaic pattern," 211) says that a "fuller appreciation of Jewish veneration of Moses" and a "closer reading of John's text" highlight the "true importance of Moses to John's Christology." Within the context of this historical, cultural, and literary backdrop, the Evangelist portrayed Jesus of Nazareth to be the embodiment and fulfillment of all that was anticipated in the Moses traditions. Jesus is shown to be the Son of God, the Messiah and King of Israel, the Father's accredited emissary, the source of truth, and the enfleshment of the divine. In short, Jesus is the perfection of the gift of the Torah; cf. Davies, *Torah*, 93–94; Evans, *Word and glory*, 135–145.

53. Beasley-Murray (*John*, lxi) states that the variety of ways the Fourth Gospel uses the Greek term rendered "law" is "characteristic of its use among rabbis." This encompasses the "narrower use to denote the Mosaic law (1:17) and its extension to include the Scriptures as a whole (12:34)"; cf. Beyler, *Torah*, 65–73.

mission of the Savior (cf. Luke 24:45–47).[54] Though Jesus was virginally conceived and born (cf. Isa 7:14; Matt 1:23; Luke 1:27), Joseph was His legal, adoptive father (cf. Matt 1:24–25). Ultimately, the revelation the Father gave to Moses and the prophets concerned the Son (cf. John 5:45–47; 7:19). Those who rejected the divine testimony, as found in the Hebrew sacred writings concerning the Messiah, made the Father out to be a liar (cf. John 9:28–29; 1 John 5:9–12). God's consistent witness in the Old Testament was that the Messiah had to die on the cross and rise from the dead so that eternal salvation could be offered to all who would believe the good news (cf. Luke 24:25–27, 44–49; Acts 2:29–32; 3:18, 21, 24; 7:52–53; 8:30–35; 26:22–23; 28:23). In short, Philip's words to Nathaniel implied that Jesus was the culmination of the Torah.[55]

Nathaniel, however, was skeptical and questioned the veracity of Philip's claims. Indeed, Nathaniel openly wondered whether anything (or anyone) "good" (John 1:46) could originate from Nazareth. The religious elite regarded it as an isolated, frontier town far from Jerusalem.[56] Perhaps Nathaniel wondered how a distinguished person as the Messiah could arise from a seemingly insignificant village as Nazareth. After all, it had a shameful reputation of being populated by crude, immoral, and unsophisticated people. The elite generally (though incorrectly) assumed that no prophet of God ever arose from Galilee, let alone one of its backwater environs (cf. 7:52). It is also possible that Nathaniel's exclamation echoed a regional saying, one that embodied longstanding rivalry between Cana (Nathaniel's hometown) and Nazareth.[57]

---

54. Cf. Boismard, *Moses or Jesus*, 25; Haenchen, *John 1*, 165; Schnackenburg, *John*, 1:315.

55. Cf. Fernando, *Relationship between law and love*, 72.

56. Cf. Lindars, *John*, 118.

57. The origin of the name "Nazareth" (John 1:45) is uncertain. One view is that it is related to the Hebrew verb *natsar*, which means "to guard" or "to watch." Accordingly, the term has been applied to watchtowers (cf. 2 Kings 17:9; 18:8). If this etymology is followed, "Nazareth" could imply that the original city was perched on or near a hill (cf. Luke 4:16-30). Another view is that "Nazareth" is related to the Hebrew noun *netser*, which means "sprout," "branch," or "shoot" (cf. Isa 11:1). According to Matthew 2:23, when Joseph and Mary relocated to Nazareth (Greek, *Nazaret*), it fulfilled prophecy; however, the prophetic declaration "He will be called a Nazarene" cannot be found in the Old Testament. One possibility is that Matthew was making a play on the Hebrew noun *netser*. Expressed differently, the *netser* (which is translated "Branch") would be called a Nazarene (Greek, *Nazōraios*; in other words, the saying is a pun; cf. Zech 6:12). In Jesus' day, Nazareth was a relatively insignificant village of Lower Galilee. The town resides in a basin north of the Valley of Jezreel / Plain of Esdraelon about 1,300 feet above sea level. Nazareth is also about 20 miles from the Mediterranean Sea and 15 miles from the Sea of Galilee, which places it near several of Palestine's key trade routes. The moderate climate

Rather than get embroiled in an argument, Philip simply invited Nathaniel to meet the Messiah.[58] When Jesus saw Nathaniel coming toward Him, the divine, incarnate Tanakh declared the young man to be a genuine son of Israel, one in whom there was not a trace of deceit or treachery (v. 47). This allusion to Psalm 32:2 implied that Nathaniel was a person of complete integrity. God the Son was able to discern Nathaniel's underlying character because Jesus intimately knew human nature (cf. John 2:24). One can only imagine how stunned Nathaniel must have felt when he encountered the Messiah. The young man was possibly a bit defensive when he asked Jesus, "How do you know me?" (1:48). The Redeemer replied by stating that before Philip summoned Nathaniel, Jesus had supernaturally seen the young man sitting alone under a fig tree.[59]

In the hot climate of Palestine, devout Jews would often sit under the shade of a fig tree to read the law of Moses, study, and pray (cf. 1 Kings 4:25; Mic 4:4; Zech 3:10).[60] Jesus' statement drew Nathaniel back to a recent occasion in which he was meditating on a portion of the Torah. Presumably it was the episode in which Jacob experienced a dream at Bethel (cf. Gen 28:10–17; 35:6–7; 48:3–4).[61] He was the first person to bear the name "Israel" (cf. 32:28), but in contrast to Nathaniel, Jacob was initially characterized by duplicity (cf. 27:34–36).[62] Nathaniel's skepticism was replaced by a profound sense of awe as he realized he was in the presence of the Anointed One. Without hesitation, Nathaniel respectfully addressed Jesus as "Rabbi" (John 1:49) and declared Him to be both the "Son of God" and the "king of Israel." Most likely, Philip had previously talked at length with Nathaniel about Jesus, and if so, this conversation established an initial foundation of understanding. Then, when Nathaniel met Jesus, he was convinced of the Nazarene's divine, exalted status as the Messiah (cf. Ps 2:6–7).

---

and ample yearly rainfall makes the area suitable for agriculture. From the third century BC until the present, people have lived in Nazareth.

58. Keener (*John*, 1:485) says that Philip's "invitation reflects the characteristic Johannine epistemology: the synagogue leadership may know the written Torah, but disciples of Jesus, Torah made flesh (1:1–18), have a personal experience with God (cf. 9:25; 10:4)."

59. Cf. Calvin, *John*, 1:78–79; Carson, *John*, 148.

60. Cf. Borchert, *John 1–11*, 148; Burge, *John*, 77; Witherington, *John's wisdom*, 71.

61. Cf. Tenney, *John*, 82.

62. Neyrey ("Jacob traditions," 423) points out that Jacob (or Israel) was "known as a crafty person who stealthily achieved his designs" (cf. Gen 27:35; Lightfoot, *St. John's Gospel*, 98; Schnackenburg, *John*, 1:316).

Jesus asked whether Nathaniel believed what he declared simply because the Nazarene had previously seen him mediating alone under a fig tree. The one who is the realization of the Tanakh would confirm Nathaniel's confession of faith by performing even "greater things than that" (John 1:50; cf. 5:20; 14:12). Jesus' miraculous changing of water into wine, which He would perform in Cana, was one of the supernatural signs Nathaniel and the rest of the Twelve witnessed over the course of the Savior's earthly ministry. Jesus solemnly affirmed that the disciples would see heaven open and God's angels going up and coming down on the "Son of Man" (v. 51). This is an allusion to Jacob's dream at Bethel (cf. Gen 28:12).

While Jacob slept, he saw a stairway that reached from earth to heaven. Some mistakenly envision this to be a wooden ladder with rungs. In actuality, Jacob's stairway resembled a large stone ramp with steps that mounted the sloping side of a Mesopotamian temple-tower called a ziggurat. Such a structure was square at its base and pyramid-like in shape. At the apex of this massive, lofty, and solid-brick edifice was a small shrine that supposedly served as the gateway between heaven and earth (cf. 11:4). Sometimes the shrine was covered with blue enamel so that it would more easily blend in with the sky, the reputed celestial home of the gods.

Jacob saw angels of God going up and coming down the other-worldly ramp (28:12). The activity in the spot where Jacob slept indicates that the locale was sacred, representing the meeting point between the human sphere and the heavenly realm (v. 19). Bethel, as the "house of God," foreshadowed Jesus as the "new temple" of the Lord.[63] The Savior has become the "place of God's revelation"[64] and the "locus for the manifestation" of God's glory[65] (John 1:51; cf. Exod 29:43). Moreover, as the ultimate reality behind all that is recorded in the Torah and the Mediator between God and people (John 14:6; 1 Tim 2:5),[66] the Redeemer enables believers to be at peace with God (Rom 5:1). The Messiah is also the believers' great High Priest who enables them to go before the throne of their gracious God to receive His mercy and help in their time of need (Heb 4:14–16).

---

63. Keener, *John*, 1:490; cf. Carson, *John*, 163–64; Köstenberger, *John*, 86.

64. Hoskins, *Jesus as the replacement of the temple*, 197.

65. Ibid., 183.

66. Hanson (*The prophetic Gospel*, 37) maintains that the one whom "Jacob saw in his vision at Bethel was the pre-existent Logos, just as Moses saw him at Sinai." Furthermore, as Whitacre (*John*) states, Jesus is "greater than Jacob (Jn 4:12), for he is the real Jacob-Israel, the locus and source of the real people of God."

The title "Son of Man" (John 1:51) was Jesus' most common self-description. He wanted to teach that, as "God's primordial Word,"[67] He combined two Old Testament roles, Son of Man (Dan 7:13–14) and Servant of the Lord (Isa 52:13—53:12). Daniel described a Son of Man to whom God gives an eternal kingdom, while Isaiah described a Servant of the Lord who suffers on behalf of others. The Lord Jesus knew that He must perform the role of the suffering Servant. This included His betrayal, rejection, crucifixion, death, and resurrection; but He also knew that eventually He would receive glory as the Son of Man. As such, He would bring salvation and judgment to the human race. Jesus did these things in accordance with the will of His Father.

Conclusion

The witness of John the Baptizer and others reinforces the portrait throughout the Fourth Gospel that Jesus is the perfection of the gift of the Torah. He is the Light of the World that shines in the darkness to dispel error and evil. As the testimony of John confirmed, the kingdom of God had entered a new and final phase in the person of Jesus as Tanakh. The ministry of all the luminaries of the Old Testament era, including the prophet Elijah, anticipated and prepared for the advent of the divine, incarnate Logos. In turn, He played a central role in the Father's plan of redemption. Indeed, the Son made the Father known and accessible to humankind. In response to the Baptizer's ministry, those who repented of their sins and turned to the Messiah in faith were pardoned.

Forgiveness is possible because Jesus is the Lamb of God who atones for the sins of the world. As the quintessential sacrifice called for in the law, the Messiah is the realization of the Torah's types, prophecies, and expectations. In order for the Son to secure redemption for God's people, He had to become the suffering Servant and Passover Lamb about whom the Old Testament prophets foretold. Through the shed blood of the divine, incarnate Logos, sin and death became vanquished foes and those once alienated from the Father could become reconciled to Him. This was possible by trusting in the Son, the person on whom the Holy Spirit descended in the form of a dove. The Baptizer was privileged to testify that Jesus, the chosen One of God, was inaugurating the promised age of covenant renewal for the redeemed.

Andrew, Simon Peter, Philip, Nathaniel, and the apostle John were the initial benefactors of the Baptizer's witness. They encountered the om-

---

67. Ratzinger, *Jesus of Nazareth*, 325.

niscient Tanakh of God, who intimately knew human nature. As a result of the Anointed One's remarkable discernment and profound insight, they affirmed Him to be the Son of God, Son of Man, and King of Israel. They discovered that Jesus of Nazareth was the person about whom Moses, the famed lawgiver, and the prophets of the Old Testament had written. In fulfillment of and as the ultimate reality behind all they had written in the Torah, the Messiah would die on the cross and rise from the dead.[68] Those who believed the good news about the Mediator between God and people, would receive the eternal life the great High Priest offered as the Lamb of God.

---

68. Cf. the appendix of this study for a discussion of a God-centered and Christ-centered view of making sense of reality.

4

Jesus as Torah in John 2–4

Introduction

A MAJOR premise of this work is that the Fourth Gospel presents Jesus as the divine, incarnate Tanakh. In particular, He is portrayed as the realization of all the Mosaic law's redemptive-historical types, prophecies, and expectations. The Evangelist's goal was to convince people to trust in Jesus as the Messiah, the Son of God, and consequently find eternal life in Him (20:30–31). The apostle's inclusion of seven signs (2:11), or attesting miracles, in the first 12 chapters of the Fourth Gospel help to accomplish that overarching purpose.[1] The wondrous deeds persuasively demonstrate the messianic identity, power, and authority of the Lord Jesus.[2] Just as in the period of Moses, the great lawgiver and leader of Israel, God intervened in human history, so now with the coming of the Logos, God involves Himself in a new way to bring about eternal redemption for those who believe (cf. Deut 11:3; 29:2).[3]

---

1. Johns ("Signs as witnesses") maintains that the "signs consistently play a positive role for faith throughout the Fourth Gospel" (521). Against the backdrop of the "juridical motif" that "dominates the Fourth Gospel," the "miracles help make the case" for the messianic identity of the Son (527); cf. Cook, *The theology of John*, 55–56; Kim, *Seven sign-miracles*, 62–64, 81–82.

2. For a discussion of the background and significance of the signs in the Fourth Gospel, cf. Brown, *John*, 525–532; Keener, *John*, 1:251–79; Kim, *Seven sign-miracles*, 28–84; Köstenberger, *Studies on John and gender*, 99–116; Nicol, *Semeia*; Schnackenburg, *John*, 1:515–28; Schnelle, *Antidocetic Christology*, 144–175; Tenney, *John*, 27–34; Van Belle, *The signs source*, 379–404; Westcott, *John*, lxxvi–lxxvii; Wright, *Jesus*, 77–81.

3. Lincoln (*John*, 61) explains that in the Septuagint, the Greek noun rendered "sign" was "particularly employed of divine actions through Moses at the time of the exodus." These miraculous deeds "attested to Moses as the divine agent, judged the Egyptians and their gods, and brought about the liberation of Israel" (cf. Exod 4:1–9, 28–31; 7:1–7; 10:1–2; 12:12–13). Similarly, in the writings of the Old Testament prophets, signs "attested to the prophets as God's agents, confirmed their message, and frequently also served as a vehicle for conveying that message" (cf. Isa 20:1–4; Ezek 4:1–4; 12:8–16). In

Jesus as Torah Changing the Water into Wine (John 2:1–11)[4]

Jesus' first recorded miracle took place at a wedding feast, which His disciples and His mother also attended (John 2:1–2). The marriage celebration was a symbolic reminder that the age of the Messiah had dawned and inaugurated the blessings of the eschatological kingdom (cf. Gen 49:11; Isa 25:6; Jer 31:5; Hos 2:22; Joel 3:18; Amos 9:13).[5] The backdrop of this wedding feast was an array of purification rites described in the Tanakh, all of which found their ultimate fulfillment in the Son. The time reference in John 2:1 suggests the Messiah arrived the third day after He and His followers left the Jordan River area, where the Baptizer had been headquartered. The presence of Mary[6] at the celebration indicates that the bride or groom (or both) was a close friend of the family, rather than just an acquaintance of Jesus and His disciples.[7] It is unclear why no mention is made of Joseph. He may have been deceased by this time.[8]

The changing of water into wine (fermented grape juice) occurred at Cana in Galilee. This village is only mentioned two other times in the Fourth Gospel (4:46 and 21:2). The latter reference identifies Cana as the home of Nathanael, who had just been chosen to follow Jesus (1:47).

---

a corresponding manner, "Jesus' signs . . . attest to his divine agency." Furthermore, the miraculous deeds He performed emphasize the "unique status of this agent as the giver of life in abundance." As the Messiah, He "exercises the divine prerogative" by "overturning dearth, disease and death."

4. The following two sections are a modified version of my journal article, "Jesus as Torah in John 2:1–22," which appears in *Conspectus* (Vol. 4, September 2007) and is reprinted with permission.

5. Cf. Bock, *Jesus*, 424; Ng, *Water symbolism in John*, 68, 70; Sanders and Mastin, *John*, 109.

6. Mary most likely belonged to the tribe of Judah, and possibly was herself a descendant of David (Matt 1:1–16; Luke 1:32). We see much of Jesus' early life through Mary's eyes, as she treasured all sorts of things that happened to Him and pondered in her heart what they might mean (Luke 2:19, 51). This information, unique to Luke, has led some to conclude that Mary was one of the eyewitnesses Luke interviewed when he gathered material for his Gospel (1:2).

7. Cf. Calvin, *John*, 1:82.

8. There is little information about Joseph in the Gospels. He was a descendant of David, the husband of Mary, and the legal guardian of Jesus. By trade, Joseph was a carpenter (Matt 13:55). It can be deduced from Scripture that Joseph possessed great integrity and firm moral conviction (1:19). Regardless of what God desired of him, Joseph was willing to obey (1:24; 2:14, 21). Because he was a devout Jew, Joseph no doubt made sure Jesus received good spiritual training during His adolescent years in Nazareth (Luke 2:39–40, 51–52). Joseph is last mentioned when Jesus was 12 years old (vv. 42–48). Many think Joseph had died by the time Jesus entered His public ministry (4:14–15).

Since Cana was a small town, more than likely Nathanael would have also known the newly married couple. The exact location of this village remains unknown. Two suggested sites are near Nazareth, where Jesus grew up with His family. One is a group of ruins called Khirbet Kana, about nine miles north of Nazareth; however, many believe that the present village of Kafr Kanna, about four miles northeast of Nazareth, is the actual location, with its abundant springs and fig trees. Some of the Crusaders identified this location as Cana, and it fits well with the descriptions of medieval travelers, who describe a church in this location supposedly containing at least one of the original water jars from the wedding.

In Jesus' day, wedding festivals could last up to a week. On such occasions, banquets would be prepared to accommodate many guests. The attendees would spend their time celebrating the new life to be enjoyed by the married couple. Archaeological evidence indicates that entire villages would be invited to a wedding celebration. Also, to refuse such an invitation was considered an insult. The wedding meal itself consisted of bread dipped in wine. Typically, the guests would call for innumerable toasts. After that, more visiting, eating, and drinking would occur (though this was rarely an occasion for drunkenness).

Wine diluted with water was the accepted beverage of the times, and people were accustomed to it. Because of a lack of water purification processes, this mixture was safer to drink than water alone. Careful planning was needed to accommodate all who came. This was imperative, for the strong, unwritten rules of hospitality implied that it was humiliating to be caught in short supply of some necessary item.[9] Even the poorest Jewish parents would scrimp and save enough money to provide plenty of food and wine for their children's wedding; yet, for some unknown reason, the bridegroom failed to supply enough of the latter for the duration of the festivities (2:3). Perhaps more guests came than he had anticipated, or perhaps they stayed longer than he had planned.[10]

Few details are given of what happened next. Evidently, someone reported the predicament to Mary, who then went to her son. Perhaps Jesus was seated at a table with His disciples and enjoying the festivities. One possibility is that Mary quietly sat down next to Jesus and discretely told Him the wine had run out.[11] It is clear from Jesus' response that

---

9. Cf. Morris, *John*, 156.

10. Cf. Nicol, *Semeia*, 53.

11. Cf. Goldsmith, *Gospel of John*. Keener (*John*, 1:503), however, observes that "women were ordinarily separated from men at such feasts (insofar as possible)." The counterpoint is that the typical Galilean home of the parents of a groom "would not be large enough to

Mary's statement implied more than a simple observation of fact. Implicit in her words was a request for Jesus to do something about the situation so that the bridegroom could avoid being socially embarrassed. According to verse 11, Jesus had not yet performed any miracles. Thus at this point in the account we can only speculate as to what Mary had observed in her son that would give her the idea He could somehow resolve the problem.

It is unlikely that Mary expected Jesus to send the people home, for that was not His prerogative. Also, Mary probably did not want Him to send His disciples into town to buy more wine, for they surely lacked the funds to do so. It is possible Mary had seen her son on other occasions do kind and helpful things for hurting people. Perhaps in the privacy of neighborhood life, Jesus was known as an extraordinary and caring person. Regardless of what Mary may have been thinking, Jesus gave her a startling and provocative answer. He did not say either yes or no; instead, He asked Mary why she had come to Him for help. Without waiting for her reply, Jesus' words indicate that He was no longer under His mother's authority. While Jesus continued to honor Mary, His actions were governed by the mission His Father in heaven had given Him (cf. 8:28–29). In brief, the goal of the divine, incarnate Torah was to die on the cross in order to atone for the sins of the world (cf. 1:29).

Jesus was neither cruel nor harsh in His remarks to His mother. "Woman" (2:4) was a common term of address that implied no disrespect (cf. Matt 15:28, Luke 13:12; John 4:21; 8:10; 19:26; 20:15).[12] In contemporary parlance, one might say, "Dear lady."[13] Such observations notwithstanding, the response "sets a peculiar distance between Jesus and his mother."[14] Jesus wanted Mary to think of Him not so much as the son whom she had parented, but rather as the Redeemer of Israel. Jesus used a social situation to point to a spiritual reality. In fact, the contrast between the wedding crisis and His mission could not have been more vivid. The Savior's query, "Why do you involve me?" (John 2:4), underscores Mary's desire that Jesus do something to help a family avoid social embarrass-

---

segregate genders." If the festivities took place "in a courtyard surrounded by homes," then "the women and food preparation could have been concentrated in one home." Given the Fourth Gospel's lack of details about the wedding celebration, any reconstruction must rely on conjecture.

12. Cf. Barrett, *St. John*, 191; Lightfoot, *St. John's Gospel*, 100–101; Schnackenburg, *John*, 1:328.

13. Cf. Beasley-Murray, *John*, 34; Brown, *John*, 99; Bruce, *John*, 69.

14. Bultmann, *John*, 116; cf. Keener, *John*, 1:504–6; Ridderbos, *John*, 105; Whitacre, *Johannine polemic*, 85.

ment. Also, the follow-up statement, "My time has not yet come," stressed that Jesus' atoning sacrifice at Calvary, resurrection from the dead, and return to the Father in glory was a more eternally relevant issue (cf. 12:23, 27; 13:1; 17:1).[15]

From what transpired, it is clear that Jesus had not offended Mary. In fact, she seemed to instinctively know that her son would intervene in a constructive manner. At this point, Mary returned to the servants and possibly told the head steward to do whatever Jesus directed. Although Mary did not know what her son might have in mind, she nevertheless trusted Him to initiate what was prudent. Here we see that despite the awkwardness of the situation, the Lord Jesus conducted Himself impeccably in the social affairs of His community. Though His redemptive mission was lofty, He was not above mingling with people on all levels, so that they might be drawn to Him in saving faith as the fulfillment of the Tanakh (2:11). Jesus' response to Mary shows that the Savior knew and controlled His eternal future (10:17–18). Mary, in turn, submitted to Jesus' decision about how to handle the situation.

The Messiah apparently wasted no time in taking action. After getting up from where He had been sitting, He went to the nearby spot where there were six empty stone jars. Perhaps after praying silently to His heavenly Father, Jesus told the servants to fill the jars with water (2:6–7). Mary's faith was honored when Jesus did His first miracle at this humble peasant wedding. Jesus performed the miracle in such a way as to not draw attention to Himself or the shortage of wine at the feast.[16] The six stone vessels at the wedding feast normally kept the family's water supply fresh and cool. The jars of varying size each could hold about 20 to 30 gallons of water (all total, roughly between 120 and 180 gallons of liquid), which the Jews used to wash their hands and vessels according to the Mosaic law's requirements.[17] Apparently, because of the number of wedding guests, the water in the six jars had been used up, so they needed to be refilled. The servants might have been puzzled by Jesus' unusual sounding command. Why take ordinary water to the master of ceremonies (v. 8)? Despite whatever doubts the servants may have had, they did not complain; instead, they did exactly what Jesus said.

After the servants filled the jars to the top with water, they then dipped some out and took it to the person in charge of the festivities (usu-

---

15. Cf. Calvin, *John*, 1:85.
16. Cf. Köstenberger, *John*, 95.
17. Cf. Thomas, "Fourth Gospel," 162–65.

ally a servant or friend of the bridegroom). When this individual tasted the water now turned into wine, he was so pleasantly surprised that he commended the bridegroom for his good taste (v. 9). The master of ceremonies noted that it was customary for the host (such as the bridegroom) to serve the best wine first and then later to bring out the less expensive wines; but the bridegroom was congratulated for the brilliant stroke of keeping the best wine until last (v. 10).

Jesus' first sign was experienced not so much as a miracle, but rather as a wonderful discovery. Only the Messiah and the servants initially knew what had happened. Jesus evidently took no unusual action, such as touching the stone jars or commanding the water to turn into wine. Most likely, Jesus' simple prayer brought about the attesting sign. Jesus did not call for a pause in the festivities, and He did not summon everyone's attention. He also did not tell those present to gather around and see how He had changed water into wine; rather, Jesus performed His miracle in a quiet and humble manner. John 1:3 reveals that the Logos is the Creator of all things. In fact, acts of creation and transformation are part of His nature (cf. 2 Cor 5:17).[18]

Jesus' turning water into wine should be understood in terms of what the Old Testament said about the coming Redeemer.[19] In the messianic age, the Lord would host a great feast complete with the best food and overflowing wine, symbolizing great joy (Isa 25:6; Joel 2:19, 24; 3:18; Amos 9:13–15).[20] In fact, one non-biblical description of the messianic age describes it as a time of great fertility, with grapes so large that just one would produce "about 120 gallons of wine"[21] (2 Bar 29:5; cf. 1 Enoch 10:19). Wine, however, could also symbolize suffering, since its color sug-

---

18. O'Day ("John," 9:538) states that the miracle Jesus performed at Cana in Galilee was not a repudiation of the Torah, but "the creation of something new in the midst of Judaism." Likewise, Silva ("Approaching the Fourth Gospel," 28) affirms that the "new order instituted by Christ must be seen as a fulfillment, not a rejection, of the OT message."

19. Smith ("Exodus typology," 334) maintains that the Johannine writer "saw Jesus' signs as antitypes of Moses' signs" recorded in the "Exodus materials." Simiarly, Lierman ("Mosaic pattern," 214) observed that "just as Moses began his ministry with signs to show that he was sent by God, so also Jesus in the Fourth Gospel performs signs to show he is sent by the Father." McGrath (*John's apologetic Christology*) offers this clarification regarding the Moses typology in the Fourth Gospel: "John makes use of a motif and imagery that is not uniquely his, and yet which he uses in his own distinctive way" (58). Indeed, in the Fourth Gospel, "the belief that Jesus is the 'prophet (like Moses)' is perhaps made more explicit than elsewhere in the New Testament" (59).

20. Cf. Westcott, *John*, 39.

21. Brown, *John*, 105.

gested blood, and drinking its dregs was a sign of punishment (Pss 60:3; 75:8; Jer 25:15–16).[22] Jesus symbolically linked wine with His blood at the Last Supper, which He celebrated when His hour had indeed come (John 2:4; 13:1; 18:11).

We do not know how Jesus changed the water into wine at Cana in Galilee, only that He did it instantaneously and without fanfare; but we do know that Jesus used this miracle to validate His claim to be the perfection of the gift of the Torah (a truth that would later lead to His crucifixion). All the miracles of Jesus were signs that He performed to demonstrate His power so that people would trust in Him.[23] It is true that Jesus healed and helped people in dire situations, and they were blessed in this way by His miracles; yet, in the end, Jesus' foremost goal was to relieve the deepest spiritual needs of people. The Messiah's changing the water into wine unveiled His glory (that is, His divine nature, presence, and power; cf. Exod 24:15–18; 34:29–35; 40:34–38), and the disciples believed in Him as the Anointed One (John 2:11).[24] His glory was seen in two aspects at Cana—His love for the neighborhood people and His control over the elements of nature.[25]

Jesus as Torah Clearing the Temple Courts (John 2:12–22)

After Jesus attended the wedding in Cana, He traveled some 20 miles northeast to Capernaum, where He stayed for a few days with His mother, brothers (cf. Matt 1:24–25; 12:46; Mark 3:21; 6:3; Luke 8:19), and disciples (cf. John 1:35–51). Capernaum, the home of some of Jesus' followers, served as the Lord's headquarters during a large portion of His public

22. Cf. Glasson, *Moses*, 26, 88.

23. Labahn ("Between tradition and literary art," 186) states that the primary objective of the Fourth Gospel is to "awaken belief or perhaps to strengthen belief." In a similar vein, Witherington (*John's wisdom*, 4) considers the Fourth Gospel to be a "dramatic biography written for Christians to use for evangelistic purposes." He also proposes a secondary purpose, namely, to "encourage those who already believe" (11). Likewise, Beasley-Murray (*John*, lxxxix) affirms "there is ground . . . for thinking that the Fourth Gospel was written with both evangelistic and didactic aims in view"; cf. Brown, *Introduction to the Gospel of John*, 152, 183; Carson, *John*, 90–95; Keener, *John*, 1:11–12.

24. Keener (*John*, 1:275) remarks that "whereas Jesus' signs in the Synoptics especially authenticate his mission, the Fourth Gospel analyzes the signs in a christological context, using them and the frequently subsequent discourses to interpret Jesus' identity and to call for faith."

25. Witherington (*John's wisdom*, 79) thinks the consequence of Jesus' glory being revealed is that "God's life-giving and joyful presence can be found" in the Messiah.

ministry (cf. Matt 4:13; Mark 1:21; 2:1). It was a fishing village built on the northwest shore of the Sea of Galilee. Capernaum hosted a Roman garrison that maintained peace in the region. Major highways crisscrossed at Capernaum, making it militarily strategic. Because of its fishing and trading industries, the city was a melting pot of Greek, Roman, and Jewish cultures.

When it was nearly time for the celebration of the Jewish Passover[26] in the winter of AD 27, Jesus traveled about 80 miles south from Capernaum to Jerusalem. Passover was one of several yearly sacred festivals the people of God observed. These special days had different purposes and varying kinds of observances, but they all were meant to deepen the people's devotion to the Lord and give them occasions for joy and celebration. Passover was the first festival on the calendar and possibly signified the most important holy feast to the Israelites. During this sacred event, they would commemorate the final plague in Egypt, when the angel of death passed over the firstborn of the Israelites, while killing the firstborn of the Egyptians (cf. Exod 12:1–30). Passover was to begin on the evening of the fourteenth day of the first month (Lev 23:5). The Israelites would kill a lamb and on that evening eat a special meal. It was designed to remind them of the meal their ancestors ate on the first Passover night, before leaving Egypt (cf. Num 9:1–14; 28:16; Deut 16:1–7; Matt 26:17; Mark 14:12–26; John 2:13; 11:55; 1 Cor 5:7; Heb 11:28).

The Fourth Gospel records at least three separate Passover celebrations that occurred during the time of Jesus' earthly ministry: the first in 2:13, 23; the second in 6:4; and the third in 11:55; 12:1; 13:1; 18:28, 39; and 19:14. Some think that the Jewish festival mentioned in 5:1 was Passover, though Pentecost and Tabernacles are two other strong possibilities.[27] Depending on the separate number of Passover celebrations appearing in John's Gospel, Jesus' ministry could have lasted as long as three and a half years.[28] This statement is based on the premise that the Passovers appear in strict chronological order. Another option is that the material in the Fourth Gospel is arranged topically. In turn, this would leave open

26. For an assessment of the relationship of the Fourth Gospel to the ancient Palestinian synagogue lectionary system, cf. Guilding, *Jewish worship*. The author's research led him to conclude that in "the Fourth Gospel the use of the Old Testament lections is entirely systematic and explicit; indeed, the Gospel might fairly be described as a Christian commentary on the lections of the triennial cycle." He also states that the "authenticity of the discourses of the Fourth Gospel, especially in relation to the circumstances in which they are said to have been spoken, has impressed Jewish scholars" (231).

27. As noted in chapter 5 of this work, Pentecost is the most likely festival.

28. Cf. Harris, *John*.

the possibility that the account of Jesus clearing the temple courts actually occurred later in His public ministry.

The Synoptic Gospels record a similar episode occurring in the week preceding Jesus' crucifixion, specifically after His triumphal entry into Jerusalem (cf. Matt 21:12–17; Mark 11:12–18; Luke 19:45–46). Those favoring the view that the episodes in the Fourth Gospel are topically arranged consider the two temple-clearing incidents as being one and the same.[29] In contrast, those who regard the material in John's Gospel as being sequenced chronologically argue for two separate episodes. This view is supported by the writer's emphasis throughout his narrative on mentioning specific times, places, facts, and details. Also, the content and wording of the Fourth Gospel and the Synoptic Gospels about the temple-clearing incident are markedly different.[30] Regardless of which view is preferred, Jesus' statement in John 2:19 most likely forms the basis for the accusations voiced by false witnesses at the Redeemer's trial before the Sanhedrin (cf. Matt 26:61; Mark 14:58) and for the spectators' taunting remarks at His crucifixion (cf. Matt 27:40; Mark 15:29).

In the Fourth Gospel, there is theological significance to the clearing of the temple courts as one of Jesus' first public acts.[31] From the start of the Savior's earthly ministry, the judgment of God rested on the established civil and religious authorities.[32] This was the reason why the old order,

29. Cf. Barrett, *St. John*, 195; Borchert, *John 1–11*, 160–62, 166; Keener, *John*, 1:518–19; Lincoln, *John*, 141–44; Schnackenburg, *John*, 1:344; Witherington, *John's wisdom*, 85–86.

30. Cf. Brown, *John*, 118–19; Carson, *John*, 177–78; Köstenberger, *John*, 111; Morris, *John*, 167–68; Tenney, "John," 9:44.

31. The importance of the temple for the Jewish people cannot be overstated. To begin, the shrine had an indispensable theological function to serve. It was the place where the Lord manifested His holy presence in Judea. It was also the spot where sacrifices were made in response to God's gracious choice of Israel as His people. In the sanctuary, God's people could spend time in prayer. Moreover, its design, furniture, and customs were object lessons that prepared the people for the Messiah. Additionally, the temple had important political and economic roles to play in Jewish society. It was the institution that held together the entire covenant community—the past as well as the present and the future. The shrine gave political identity to the people. Access to its courts identified who was properly a citizen and who was excluded. From an economic perspective, rooms in the temple functioned as a treasury—in effect, the society's bank. Because of the sanctuary's demands for tithes and offerings, a large portion of the Jewish economy passed through the temple personnel and storehouses. In brief, without the shrine, God's people had little opportunity to pull together as a coherent society to face the challenges of the future.

32. Kerr (*Temple theme*, 67) maintains that Jesus' bold action at the Jerusalem shrine heralded the "eschatological hour, the hour that comes to dominate the Gospel as Jesus moves towards the cross and the resurrection." Expressed differently, the cleansing of the

represented by the temple built by Herod the Great, would give way to the new order, represented by the temple of Jesus' body.[33] With the advent of Jesus as the final expression of God's Tanakh, all the divine blessings anticipated under the old covenant were brought to fruition, including being cleansed from sin, experiencing the delight of salvation, and enjoying unbroken fellowship with the Lord (cf. Isa 25:6–9; 56:7; Jer 31:31–34; Rev 21:22).

The temple area Jesus entered with His disciples was a complex of courts, porticoes, and buildings on a large raised platform. The place was filled with activity and noise as merchants and bankers did business with worshipers. Every day, and especially during the Passover celebration, pilgrims who had traveled from near and distant locations offered many types of sacrifices. Vendors close to the temple sold ceremonially pure animals to the worshipers for this purpose. Money changers converted foreign coins into the proper currency so that visitors could buy the animals they need-

---

temple in John 2:13–22 is an end-time event that "signals that the day of the Lord has come or is very near." It is in this "eschatological ethos" that "judgment will begin at the house of the Lord and a new Temple will be raised." According to Köstenberger (*John*, 102), the literature of the Old Testament and Second Temple Judaism "express the expectation of the establishment of a new temple for the messianic age" (cf. Ezek 40–44; 1 Enoch 90:28–36; Pss Sol 17:30). Burge (*John*, 95) advances the discussion by noting that the members of the "Dead Sea community of Qumran" not only were harsh in their criticism of "Herod's temple project," but also included in their belief system the "hope and plans for a new temple." Moreover, despite the razing of Jerusalem and its temple by the Romans in AD 70, the Jewish longing remained strong for the Messiah to appear and rebuild the shrine in the holy city. In point of fact, towards the latter part of the century, the Jewish people "confessed the 'Eighteen Benedictions'" (also called the *Amidah,* or the prayer that is said while standing and facing toward Jerusalem), some of which petition the Lord for Israel's salvation and the exiles' return. The fourteenth benediction, which "looks forward to the new temple and Messiah," offers the following prayer to God: "And to Jerusalem, your city, return in mercy, and dwell therein as you have spoken; rebuild it soon in our days as an everlasting building, and speedily set up therein the throne of David. Blessed are you, O Lord, who rebuilds Jerusalem."

33. Hanson (*The prophetic Gospel*, 43) thinks that the Evangelist's intent in John 2:17–22 was to "present Jesus as the true Temple, the house of God." Likewise, Coloe (*God dwells with us*, 3) states that the "Temple, as the dwelling place of God, points to the identity and role of Jesus." Moreover, Hoskins (*Jesus as the replacement of the temple*), based on his analysis of John 1:14, 1:51, 2:18–22, and 4:20–24, concluded that the Messiah's advent "inaugurates a new phase in the relationship between God and his people" (157). The Son, as the "true Temple" of God, "fulfills, surpasses, and replaces" the shrine in Jerusalem (iv), along with the religious festivals associated with it, namely, "the Passover, Feast of Tabernacles," and "Feast of Dedication" (v). It is through the death, resurrection, and exaltation of the Son that the Father replaces the old temple order with the new temple order. Jesus, as the "antitype" of the Jerusalem sanctuary, has become the "locus of God's presence, glory, revelation, and abundant provision" (iv); cf. Hakola, *Identity matters,* 88.

ed and also pay the required half-shekel temple tax (cf. Exod 30:13–16). Tragically, the presence of all this commercial activity prevented Gentile converts to Judaism from being able to worship and pray in the only approved spot of the temple area (John 2:14).[34]

The Messiah, being filled with indignation at the enormity of the injustice, took bold and decisive action. To symbolize God's authority and judgment,[35] Jesus made a whip out of cords of rope and began to flail it in the air, perhaps in a wide, circular motion. He chased people out of the temple area, and opened the pens housing their sheep and cattle to let these animals escape. He also turned over the tables of the moneychangers and scattered their coins on the ground (v. 15). Next, Jesus went to the merchants selling doves and ordered them to remove the birds from the area. Perhaps He opened some of the cages in which the doves were kept so they could more easily fly away. He ordered that the rest be removed and that the house of His Father no longer be turned into a marketplace of merchants (v. 16). This is possibly an allusion to Zechariah 14:21, wherein the Hebrew term rendered "Canaanite" could also be translated "merchant" or "trader." The idea is that in the day the Lord established His messianic kingdom, He would remove all those involved in commercial activity from His temple.[36]

From Jesus' earliest years, He was aware of His special relationship with His heavenly Father, including God's desire that the temple in Jerusalem be a sacred place for worship and prayer (cf. Luke 2:49). This attitude is reflected in Jesus' efforts at the start of His earthly ministry to clear the temple area of all profane activity. This set in motion a long chain of events that led to His atoning sacrifice on the cross.[37] After the Messiah's

---

34. The court of the Gentiles, where the money changers and merchants were set up, was the outermost section of the temple complex. It was paved with marble and formed a square three-quarters of a mile in circumference. Several porticoes or meeting places located there were often used by Jesus for teaching. According to Jewish tradition, this was also the place where the Levites who assisted the priests ate and slept. This outer court was the only spot in the temple where the Gentiles were allowed. It was separated from the inner courts by a stone balustrade a few feet high. Warnings were posted along the balustrade in Greek and Latin, telling Gentiles they would be put to death if they entered any of the other, inner courts.

35. Cf. Bruce, *John*, 75.

36. Jesus' cleansing of the temple did not mean that no true worship of God was occurring there. For example, there are Gospel accounts of devout people such as Zechariah, Simeon, and Anna humbly worshiping God in the temple (cf. Luke 1:8–10; 2:25–38).

37. Burge (*John*, 94) clarifies that Jesus, in "attacking the financial machinery of the festival system," placed Himself "at odds with Caiaphas and the temple leadership." Furthermore, Kerr (*Temple theme*) argues that John 2:17 "brings the death of Jesus into

resurrection from the dead, His disciples remembered the prophecy recorded in Psalm 69:9, which foretold that Jesus' fervent devotion for the Lord's house burned in Him like a fire. As the second half of this verse prophesies, the Redeemer's love for the things of God would raise the ire of His enemies (cf. Rom 15:3). The antagonists did not realize that the insults they hurled at the Father, fell on the Son.

As the divine, incarnate Torah, Jesus is the Lord and the Messenger of the covenant about whom Malachi 3:1–4 said would come to spiritually purify and morally refine God's people. This is in keeping with the Old Testament teaching that God maintained a burning zeal and passion for the covenant community and would deal with all rivals firmly. As John 2:17 indicates, anyone who was spiritually unfaithful to the Lord Jesus would experience His hand of discipline (cf. Prov 3:11–12; Heb 12:5–6). Similarly, James 4:5 states that God "jealously longs for the spirit he has caused to dwell in us." The idea is that when God's people become unfaithful in their commitment, He zealously desires to have them return to Him in faithfulness and love. For that reason, when they opt for friendship with the world, it provokes God to anger. Indeed, He will not permit them to have divided loyalties between Himself and the world.

At some point, the temple authorities were alerted to the unfolding events and began to rush to the scene to investigate. When "the Jews" saw what Jesus had done, they demanded an explanation for His actions (John 2:18). In the New Testament, the Greek noun *Ioudaioi* (rendered "Jews") has a range of meanings, including the Jewish people as a whole, the inhabitants of Jerusalem and its environs, the religious leaders headquartered in Jerusalem, or simply those who were antagonistic toward Jesus.[38] Often in the Fourth Gospel, references to "the Jews" are not only an "ethnic designation," but also a "symbol of Jesus' opponents."[39] Put differently,

---

view and that his death is the death of God's Paschal Lamb" (67). Accordingly, there is "no future for the old Temple and its sacrifices. God no more dwells within its walls, and its sacrifices have been replaced by Jesus, the Passover sacrifice. Jesus is now the house of the Father. God dwells in Jesus" (82).

38. Carson, *John*, 141–42; Stern, *Jewish New Testament commentary*, 158–59; Whitacre, *Johannine polemic*, 20; cf. the discussion provided by Brown, *Introduction to the Gospel of John*, 157–175; Kierspel, *The Jews and the world*, 13–36.

39. O'Day, "John," 9:617. Keener (*John*, 1:222) states that the "primary issue is not ethnic (both persecutor and persecuted are Jewish) but power." Kierspel (*The Jews and the world*) clarifies that maintaining a historical reference for *Ioudaioi* does not encourage anti-Semitic interpretations, for the Evangelist used *Ioudaioi* "in parallel position to *kosmos* throughout the Gospel" (214). Moreover, an examination of the way in which *kosmos* is used "reveals the author's intent to translate the particulars of Jesus' life *throughout* the text

while *Ioudaioi* retains its normal empirical reference to a religious-ethnic body of people, "the Jews" are also "symbols of human rejection of God's revelation in Jesus." In a "negative sense," the antagonists in the Fourth Gospel become "representatives of the world."[40]

In this verse, the apostle was referring to the Jewish authorities who had oversight of the Jerusalem shrine. Because they considered Jesus to be a counterfeit rabbi who operated "without being ordained,"[41] they wanted proof of His legal right to disrupt the commercial activities occurring in the temple area. The Greek word rendered "sign" most likely refers to some sort of miracle that would certify Jesus' status as the Son of God (cf. 1 Cor 1:22). Ironically, Jesus' resurrection is the only authentication of His divine nature that He promised to give the religious leaders (cf. Rom 1:3). They failed to understand His claim that if they tore down the temple of His body, He would build it again within three days.[42] The Jewish authorities thought the Messiah was referring to the temple of Herod the Great, which the king began to renovate and reconstruct around 19 or 20 BC. The shrine was not completed until AD 64, during the reign of

---

into universal notions that apply to Jews and Gentiles alike" (215; italics are his). Attention is deflected away from the Jews as a race to the whole world as the reason for Jesus' coming (His mission) and going (His death). Consequently, the audience in the Fourth Gospel is cosmopolitan irrespective of the ethnic origin of its members (cf. John 3:16, 19; 4:42; 12:19–20).

40. Smith, *John*, 56; cf. his discussion of anti-semitism, 169–173. Lincoln (*Truth on trial*, 45) notes that the lawsuit motif found in the Fourth Gospel is a reworking of the lawsuits recorded in Isaiah 40–55. Moreover, in the Fourth Gospel, Israel becomes the "representative of the world" (46), especially as the evidence is presented in the universal court of justice regarding Jesus and His messianic claims. The nations are "represented through the Samaritans," who affirm that Jesus is the Savior of humankind (John 4:42), and the Greeks, who want to meet Jesus (12:20–22). Furthermore, Jesus' "climactic trial before Pilate . . . sets the lawsuit squarely on the world stage and in the context of the nations" (256). Throughout the forensic process (as seen in the Fourth Gospel's cosmic-trial metaphor), Jesus functions as "God's authorized agent and chief witness" (46). The irony is that the person who is eventually tried and condemned by the religious and civil authorities of the day turns out to be their Creator and Judge (as well as that of all humankind). Also, cf. Bultmann, *John*, 86; De Jonge, "Jewish expectations," 265; Keener, *John*, 1:214–228; Lightfoot, *St. John's Gospel*, 130; Meeks, *The prophet-king*, 41, 82–83, 305–6; Ridderbos, *John*, 62–63, 324–330; Schnackenburg, *John*, 2:200; Trites, *Witness*, 79, 112–13.

41. Daube, *Rabbinic Judaism*, 217. According to the author, the religious leaders were convinced that whatever claim Jesus made to exercise divine authority was illegitimate. In short, they regarded Him to be a "false prophet" (219).

42. Cf. Lightfoot, *St. John's Gospel*, 113–14.

Herod Agrippa. A 46-year timeline implies a date of around AD 27 for the Passover mentioned in John 2:13.[43]

On other occasions (recorded in the Synoptic Gospels), Pharisees and teachers of the law demanded to see Jesus perform a sign to authenticate His divine authority. In response, He declared that the only certifying mark they would receive was that of Jonah. The prophet was facing certain death during the three-day period in which he lay entombed in the belly of a huge sea creature (cf. Jonah 1:17). The Lord restored Jonah to life by setting him free from his predicament. This foreshadowed Jesus spending a similar amount of time buried in the depths of the earth. His own resurrection from the dead would be the supreme validation of His messianic power and authority and serve as a sign that He was superseding the "old temple order"[44] (cf. Matt 12:38–41; 16:1–4; Luke 11:16, 29–32). After Jesus' body was raised from the dead, the Holy Spirit enabled the disciples to remember what the Redeemer had said, including the meaning and significance of His teachings (cf. John 14:26). What the embodiment of the Tanakh had prophesied, fulfilled what God had promised in the Old Testament.[45] Jesus' disciples believed the Scriptures and the sayings Jesus had spoken about them.

Jesus as Torah Teaching Nicodemus (John 2:23—3:21)

John 2:23 makes reference to miraculous signs that Jesus performed during the festival of Passover in the winter of AD 27. Many of those who witnessed these began to trust in His name. "Jesus" is the Greek form of the Hebrew name "Joshua," which means "the Lord is salvation" or "the Lord saves" (cf. Matt 1:21; Luke 1:31). It appropriately emphasized the redemptive identity and mission of the Son. Regrettably, though, the belief referred to in John 2:23 tended to be superficial, fickle, and distorted (cf. 6:60–66),[46] for the respondents most likely regarded Jesus to be some sort of end-time, political figure who would liberate them from bondage to Rome (cf. vv. 14–15). Because God the Son knew what was in their hearts (cf. 1 Sam 16:7; 1 Kgs 8:39), He refused to entrust Himself to or seek approval from these or any other would-be followers (John 2:24). In

---

43. Cf. Haenchen, *John 1*, 184; Schnackenburg, *John*, 1:351.
44. Keener, *John*, 1:517; cf. Ridderbos, *John*, 120.
45. Cf. Calvin, *John*, 1:98; Keener, *John*, 1:174.
46. Cf. Carson, *John*, 184.

fact, the Messiah did not need anyone to tell Him about the true nature of people, for He already knew it perfectly (v. 25).

The phrase rendered "human testimony" is more literally translated "testify about man." Likewise, the remainder of the verse is more literally rendered, "for he knew what was in a man." This observation helps to stress the strong literary connection between John 2:23–25 and 3:1–21. Verse 1 of the latter passage is literally translated, "now there was a man."[47] The reference is to Nicodemus, who was both a Pharisee and a member of the "Jewish ruling council," or Sanhedrin.[48] Also, verse 10 reveals that Nicodemus was "Israel's teacher." This reference has led some to think that he had a special position as the premier instructor to the nation. The more likely option is that Jesus affirmed the status of Nicodemus as a highly esteemed rabbi among his religious peers. In a later episode, Nicodemus defended Jesus before the Sanhedrin (cf. 7:51). The faith of Nicodemus eventually progressed to the point where he openly assisted in the burial of the Messiah (cf. 19:39–42).[49]

Nicodemus might have been one of the religious leaders who saw Jesus clearing the temple area and performing various signs during the Passover Festival. Evidently, Jesus' miracles had impressed the esteemed Pharisee (3:2). In brief, Nicodemus had seen the signs as the Lord's seal of approval on Jesus. Perhaps Nicodemus also felt that with all his self-righteousness, something was still missing; or possibly Nicodemus was questioning Jesus on behalf of some members of the Sanhedrin. The night visit may mean that Nicodemus did not want to be seen publicly talking with Jesus; or it may mean that Nicodemus wanted a long conversation, which would be more possible at the end of the day.[50] In any case, the Light of the world was about to illumine this seeker of truth with good news of the new birth and the new order He was about to inaugurate.

Nicodemus addressed Jesus with high respect by calling Him "Rabbi" and acknowledging that God had sent Him to teach the Jewish people; but at this point, Nicodemus did not realize he was in the presence of the one who is the culmination of the Torah.[51] In fact, the Pharisee regarded

---

47. Cf. Ridderbos, *John*, 123; Westcott, *John*, 47.

48. Cf. Stern, *Jewish New Testament commentary*, 165.

49. For a discussion of the role of Nicodemus in the Fourth Gospel, cf. Ridderbos, *John*, 282–285.

50. Cf. Brown, *John*, 130; Hoskyns, *The Fourth Gospel*, 211.

51. Lindars thinks Nicodemus "represents official Judaism in a situation of openness before the claims of Christ" (*John*, 149); cf. Julian, *Jesus and Nicodemus,* 77; Köstenberger, *John*, 117.

his conversation with Jesus as one peer discussing doctrine with another.[52] Undoubtedly, to the surprise of Nicodemus, Jesus did not respond to his flattering remark, but spoke directly to the subject at the heart of the ruler's greatest need—eternal salvation. Jesus' statement immediately undercut what Nicodemus had believed and taught as a Pharisee, namely, that if one wanted to be right with God, he or she must strive to perfectly obey the Mosaic law. With profound insight, Jesus told Nicodemus that, in order to see God's kingdom, a person must be "born again" (v. 3).[53]

The Greek word rendered "again" (*anōthen*) can also mean "from above" (cf. 3:31; 19:11) and probably both meanings are operative here.[54] Scripture teaches that in a sovereign act of grace, the Holy Spirit entirely revitalizes the fallen human nature of believing sinners (cf. Rom 12:1–2; Eph 4:22–24; Col 3:9–10; Titus 3:5–7; 1 Pet 1:3). In this decisive intervention, God miraculously raises them from spiritual death to new life. The desires, goals, and actions of the regenerate are so radically changed that they want to live for God and serve others. To see God's kingdom (as a result of the new birth) means to experience fully the redemptive blessings associated with the rule of the Lord in one's life, both in the present and throughout eternity. Even such a respected religious leader as Nicodemus needed to be spiritually reborn; and only God's power, not human effort, could transform the Pharisee's sinful heart (as well as that of all people).

Nicodemus interpreted Jesus' statement in an overly literal way. Specifically, the religious leader thought the Savior was talking about an adult reentering the womb of his or her mother and going through the process of physical birth a second time (John 3:4). Perhaps Nicodemus had been attempting to earn God's favor for years and had failed. To strive to do even more would seem like an act of futility. The response of

---

52. Cf. Bruce, *John*, 82; Köstenberger, *Studies on John and gender*, 77–78.

53. Keener (*John*) points out that the Evangelist "develops most of his discourses the same way: Jesus' statement, then the objection or question of a misunderstanding interlocutor, and finally a discourse." The latter is "either complete in itself or including other interlocutions (1:68). Neyrey ("Jesus the judge," 515) identifies the following passages in the Fourth Gospel as fitting the "statement/misunderstanding/explanation . . . mode of inquiry and proof": 3:3–5; 4:10–12, 32–38; 6:41–51; 8:32–58; 11:11–15. Keener (*John*), in agreement with many scholars, thinks that "Jesus' discourses in the Fourth Gospel reflect Johannine editing or composition." Keener notes that "such stylistic adaptation and interpretive amplification did not violate the protocols of ancient historical writing" (1:69).

54. Stern (*Jewish New Testament commentary*, 165) sees a parallel between Jesus' statement in John 3:3 about "being born again" and Paul's declaration in 2 Corinthians 5:17 that "if anyone is in Christ, the new creation is here." Also, according to Stern, the concept of the new birth is Jewish, being "found in rabbinic literature," such as Gen Rab. 39:11; cf. Morris, *John*, 188–89; Ridderbos, *John*, 125; Tenney, "John," 9:46; Westcott, *John*, 63.

Nicodemus to Jesus can be viewed in at least two ways: either Nicodemus did not understand Jesus; or Nicodemus did not like where the conversation was headed and chose to be ignorant of Jesus' true meaning. In either case, Nicodemus was searching for more information from the Messiah.

Jesus noted that the rebirth was spiritual, not physical, and could only be accomplished by the Holy Spirit (v. 5). There are three noteworthy views concerning the meaning of the phrase rendered "of water and of the Spirit." Some think Jesus was referring to the meaning behind baptism. Since Jesus' ministry came shortly after that of John the Baptizer, John's baptism of repentance was on everyone's minds. Thus, Jesus' reference was to baptism, which signified repentance. Put another way, Nicodemus needed to repent and be born of the Spirit to see God's kingdom. Others maintain the reference is to water (the fluid in the amniotic sac) associated with the birth of a child. Thus, Jesus was referring to both physical and spiritual births. Still others note that Nicodemus, as a scholar, should have known those Old Testament passages where "water" (as cleansing) and "spirit" (or "wind") are both mentioned (e.g. Isa 32:15; 44:3–5; Ezek 18:31; 36:25–27; 37:9–10; cf. Titus 3:5). These symbolize new life from above and anticipate the coming age in which the Messiah brings redemptive blessing to God's people.[55]

Jesus' main point was that entrance into the divine kingdom could not be obtained by keeping the law or by belonging to the right race or people. The very enfleshment of the Father's truth to the world explained that what is born of physical heritage is physical (namely, weak and mortal in nature); in contrast, what is born of the Spirit is spiritual (namely, eternal and immortal in nature; John 3:6). Jesus urged Nicodemus not to be amazed that the new birth was a necessity for anyone to enter God's kingdom (v. 7). Perhaps the two were standing on the flat roof of a house and talking when a gust of wind arose.[56] Accordingly, the Messiah took the opportunity to compare the work of the Spirit to the wind (v. 8). In fact, in both Hebrew (*ruah*) and Greek (*pneuma*) the same word can mean either "spirit" or "wind." One cannot see the wind or understand its origin, but its effects can be seen. In the same way, people cannot see the Spirit at work within someone's heart, but people can watch the dramatic changes in that individual's life. Just as people cannot control the wind, so the Spirit does as He pleases in regenerating believing sinners.

---

55. Cf. Barrett, *St. John*, 208–209; Beasley-Murray, *John*, 48–49; Bultmann, *John*, 138–39; Calvin, *John*, 1:109–112; Carson, John, 191–95; Julian, *Jesus and Nicodemus*, 91–197; Ng, *Water symbolism in John*, 70–75.

56. Cf. Goldsmith, *Gospel of John*.

Nicodemus admitted that he did not understand Jesus' words (John 3:9). The religious leader's reply should probably be taken as a sincere plea for help, not as a sarcastic questioning of Jesus' response. Nicodemus wanted to know how he could experience this seemingly mysterious and enigmatic new birth. Jesus, in turn, was surprised that Nicodemus did not understand the concept of the new birth (v. 10). As a prominent teacher, he should have been familiar with Old Testament prophetic passages that speak of a new life and a new heart (Jer 31:33).[57] The second member of the Trinity noted that He and the other persons of the Godhead spoke about what they knew and testified about what they had seen.[58] Regrettably, though, many of the Pharisee's contemporaries did not accept the testimony of the one who is the perfection of the gift of the Tanakh (John 3:11). If they did not believe what Jesus said about things that happen on earth (particularly, spiritual regeneration), they would have much more difficulty in believing what He said about things that happen in heaven (v. 12).

Thankfully for Nicodemus, he was talking with someone who could speak with authority regarding eternal matters. While the Jews possessed God's revelation in the Mosaic law (cf. Rom. 9:4), no one but the Son of Man had ever gone into heaven or come back to describe it (cf. John 1:51; 3:31; 6:41–42).[59] Also, because Jesus is the divine, incarnate Torah, He alone can unveil heaven's true nature to humanity (3:13). He revealed to Nicodemus truths that cannot be discovered by experience or logic, including how the new birth is possible. Jesus referred to an historical event recorded in the Pentateuch involving the Israelites. As they were about to go around Edom in their path to the promised land, the people grumbled against God and Moses. The people also complained about the "miserable food" (Num. 21:5) they had to eat in the wilderness.

---

57. Burge (*John*, 116) spotlights the contrast between John 3:2 and 10. Nicodemus, a distinguished rabbi, was ignorant of the most fundamental truths about the new birth. Consequently, he had to depend upon the eschatological Tanakh, who was the "only 'true rabbi,'" to "explain the deeper mysteries of God."

58. Keener, *John*, 1:785; Tenney, "John," 9:48. It is less likely that Jesus was referring to John the Baptizer, the first disciples of Jesus, the so-called Johannine community, or the witness of the early church; cf. Brown, *John*, 132.

59. Harris (*John*) states that in "both Jewish intertestamental literature and later rabbinic accounts, Moses is portrayed as ascending to heaven to receive the Torah and descending to distribute it to men (e.g. Targum Psalms 68:19). In contrast to these Jewish legends, the Son is the only one who has ever made the ascent and descent"; cf. Heschel, *Heavenly Torah*, 291–92, 324–25, 343–347; Lierman, "Mosaic pattern," 212.

In response, God sent "venomous snakes" (v. 6) into the Israelite camp until the people cried out in repentance. The number and variety of snakes in Israel, Sinai, and Egypt are numerous, but only a small percentage are potentially lethal. One of the most poisonous species in the Middle East is the cobra. Another deadly species is the viper. The adder, which is mentioned in Jeremiah 8:17, was possibly the desert viper. The snakes that attacked the Israelites in the desert (Num 21:6) were probably carpet vipers. Vipers can strike without provocation and their bite can kill within a few days. The Bible almost always portrays the snake as a symbol of evil, so the analogy that Jesus makes in John 3:14 is unusual.

Next, the Lord instructed Moses to make a bronze replica of a poisonous snake, attach it to a pole, and lift it up so everyone could see it. Those who were bitten could look at the object and live (Num 21:8). Jesus as Torah equated His coming death on the cross to Moses lifting up the snake in the wilderness.[60] The word translated "lifted up" (John 3:14) can mean both lift up (as on a cross) and exalt (as to heaven; cf. 8:28; 12:32, 34). This lexical data serves as a reminder that the Messiah's death became the steppingstone to His exaltation. Furthermore, through the Son's death on the cross, believing sinners become citizens of the divine, heavenly kingdom. They realize their condition as being similar to that of the ancient Israelites. Regardless of the age in which people live, they are guilty of disobedience, under God's judgment, and unable to rescue themselves. Their only hope is to accept the provision of salvation the Father makes in the Son. In particular, when they look to the Cross in faith, they are saved, just as looking at the bronze snake brought relief to the Israelites (3:15).

It is quite probable that Jesus was still speaking until the end of verse 15, for only He used the phrase "Son of Man" in the four Gospels. It is also probable that the Evangelist's reflection commences with verse 16, since Jesus' death is spoken of in the past tense after verse 15. Regardless of whether John was recording Jesus' words to Nicodemus in verses 16–21 or adding to this dialogue what Jesus had taught him, these verses reveal the truth about the nature and extent of God's love for the lost. The Father, being motivated by His infinite love for humanity, sent His "one and only

---

60. Harstine (*Moses*, 56) comments that the "introduction of Moses by name reinforces the veracity of Jesus' statements about rebirth: the law is not sufficient to save people from death." Also, whereas "Moses' standard could only provide earthly life," the "standard of the Son of Man provides eternal life." In a similar vein, Keener (*John*, 1:563) noted that Jesus is "greater than Moses because Jesus parallels the Torah or Wisdom which Moses merely mediated." Also, Jesus is "greater than Moses because he parallels the instrument of salvation which Moses merely lifted up."

Son" to die for the sins of the world.⁶¹ God summons all people on earth to put their faith in Messiah—not only assenting to what He said as true, but also entrusting their lives to Him. Those who believe in the Redeemer will not suffer eternal separation from God, but will enjoy a reconciled, deeply satisfying relationship with the Son and His heavenly Father.⁶²

Verse 17 explains that the Father's ultimate purpose in sending His Son into the world was not to condemn humankind for its guilt and eternally punish the lost; rather, it was to provide the way of salvation for them. This has been the Lord's supreme desire since Adam and Eve sinned in the garden of Eden. Those who refuse God's provision will perish. The fact that salvation is for all who believe implies judgment for those who reject the Messiah. While John emphasized that the Redeemer came to offer eternal life, the apostle could not ignore the destiny of those who spurned the "one and only Son" (v. 18; cf. 1 Pet 2:8; 1 John 5:10–12). He alone is God's provision for salvation (Heb 6:4–8).

The heavenly court of divine justice forms the backdrop of the Father's condemnation of those who reject the Son. The fact is that God sent the one who is Light into the world (cf. John 1:2–5, 9). Tragically, though, morally depraved people love the darkness of Satan and sin (John 3:19). Because their lives are characterized by disobedience (cf. Eph 2:2) and steeped in wickedness (cf. Rom 1:32), they dread the possibility of coming in faith to the Light. Also, because they realize He will expose their sins, they hate Him and His followers all the more (John 3:20; cf. 15:18–25). In contrast are those who practice the truth revealed by Jesus as Tanakh.⁶³ They demonstrate by their lives of piety and integrity that they readily come to the Light. They do not fear any kind of exposure—not because they are free from sin, but because they want to be cleansed by God's grace. When others see that God enables them to be people of rectitude and virtue, He is glorified (3:21).⁶⁴

---

61. MacRae ("Theology and irony," 94) observes that the "heart of the Johannine theology is itself the irony of the Logos becoming flesh and dwelling among" humankind. The "revealing Word graciously" heralded to people "their own potential for eternal life in the self-giving act of love that is the return to the Father." Likewise, Duke (*Irony*, 111) says that the incarnation of the Word "is the irony of all Christian proclamation." For a discussion of the use of irony as a literary technique in the Fourth Gospel, cf. Duke, *Irony*; MacRae, "Theology and irony," 83–96, Wead, *Literary devices*, 47–68.

62. For an examination of the Johannine concept of life, cf. Dodd, *Fourth Gospel*, 144–150; Schnackenburg, *John*, 2:352–361; Wright, *Jesus*, 88–96.

63. For an examination of the Johannine concept of truth, cf. Dodd, *Fourth Gospel*, 170–78; Schnackenburg, *John*, 2:225–237.

64. A discussion of the testimony offered by John the Baptizer to Jesus as Torah (John

Jesus as Torah Revealing Himself as the Messiah to a Samaritan Woman (John 4:1–42)

The Samaritan Woman's Conversation with Jesus as Torah (John 4:1–26)

The Fourth Gospel leaves as indefinite the time interval between the visit of Nicodemus to Jesus and the testimony of John the Baptizer concerning the Savior (John 3:22–36). In turn, the chronological relation between these sections and Jesus' conversation with a Samaritan woman (4:1–42) is not specified. Most likely, the latter occurred sometime during the winter of AD 27. Even at this early stage in Jesus' ministry, He encountered opposition from the Pharisees and scribes. They began to envy His growing popularity. They also resented His challenges to their traditions and hated His exposure of their hypocrisy. Undoubtedly, the religious leaders wondered whether Jesus had political aspirations and worried about how His increasing influence would affect their control over the people. The Pharisees and scribes allowed their petty concerns to blind them to the truth that Jesus is the fulfillment of the Mosaic law.

Perhaps sympathizers within the Sanhedrin (e.g. someone such as Nicodemus) kept Jesus informed of the consternation of the Jewish leadership over His activities. For instance, the Pharisees were alarmed by the many disciples He won and baptized, particularly that they exceeded the number of followers John had gained (v. 1). Verse 2 is the author's parenthetical clarification that it was Jesus' disciples, not the Savior Himself, who actually baptized others in His name. Elsewhere it is revealed that He gave the Twelve authority to cast out evil spirits and heal every kind of disease and sickness (cf. Matt 10:1; Mark 3:14). John had already provoked the Pharisees, and Jesus probably did not want to clash with the religious establishment of Jerusalem at this time. Thus, He decided to return to Galilee by the shortest route, which was through the province of Samaria, a journey that took about three days (John 4:3–4; cf. 7:1).[65]

As noted in chapter 3, Palestine in Jesus' day consisted of three major provinces. Galilee was to the north, Samaria occupied the central highlands, and Judea was to the south. Many Jews would not enter Samaria

---

3:22–36) appears in chapter 1 of this study.

65. Cf. Barrett, *St. John*, 320; Bultmann, *John*, 176; Calvin, *John*, 1:143; Haenchen, *John 1*, 218; Sanders and Mastin, *John*, 138.

because they believed that they would be defiled if they had any contact with the region's inhabitants. The mutual hatred between these two people groups can be traced back several hundred years before the advent of the Messiah. For instance, in 722 BC, the Assyrian Empire defeated the northern kingdom of Israel and deported most of the Israelites to other parts of their realm. The Israelites who remained intermarried with foreigners. Out of these marriages came a religion that mixed the worship of Yahweh with that of other pagan deities. Later, in 539 BC, when the Jews returned to Jerusalem from Babylonian captivity, they encountered Samaritans who were hostile to them and their religion.

By the first century AD, the Jews had cultivated and nurtured a deep animosity for the people who lived in Samaria. Amazingly, it was of divine necessity for Jesus to travel through the province. Expressed differently, it was the Father's will and plan that compelled the Son to break with convention, enter Samaria, and stop at Sychar. This small village (somewhere near Shechem on the slope, or shoulder, of Mount Ebal) was famous because Jacob, ancestral patriarch of the Jews and the Samaritans, had bequeathed some of the nearby land to his son Joseph (John 4:4–5; cf. Gen 33:18–19; 48:21–22). After the Israelites returned to the promised land from Egyptian bondage, Joseph was buried in this plot of ground (cf. Josh 24:32). The Samaritans claimed that they were direct descendants of Joseph.

One of the historic landmarks in Palestine was Jacob's well at the foot of Mount Gerizim (located southwest of Mount Ebal).[66] Centuries earlier, after the Israelites entered the promised land, they gathered in front of Mount Gerizim and Mount Ebal to hear Joshua read the blessings and curses recorded in the Mosaic law (Deut 27:12–13; Josh 8:33–35). This incident was one reason why the Samaritans insisted that God had to be worshiped on Mount Gerizim rather than in Jerusalem (cf. John 4:20). Despite this difference of opinion between the Jews and the Samaritans, there were similarities between their faiths. For instance, both practiced circumcision as a religious rite and both looked for the Messiah. Also, like the Jews, the Samaritans believed in a final judgment with the Messiah handing out rewards and punishments. Moreover, by Jesus' day they had forsaken all idolatry, as had the Jews.

It was around noon when Jesus came to Jacob's well. Most likely, it was a shaft that burrowed deeply (perhaps more than 100 feet) into solid limestone rock.[67] A low stone wall possibly encircled the spring-fed well

---

66. Köstenberger (*John*, 147) suggests that "Jacob's well was a convenient stop for pilgrims traveling between Galilee and Jerusalem."

67. Cf. Brown, *John*, 169; Tenney, "John," 9:55; Westcott, *John*, 69–70.

(cf. vv. 11–12) and formed a ledge upon which a weary and exhausted traveler such as Jesus could sit (v. 6). In that culture, it was the job of women to draw water from wells by using jugs or animal skins attached to ropes. Because the heat was probably most intense at this time of the day, women normally drew water at sunset (cf. Gen 24:11). Thus, it was unusual for the Samaritan woman to come at midday. Perhaps she had an urgent need for the water; but since there were other wells nearer to Sychar (less than a mile away to the northeast), she probably came to this well at that moment in order to avoid the other women of the community. The woman at the well might have been shunned by the other women because of her apparently tainted character.

By that point in the exchange, the Savior's disciples had gone into the village to buy food (John 4:8). This left Jesus alone at the well when He asked the Samaritan woman for a drink (v. 7).[68] Respected Jewish teachers of that day rarely, if ever, volunteered to speak with a woman in public; and no Jewish man would ever make himself ceremonially unclean by drinking from a Samaritan's cup.[69] Given this cultural context, it is understandable why the woman at the well was astonished by Jesus' request. She even noted the centuries-old wall of enmity between the two groups of people (v. 9). Incidentally, to be called a Samaritan was the worst form of insult (cf. 8:48). In fact, some religious leaders would not even say the name "Samaritan" (cf. Luke 10:37).

Rather than get drawn into a longstanding racial conflict, Jesus redirected the woman's attention to her deepest spiritual need. By referring to Himself as "living water" (John 4:10), Jesus wanted the woman to recognize Him as God's gracious provision of salvation to the lost (cf. John 3:16; Gal 2:20; Eph 5:25). Ng points out that in Jewish "literature 'water' is very frequently used to refer to the 'Torah'" (cf. 1 Enoch 48:1; 49:1).[70] The Messiah implied that because He is the perfection of the gift of the Tanakh, He could give the woman water much greater than that from the well.[71] In the original, the phrase rendered "living water" (John 4:10) typi-

68. Carson (*John*, 216) thinks the Evangelist intended a "contrast between the woman of this narrative and Nicodemus" in John 3. The latter was "learned, powerful, respected, orthodox, [and] theologically trained." In contrast, the Samaritan woman was "unschooled, without influence, despised, [and] capable only of folk religion." While Nicodemus was male, Jewish, and a highly respected religious leader, his counterpart was female, Samaritan, and a "moral outcast." Such observations notwithstanding, both individuals "needed Jesus."

69. Cf. Thomas, "Fourth Gospel," 165–69.

70. Ng, *Water symbolism in John*, 139; cf. Balfour, "John's use of the Scriptures," 378; Beasley-Murray, *John*, 60; Fernando, *Relationship between law and love*, 123–24.

71. Casselli ("Jesus as eschatological Torah," 34) maintains that the Evangelist, in recount-

cally referred to fresh, pure water that flowed in rivers, streams, and springs. In the Old Testament, the Lord referred to Himself as "the spring of living water" (Jer 2:13). He also described the heavenly blessings He offered as "living water" (Zech 14:8). These metaphors would have resonated with those living in the hot, arid climate of Palestine. The community of faith would depend on the Lord to nourish and refresh them spiritually for all eternity (cf. Ps 36:9; Isa 12:3; 44:3; 49:10; 55:1; Jer 17:13).[72]

The woman responded to Jesus' peculiar statement with two questions. First, she asked how He planned to get this drinkable water, especially since He was without the means to obtain it from the well (John 4:11). Second, the woman attempted to provoke Jesus by asking whether He was greater than Jacob. The well he left for the Samaritans to enjoy had provided water for the famed patriarch, his family, and their livestock.[73] The woman became incredulous at the possibility that Jesus imagined Himself to be superior to Jacob (v. 12; cf. 8:53).[74] The woman may have been comparing Jesus' apparent unimportance with the Samaritans' importance as descendants of Jacob and Joseph. This would imply that the woman did not need what the Messiah offered.

In point of fact, Jesus was infinitely greater than Jacob and all other esteemed individuals in the Old Testament. By way of example, the prophet Isaiah had promised that a virgin would conceive and bear a son (Isa 7:14). Mary's Son would be that child, the absolutely great Messiah of Israel. This miracle was possible because He would also be the "Son of the Most High" (Luke 1:32). Furthermore, He would fulfill what Isaiah had prophesied about the one who would rule on David's throne (Isa 9:6–7). God had promised David that his kingdom would be established forever (2 Sam 7:16). As it

---

ing Jesus' statement to the Samaritan woman, portrayed the Son as the "replacement/fulfillment of Torah and all that it represents." In short, the Messiah is the "realization of the eschatological waters of life, which were connected, in the Jewish mind, with the Torah itself."

72. Cf. Bock, *Jesus*, 436; Ng, *Water symbolism in John*, 76.

73. Schnackenburg (*John*, 1:429) notes that there is no specific Old Testament reference to Jacob either giving his descendants the well named after him or "drinking from it, along with his sons and flocks." One possibility is that the Samaritan woman's assertion could have reflected a local "popular tradition." Schnackenburg also points out that the "theme of 'digging the well' is of some importance in the Qumran texts."

74. For the Jewish background that lay behind the Samaritan woman's question recorded in John 4:12, cf. Neyrey, "Jacob traditions." He specifically examines "interpretations of that text found in sources such as targum and midrash" (420). He concludes that Jesus "supplants Jacob's well and water" by replacing the "reality for which well/water are symbols." Jesus also "supplants the old traditions of spirit, cult and knowledge which were associated with Jacob's well" (436).

happened, David's descendants reigned over Judah until the Exile (586 BC). The angel's reference to the "throne of his father David" (Luke 1:32) meant that God would now restore the broken line of David's succession. Indeed, Gabriel revealed to Mary that her Son would fulfill that promise, most of all as He ruled forever in majestic splendor (v. 33).

Jesus adroitly sidestepped the Samaritan woman's provocation by noting that even water from Jacob's well quenched thirst for only a short time (John 4:13); but the eternal life Jesus offered would abundantly satisfy the spiritual thirst of people forever (cf. 10:10). God's gift of salvation was comparable to a fountain of water that vigorously welled up in believers in an inner, unending, and overflowing supply (4:14). The idea of a perpetual torrent of water intrigued the woman, who pictured it as something that would replace her daily trips carrying a heavy pot to and from the well. She took Jesus literally and focused on personal convenience rather than anything spiritual (v. 15).

The Redeemer, however, had a different agenda, one that involved getting the woman to see her need for eternal life.[75] To achieve this goal, Jesus focused on the woman's sin, which stood in the way of her receiving what He offered. Jesus began by telling the woman to go and get her husband (v. 16). In turn, she stated that she was not married. The omniscient Torah of God affirmed the truthfulness of the woman's statement, adding that she had been divorced five times and was now living immorally (vv. 17–18). Suddenly it dawned on the woman that Jesus was not an ordinary person. Indeed, to have such remarkable discernment, He must be a prophet (v. 19; namely, a divinely inspired person with supernatural knowledge and insight).[76] Perhaps in an attempt to deflect the conversation away from her sinful lifestyle, the woman brought up the controversy between Samaritans and Jews regarding the proper place to worship (v. 20). To her it was a suitable religious question for a prophet to give his authoritative assessment.

The Jews recognized that God had instructed Solomon to build a temple in Jerusalem. They could go there to offer sacrifices and to worship

---

75. Cf. Calvin, *John*, 1:152; Ridderbos, *John*, 159.

76. According to de Jonge ("Jesus as prophet," 161), the title "prophet" (John 4:19) is "neither the most suitable nor the final title for Jesus." Likewise, the Evangelist does not intend it to "indicate the essential meaning of Jesus' mission in the world." Reinhartz ("Jesus as prophet," 10) advances the discussion by explaining that in the Fourth Gospel, Jesus is "not only the prophet, but the prophesied." He is "not only the mouthpiece for the divine word but the content of the message itself." His "divine identity" is proven or demonstrated by the "fulfillment of his words." The author's intent is to encourage readers to put their "faith in Jesus as the divinely sent redeemer and revealer."

Him. Meanwhile, the Samaritans argued that worship of God should be performed at Mount Gerizim, where they claimed many blessed events occurred. The Samaritans taught that Abraham proved his faithfulness and obedience to God when the patriarch offered his son, Isaac, on Mount Gerizim. The Samaritans also taught that Abraham and Melchizedek met on this mountain. More importantly, the Samaritans believed the Lord commanded Moses to build an altar on Mount Gerizim for God's people to worship Him. Since the Samaritans regarded only the Pentateuch as sacred, they naturally dismissed the Jewish belief that the center of worship should be at the temple in Jerusalem. In contrast, the Jews claimed that the Samaritans distorted the Scriptures. This controversy over the proper place to worship God only added to the enmity between the Jews and Samaritans.

Jesus used the mention of the inter-racial debate to strike at the heart of the woman's problem. She was concerned with an external aspect of worship, that is, the right place to worship God. Jesus made her focus on the internal aspect of worship, namely, worshiping God with a cleansed heart. Here we see that the woman's frame of reference needed to be adjusted. Jesus began to do this by bluntly stating that in the coming day of eschatological fulfillment, it would not matter where people worshiped—be it Mount Gerizim or Mount Zion (v. 21). After all, the Messiah surpassed in importance all earthly shrines and sanctuaries, even the temple in Jerusalem.[77] Next, He who is the culmination of the Tanakh addressed the issue the woman had raised. The Samaritans acknowledged the true

---

77. Kerr (*Temple theme*, 167) states that with the advent of the Messiah, a "new era" has dawned. From the post-resurrection perspective of the Evangelist, "Moses and the law, including the Temple and associated rituals and festivals, are not ends in themselves, but signposts pointing towards Jesus Christ." The Son becomes "the *raison d'être* of Judaism" in which worship is "no longer centered in a place, but in Spirit and truth." An analogous outlook is found in the concluding portion of the book of Revelation (cf. deSilva, *Introduction*, 424). In the eternal state, there will not only be "a new heaven and a new earth" (21:1), but also "the Holy City, the New Jerusalem" (v. 2), which God sends down out of heaven. The Lord magnificently adorns the new Jerusalem (the bride) for her husband (the groom). The implication is that the city surpasses the beauty of everything else God has made. Regardless of whether the new Jerusalem is a symbol of the Christian community in heaven or a literal city, God permanently dwells among the redeemed of all ages (v. 3). Unlike the Jerusalem of Bible times, the new Jerusalem of the eschatological future does not have a temple within it (v. 22). The reason is that "the Lord God Almighty and the Lamb" are the city's temple. Similarly, the new Jerusalem has no need for the sun or the moon, for "the glory of God" (v. 23) illuminates the city and "the Lamb" is the city's source of light. In the new creation, the Father and the Son are seated on their thrones, and the redeemed worship and serve them continually (22:3). God establishes unbroken communion with His people, and He claims them as His own (v. 4).

God, but they worshiped Him in ignorance. Since they considered only the Pentateuch as sacred, they ignored the prophets. The Jews worshiped God as He revealed Himself in the entire Hebrew Bible. The Messiah clearly sided with the Jews on this issue by identifying Himself with them through the emphatic use of the Greek word rendered "we" (v. 22). God had chosen the Jews to be the vehicle through which He would reveal His plan of redemption. Put another way, "Judaism is the trajectory of religious history through which God has been at work."[78]

The time was soon coming, however, when a Jew, a Samaritan, or any other person could freely worship the Lord—as long as that person did so in spirit and truth (v. 23). Indeed, the opportunity had been inaugurated with the Messiah's advent (which included His death, resurrection, and ascension).[79] To worship in spirit is to do so from the heart, not merely to go through the motions of worship. The latter is frequently characterized by an obsession with being at the right place and performing approved rituals. To worship in truth is to reverence the Father as He has disclosed Himself in the Son (cf. 1:18), not as would-be worshipers have created God in their own minds.[80] Indeed, He actively seeks people who worship Him with sincerity and dedication.

The essential nature of God is "pure spirit,"[81] which means the divine is immaterial in His existence (4:24).[82] This verse "points to the reality of God as the absolute Power and Life Giver."[83] It would be incorrect

---

78. Burge, *John*, 145.

79. Schnackenburg (*John*, 1:438) comments that Jesus' "revelation of the true worship of God is well illustrated by the Qumran texts, but it goes beyond them, since Jesus proclaims that the eschatological fulfillment has come."

80. Cf. Bultmann, *John*, 190–91.

81. Bruce, *John*, 111. Westcott (*John*, 73) notes that God is "absolutely free from all limitations of space and time."

82. Deuteronomy 6:4 is a key verse concerning the nature of God, for it affirms His uniqueness. Despite the world's worship of many gods and many lords, Yahweh alone is God (cf. 1 Cor 8:4–6). Deuteronomy 6:4 also affirms the unity, or singularity, of God's being (cf. Mark 12:29). This means He is simple and unchanging in His essence. He is not composed of different elements, and nothing can be added to or taken away from Him. Scripture also teaches the existence of three persons in the Godhead. This is called the doctrine of the Trinity (from the Latin word *trinitas*, which means "threeness"). The notion of the three-in-oneness of God is nowhere fully formulated in the Bible; yet Scripture provides ample evidence to support the doctrine. It affirms that the Lord exists in three personal distinctions known respectively as the Father, the Son, and the Holy Spirit (cf. Matt 28:19; 2 Cor 13:14). Each person is co-equal and co-eternal with the other two (cf. Isa 48:16; Matt 3:16–17).

83. Saucy, "Biblical concept of God," 91; cf. Packer, "God," 276–77; Saucy, "God,

to conclude that God is merely an impersonal force that gives existence to everything else; instead, He is a personal, sentient being who is "self-existent, eternal, and unchanging." Metaphysically speaking, while He transcends the world, He remains actively involved in providentially sustaining, guiding, and governing His creation according to His will and purpose. Intellectually, He is "omniscient, faithful, and wise." From an ethical standpoint, God is "just, merciful, and loving." With respect to emotions, He "detests evil," is infinitely patient, and full of compassion. From an existential perspective, God is "free, authentic," and all-powerful.[84] Because of who God is and what He does,[85] He expects the worship offered by believers to be spiritual and not merely a ritualistic duty.

Upon hearing the truths Jesus declared, the Samaritan woman started to wonder whether He was more than just a prophet (v. 25). The woman thus voiced the hope of both Samaritans and Jews, namely, that the Messiah would come.[86] In Bible times, it was commonly believed that whenever the Anointed One came, He would explain all the conundrums of life.[87] At this point, Jesus directly told the Samaritan woman that He

---

doctrine of," 501–02.

84. Lewis, "Attributes of God," 98; cf. Bray, "God," 514–19; Lewis, "God, attributes of," 492.

85. Park (*Transcendence and spatiality*) affirms that a "creative tension" exists between "God's transcendence and his immanence" (268). On the one hand, God exists independently from the material universe and is not subject to its limitations. On the other hand, He is "present and interacts with the world" (263). Indeed, the glory of God is "embodied through material things, including the human body" (258). Markus (*Beyond finitude*) uses the following four categories to frame his understanding of the transcendence of God: "ontological, moral, capacity and conceptual." He clarifies that while "God's existence transcends all creaturely existence," He is also "intimately present" and "engaged in personal relations with human beings." Because "God is perfectly good," it is impossible for Him to "commit moral evil." Likewise, He is the "source of moral norms" (357). Furthermore, since God is all-powerful and all-knowing, He has the capacity to bring about whatever He wills, "both indirectly and directly." He "perfectly knows all possibilities" and "all future contingent events." Moreover, God is incomprehensible in that He surpasses the "limits of [human] thought." At the same time, the "concepts and conceptual abilities" of people are sufficient for them to "have a limited understanding of God" (358).

86. Whitacre (*John*) comments that the Samaritans did not expect a "Davidic king, but rather the *Taheb*," a name that means the "one who returns." This person "would be primarily a lawgiver, teacher, restorer, revealer."

87. Teeple (*Mosaic eschatological prophet*, 114) points to the common belief of the day that the "Samaritan Prophet-Messiah will teach the existing Samaritan law to Jews and gentiles." Ellis (*Genius of John*, 71) adds that while "little is known about the messianic expectations among the Samaritans," the Evangelist "makes it clear that Jesus is the fulfill-

was the Messiah (v. 26). Evidently, the political overtones associated with Jewish misconceptions of the Messiah did not prevail in Samaria, thus making it relatively safe for Jesus to identify Himself unambiguously in this way.

The Belief of Many Samaritans in Jesus as Torah (John 4:27–42)

Just as Jesus was finishing His conversation with the woman, His disciples returned with some food. Because of cultural prejudice against women, His disciples were astonished to discover Him talking to the Samaritan woman in public; yet they had been with Him long enough to know not to question their Master, who by His actions was teaching them to break down the walls of prejudice (John 4:27). Meanwhile, the woman abandoned her jug of water at the well and hurried back to the village. Her excited response shows the profound impression Jesus as Torah had made on her (v. 28). In the woman's effort to tell others in the village about the newcomer, she completely forgot about her initial reason for going to the well (v. 29). (Undoubtedly, she planned to return to it.) Meeting Jesus also helped the woman forget the shame she may have carried for years. She seemed thrilled that Jesus was able to tell her everything she ever did (a slight overstatement) and still talk with and accept her. The woman did not say to the villagers, "I have found the Messiah," but asked humbly, "Could this be the Messiah?" (v. 30). This indirect approach aroused the interest of the Samaritans without overtly stating any conclusion. Because of the woman's reputation, it is doubtful her neighbors would have accepted her assessments; but by simply relating what had happened, the woman generated considerable interest. While the text does not indicate how many came, it gives the impression that a large number of residents from Sychar responded to the woman's invitation.

Previously, Jesus' disciples had left Him weary and hungry. When they returned with the food they had bought, they kept urging their Rabbi to eat (v. 31). Jesus declined their offer by stating that He had food to eat about which they were unfamiliar (v. 32). Because His disciples took Him literally rather than figuratively, they misunderstood what He meant (v. 33). The Son explained that His nourishment came from doing the will of His Father, who sent Him, and accomplishing His redemptive task (v. 34). Jesus would

---

ment of whatever the Samaritans expected in the way of a Messiah"; cf. Boismard, *Moses or Jesus*, 3–4, 30–32, 36; Carson, *John*, 223–24, 226, 231–32; De Jonge, "Jewish expectations," 269; Hakola, *Identity matters*, 102–3.

bring His saving mission to completion at Golgotha (cf. 19:30). A straightforward connection exists between work as food and the fruit of one's labor as something to be harvested. In the present case, the eternal harvest would be the Samaritans approaching in the distance (4:30).

The Redeemer might have pointed to the townspeople as He told His disciples to open their eyes and see the ripe harvest coming toward them. "It's still four months until harvest" (v. 35) may have been a common proverb among the farmers just after they planted their grain; but Jesus' disciples did not have to wait that long before the spiritual harvest was ready to be picked. The Savior urged His followers to look and see that the evangelistic fields were ripe and ready to yield an abundant crop of believers. Both those who sowed the seed of the gospel and those who reaped the harvest of many converts were overjoyed that so many were brought to eternal life (v. 36). In fact, others such as John the Baptizer (and the Old Testament prophets who lived prior to him) had planted the seeds and sown the crops before Jesus' disciples. Now they could reap the benefits of the work of others (vv. 37–38; cf. Matt 9:37–38; Luke 10:2; 1 Cor 3:5–9).

The residents of Sychar were amazed that Jesus had such incredible insight into the personal life of the woman they knew so well. As a result of her testimony, many Samaritans put their faith in Jesus as the Messiah (John 4:39).[88] They were even more impressed with Him when they met Him face-to-face. They insisted that He remain with them, so Jesus stayed for two days (v. 40). Previously, they had considered the law as the full expression of God's will for His people. Now as more villagers heard the teaching of the one who is the embodiment of the Tanakh, they believed in Him for eternal life (v. 41). This personal encounter with Jesus became the basis for the Samaritans declaring Him to be far more than a prophet. He was "the Savior of the world" (cf. 1 John 4:14). From the beginning of His earthly ministry, Jesus extended His hand to people steeped in sin and lost in false doctrine. Truly there is no one Jesus cannot reach.

The response of the Samaritans to the presence of Jesus contrasts with that of Nicodemus. Though the former were social outcasts due to their unorthodox beliefs and mixed Jewish heritage, they not only believed that Jesus is the Messiah but also openly declared so to others. Nicodemus, on the other hand, while being of pure Jewish heritage and a highly respected religious leader in Judah, responded to the Savior of the world tentatively

---

88. Köstenberger (*John*, 165) thinks the spiritual harvest Jesus reaped "among the Samaritans . . . signals the return of a part of the unbelieving world to God as a first sign of the universal scope of Jesus' saving mission."

and remained a secret disciple throughout the duration of Jesus' earthly ministry. Even more sobering is the truth recorded in John 1:11 that many among Jesus' own people rejected the one who is greater than all the luminaries of the Old Testament, including the patriarchs and Moses. The religious specialists of the day remained unconvinced that the life, witness, and promises made to these Old Testament saints pointed to the Anointed One, who is the quintessential hope of Israel as well as all humanity.

Jesus as Torah Healing a Government Official's Son (John 4:43–54)

After Jesus spent two days with His new followers in the province of Samaria, He continued His journey north to Galilee (John 4:43). The author inserted a parenthetical note recalling Jesus' observation that prophets of God often received no honor in their own country (v. 44; cf. Matt 13:57; Mark 6:4; Luke 4:24). While the saying itself is sufficiently straightforward, it remains unclear whether Jesus was referring to Judea or Galilee. On the one hand, Bethlehem in Judea was the Savior's birthplace (cf. Matt 2:1; Luke 2:4); On the other hand, Nazareth in Galilee became His hometown (Matt 2:22–23; Luke 2:39, 51; 4:16; John 1:46; 7:42, 52).

In the winter of AD 27, the Messiah decided it was prudent to leave Judea and minimize provoking a conflict with the religious establishment there (cf. John 4:3). In fact, throughout Jesus' earthly ministry He tended to be unwelcome in Judea (cf. 1:11). In contrast, the residents of Galilee initially welcomed Jesus (4:45); but this was mainly due to their witnessing the miracles He performed at the Passover Festival in Jerusalem. Jesus seemed to suggest in verse 48 that in the absence of signs and wonders, the Galileans would also refuse to believe. As a matter of fact, later in the spring of that year, the people of Nazareth tried to kill the Redeemer (cf. Luke 4:16–30).[89]

Jesus' first recorded miracle in the Fourth Gospel occurred in Cana of Galilee (cf. 2:1–11) and it is to that place that the Messiah returned (4:46). Stationed 20 miles away at Capernaum was an unnamed government official with a gravely ill son. The officer (possibly a Gentile) was a servant of Herod Antipas, the tetrarch of Galilee (and son of Herod of the Great), who was often referred to as king (cf. Matt 14:9; Mark 6:14; Luke 23:7).[90] In Jesus' day, there were many diseases and infirmi-

---

89. Whitacre (*John*) observes that "both Judea and Galilee are viewed as Jesus' own country because in neither does he receive real honor."

90. Cf. Witherington, *John's wisdom*, 128.

ties that plagued people. Ill individuals selected eclectically from whatever was available. These sources included a number of healing cults and their shrines, various magical potions, spells, amulets, and sacred inscriptions, and a hodgepodge of physicians who tended to be rather inept in the science and art of healing.[91]

When the distressed father learned from his staff that Jesus was in the area, the man possibly rode out on his horse, accompanied by a few servants, to meet Him.[92] The official repeatedly implored the worker of miracles to come to his residence and heal his son, who was near death (John 4:47). Jesus lamented that in the absence of "signs and wonders" (v. 48), few people responded to Him in faith. This statement "recalls the story of the exodus" and the refusal of the Israelites to believe in the Lord, despite all the signs He had performed through Moses in their presence (cf. Num 14:11).[93] Jesus' ambivalent response no doubt increased the sense of desperation and urgency felt by the official (John 4:49). Even so, the father remained respectful in his demeanor. Likewise, Jesus showed compassion when He told the official to return home, encouraged by the promise that his son would live (v. 50).

The Messiah was not declaring a prophecy that the gravely child would soon recover; instead, He spoke simply, powerfully, and directly, and His command resulted in the healing of the official's son. The father, in turn, believed what Jesus said and started back home with his entourage. While on the way, he met some of his other servants, who enthusiastically conveyed the good news that his son was alive and well (v. 51). When the official asked when the child began to improve, the servants replied that the boy's fever left him at one o'clock the preceding afternoon (v. 52). This information prompted the official to recall that this was also the precise hour when Jesus had said the child would live. The grateful father, along with his entire household, trusted in Jesus as the Messiah (v. 53; cf. Acts 10:2, 44–48; 11:14; 16:15, 31–34; 18:8).

Among the many signs the Redeemer performed (cf. John 2:23; 4:45; 21:25), the healing of the government official's son in Cana was the second one John recorded in the Fourth Gospel (4:54). It authenticated the truth that Jesus, as the Torah of God, has the power and authority to impart life, whether physical or spiritual in nature.[94] Not even distance (such as the 20

---

91. Lioy, "Spiritual care in a medical setting."
92. Cf. Goldsmith, *Gospel of John*.
93. Johns, "Signs as witnesses," 531; cf. Köstenberger, *John*, 170.
94. Cf. Bock, *Jesus*, 440.

miles separating Cana from Capernaum) prevented Him from bringing His will to pass. This was in fulfillment of Scripture, which revealed that the Savior came to bring healing and wholeness to the poor and oppressed of society, including Gentiles (cf. Isa 35:5–6; Matt 11:5; Luke 7:22).

Conclusion

As noted at the beginning of this chapter, the Fourth Gospel presents Jesus as the divine, incarnate Tanakh. The apostle recorded a number of witnesses from the first year of the Messiah's earthly ministry to substantiate this truth. The miracle of changing water into wine at a humble peasant wedding in Cana of Galilee revealed that the Logos is the Creator of all things. He also demonstrated that acts of creation and transformation are part of His nature; but in order to bring about overflowing joy associated with the fulfillment of the law's messianic promises, it was necessary for Jesus to atone for the sins of humanity, particularly through the shedding of His blood on the cross.

Jesus' clearing the temple courts in Jerusalem validated His claim to be greater than this shrine and to have authority over all the religious institutions associated with it. By His bold act, the one who is the culmination of the Torah signaled that the judgment of God rested on the established civil and religious authorities. They were giving way to the new order of forgiveness from sin and fellowship with the Lord. It was to be an era characterized by spiritual purity and unmitigated zeal for God.

Jesus' encounter with Nicodemus showcased the Son as the true Rabbi of Israel and the one who had the Father's seal of approval on His ministry. In addition, Jesus as Tanakh alerted Nicodemus to the necessity of the new birth. The one who is Light noted that spiritual regeneration was a sovereign act of God's grace and a prerequisite to entering the divine kingdom. Likewise, only the enfleshment of the Father's truth to the world could unveil heaven's true nature to humanity.

While most within the religious establishment of Jesus' day rejected His messianic claims, numerous others who were social outcasts put their faith in Him. The Samaritan woman is a prime example. From her encounter with the one who is the perfection of the gift of the Torah, she recognized the Son as the Father's gracious provision of salvation to the lost. Regardless of one's gender, race, or social standing, they could depend on the Redeemer to nourish and refresh them spiritually for all eternity.

The woman learned that Jesus is superior to all the luminaries of the Old Testament era, including Jacob, whose name was associated with the well where the woman encountered Jesus. The omniscient Tanakh of God demonstrated this by the supernatural knowledge and insight He manifested. Because Jesus surpassed in importance all earthly shrines and sanctuaries (including the Jerusalem temple), He was the one who would bring about spiritual wholeness to the lost. The Savior would enable them to worship the Father from the heart (in spirit) with sincerity and dedication (in truth). These messianic verities were confirmed by the government official's encounter with Jesus. By healing the father's son at a distance, Jesus as Torah showed that He has the power and authority to impart life, whether physical or spiritual in nature.

5

Jesus as Torah in John 5–6

Introduction

IN JOHN 1–4, the Evangelist compared the eternal Tanakh with "institutions of Jewish piety and history."¹ Beginning with chapter 5, the comparison is between Jesus and "some of the major festivals of Judaism."² John 5 specifically deals with the Torah of God healing a paralytic at the pool of Bethesda and His divine authority to perform the miracle on the Sabbath. Chapter 6 narrates the Messiah's feeding of a multitude, walking on the water, and declaring Himself to be the Bread of Life. In each of these episodes, Jesus encounters and engages both Jewish clergy and laity. Through these varied exchanges, the author of the Fourth Gospel validated the theological truth that the Son as Tanakh is the culmination (that is, the destination, goal, outcome, and fulfillment) of the law for believers. As the Lord of the Sabbath, He provides eternal rest for His disciples. Also, as the Bread of Life, He eternally satisfies the deepest spiritual needs of believers.

---

1. Burge, *John*, 170. According to the author (41), these longstanding Jewish institutions would include traditions connected with ceremonial cleansing (John 2:1–12), the temple and its ritualistic practices (vv. 13–25), the rabbinic establishment and its understanding of spiritual regeneration (chap. 3), and the sacred institutions associated with the proper worship of God (chap. 4).

2. Burge, *John*, 170. The author lists the following Jewish festivals: the "Sabbath Festival in Jerusalem" (John 5); the "Passover Festival in Galilee" (chap. 6); the "Tabernacles Festival in Jerusalem (chaps. 7–8); and the "Hanukkah Festival in Jerusalem" (chap. 10). Regardless of the "various institutions and festivals of Judaism" being highlighted in the Fourth Gospel, Jesus makes them "interpretive vehicles for his self-revelation" (310).

Jesus as Torah Healing a Paralytic at the Pool of Bethesda (John 5:1–47)

The Healing of the Paralytic by Jesus as Torah (John 5:1–15)

The mention of "some time later" (John 5:1) is an indefinite temporal reference. Most likely, the incident occurred between AD 27 and 29. Uncertainty also exists concerning which of the three major annual Jewish festivals—Tabernacles, Pentecost, or Passover—is in view.[3] Because Passover occurred toward the end of winter, when the weather was still uncomfortably cooler, this sacred feast seems less likely. Also, because Tabernacles forms the backdrop for the narrative recorded in chapter 7, it probably was not the annual event under consideration in 5:1. Pentecost, then, is the remaining likely alternative.[4] In Jewish writings penned during the intertestamental period, some practitioners associated this festival with God's issuance of the law to Moses on Mount Sinai, which may have occurred on the fiftieth day after the Exodus.[5] This possibly accounts for Jesus' mention of Moses in verses 45 and 46.[6] Pentecost was basically a celebration of the grain harvest, a period that lasted about seven weeks. Barley and wheat were the primary harvest foods. Strangers and the poor were especially welcome during this festival.

The previously mentioned, debated issues notwithstanding, John was clear that the healing took place on the Sabbath (vv. 9, 16). In turn, this sparked a dispute with the Jewish leaders. It is not known when the Hebrews began keeping the Sabbath. From Exodus 16:27, however, it is known that they began to do so before God gave the fourth commandment to require Sabbath observance. In the four or five centuries before the advent of the Messiah, Jewish religious teachers debated at length what actions should and should not be permitted on the Sabbath. They formulated 39 articles prohibiting all kinds of agricultural, industrial, and domestic work. The teachers also developed ways of getting around their own rules. For instance, they taught that no one should travel more than 2,000 cubits on the Sabbath; but if people were to deposit food 2,000 cu-

---

3. Cf. Lenski, *St. John's Gospel*, 359.

4. Cf. Calvin, *John*, 1:184–85; Lindars, *John*, 211; Ratzinger, *Jesus of Nazareth*, 237; Schnackenburg, *John*, 2:93.

5. Cf. deSilva, *Introduction*, 422; Harris, *John*; Witherington, *John's wisdom*, 384.

6. Cf. Brown, *John*, 206; Ellis, *Genius of John*, 88.

bits from their home before the Sabbath, then on the Sabbath they could declare the spot a temporary residence and act as though they had not traveled up to that point. Over time, the Pharisees and some other sectarian groups thought these humanly-devised interpretations (called the oral law) had as much force and authority as the written law.[7] In contrast, Jesus called them—perhaps with some disdain—"traditions" (Mark 7:9). It is no wonder Jesus felt He had to put the Sabbath back into perspective.[8]

There is uncertainty regarding the name of the pool where Jesus healed the paralytic. The various textual readings include Bethesda, Bethsaida, Bethzatha, and Belzetha.[9] John 5:2 says the pool was in the northeastern part of Jerusalem near the sheepgate. The latter provided an entrance to the temple complex (cf. Neh 3:1, 32; 12:39). Encircling the double-pool were four colonnades or porticoes, with a fifth one between the two pools. A colonnade was a partial roof supported by rows of columns separated at regular intervals. As people milled about the pool, the overhang gave them some shelter from the elements (such as rain, heat, and so on). Those who were blind, lame, or paralyzed would lay about under these covered walkways and enter and exit the pool's water, believing it to have curative powers (John 5:3). Later textual tradition, as reflected in verse 4, adds that the disabled would wait for the water in the pool to be stirred. Supposedly, an angel from the Lord would occasionally appear and cause the water to be moved. Then, the first person to enter the pool after that would be healed. The authenticity of this verse, however, is doubted, especially since it does not appear in the earliest and best Greek manuscripts and its vocabulary is dissimilar to the remainder of the Fourth Gospel.

One man who had been disabled for 38 years (most likely his entire life), was lying on a straw mat beside the pool. It is not difficult to imagine

---

7. According to Neusner ("Pharisaic law," 331), the "legal sayings in Talmudic literature" penned "before 70 AD" are predominately concerned with "agricultural tithes, offerings, and other taboos, and rules of ritual purity." Corbett ("The Pharisaic revolution," 376) adds that the written and oral Torah represented "more than a system of faith." Collectively, the laws were a "guide to the ideal life" that promoted such virtues as "piety, justice, work, self-reliance, positive action (rather than mere reflection), love of harmony, scorn of death in war, and devotion to the arts of peace, especially the crafts and agriculture." Also, cf. Meir, "The historical Jesus," 57–58; Stern, *Jewish New Testament commentary*, 169; Thomas, "Fourth Gospel," 169–172.

8. In the view of Schoneveld ("A new reading," 90), the Fourth Gospel presents Jesus as "the Torah in the flesh, the incarnate Word of God." He alone provides the "true and authoritative interpretation" of the commandments of Scripture. Furthermore, the "Oral Torah . . . embodied in Jesus" is superior to the "Oral Torah" found in "Pharisaic and rabbinic Judaism."

9. Cf. Sanders and Mastin, *John*, 159.

him giving up hope of ever being cured of his paralysis after so long a period of time. While verse 5 does not specify the nature of his impairment, it was possibly some form of paralysis. According to verse 7, the invalid needed the help of others to enter the pool. Also, verse 8 reports that the nature of the healing he received from Jesus was the ability to walk. After the Messiah entered the area, He possibly saw the paralytic struggling to get himself into the water; but his repeated efforts were frustrated. Whenever the water bubbled up, he had no benefactor to help him. In the meantime, others would enter the water.

How Jesus came to the realization that the man had been crippled for many years is unclear (v. 6). Though the paralytic did not solicit help from the Redeemer, Jesus offered it anyway without any preconditions. Also, despite the lame man's somewhat ambivalent response, Jesus still extended to him the opportunity to be healed. Perhaps while looking directly at the man,[10] the Son plainly commanded him to pick up his mat and start walking (v. 8). Instantly, once useless limbs were healed. They were now sufficiently strong for the formerly handicapped man to do exactly as Jesus said (v. 9). Undoubtedly, the cured man was overjoyed by what had just happened. It remains unclear, though, whether the man had any faith in the Son and whether this played any role in the miracle that occurred (cf. Matt 9:22; 13:58; Mark 6:5–6).[11]

Without giving thought to the fact that it was the Sabbath, the man rolled up his mat and started to walk. Then, as he made his way through the temple complex, some religious authorities spotted him and censured him for his activity. Their rabbinic interpretations, which were elaborations on the Mosaic law and considered just as binding, did not permit the carrying of any kind of burden (John 5:10; cf. Neh 13:15; Jer 17:21–27). This was a situation in which He who is the embodiment of the Torah—and thus Lord of the Sabbath (cf. Matt 12:8; Mark 2:28; Luke 6:5)—contradicted the narrow, reductionistic, and legalistic views of the religious establishment. They failed to appreciate and accept that God instituted the Sabbath to meet the physical, mental, and spiritual needs of people, not for individuals to be enslaved to a distortion of the truth (cf. Matt 12:12; Mark 2:27). Unlike the elitists of the day, the Son cared more about heeding the will of the Father, as reflected in His holy Word, than conforming to externally imposed human standards (cf. John 7:24).

The cured paralytic noted that someone else had directed him to pick up his mat and walk (5:11). His response seems to suggest that he "felt no

10. Cf. Goldsmith, *Gospel of John*.
11. Cf. Köstenberger, *John*, 180.

particular gratitude to Jesus for his healing."[12] Because this circumstance represented a challenge to the authority of the Jewish leaders, they wanted to know the name of the person who had issued the controversial directive (v. 12); but the healed man was unable to identify his benefactor, for Jesus had quietly slipped away. Presumably, He wanted to avoid drawing unwanted attention to Himself, especially since it could precipitate a crisis with the religious establishment, particularly as a sizable crowd looked on (v. 13; cf. 6:15; 8:59; 10:39; 12:36). Sometime afterward, Jesus took the initiative to locate the former invalid walking in the temple area. In contrast to those who presumed they were the arbiters of the Mosaic law, He who is sovereign over the proper interpretation of the Tanakh confronted the man about the deeper spiritual issue of sin in his life. Rather than living in a manner characterized by iniquity and thereby facing the prospect of suffering God's eternal condemnation, the man was urged to sin no more (5:14). It remains unclear whether the man's disability was a direct consequence of a particular transgression in his life (cf. 9:1–3).[13]

The Divine Authority of Jesus as Torah (John 5:16–30)

The incident of the Redeemer's healing on the Sabbath was not a one-time event. Because it was something He did on numerous occasions, it challenged the authority of the religious leaders. They responded by persecuting Him. This included not only opposing Him verbally, but also exploring ways to have Him tried, convicted, and executed (John 5:16, 18). The Jewish authorities were convinced that Jesus stood condemned for violating their Sabbath traditions.[14] In His defense, the Savior noted that His acts of mercy on such a sacred day harmonized with the will of

---

12. Tenney, "John," 9:62. Carson (*John*, 243) observes that the cured paralytic "tries to avoid difficulties with the authorities by blaming the one who had who has healed him" (John 5:11). Likewise, the former lame man is "so dull he has not even discovered his benefactor's name" (v. 13). Moreover, "once he finds out he reports Jesus to the authorities" (v. 15). In short, the restored "invalid is the painful opposite of everything that characterizes" the cured blind man described in John 9. The latter is known for his "initiative, quick-wittedness, eager faith and a questing mind." Even so, Borchert (*John 1–11*, 235) notes that in both episodes, Jesus refused to abandon those whom He healed to the predatory clutches of the religious leaders. The good Shepherd, after seeking and finding the cured paralytic and the healed blind man, ministered to them spiritually (cf. John 5:14; 9:35).

13. Cf. Beasley-Murray, *John*, 74; Calvin, *John*, 1:192–94; Witherington, *John's wisdom*, 138–39.

14. Cf. Asiedu-Peprah, *Johannine sabbath conflicts*, 24.

His Father, who never stopped working (v. 17).[15] Even at the dawn of time, when the Father ceased from His creation activity, He still remained active in overseeing the universe and sustaining life on earth (cf. Gen 2:2–3). The Son, by making such a strong association with the Father, was asserting a similar divine prerogative. This enraged the Messiah's critics, for they saw Him not only violating the Sabbath law, but also committing the capital offense of blasphemy, for He made Himself equal with God (John 5:18). It was inconceivable to Jesus' opponents that He who is the embodiment of the Torah would have the same authority as the one who not only gave the Mosaic law but also established the Sabbath.[16]

Perhaps while still in the temple complex, Jesus declared to the religious leaders the solemn truth that He, the Son, did nothing on His own initiative; instead, He only did what He saw His Father doing (v. 19). The Father commissioned His Son to be His "sole agent on earth"; also, the Father authorized and empowered His Son to "convey God's life and light to humankind."[17] It would be incorrect to conclude that Jesus was unable to make decisions on His own. More accurately, He submitted to the will of His Father in everything He did (cf. 4:34; 8:28; 12:50; 15:10). This relational closeness is evident in Jesus' assertion that the Father loved Him and showed Him all His plans and purposes (5:20).[18] The Son's healing of

---

15. Whitacre (*Johannine polemic*, 36) remarked that "Jesus' work on the Sabbath is his Father's work in that it reveals the Father's gracious love."

16. According to Ratzinger (*Jesus of Nazareth*), the Savior "understands himself as the Torah—as the word of God in person" (110). Furthermore, Jesus openly asserted through His discourses to be "on the same exalted level as the Lawgiver—as God" (102). In short, the words that Jesus spoke "constitute the definitive Torah" (68).

17. Witherington, *John's wisdom*, 140. McGrath (*John's apologetic Christology*, 77) notes the looming issue was that Jesus' interlocutors did not acknowledge Him to be "God's agent." Instead, they regarded Jesus to be "an upstart, one of a number of messianic pretenders and glory-seekers to appear on the scene during this period of Jewish history."

18. According to Borgen ("God's agent"), there is a rabbinic halakhic principle that forms the historical and cultural backdrop to Jesus' status as the divine and heavenly agent of God in the Fourth Gospel. In particular, the agent is "like his sender" with respect to the "judicial function and effects." Some rabbis went even further by declaring that the "agent is a person identical with the sender." Thus, the agent derives his "authority," "function," and "qualities" from the sender. For example, one ancient Jewish marriage rite asserted the following: "the agent ranks as his master's own person." This principle is evident throughout the Fourth Gospel (139; cf. 5:23; 10:30, 38; 12:45; 14:9; 15:23). Borgen adds that the "idea of the Son-Father relationship also implies that the Son is subordinate to the Father" (cf. 10:29; 13:16) and obedient to His will (140; cf. 6:38; 8:29). Other "striking similarities between the halakhic principles of agency and ideas in the Fourth Gospel" include the agent's "return and reporting back to the sender" (cf. 13:3) and the agent's appointment of "other agents as an extension of his own mission in time and space" (143–44; cf. 17:18;

a 38-year-old paralytic on the Sabbath, in accordance with the will of the Father, was an amazing miracle, one that showed the Son to be the master over time. Nevertheless, Jesus' antagonists would hear about even more remarkable works, such as His raising Lazarus from the dead (cf. 11:38–53) and one day judging all humankind (5:28–30).

One can only imagine how increasingly agitated the authorities became as they heard the one who is the realization of the Tanakh claim for Himself the prerogatives of God. For instance, in verse 21, the Son declared that He, like the Father, gives life to whomever He wishes. This includes physical and eternal life (cf. Deut 32:39; 1 Sam 2:6; 2 Kgs 5:7; Isa 26:19; Ezek 37:3–12; Dan 12:2; Tob 13:2; Wis 16:13).[19] In fact, He alone is the resurrection and the life (cf. John 11:25). Undoubtedly, the religious leaders bristled at Jesus' claim to exercise the divine right to raise the dead; but perhaps even more outlandish to them was His assertion that the Father had assigned all judgment to the Son (cf. Pss 43:1; 109). On behalf of the triune Godhead, the Son would one day evaluate how all people lived, including His antagonists, and determine their eternal future (John 5:22; cf. Acts 17:31). John 5:23 records further claims Jesus made about His equality with the Father and equal status as God. It was the divine will that all would honor the Son to the same extent as they honored the Father. In fact, those who failed to accord the Son the honor He deserved, dishonored the Father, who had commissioned and sent Him. In this context, Jesus' critics blasphemed the Lord by rejecting the truth of the Son's divinity.[20]

It is amazing how patient and measured Jesus remained in the midst of His audience's opposition. With grace and compassion, He stressed the importance of people heeding His message and putting their faith in the Father, who sent Him.[21] Those who did so received eternal life. From that

---

20:21; also, Borgen, *Bread from heaven*, 158–164).

19. Köstenberger (*John*, 187) notes the agreement between the Old Testament and the writings of the Second Temple period of Judaism that "raising the dead and giving life" were the "sole prerogatives of God."

20. Keener (*John*, 1:650) remarks that "worshiping humans who wanted to be divine was certainly idolatry, but the informed reader knows that Jesus was actually of divine rank and became human" (cf. John 1:1, 14).

21. The dual themes of belief and faith dominate the Fourth Gospel. In point of fact, it contains the New Testament's most probing treatment of the experience of faith. A range of meanings and nuances are implied, from mere assent to complete dependence. In turn, these form the biblical basis for having eternal life, knowing the truth, receiving the Son, obeying His teachings, encountering the Father, and averting judgment. It would be incorrect to assume that the concept of faith, as found in the Fourth Gospel, is

moment on, they were no longer in the realm of death but abided in the realm of life. They could rest assured that they would not be condemned in the judgment of the wicked on the last day (v. 24). In brief, the Evangelist was urging his readers to believe that Jesus is the Messiah, the Son of God. By depending on and remaining vitally committed to Him, they would have eternal life. There are no religious, cultural, or economic barriers associated with this kind of faith. Jesus is available to all who are willing to come to Him in simple trust and unwavering devotion.[22]

The implication of Jesus' message is clear. Those who believe in Him have eternal life, both now and on the last day. Conversely, those who reject Him will be judged and condemned to an eternity without the Son. Jesus solemnly affirmed to His audience that now was the time for them to come to Him in faith and receive eternal life. They were foolish to delay such a decision, for a day of judgment was coming; in fact, from the divine perspective, it was already at hand. In that moment of reckoning, the Son will issue His summons, and those who hear will live forever with Him in heaven (v. 25). This group will be comprised of believers, namely, those who heeded Jesus' declaration to put their faith in Him. Despite the objections of His opponents, Jesus did not shrink back from making such claims. Moreover, He asserted that the Father, who had life in Himself, had granted that the Son also have life in Himself (v. 26).[23] Only Jesus, as the final expression of God's Torah, could rightfully claim that He is the way, the truth, and the life, and that it is only through faith in Him that people receive access to the Father (cf. 14:6). The Father had also given Jesus authority to one day judge humanity, for He is the "Son of Man" (5:27; cf. 1:51).

---

static or passive. Instead, saving faith is dynamic and active. Moreover, this vibrant belief reaches out to appropriate the object of faith, namely, the Redeemer. Likewise, this kind of faith is much more than a mental comprehension of what one believes. Biblical faith makes a wholehearted commitment to the divine, incarnate Tanakh. For a discussion concerning the notion of faith in the Fourth Gospel, cf. Adkisson, *Believing as a dominant motif*, 49–90; Dodd, *Fourth Gospel*, 179–186; Hawthorne, "Faith in the Fourth Gospel," 117–126; Keener, *John*, 1:325–28; Painter, "Eschatological faith," 36–52; Morris, *John*, 296–98; Schnackenburg, *John*, 1:558–575.

22. Cf. Cook, *The theology of John*, 97–100.

23. Thompson ("The living Father") clarifies that the intent of John 5:26 is not to address "the nature of the relationship or the unity of the Father and Son"; rather, it is to characterize "the unity of their work" (24). Moreover, through Jesus' words and works, "the Father's life-giving power becomes embodied, rather than remaining merely a cipher or idea." In this way, "God's identity as Father is concretely realized" (25).

Many of Jesus' contemporaries would have agreed with Him that there was a future day of reckoning; but they would have contested His assertion that He would be judging them as well as all humanity. In that time of judgment, the Lord Jesus will summon all the dead from their graves (5:28). Such a notion is not preposterous when one realizes that the Tanakh of God is the Lord of life; and as the Creator, He has the power and authority to raise the dead. Verse 29 differentiates two separate ends for resurrected humanity. Those who have trusted in the Messiah—as evidenced by their life of doing good—will be raised to spend eternity with the triune God in heaven. Conversely, those who rejected the Son—as evidenced by their life of doing evil—will be raised and condemned to spend eternity in hell. The judgment the Son renders in the last day will not be an independently made, self-initiated evaluation; rather, it will be in accordance with the will of His Father (v. 30). The Son's assessment will be impartial and fair, for He seeks to please the Father, not Himself, in whatever He does. It is little wonder then that the Father has made His resurrected Son both Lord and Messiah (Acts 2:36).

The Multiple Witnesses to Jesus as Torah (John 5:31–47)

Like a skilled defense attorney, Jesus acknowledged that if He alone testified about Himself, what He declared would be invalid (John 5:31; cf. 8:13). This is because the Old Testament required at least two confirming witnesses to validate whatever testimony was given in a court of law. Adhering to this requirement would help to ensure the integrity and accuracy of the assertions being made (cf. Num 35:30; Deut 17:6; 19:15). Regrettably, the experts in the law did not accept the truth regarding the Son's relationship with the Father. The elitists also failed to recognize Jesus as the Prophet of Deuteronomy 18:15 and 18, whom God promised to send and whom Moses commanded God's people to heed (cf. Acts 3:22; 7:37). The religious leaders' stance of unbelief openly disregarded the corroborating witnesses provided by John the Baptizer (John 5:33), the Redeemer's own miracles (v. 36), the Father in heaven (v. 37), and Scripture (particularly through Moses; vv. 39, 46).[24]

The one who is the realization of all the types and prophecies recorded in the law declared that the testimony offered by the Father about the Son was true (John 5:32).[25] Neither did it matter whether the religious lead-

---

24. Cf. Asiedu-Peprah, *Johannine sabbath conflicts*, 27–28.
25. Köstenberger (*John*, 191) states that Jesus, in saying "there is another" (John 5:32),

ers accepted the assertions made by the Father, for whatever He declared remained intrinsically valid (cf. Rom 3:3–4). In 1 John 5:9, the writer declared that if we accept human testimony in a legal proceeding, which is far inferior to what God provides, how much more should people accept the Father's testimony about His Son? For those who accept the Father's witness, the love of the Messiah becomes a reality in their hearts. Those who reject it are in effect calling God a liar (v. 10). For the apostle John, there was no room for wavering, no ambiguous middle ground when it came to one's position on the Father's testimony about His Son. Rejecting the perfection of the gift of the Torah contradicted the testimony of the Father regarding the Son, namely, that eternal life is in Him (v. 11). This is the heart of biblical faith. Christianity is not just a philosophy, religious system, or set of beliefs. It is most of all a relationship with the Lord Jesus. Salvation can only come in the context of that personal relationship. Accordingly, to believe in the Son is to be truly born again. Likewise, to reject the Son is to be eternally lost (v. 12).

In John 5:33, the Messiah noted that previously the religious leaders in Jerusalem sent a delegation of priests, Levites, and Pharisees to interrogate John the Baptizer and he testified to the truth about the Son (cf. 1:19, 24). This observation did not mean Jesus had an implicit need for any human witnesses. Instead, His motive was to use these to convince His opponents to accept Him as the divine, incarnate Tanakh and as a result be saved (5:34). When Gabriel foretold the birth of John, the angel said the Baptizer would operate in the spirit and power of Elijah (Luke 1:17). In Sirach 48:1, Elijah is portrayed as a "prophet like fire" whose declarations "burned like a torch" (NRSV). Similarly, Jesus said His forerunner had been like a beacon of light—a burning and shining lamp—to the truth about the Messiah (cf. Ps 132:17; Bar 4:1–2). For a short while, people were excited by John's ministry and rejoiced in the message he declared (John 5:35). Regrettably, though, their positive response seemed fickle and short-lived. The religious leaders were especially ambivalent about John's testimony concerning the Savior. It is not clear whether by this time, John had been imprisoned and executed at the Machaerus fortress (about AD 28; cf. Matt 11:2; 14:3–12; Mark 1:14; 6:17–29; Luke 9:9).

Jesus' teachings and miracles were an even greater witness verifying His messianic claims (cf. John 10:25). The Father decreed these works for the Son to perform—especially His atoning sacrifice at Calvary and resurrection from the dead—and confirmed that the Father had sent the Son (5:36). Tragically, though, the religious leaders refused to believe the one

---

reflected the contemporary Jewish custom of "avoiding the name of God."

who is the enfleshment of the Torah. By their actions, Jesus' antagonists proved they had never heard the voice of God nor seen His form at any time (v. 37; cf. Num 12:8; Deut 4:12, 15; 5:24–27).[26] Otherwise, they would have trusted in the "one and only Son" (John 1:18) who had made the Father known (5:38; cf. 14:9). The paradox of the circumstance is even greater if Pentecost was the Jewish festival mentioned in 5:1, in which the Jews commemorated the giving of the Mosaic law at Mount Sinai. Jesus affirmed the diligent and thorough manner in which the religious leaders scrutinized the Tanakh, noting that they believed they would somehow find eternal life in these ancient sacred texts.[27] Ironically, these Scriptures pointed to the Son, the same person whom His detractors refused to trust in for eternal life (vv. 39–40; cf. Luke 16:31; 24:25–27, 44–47; Acts 10:43; Rom 1:2; 3:21; 10:4).[28]

Jesus' remarks did not mean He solicited the approval and praise of any human being, least of all the religious leaders (John 5:41). His decision was especially prudent, given how deeply He knew their hearts. In particular, the omniscient Torah discerned that His opponents were devoid of love from God and for God (v. 42). After all, they rejected the Son, who came in the authority of the Father. In contrast, Jesus' antagonists welcomed those who came in their own lesser authority (v. 43). With such rampant hypocrisy, it is no wonder the legalists refused to believe in the Redeemer. Tragically, they more highly valued obtaining respect and praise from their peers than caring about the honor that came from the true and living God (v. 44). In a sense, then, they idolized one another, rather than loving the triune God with all their heart, soul, and strength (cf. Deut 6:4–5). Failing to do the latter was a fundamental breach of the foremost commandment of the law they highly venerated (cf. Exod 20:3–6; Deut 5:7–10; Matt 22:36–38; Mark 12:28–30).[29]

---

26. For a discussion of contrasting rabbinic points of view as to whether the Israelites saw the glory of the Lord at Mount Sinai, cf. Hakola, *Identity matters*, 151–52; Heschel, *Heavenly Torah*, 315–18.

27. Evans (*Word and glory*) thinks Jesus' comment in John 5:39 "refers to rabbinic interpretation known as 'midrash'" (151), the main objective of which "was to find life" (152).

28. Cf. Calvin, *John*, 1:217–18.

29. Keener (*John*, 1:659) observes that to "reject the Word in flesh is to show that one does not heed the less complete revelation in the law, either" (cf. John 1:17–18). Similarly, Lierman ("Mosaic pattern," 216) emphasized that in the Fourth Gospel, "the Son is a superior focus of faith than Moses ever could have been, and his words are superior to Moses' writings." Furthermore, as Casselli ("Jesus as eschatological Torah," 24) points out, while the "Rabbinic traditions" portrayed Moses as a "divine-like figure," the Evangelist presented the Son as "truly and fully Divine."

Once again, like a skilled prosecuting attorney,[30] Jesus as Tanakh declared that in the day of judgment, He would not be the one to accuse His opponents of sinning against the Father. Instead, it would be their esteemed lawgiver, Moses, in whom the religious authorities of the day had pinned their hopes of salvation (John 5:45).[31] In the eschatological time of reckoning, the critics would not be able to look to Moses as their intercessor before God (cf. Exod 32:30–34; Ps 106:23), for ultimately what Moses penned concerned the Messiah. The two are so intertwined that to receive or reject the former is to receive or reject the latter (John 5:46–47).[32] He who is the only mediator between God and humanity is also the same person the elite spurned (cf. 1 Tim 2:5). In short, to reject the Son—the Father's only provision of salvation—was to leave oneself eternally condemned (cf. Heb 6:4–8; 1 Pet 2:7–8).[33]

Jesus as Torah Offers the Bread of Life (John 6:1–71)

The Feeding of the Multitude by Jesus as Torah (John 6:1–13)

The context of John 6 is the Savior's feeding of over 5,000 people. It also represents a major turning point in the thematic development of the Fourth Gospel. Up until this time in the narrative, Jesus' ministry was primarily in Jerusalem; but now it shifts to Galilee. This change of venue brings the Son's identity as the divine, incarnate Torah into sharper relief. For instance, the signs He did recalled the miraculous ways in which God intervened on behalf of His people in the book of Exodus, specifically the first Passover event, the exodus from Egypt, and the provision of manna

---

30. Harstine (*Moses*, 57) comments that "Jesus' defense is based on his divine Sonship."

31. Meeks (*The prophet-king*, 307) states that "Judaism and Samaritanism regarded Moses as the 'defense attorney' for their respective groups in the heavenly court" (cf. T. Moses 12:6; Exod Rab. 18:3; 43). Köstenberger (*John*, 194) builds on this thought by noting that the "widespread confidence in the efficacy of Moses' intervention" underscores "how shocking Jesus' statement would have been for his Jewish audience."

32. Keener (*John*, 1:662) indicates that Jesus' "closing appeal to Moses," which is recorded in John 5:45–47, "paves the way for John's narrative about the one greater than Moses who gives new manna," which is found in chapter 6.

33. Whitacre (*Johannine polemic*, 43) comments that in the Fourth Gospel, the Evangelist uses the Hebrew sacred writings to testify about Jesus' critics by predicting their "unbelief and opposition." Furthermore, the Torah bears witness against Jesus' interlocutors by affirming the validity of His messianic claims; cf. Calvin, *John*, 1:224–25.

in the desert.³⁴ In the first century AD, it was "quite common among the Jewish literate circles" to regard "bread as a metaphor for the Torah" (cf. Sir 15:1-3; 24:20-23; Wis 16:26; Gen Rab. 70:5).³⁵ Jesus is shown to be the fulfillment of the law's types and prophecies, the one whom the Father has sent into the world to do His will. Perhaps more than before, the distinction between and consequences of belief versus unbelief are differentiated. People in the category of unbelief become increasingly intense in their rejection of and hostility toward the Messiah.

Apart from the Resurrection, Jesus' feeding of over five thousand people is the only miracle that is recorded in all four Gospels.³⁶ It shows the Redeemer to be the Bread of Life. The fact that John retold an incident that was probably already well-known is an indication of the impact this miracle had on people. The "some time after this" (John 6:1) reference is indefinite, though verse 4 says it was near the time when the Passover was about to be celebrated in Jerusalem. A probable date for the episode is the spring of AD 29, which was just one year before the crucifixion of the Anointed One.

The author provided no explanation concerning the Messiah's journey north from Jerusalem to Galilee. According to Matthew 14:13, Jesus retreated from the crowds to a remote place after hearing about the execution of John the Baptizer. The solitary spot was likely in the area of Bethsaida (cf. Luke 9:10), a town located on the northeast shore of the Sea of Galilee. John 6:1 notes that Jesus withdrew by crossing over to the far side of the lake; but by the time the Fourth Gospel was written, the lake was called "the Sea of Tiberias," named after the Roman emperor who reigned during Jesus' earthly ministry.

Initially, the Savior traveled alone to an isolated location; but it was not long before large crowds of people heard of His whereabouts and fol-

---

34. Smith ("Exodus typology," 329) observes that some scholars consider the miracle of Jesus feeding over 5,000 people to be an example of exodus typology occurring throughout the Fourth Gospel. By this is meant "instances of typology related to the exodus traditions" as well as "running parallelisms" with the content of the book of Exodus (and possibly other portions of the Old Testament historical record; e.g. the paschal lamb, the bronze serpent, and the manna from heaven). Smith notes that because the "Johannine imagery is often subtle and complex," it has resulted in numerous "competing theories" (330) that are methodologically weakened by their "arbitrary selection of evidence" (332).

35. Fernando, *Relationship between law and love,* 112; cf. Beasley-Murray, *John,* 92; Hakola, *Identity matters,* 166–67.

36. According to Keener (*John,* 1:79), the Evangelist—even in recounting an episode such as the feeding of over 5,000 people—"goes his own way, writing in his own idiom and connecting the events and teachings to theological motifs that run throughout his Gospel."

lowed Him on foot from the nearby towns of Galilee (Matt 14:13). Many of them had seen Jesus miraculously heal the sick (John 6:2). Some probably wanted to be healed of an illness themselves. Others no doubt were curious to see the Redeemer perform more miraculous signs. Still others may have believed He was the promised Messiah and wanted to witness the deliverance of God's people from foreign oppression (v. 3). Whatever their motives, Jesus had compassion on them when He saw them. Matthew 14:14 notes that Jesus showed His concern by meeting them and healing the sick among them.

John 6:3 states that at some point, Jesus climbed up a mountainside or hillside, a detail that recalls Moses' ascent of Mount Sinai. The apostle did not specify the identity of this elevated region. While Jesus sat down with His disciples around Him, large crowds flocked toward Him. By this time, Jesus had become tremendously popular among the people, who looked to Him to fill a spiritual vacuum in their lives. Evidently, the numbers grew as Jewish pilgrims eagerly joined the throng on their way to Jerusalem to observe Passover at the temple (v. 4). Jesus saw the people as sheep without a shepherd (Mark 6:34). He delayed meeting His own needs for privacy and rest so that He could minister to the people's need for teaching, especially about the kingdom of God (Luke 9:11).

At some point, Jesus asked Philip where they could get enough bread to feed the vast crowd (John 6:5). Philip was a good person to query since he was from nearby Bethsaida and would know the area well (cf. 1:44). Though the Messiah had already decided what He was about to do, He still asked the question because He wanted to test and refine the faith of Philip and the other disciples (v. 6; cf. Jas 1:3; 1 Pet 1:7). This calls to mind the query Moses asked the Lord during an episode in the Sinai desert involving the manna and quail (cf. Num 11:13). Philip's answer highlighted the cost involved in buying enough to feed the huge crowd. Eight months' wages (about 200 denarii) would be insufficient (John 6:7). A denarius was a day's wage for an unskilled laborer or a soldier at that time (cf. Matt 20:2). Two hundred denarii was far beyond the financial resources of the Redeemer's followers. Then, Andrew, the brother of Simon Peter, brought a young boy to Jesus who had something to offer. The child, who was undoubtedly poor, had five small, flat barley loaves and two sardine-sized pickled fish (John 5:8–9; cf. Matt 14:17; Mark 6:38; Luke 9:13).[37]

---

37. In the region of Palestine, bread was essential to life. Grain was usually ground with a millstone, kneaded in a wooden bowl, and baked as circular cakes. Bread was so important to the people of the region that it was baked daily. Other foods, like fish or meat, were wrapped inside bread. The latter was also used as an eating utensil for stews and soups.

Jesus saw that His disciples were at a loss as to how all the people could be fed. Thus the Torah of God took charge by instructing His disciples to get everyone to settle on the expanse of grass carpeting the hillside (John 6:10). They sat down in groups numbering between 50 and 100 people (cf. Mark 6:40; Luke 9:14). John numbered the men[38] at about 5,000, but women and children were also present (cf. Matt 14:21; Mark 6:44; Luke 9:14), so there could have been 10,000 to 15,000 people there. In the culture of that day, the men often ate separately from the women and children. As they were all seated, Jesus blessed the food with a prayer of thanksgiving.[39] He then handed the bread and the fish to His disciples, who distributed them among the people until they were all fully satisfied (John 6:11). This episode was possibly reminiscent of the incident in which Elisha the prophet multiplied 20 loaves of barley bread to feed 100 men (cf. 2 Kgs 4:42–44).[40] The enfleshment of the Tanakh, however, did a far more amazing feat, one that demonstrated His deity as the Creator.

Unleavened bread was conveniently used at harvesttime when families were too busy to wait for bread to rise. When a long trip was planned, unleavened bread was practical to bring along. Bread was used in temple offerings and placed daily inside the sanctuary. It was also used to offer blessings within the Jewish family. Wheat was the grain most commonly used to make bread. Barley was also used for making bread, but only for the poorest people, since it was typically used to feed livestock.

38. Köstenberger (*John*, 202) thinks the men were "heads of households."

39. Jesus' distribution of the "loaves" (John 6:11) and "fish" mirror what the host at a Jewish meal would do. Perhaps Jesus said something similar to the following refrain, which would have been offered in that day during the celebration of the Passover Seder (ceremonial meal): "Blessed are you, O Lord our God, King of the universe, who brings forth bread from the earth" (cf. David's prayer of thanksgiving recorded in 1 Chron 29:10–13). The eternal Tanakh, who is the "bread of life" (John 6:35), invited and welcomed people to share in the abundance of God's provision.

40. Elisha (848–797 BC), whose name means "God is salvation," was the son of Shaphat from Abel Meholah, a town located on the western side of the Jordan River. Elisha was also a statesman and prophet who succeeded Elijah (875–848 BC) in being God's official spokesperson (1 Kings 19:16-21). Before Elijah was taken up to heaven, he gave Elisha a double share of his prophetic spirit (2 Kings 2:9-15). The implication is that God blessed Elisha's ministry as Elijah's replacement. Elisha, as a holy person, devoted himself in service to God (cf. 4:9). While all who belong to the community of faith are called to serve the Lord and their fellow human beings, prophets such as Elisha were consecrated to God's work in a very special way. Elisha's 51-year ministry in the northern kingdom of Israel encompassed the reigns of Jehoram, Jehu, Jehoahaz, and Joash. Elisha declared the divine message, lead a prophetic order, advised monarchs, and anointed kings. Elisha's access to the royal court neither corrupted him nor diminished his piety, as seen in his concern for the poor and oppressed. His efforts to assist the disadvantaged often came through the performance of miracles.

After the people had eaten, Jesus told His disciples to gather the fragments that were left on the ground so that none of the food would go to waste (John 6:12). This instruction would not have seemed unusual to His disciples since it was customary for servants to pick up and eat the leftovers after a Jewish feast. It was also in keeping with the Jewish belief that bread is a gift from God and must not be left lying around.[41] Most likely, the disciples did not use small wicker baskets, but rather larger ones normally used for carrying sizable quantities of food and other supplies. The disciples filled their twelve baskets with the remaining pieces of bread (v. 13).

The feeding of the multitude was clearly a miracle from the hand of the Messiah; yet He did not perform it in isolation. He let the Twelve have a part in working the miracle, such as by setting out the food for the people; and even before Jesus began to perform the miracle, He challenged His followers to come up with their own plan for feeding the crowd. In this way the deed became a collaborative effort from beginning to end. Imagine the disciples' feeling of excitement in cooperating with the Redeemer in feeding the multitude. That thrill, that sense of involvement, was necessary to their training. Jesus had not called them to stand aside and watch Him work. Neither was He sending them to work without His help. The disciples were partners with the Lord Jesus in His ministry of redemption.

The Walking on the Water by Jesus as Torah (John 6:14–21)

The miraculous supply of food prompted many to wonder if Jesus was the prophet that Moses referred to in Deuteronomy 18:15 and 18 (John 6:14).[42] Whether this prophet was to be a forerunner of the Messiah or the Messiah Himself is unclear, though the Pharisees questioned John the Baptizer as if the Prophet and the Messiah were separate people (cf. John 1:20–21). In any case, the crowd saw significant signs in Jesus' ministry that He was someone worthy of being the Prophet whom Moses described. For instance, Jesus miraculously fed the people a kind of Passover (6:4) that filled 12 baskets with leftovers—symbolically, one for each of the 12 tribes. Further, Jesus' miracles hinted at what the people were expecting

---

41. Stern (*Jewish New Testament commentary*, 171–72) indicates that the prohibition in rabbinic law against the "destruction of food" is part of the cultural backdrop of Jesus' command.

42. According to Ratzinger (*Jesus of Nazareth*), the Savior, as the "Chosen Prophet who sees God face-to-face" (126), claimed to be "Temple and Torah in person" (111). Moreover, in Him, as the true "eternal Israel," the divine Word is "actualized" for the redeemed, who are the "newly reborn People of God" (171).

when the Messiah would come, namely, that abundant wine would flow and enough food to feed all Israel would fall like manna from the heavens (cf. Amos 9:13; 1 Enoch 62:14). In their desperation, the people wanted to force Jesus to be their king; but the kind of ruler they wanted, a brigand who would overthrow Israel's oppressors, was not in God's plan (cf. John 18:36–37; Acts 1:6; Rom 14:7).[43]

The one who is the perfection of the gift of the Torah came to offer forgiveness from sin and an enduring relationship with God (cf. Jer 31:31–34). Thus, the Son retreated into the hills to spend the night in prayer with His Father (Matt 14:23; Mark 6:46; John 6:15). Just prior to this, Jesus dismissed the crowds. He also directed His disciples to get into a boat without Him, cross over to the west side of the lake, and head to Capernaum (Matt 14:22; Mark 6:45; John 6:16–17). As the Twelve made their way, a gale-force wind sent huge waves crashing against the sides of the boat (Matt 14:24; John 6:18). At times on the Sea of Galilee, the sudden appearance of violent storm episodes occurred. Evidently, the disciples spent most of the night fighting the elements as they tried to cross. Despite their efforts, they only went about three miles, which placed them near the middle of the lake (Mark 6:47; John 6:19).

In the hours immediately preceding dawn, Jesus saw the trouble His disciples were in and came to them by walking on the lake (Matt 14:25; Mark 6:48; cf. Job 9:8). Ridderbos notes that the Greek word translated "walking" (John 6:19) indicates "the effortlessness of Jesus going over the sea."[44] Not even the wind, waves, and gravity could stop the one who is the Lord of all creation (cf. Job 38:8–11; Pss 29:3–4, 10–11; 65:5–7; 77:19; 89:9; 107:23–32; Isa 43:2, 16).[45] When Jesus' form appeared mysteriously out of the darkness like a ghost, the disciples' minds must have turned to the old Jewish superstition that a spirit seen at night brings disaster. In this case, they mistook Jesus for a ghost (Matt 14:26; Mark 6:49–50). It seems that whenever the Savior was absent, the Twelve fell into distress through lack of faith. Jesus quickly calmed their fears. Undoubtedly, the familiar sound of His voice identifying Himself reassured His disciples that they

43. Köstenberger (*John, 203*) postulates that in the time of Jesus, the people could have amalgamated the popular concept of the "prophet" with that of a "king." Likewise, Beasley-Murray (*John*, 88) states that the "step from a prophet like Moses (v 14), the first Redeemer and worker of miracles, to a messianic deliverer was a short one for enthusiasts in contemporary Israel to make."

44. Ridderbos, *John*, 217.

45. Keener (*John*, 1:673) observes that while God used Moses to part the waters of the Red Sea, not even the famed leader, liberator, and lawgiver of Israel could claim authority and control over the elements the way Jesus did.

would not be harmed (Matt 14:27; John 6:20). After Jesus entered the boat, the turbulent wind died down (Matt 14:32; Mark 6:51). The Twelve were completely dumbfounded over what had taken place, including the episode in which Jesus rescued Peter as he attempted to walk on the water (Matt 14:28–31). On impulse, the disciples worshiped the divine, incarnate Torah, exclaiming Him to be the Son of God (v. 33). Then, perhaps in what seemed like a moment of time, the boat and all its passengers immediately reached the shore of the lake (John 6:21).

The Declaration of Jesus as Torah to Be the Bread of Life (John 6:22–59)

The next day, the crowds who had stayed on the east side of the lake realized that there had been only one boat there. They saw that the Twelve set off in the vessel and that Jesus had not gone with them (John 6:22). Several boats from Tiberias landed near the spot where Jesus had miraculously fed thousands of people (v. 23).[46] When the crowd saw that Jesus and His disciples had left, some of the people embarked in the boats, went across the lake, and began looking for the Savior at Capernaum (v. 24). Once they found Jesus, the people asked when He had arrived (v. 25). In addition to those who had witnessed the multiplication of bread and fish, others from Capernaum also likely showed up. After they heard what Jesus had done the previous day, they probably wanted to see Him perform the same kind of miracle for them (cf. the demand of the crowd recorded in v. 30). Though Capernaum was Jesus' headquarters during His Galilean ministry, and though Peter and some of the other disciples had their families there, the residents of the city rejected the one who is the embodiment of the Tanakh. Their unbelief prompted Jesus to foretell Capernaum's destruction (Matt 11:23–24; Luke 10:15).

Jesus, who knew the hearts of all people (John 2:24), sidestepped the issue of when He arrived on the other side of the lake; instead, He dealt directly with the people's motives for seeking Him. Since the Redeemer had provided them with a miraculous meal, they wanted more (6:26). They were so focused on satisfying their physical needs that they did not even consider the spiritual implications of this sign. Jesus admonished them not to put a priority on obtaining material desires, which had no lasting value, but to seek eternally lasting spiritual nourishment. Jesus was speaking metaphorically of everlasting life, which He, as the Son of Man, gave

---

46. Between AD 18 and 22, Herod Antipas founded the city and named it after the Roman emperor, Tiberius Caesar.

to believers. He had the right to do so because God the Father had placed His seal, or mark, of approval on the Son's ministry and messianic claims (v. 27).[47] In ancient times, a seal, or signet, was a small engraved object that was created to produce an image in soft clay or wax. The presence of a seal on a document, container, or storage compartment guaranteed that the contents were authentic and carried the endorsement of the monarch or emperor.

The crowds misunderstood Jesus when He talked about working for the food that endures forever. They thought He meant rules and regulations they had to keep in order to earn God's favor. Thus, they wanted to know exactly what God demanded of them (v. 28). In response, Jesus explained that the "work" of God was simply to trust in His emissary, the one who is the embodiment of the Torah (v. 29).[48] Faith in Him would lead to eternal life (cf. Eph 2:8–9; Titus 3:5). Rather than entrust their eternal future to Jesus, the throng demanded to know what miracle He would perform to convince them to make such a commitment (John 6:30). Unless He could prove to them that He was greater than Moses, the famed lawgiver and leader of Israel, the crowd refused to accept Jesus' claim to be the promised Redeemer (v. 31). This is because popular opinion among some Jews of the day was that when the Messiah came, His arrival would be accompanied by a miracle that exceeded the feat God performed in the desert on behalf of Moses (cf. 2 Bar 29:8).[49] For 40 years, God rained down heavenly food, in the form of manna, for an entire nation (cf. Exod 16:4, 15; Neh 9:15; Pss 78:24–25; 105:40). By comparison, Jesus' one-time provision of inexpensive barley bread to a multitude of people seemed junior-grade; but in point of fact, the eternal Tanakh performed other miraculous signs that exceeded anything ever done by Moses.[50] This included giving sight

---

47. Borgen ("John 6," 273–74) suggests that the reference to the Father placing His seal on Jesus denotes "the Son of Man as the Father's emissary, as the Son of Man who descended from heaven" (cf. John 3:13).

48. According to Ratzinger (*Jesus of Nazareth*, 268), "the Law has become a *person*" (emphasis his). Through the believers' encounter with the divine-human Tanakh, they spiritually "feed on the living God himself." Such intimate communion with the Father "happens in the context of faith in Jesus." He alone enables the redeemed to experience a "living relationship with the Father." Also, cf. Calvin, *John*, 1:244–45; Carson, *John*, 285; Keener, *John*, 1:574.

49. Glasson (*Moses*, 45) points out that there is a substantial amount of "Rabbinic evidence of the expectation that the Messiah, the second Deliverer, would repeat the signs of Moses, the first Deliverer"; cf. Witherington, *John's wisdom*, 156.

50. Cf. Beasley-Murray, *John*, 98.

to a man born blind (cf. John 9:1–7, 30–32) and restoring Lazarus to life (11:1–44).[51]

Jesus solemnly assured the crowd that it was actually God, not Moses, who gave their ancestors manna to eat (cf. Deut 8:3). The latter, while the Father's genuine and gracious provision, was not meant to be an end in itself; rather, the manna foreshadowed the ideal and eternally satisfying life now made available in the Messiah. In the fullest and most perfect way, He is the "true bread from heaven" (John 6:32). The Son came to earth as the enfleshment of the Torah to make new life available to the world (v. 33).[52] Despite the clarity of the Savior's explanation, the crowds misunderstood Him to be referring to literal, physical loaves of bread. They even asked Jesus to give them this source of nourishment from then on (v. 34; cf. 3:4; 4:15). Jesus' response in 6:35 is the first of the seven "I am" declarations in the Fourth Gospel that point to the Son's divine nature.[53] With Exodus 3:13–15 as the contextual backdrop, the Lord Jesus revealed Himself to be the ever-present, ever-living God of Israel (cf. John 1:1–2; 8:58; Heb 13:8; Rev 1:4, 8; 4:8; 11:17; 16:5).[54] By declaring Himself to be the "bread of life" (John 6:35), the divine-human Tanakh revealed that only in Him can a person find the sustenance necessary to nourish one's soul. Specifically, Jesus' statement was an invitation for the crowd to place their faith in Him. All who did would never be spiritually hungry or thirsty again (cf. Sir 24:21).

---

51. Cf. Balfour ("John's use of the Scriptures," 368), who notes that the key issue concerned Jesus' "role and identity" as the Messiah: "He, not Moses, is the messianic, eschatological figure who, like his Father, provides manna from heaven, by feeding the 5,000; he, the last redeemer, marks the inauguration of a new age; he himself becomes the bread that the Father provides." Ellis (*Genius of John*, 26) clarifies that the "contrast between Moses and Jesus is not meant to denigrate Moses but rather to extol Jesus."

52. Keener (*John*) remarks that Jesus "is not merely, like Moses, the mediator of God's gift; rather he himself is God's gift" (1:675). For that reason, what the crowds should "seek is not a wilderness prophet like Moses but the gift of God which is greater than the earthly manna in the wilderness" (1:680).

53. Cf. Cook, *The theology of John*, 56–59; Hurtado, *Lord Jesus Christ*, 370–73.

54. Lioy, *Decalogue in the Sermon on the Mount*, 53. For a discussion of the origin and meaning of the "I am" divine revelation formula, cf. Barrett, *St. John*, 291–93, 342; Brown, *John*, 533–38; Bultmann, *John*, 225–27; Ridderbos, *John*, 300–301; Schnackenburg, *John*, 2:79–89; Smith, "Exodus typology," 341–42; Williams, *I am he*, 255–303. Daube (*Rabbinic Judaism*, 325) maintains that the "I am" pronouncement denotes "the personal presence of the redeeming God." Williams (*I am he*) adds that the declaration "serves as a succinct expression of the unique and exclusive divinity of Yahweh" (302). Furthermore, "all the Johannine *ego eimi* pronouncements . . . convey the message that God's saving promises are made visible and accessible in Jesus" (303).

The various "I am" declarations in the Fourth Gospel are accompanied by discourses. These help to contrast Jesus with the legalistic religious practices of His day, especially obsolete rituals. For example, Jesus being the bread of life implies that He satisfies the longings of people in a way that no other person or group could ever do. His being the good Shepherd (cf. John 10:11) indicates that other spiritual shepherds were untrustworthy and self-serving. Together, the "I am" declarations in the Fourth Gospel make a profound theological claim for Jesus. As the culmination of the Torah, He does not just represent the Father, but also manifests His presence in the world (1:18). Also, because Jesus is the radiance of God's glory and the exact representation of His being (Heb. 1:3), the Son can work, speak, and act as the Father's counterpart. People should direct their spiritual longing and need to Jesus because He is the Logos (John 1:1, 14).

As the Son of God, Jesus was no mere human; yet the crowds, having experienced His words and works, still refused to trust in Him as the Messiah. This applied to both the people in general and the religious elite among them. Despite the widespread presence of unbelief, Jesus remained unswerving in His exhortation that all should come to Him in faith (6:36). The Messiah noted that ultimately it was the Father who enabled the lost to respond in trust to the message of hope. Indeed, all whom the Father gave to the Son would surely receive the good news of salvation. In turn, Jesus would welcome them, not send them away (v. 37). This contrasted sharply with the practices of the religious elite, who threatened to banish people from the synagogue if they acknowledged Jesus as the Messiah (cf. 9:22). The balance between divine sovereignty and human responsibility can be seen in 5:35–37. The commitment of the triune God to extend salvation to the lost is unconditional and unwavering. As well, all are invited to come to Jesus and put their faith in Him for eternal life. When they do, their spiritual hunger will be met and their spiritual thirst will be satisfied. The tragedy is that many close their hearts to the truth and refuse to believe in the Messiah.

The opening verses of the Fourth Gospel reveal that the divine Word came to earth as a human being and made His dwelling among people. Furthermore, He made the Father known by manifesting His glory, grace, and truth. While many rejected the perfection of the gift of the Tanakh, others turned to Him in faith and became members of God's spiritual family (1:1–14). It is disclosed in 6:38 that Jesus' advent—His coming down from heaven as the Father's "commissioned envoy"[55]—was an occasion

---

55. Borgen, "John 6," 281. He also refers to Jesus as "the Father's accredited envoy" (290); cf. Boismard, *Moses or Jesus*, 59–65.

for the Son to execute the will of His Father, not His own will. To those who might have been hesitating to make a faith commitment to Jesus, the Savior issued an emphatic promise. It was God's will that the Son would never lose any whom the Father had given to Him. Believers had the firm assurance that at the Messiah's second advent, He would resurrect them all (v. 39). The Lord's part was to promise eternal life and guarantee His intention to fulfill His pledge. The sinners' part was to make the Son the object of their faith and believe in Him. Those who did so could rest assured that the Messiah would raise them up on the last day (v. 40). This is the time when the wicked will be vanquished, the righteous will be vindicated, and the kingdom of God will be established. The Savior promised that He will not abandon His followers to death and eternal condemnation. The disbelief of the crowd now surfaced as they murmured among themselves their skepticism about Jesus' claim to be God's bread from heaven (v. 41).[56] They regarded Jesus from a merely human perspective as the son of Joseph and Mary (v. 42).[57] Evidently, some of the residents of Capernaum had known Jesus for years as the son of a carpenter from Nazareth. Their cynicism compelled them to oppose Him. In turn, Jesus chastised His listeners for their grumbling (v. 43).

---

56. O'Day ("John," 9:603) notes that the Greek verb rendered "grumble" (John 6:41) is used in the Septuagint to "describe the Israelites' grumbling and complaints in the wilderness" (cf. Exod 15:24; 16:2, 7, 12; Num 11:1; 14:2, 27; Ps 105:24–25). In short, John 6:41 is an example of "exodus imagery" in which the "crowd demonstrates the same recalcitrance as their forbearers"; cf. Beasley-Murray, *John*, 93; Glasson, *Moses*, 101–102; Hanson, *The prophetic Gospel*, 87–88; Lightfoot, *St. John's Gospel*, 162.

57. According to Harstine (*Moses*, 62), the Evangelist "treats Jesus like a diamond that has a noticeable appearance, but whose inward qualities define its value." Paradoxically, Jesus' true identity remained a mystery to the throng. Köstenberger (*John*, 213) points out that the crowd's remark about Jesus being "the son of Joseph" (John 6:42) is "another example of Johannine irony."

Perhaps it was at this point that Jesus resumed His teaching in the synagogue[58] in Capernaum (cf. v. 59).[59] The Messiah noted that unless the Father draws people to the Son, they will show no interest in belief and thereby forfeit the opportunity to receive eternal life (v. 44). To support His statement, Jesus as Torah paraphrased Isaiah 54:13, which says, "All your children will be taught by the LORD."[60] A future time of redemption, restoration, and renewal is the literary context of the verse. In John 6:45, the Son was implying that He is the one who brings to pass these divine promises for all who come to Him in faith. In so doing, they likewise demonstrate that they listen to the Father and learn from Him. Despite the singular importance of the Messiah as the Father's true emissary, many in the audience remained unconvinced.

In Exodus 33:20, the Lord said to Moses that no one could see the face of God and live. No person except the Son has seen the heavenly Father. Jesus was describing to His listeners the intimacy that exists between the Father and the Son. This closeness gave Him the authority to speak as He did (John 6:46). To emphasize what He was about to say, Jesus said, "Very truly I tell you" (v. 47). He wanted to make it clear to His listeners that He would give eternal life to those who put their faith in Him.

---

58. The word *synagogue* means "assembly," coming from a Greek verb that means "to bring together." The Jews probably established synagogues during the Exile. The Babylonians had destroyed Jerusalem and its temple and deported most of the inhabitants of Judah. In order for the Jews to preserve their religious teachings and practices, they established synagogues as local places for worship and instruction. Most communities where Jews lived had at least one synagogue, and some had two or more. According to tradition, the Jewish leaders in a community were to establish a synagogue if at least 10 Jewish men lived in the town. In New Testament times, Jews would meet in the synagogue principally on the Sabbath. During the worship service, men sat on one side and women on the other. The participants would recite the Shema (a confession of faith in the oneness of God, based on Deuteronomy 6:4–9), prayers, and readings from the Law and the Prophets. A speaker would deliver a message and then give a benediction (Luke 4:16–21). The elders of the town selected layman to oversee the care of the building and the property, to supervise the public worship, to choose people to read Scripture and pray, and to invite visitors to address the congregation. An attendant would hand the sacred scrolls to the reader during the service. After the reader finished, the attendant would return the scrolls to a chest mounted on a wall.

59. Borgen ("John 6," 274) observes that "questions and answers, direct exegesis and problem-solving exegesis were part of the discourses in the synagogue. All these elements are found in rabbinic midrashim"; cf. Goldsmith, *Gospel of John*.

60. According to Köstenberger (*John*, 214), during the Second Temple period of Judaism, "it was held that to learn the Torah was to be taught by God himself." To those willing to accept the truth, the Messiah fulfilled this expectation as the embodiment of the Tanakh.

Then once more, the Torah of God declared that He was the bread of life (v. 48). The manna the Father gave the Israelites in the desert provided only temporary nourishment and did not prevent them from dying (v. 49); but those who by faith appropriated the bread of life that comes from heaven would never die in the eternal sense (v. 50). Though both the manna and the Messiah had come from the Father, only the Son could provide and sustain eternal life. Jesus declared that His physical body was the "living bread that came down from heaven" (v. 51). When the Jewish backdrop for this statement is considered, it is clear "the Evangelist has set out to present Jesus as the final realization of Torah itself."[61] The Redeemer foretold that He would sacrifice His body so that others might live. Indeed, anyone who partook of His body—that is, appropriated the eternal life He offered—would live forever.

The audience took Jesus' remarks in a crassly literal sense.[62] This caused an intense argument to erupt among them over the meaning and implication the Savior's teaching. They thought He was talking about cannibalism, when in reality He was referring to people trusting in Him as the crucified and resurrected Lamb of God (v. 52).[63] Jesus did not make it any easier for His offended listeners when He told them that they also had to drink the blood of the Son of Man in order to receive eternal life (v. 53).

---

61. Casselli, "Jesus as eschatological Torah," 32.

62. Based on Stern's examination of rabbinic writings, he concludes that "Jewish understanding allows for symbolic interpretation" of Jesus' statement in John 6:51 (*Jewish New Testament commentary*, 173–74).

63. A less likely option is the view that Jesus giving His "flesh to eat" (John 6:52) is an allusion to taking Communion, or at least to what Communion represents. Burge (*John*) observes that the presence of "eucharistic language" in "John's literary imagery" is only a "secondary" emphasis (199; cf. 201). In point of fact, the Evangelist regards all of history to be "sacramental." This is especially manifest with the Savior's coming to earth. His incarnation "means the genuine appearance of God in history" (30). In a similar vein, Vander Zee (*Christ's baptism*) considers the entire world to be a "sacramental place by virtue of its creation by God" and "its ultimate recreation through the incarnation of Jesus Christ" (11). He is the "new and final sacrament" who offered Himself in "perfect obedience and love to God" (17). Jesus is also the "new human who clothes himself again in the priestly role to which God called humanity in the beginning" (19). Keener (*John*, 1:690) explains that the words of the Evangelist "invite his audience to look to Christ's death itself, not merely those symbols which point to his death." DeSilva (*Introduction*, 429) adds that "John's fundamental preoccupation" is "with the greater 'sacrament,'" namely, "the Word made flesh." Only He, as the eschatological Tanakh, reveals the Godhead and gives believers access to the throne of grace. Also, cf. Calvin, *John*, 1:266–67; Carson, *John*, 277–282; Harris, *John;* Tenney, "John," 9:78; Morris, *John*, 300, 311–15; Westcott, *John*, 113–14; Witherington, *John's wisdom*, 95–97, 150.

The Redeemer's statement about drinking His blood metaphorically referred to the close spiritual union that existed between Himself and His followers. The Savior's Jewish audience found His remarks disgusting, for the law of Moses had prohibited them from ingesting any blood when they ate. The penalty for breaking this law was for the wrongdoer to be treated as an outcast (cf. Lev 7:26–27; 17:10–14; Deut 12:23–24; Acts 15:29). Jesus as Tanakh remained undeterred by whatever offense His teaching may have caused, for the eternal future of all believers was at stake. He promised that at the end of the age, He would resurrect those who received by faith the new life He offered (John 6:54).

For the rest of this discourse, Jesus used a Greek word for "eating" that conveyed the notion of feasting with enjoyment. The idea is that when believers take the Messiah into their innermost being and abide in Him, they do so with great pleasure. To a first-century Jewish audience the real food was the manna in the wilderness. They needed to know that Jesus Himself—His flesh and blood—were the true food and drink necessary to receive eternal life (v. 55). As a result of believing in the efficacy of His atoning sacrifice, they remain in vital spiritual union with Him (v. 56). Although there is a mutual indwelling between the Messiah and His followers, believers must not be confused about their distinctive roles. Jesus is like a vine and His disciples are like branches. Though believers abide in Him and He in them, His disciples still can accomplish nothing apart from Him (cf. 15:5).

In 6:57, Jesus again emphasized His redemptive mission. The Father had sent the Son to give eternal life. Indeed, apart from the Father, the Son had nothing to offer.[64] Likewise, apart from the Lord Jesus, believers are devoid of new life and the spiritual fruit it bears (cf. 15:8, 16). Furthermore, just as the Son lived to do the will of the Father, so too believers lived to do the will of the Son (6:57). At the end of His discourse, Jesus returned to the original demand of His audience. They placed a great emphasis on the manna their ancestors ate in the wilderness, yet all those people eventually died. The manna sustained them only temporarily; but the divine, incarnate Torah, who had come down from heaven and stood before them, offered them eternal life. The challenge was now before Jesus' listeners. Would they partake by believing and living in Him, or would they turn their backs and walk away, rejecting the bread that the Father offered to the entire world (v. 58)?

64. Thompson ("The living Father," 23) clarifies that when the Evangelist refers to God as "the living Father" (John 6:57), the "epithet embodies within it the conviction that as the eternally existent, living God, God alone is the source of all life."

The Varying Responses of the Disciples to Jesus as Torah (John 6:60–71)

A number of those who had been following Jesus objected to His teaching, for they found it difficult to accept (John 6:60). The omniscient Messiah, without being told, was aware of their complaints (v. 61). He noted that if what He had declared upset them, then they would become even more offended over seeing the crucified and resurrected Son of Man ascending in glory to His Father in heaven (v. 62). Paul later noted that the message of the cross was a stumbling block to the Jews and foolishness to the Gentiles; but to all those who believed, the Lord Jesus was the epitome of God's power and wisdom (1 Cor 1:23–24).[65] Earlier, people asked Jesus what works they should perform to win God's approval and the eternal life He offered (John 6:28). In response, Jesus emphasized the necessity of believing in Him (v. 29). He built on that truth by noting that human power, will, and initiative were ineffective in bringing about regeneration (cf. Phil 3:3). It was the Father, sovereignly working through the Spirit, who made the heavenly new birth a reality (cf. John 1:13; 3:3, 5–8). These truths, as reflected in what the Torah of God declared at Capernaum, were spirit-giving and life-producing (6:63).

The Evangelist noted that from the start of Jesus' earthly ministry, He knew who would reject Him, including the person who would betray Him—Judas Iscariot (v. 64).[66] Rather than avoid this sobering prospect, the Messiah openly confronted the unbelief of His detractors. He saw them as living proof that only those whom the Father had permitted actually received the ability to trust in the Son for eternal life (v. 65). Because of what the Logos had taught, many would-be disciples quit following Him and even deserted Him (v. 66).[67] Since this development represented

---

65. Cf. Boismard, *Moses or Jesus*, 72–84.

66. Judas Iscariot is identified as the son of Simon (John 6:71; 13:2, 36). Most likely, the term "Iscariot" refers to the town of Kerioth, which was located near Hebron in southern Judah (Josh 15:25). Among the 12 disciples, Judas was their treasurer. He carried the moneybag and sometimes would steal from it (John 12:6). The three Synoptic Gospels detail how Judas plotted with the Jewish leaders to bring about Jesus' arrest. Judas received a payment of 30 silver coins (Matt 26:14–16; Mark 14:10–11; Luke 22:3–6) for leading the authorities to Jesus (John 18:1–2).

67. Domeris ("Confession of Peter," 167) uses the phrase "the scandal of the incarnation" to refer to the "paradox of a human agent" such as Jesus performing "divine deeds," making "divine claims," and experiencing either acceptance or rejection. For an overview of the differing public responses to the signs Jesus performed, cf. Umoh, *The plot to kill Jesus*, 166–171. He notes that Jesus, by means of His signs, "interacts with almost every cadre of society," with some people responding positively to Him and others negatively (170).

a turning point in the Redeemer's ministry, He asked the Twelve whether they also wanted to abandon Him (v. 67).[68]

Peter, perhaps taking on the role of a spokesperson for the rest (cf. Matt 16:16; Mark 8:27; Luke 9:20),[69] noted that there was no one else like the Prophet from Nazareth. Jesus alone heralded a message that genuinely offered eternal life (John 6:68). After spending several years of ministry with Jesus, the Twelve (except for Judas Iscariot) were convinced that the Son was the Holy One of God (v. 69; cf. Mark 1:24; Luke 4:34; Acts 2:27). As such, Jesus' origin is divine. He is absolutely perfect and infinitely transcends all that is fallen and finite. Only He is deserving of worship and adoration, for He alone is utterly sacred and set apart as the Creator and Lord of the universe (cf. Isa 41:14; 43:3; 47:4).[70] The truthfulness of Peter's affirmation notwithstanding, Jesus affirmed that one disciple among the twelve He had chosen was a "devil" (John 6:70; cf. 13:2, 27). The Greek noun is *diabolos* and literally means "slanderer" or "accuser."[71] It refers to an evil entity who opposes God, His will, and His people. Those who sought to thwart the Son and His redemptive mission operated as agents of Satan, the Holy One's doomed arch-rival (cf. Matt 4:1–11; 16:23; Mark 1:13; 8:33; Luke 4:1–13). Judas Iscariot, while being one of the Twelve, planned to betray the Savior.

Conclusion

The episodes from John 5 and 6 portray Jesus as the Tanakh of God who is both Lord of the Sabbath and the one who satisfies the deepest spiritual needs of believers. With Pentecost as the most likely backdrop for the incident involving the Messiah's healing of the paralytic, God's issuance of the Mosaic law on Mount Sinai would have also loomed large in the

---

68. Cf. Sanders and Mastin, *John*, 198.

69. Cf. Borgen, "John 6," 286; Calvin, *John*, 1:278.

70. Domeris ("Confession of Peter") stresses that the title, "Holy One of God" (John 6:69), when applied to Jesus, "sets [Him] apart from all that is profane" (157). As God's chosen and authorized agent, the Messiah represents the "sphere of the holy" (159). He is more than simply a "worker of miracles"; He is a "teacher with authority" who heralds a "new message to the people" (160; cf. Mark 1:27). He also champions the cause of God (161). Jesus, as "God's special Holy One," is "destined to judge the world" (162). The "Wisdom of God," after coming to earth to reveal Himself to the world, ascended to His throne in heaven (164). Accordingly, when Peter declared that Jesus had "the words of eternal life" (John 6:68), Domeris maintains the disciple was responding to Jesus as the incarnation of wisdom (163; cf. Prov 8:35; Bar 3:37—4:1; 1 Enoch 42:1–3).

71. Danker, *A Greek-English lexicon*, 226.

minds of the Jewish practitioners attending the annual festival. On the one hand, they revered the famed lawgiver and leader of their ancestors in the wilderness. On the other hand, they encountered the embodiment of the Torah, about whom Moses wrote.

The dispute over the Son's messianic claims and authority came into sharp relief as a result of His enabling the paralyzed man to walk. While the Father approved this act of mercy, the religious hierarchy did not, for it clashed with their rabbinic tradition; and since the latter was accorded the same respect as the Torah itself, violating the oral law was considered as much of an offense as transgressing the commands recorded in the Pentateuch. While the authorities remained legalistic and reductionistic in their interpretation of the law, the one who is the enfleshment of the Tanakh conveyed the divine perspective by urging the former paralytic to sin no more.

What particularly enraged the Messiah's critics was His outrageously sounding claims. He maintained the right to heal on the Sabbath and to presume to urge God's people to live righteously. Perhaps worst of all to the religious leaders was the hubris they felt stood behind the Son as Torah's claim to have God as His Father. To Jesus' opponents, this was tantamount to claiming equality with God; and since they rejected such an assertion, they accused the Son of blasphemy, a charge they leveled more than once against Him. Just as slanderous to their ears was the Messiah's assertion to raise the dead and judge all humankind. While Moses and other luminaries of the Old Testament era acted as judges and arbitrators within the covenant community, they never claimed the level and extent of authority Jesus maintained belonged to Him.

Even when many would-be disciples abandoned Him, Jesus as Torah remained unwavering in declaring the necessity of spiritually appropriating Him in order to have eternal life. His decision was confirmed by the affirmation of Peter, who perhaps spoke for the rest of Jesus' loyal disciples. The fisherman from Galilee affirmed the Son to be the Holy One of God. Even the betrayal of a renegade follower such Judas Iscariot could not undermine the conviction of the other eleven regarding the Savior's divine origin, holy life, and infinite authority. Moreover, the diabolical schemes of the evil one to somehow thwart the Son in His redemptive mission would not prevent Him from securing eternal life for all who would put their trust in Him as the Light of the world.

6

Jesus as Torah in John 7–9

Introduction

Tabernacles is the major event that forms the backdrop of John 7 through 9. Despite the growing threat of being arrested, the Torah of God still attended the Jewish festival. In addition, Jesus' decision to teach in the temple courts enraged the religious hierarchy and incited squabbling among the laity concerning the Messiah's identity. There were disputes over His testimony, the paternity of His critics, and the legitimacy of His claims. Not even His miraculous healing of a man born blind resolved the sharp disagreement regarding the true status of the Son; but all who objectively considered the evidence came away convinced that Jesus, as the embodiment of Light, provides the Spirit of truth in abundance to the community of the redeemed.[1]

Jesus as Torah Ministers at the Festival of Tabernacles (John 7:1—8:59)

Jesus as Torah Attending the Festival Secretly (John 7:1–13)

After giving His discourse at the synagogue in Capernaum, Jesus spent approximately the next six months traveling around Galilee. Because the Jewish authorities were plotting to kill Him, He did not travel in Judea (John 7:1). It would not be until the Jewish Festival of Tabernacles in October, AD 29, that Jesus traveled to Jerusalem (v. 2). This feast (also known as Sukkoth, Ingathering, Shelters, Booths, and Tents) was celebrat-

---

1. Bruce (*John*, 13) asks the probing question, "Whom are the arguments deployed in the great debate of [the Evangelist's] central chapters designed to convince?" In part, it is "the religious leaders in Jerusalem," who engage in a "sustained debate" with Jesus over His messianic identity and claims.

ed in autumn after the harvest. The observance lasted seven days, making it the most extended festival of the Jewish year. During this time, participants lived in tents or shelters made from branches and leaves. It was a sacred season when God's people commemorated the way the Lord graciously provided for the Israelites during their years of wilderness wandering. The feast was also a time to thank God for allowing the year's harvest to be completed (cf. Lev 23:33–43; Num 29:12–39; Deut 16:13–17).

Evidently, in the fall of AD 29, Jesus was intermittently working as a carpenter with His brothers (in reality, His half-brothers).[2] As the Festival of Tabernacles drew near, they urged Him (perhaps with a bit of sarcasm) to leave the area and go to Jerusalem so that His disciples could see Him perform more miracles (John 7:3). The siblings reasoned that no Jewish messianic figure who sought to become well-known operated in the relative obscurity of a distant region such as Galilee. In order to make a convincing case for one's divine status, it was necessary to perform signs and wonders openly in the capital of the Jewish state (v. 4). The brothers of the Lord Jesus did not offer this advice because they accepted His messianic claims, for as verse 5 explains, they had not yet trusted in Him for eternal life. It would only be after His resurrection from the dead that they would become His disciples (cf. Acts 1:14; 1 Cor 15:7).

The Son knew that He had to operate in harmony with the Father's redemptive plan. In this case, the appointed time for the Redeemer's death on the cross had not yet come.[3] Thus, it was not the right moment for Him to openly travel to Jerusalem.[4] Things were different, though, for His siblings. They could immediately make the journey without fear of experiencing retaliation from the Jewish authorities in Jerusalem (John 7:6). Jesus noted that the people of the world did not hate His brothers, for the latter identified with those who rejected the Son's messianic claims and opposed His redemptive mission (cf. John 15:18–19; 1 John 5:19). In contrast, the unsaved hated the Tanakh of God, for He accused them of doing evil (John 7:7). Regardless of whether their works were characterized by injustice, immorality, or iniquity, the moral governor of the universe declared all such activities to be wicked (cf. Rom 3:9–18).

---

2. Cf. Goldsmith, *Gospel of John*.

3. Köstenberger (*John*, 230) notes the "well-established Jewish belief that every man had his time" (cf. Eccl 3:1; Eccl Rab. 3:1); also, cf. Haenchen, *John 2*, 7.

4. O'Day ("John," 9:616–17) comments that "Jesus' self-revelation at any given moment belongs to the larger framework of the time of glorification" through His "death, burial, resurrection, and ascension" into heaven.

In light of this circumstance, Jesus declined to attend the festival in the overt way proposed by His brothers. Instead, the Son would make His appearance in a manner approved by His heavenly Father (John 7:8). Thus, Jesus waited for a while in Galilee (v. 9) before making the journey south in secret and staying out of public view (v. 10). Meanwhile, at the Festival of Tabernacles, the religious leaders actively searched for the Nazarene. This included asking whether any pilgrims had seen Him (v. 11). The laity (who were from all parts of the Roman empire) debated whether Jesus was the Messiah or a fraud. Some asserted He was a good person, while others claimed He deceived the common people (v. 12). No one, however, spoke openly about Jesus, for they feared the possibility of getting into trouble with the Jewish hierarchy who opposed Jesus (v. 13).

Jesus as Torah Teaching Openly at the Festival (John 7:14–24)

According to Deuteronomy 16:13, Tabernacles lasted seven days. By the time the festival was nearly half over, a large number of pilgrims would be present. Accordingly, the Tanakh of God strategically chose this moment to go into the temple courts and begin teaching any who would listen to Him speak (John 7:14). Though the Jewish authorities opposed the Messiah, they were nonetheless astonished by His instruction from the Mosaic law. They noticed that while He never received advanced training in a rabbinic school, He demonstrated profound knowledge, understanding, and wisdom (v. 15; cf. Luke 2:47).[5] Supposedly, the only schooling Jesus ever received was that provided at the local synagogue in Nazareth, where He spent His childhood.[6] According to Matthew 7:28–29 (cf. Mark

---

5. Köstenberger (*John*, 233) observes that in Jesus' day, "it was not enough for a Jew to master the written Scriptures or even the oral law; formal rabbinic training became the norm." Nonetheless, as Haenchen (*John 2*, 13) remarked, "Jesus proves to be an effective haggadist, although he did not enjoy rabbinic training; cf. Brown, *John*, 312.

6. During Jesus' time growing up in Nazareth, He learned the carpenter's trade (Mark 6:3). He also continued His religious studies in the prescribed Jewish fashion. With reference to Jesus' human nature, He physically matured and became strong (Luke 2:40). Indeed, Jesus experienced normal development in body, mind, spiritual awareness, and social acceptance. All these things occurred with the perfection that is suited to each phase of life through which He passed (vv. 40, 52). As Jesus gained knowledge through observation, asking questions, and seeking instruction, He progressively became filled with wisdom (vs. 40). Jesus' wisdom was more than mere intellectual knowledge. It included the ability to use the knowledge He acquired to the best advantage. Though He did not attend a rabbinical college, the Messiah received a common education, which was primarily religious and which prepared Him for the practical duties of life. During Jesus' adolescence, He kept

1:22), at the end of Jesus' discourse called the Sermon on the Mount, the crowds were amazed that such an unschooled person could teach so powerfully and persuasively. Unlike the legal experts of the day, who cited other scholars to support their statements, Jesus taught as the one who is the culmination of the Torah.[7] Also, because His authority was divine, it not only exceeded that of the legalists of the day, but also that of Moses, Israel's noteworthy lawgiver.[8]

The question the religious leaders asked in John 7:15 was meant to openly challenge Jesus' authority and call into question His qualifications as a rabbi. In response, Jesus noted that He did not conjure up His teaching; rather, His message came directly from God the Father, who had sent the Son as His emissary (v. 16; cf. 12:49). More generally, regardless of whether one is considering the Old or New Testaments, all of it is God-breathed (cf. 2 Tim 3:16–17; 2 Pet 1:20–21). The Messiah was confident that everyone who genuinely sought to do the will of God would recognize the divine origin of Jesus' teaching (John 7:17). The Son explained that those, like the religious elite of the day, who presumed to speak on their own authority, sought to obtain honor for themselves. In contrast, the one who fulfills all the types and prophecies recorded in the law[9] sought to honor the Father, who sent Him. In turn, this proved that what the Son declared was true and that He was honest, not a liar (v. 18). Put another

---

the law perfectly, for He was without sin (2 Cor 5:21; Heb 4:15; 7:26). He also observed the religious festivals and rituals of the Jews, for He said that He had come to fulfill the Mosaic law, not to break it (Matt 5:17). Jesus evidently did not do any miraculous works in the years preceding His public ministry. He lived a quiet, ordinary life, fulfilling His domestic, professional, and religious duties until the time when His Father summoned Him to complete His redemptive mission.

7. Carson (*John*, 312) remarks that "one of the consequences of studying for years in the rabbinical centres was the tendency to substantiate every pronouncement by appealing to precedent, to earlier rabbinic judgments." Indeed, failure "to do so might indicate a certain arrogance, an independence of spirit in danger of drifting from the weight of tradition."

8. Lioy, *The Decalogue in the Sermon on the Mount*, 186. Harstine (*Moses*, 46–47) points out that "in the first century," the identity of Moses was "inextricably linked to his giving of the law." Additionally, the "mere mention of his name simultaneously recalls the two themes of Jewish law and religious authority." Stern (*Jewish New Testament commentary*, 176) carries the discussion further when he indicates that Jesus not only had "wide knowledge of both biblical and traditional materials," but also "wisdom from God transcending academic credentials."

9. Contra Lindars (*John*, 287), who maintains that Jesus "supersedes the Law" because He is the Son of God. As Ratzinger (*Jesus of Nazareth*, 235) notes, the Savior "does not break the Torah, but brings its whole meaning to light and wholly fulfills it." Similarly, Lenski (*St. John's Gospel*, 556) asserts, "Moses upholds Jesus, and Jesus upholds Moses."

Jesus as Torah in John 7–9

way, Jesus was a person of integrity in whom there was no trace of unrighteousness. Indeed, the Son was the source and quintessence of the truth that characterized all three persons of the Godhead (cf. 1:14, 17; 3:33; 7:28; 8:26; 14:6, 17; 15:26; 16:13; 17:3; 18:37).

The looming issue was the guilt of the religious hierarchy, who sought to kill Jesus, an innocent person (7:19). The irony is that while the elite prided themselves on their possession of and devotion to the Mosaic law (cf. Ps 103:7; Rom 3:2; 9:4), they were violating the commandment against murder (cf. Exod 20:13; Deut 5:17; Rom 2:17–29).[10] Furthermore, their intended victim was the one to whom the entire law bore witness.[11] At the this point, some pilgrims in the onlooking crowd—who would not necessarily be aware of the plans of the Jewish leaders—accused Jesus of having a demon in Him (cf. Matt 12:24–32; Mark 3:22–30; John 8:48–52; 10:19–21). The general populace thought He was crazy to imagine that anyone would try to kill Him (John 7:20). The real issue was not Jesus' sanity, but His decision to go against rabbinic tradition by healing a paralytic on the Sabbath (v. 21; cf. 5:1–15). The miracle He performed represented a challenge to the legalists who claimed they operated in the authority of Moses.

The Torah of God directed the attention of His listeners to an inconsistency. The patriarchs began the tradition of circumcising male infants on the eighth day after birth, and Moses in the law codified the practice (7:22; cf. Gen 17:1–14; 21:4; Exod 12:44, 48; Lev 12:3). In some situations, the appointed time to perform the rite of circumcision fell on the Sabbath. Rabbinic Judaism took this directive so seriously that they believed observing it had greater precedence than refraining from doing any form of work on the Sabbath.[12] Given the legitimacy of this course of action, Jesus questioned why the religious hierarchy were irate over His decision to heal a lame man on the Sabbath (John 7:23). Expressed differently, if the less important deed was permissible on the Sabbath (namely,

---

10. Keener (*John*, 1:714) explains that for "early Judaism in general, including the early Jewish Christians, the Law was the supreme written embodiment or description of God's will."

11. Harstine (*Moses*, 67) maintains that the choice facing Jesus' interlocutors was not between Himself and Moses, through whom God mediated the law, for the teaching of both Jesus and Moses had "the same source." Instead, the real choice was "between obeying the traditions of the rabbis and fulfilling the purpose of the law"; cf. Fernando, *Relationship between law and love*, 78.

12. As noted by Keener (*John*, 1:716), a "well-attested principle of rabbinic ethics" is that "some commandments must override some other commandments." Indeed, "matters such as which rules took priority were too critical to be left to a moment's personal discretion"; cf. Bruce, *John*, 177; Carson, *John*, 315–16; Thomas, "Fourth Gospel," 173–74.

removing the foreskin from the organ of procreation on a male infant), then why was the more important act considered illegal on the same day (namely, curing an invalid's entire body)?[13] The Messiah urged His listeners to stop judging Him by mere external standards and begin evaluating His words and works by the true standard reflected in God's law (v. 24; cf. Deut 16:18–19; Isa 11:3–4; Zech 7:9). In this case, displays of mercy were legal and sometimes necessary to perform on the Sabbath (cf. Matt 12:1–14; Mark 2:23—3:6; Luke 6:1–11).

Squabbling over the Identity of Jesus as Torah (John 7:25–36)

Some of the residents living in Jerusalem began asking one another whether Jesus was the person the religious authorities were seeking to arrest and put to death (John 7:25). They were amazed that the Jewish leaders had not yet taken any overt action to put a stop to the Nazarene's public teaching. These befuddled onlookers wondered how likely it was that the experts in the law accepted Jesus' messianic claims and authority (v. 26). It was well known that Jesus came from Galilee (cf. vv. 41, 52). Some were convinced that the Old Testament did not reveal the place where the Messiah would originate (v. 27; cf. Isa 53:8; Mal 3:1).[14] In contrast, others held the view that the Messiah would be a descendant of David and born in Bethlehem[15] (John 7:42; cf. 1 Sam 20:6; 2 Sam 7:12–16; Ps 89:3–4; Mic 5:2, 4; Matt 2:5–6; Luke 2:1–7).[16] Both groups felt they had legitimate reasons to re-

13. Cf. Lenski, *St. John's Gospel*, 553–554.

14. Harris (*John*) points out that some of the religious experts of the Second Temple period of Judaism held to the "idea that the origin of the Messiah [was] a mystery." For instance, Harris mentions the teaching of Rabbi Zera in the Babylonian Talmud (Mishnah Sanhedrin 97a): "Three come unawares: Messiah, a found article, and a scorpion" (cf. 1 Enoch 48:6; 4 Ezra 13:51–52).

15. Bethlehem is located on the edge of the Judean desert about five mile southwest of Jerusalem. It is also situated on a high ridge of mountains about 2,500 feet above sea level, near the main road linking Hebron and Egypt. The climate of Bethlehem is somewhat Mediterranean; however, the town's higher elevation moderates the summer temperatures it experiences. This milder climate, along with fertile surrounding hills, makes the area ideal for growing grapes and figs and for grazing sheep and goats. Bethlehem was the burial place of Rachel, the wife of Jacob (Gen 35:19). The city was also the setting for much of the Book of Ruth. Bethlehem later became the ancestral home of David, and it was there that Samuel the prophet anointed David as Saul's successor (1 Sam 16:1, 13; 17:12). King Rehoboam subsequently rebuilt and fortified the city (2 Chron 11:5-6). Micah 5:2 foretold that Bethlehem would be the birthplace of the Messiah, and Luke 2:11 records the fulfillment of this prophecy.

16. Meeks (*The prophet-king*, 35) states "there is evidence that Micah 5:1–5 was inter-

ject Jesus' claim to have come down from heaven and to have supreme authority over the law as the final expression of God's Tanakh.

While still teaching in the temple courts, Jesus directly answered His critics by drawing attention to their superficial awareness of His origins.[17] On a purely earthly level, He lived for a while in Nazareth of Galilee; but on a spiritual level, the Son—in His preincarnate state—eternally lived with the Father and the Spirit in heaven. The Father, who is true, sent the Son to earth and authorized Him to minister the truth to others (cf. 1 Enoch 48:6–7; 2 Bar 29:3; 4 Ezra 7:28; 13:51–52). Consequently, those who rejected the Son also rejected the Father and showed that they did not know either member of the Godhead (John 7:28–29). In response, some of the religious leaders tried to have Jesus arrested; but the attempt failed because the divinely appointed time for the Son to bring glory to the Father through the Crucifixion had not yet arrived (v. 30).[18] Despite the confrontation surrounding Jesus, many of the pilgrims in the crowd put their faith in Him as the Messiah. They reasoned that all the miraculous signs Jesus performed validated His claim to be the Son of God (v. 31).

The Pharisees were angered by the fact that so many in the crowd were whispering positive things about Jesus. For that reason, they joined with their perennial religious and political rivals, the chief priests (who were primarily Sadducees), to dispatch some temple guards (who were religiously trained Levites) to arrest the Nazarene (v. 32). The Messiah told these agents of the ruling council, or Sanhedrin, that He would be among them for a relatively short while longer and then He would return to the one who sent Him (v. 33). Jesus was referring to His upcoming crucifixion, resurrection from the dead, and ascension to heaven. He explained to the police that even though their superiors might try to search for Him, they would do so in vain, for they would be unable to enter heaven (v.

---

preted messianically in relatively old rabbinic traditions."

17. Beasley-Murray (*John*, 122) observes that in the exchange between Jesus and His detractors, the author of the Fourth Gospel did not "represent Jesus as standing pathetically before the bar of his people and their rulers." Instead, the Tanakh of God responded to the accusations of His critics by raising the "question of *their* integrity." He also confronts "them with a revelation that demands an answer from them." In short, "*His* trial becomes *their* trial!" (emphasis is his). Burge (*John*, 178) explains that this phenomenon was in keeping with the way the Jewish court system functioned. In that era, "defendants did not simply prove their innocence and thus end the trial." Because the judicial process sought to "uncover the truth," disputants who put forward trumped-up charges "in court could find themselves placed in the defense and subject to serious jeopardy." In a reversal of fortunes, the penalties they sought to "inflict on their opponent now could turn back on them."

18. Cf. Bock, *Jesus*, 468.

34). Instead of arresting Jesus, the temple guards returned to the religious leaders empty-handed and reported what they heard Him say (cf. v. 45). The Jewish authorities puzzled over Jesus' statements and interpreted them in a completely literal manner. They wondered whether He planned to leave Palestine, travel to foreign locales of the Roman Empire where ethnic Jews lived among Gentiles, and teach those who followed Greek customs, whether Jews or Gentile proselytes (v. 35). Undoubtedly, such a thought was objectionable to the elitist hierarchy in Jerusalem. Perhaps this explains why they continued to ponder without any success the exact meaning of Jesus' statements (v. 36).

Differing Responses to the Declaration Made by Jesus as Torah (John 7:37–52)

In that day, one prominent ritual the people performed during the Jewish Festival of Tabernacles included a ceremonial drawing of water. This commemorated the Lord's provision of water to the Israelites in the desert (cf. Num 20:2–13). Another prominent ritual was a ceremonial lighting of lamps.[19] The first ritual formed the context for Jesus' statement in John 7:37–38, while the second ritual is the backdrop for His declaration recorded in 8:12. According to 7:37, Jesus waited until the last day of the feast, which was the greatest day of the festival, to make an announcement. According to Deuteronomy 16:13, Tabernacles lasted seven days; but according to Leviticus 23:36, there was a holy assembly on the eighth day. It is unclear whether the seventh or eighth day was the climax of the feast.[20] Mishnah Sukkah 4:1 indicates that the rituals involving water and lights did not continue beyond the seventh day, so perhaps this is what John meant. In any case, the Torah of God stood (rather than sat, which most rabbis did when they taught) and declared in a loud voice that whoever had spiritual thirst should come to Him and drink. After all, He was the spiritual rock from which the water flowed to nourish the Israelites who were wandering in the Sinai desert (cf. Exod 17:6; Num 20:7–11; Neh 9:15; Pss 78:15–16, 20; 105:40–41; 1 Cor 10:4).[21]

---

19. Cf. Beasley-Murray, *John*, 106.
20. Cf. Tenney, "John," 9:86.
21. Glasson (*Moses*, 50) discusses "the Rabbinic evidence for a connection between the water ceremony" observed during the Festival of Tabernacles and "the rock of the wilderness" (in particular, 58–59); cf. Hanson, "John's use of Scripture," 366; Ratzinger, *Jesus of Nazareth*, 244, 264–65; Westcott, *John*, 123.

Since the crowds had a tendency to take Jesus' metaphorical statements in a narrow, concrete sense, He clarified what He meant. The Savior was inviting all to put their faith in Him. When they did, He pledged that from within such believers (as opposed to the view that Jesus was referring to Himself in John 7:38) would flow rivers of living water.[22] This statement does not represent an exact quotation from any particular Old Testament text.[23] Perhaps Jesus was referring to several verses.[24] There are some that associate water with the gift of the Spirit at the end of the age (cf. Isa 32:15; 44:3; Ezek 36:25–27; 39:29; Joel 2:28–32). Other passages metaphorically refer to water in connection with the blessings of the messianic age (cf. Isa 12:3; 55:1; 58:11; Ezek 47:1–12; Zech 13:1; 14:8).[25]

Regardless, the thrust of the Messiah's promise is that in fulfillment of the types and prophecies recorded in the Old Testament, the Holy Spirit would be abundantly present in believers, benefiting both them and those around them (John 7:38). The water "anticipates the eschatological means of purification" through the permanent indwelling of the Spirit.[26] Verse 39 is the apostle's parenthetical note in which he explained that, prior to the day of Pentecost, the era of the Spirit had not yet arrived. Once the Son had experienced His death, resurrection, and ascension in glory to the Father, the presence and power of the Spirit would be manifested in a way not yet seen to that point in salvation history (cf. Acts 2:1–4).

Some pilgrims in the crowd who heard Jesus speak concluded that He had to be the eschatological Prophet about whom Moses foretold in Deuteronomy 18:15 and 18 (John 7:40; cf. Acts 3:22).[27] While some were convinced of Jesus' messianic claims, others doubted whether these could

---

22. Contra O'Day, "John," 9:623; cf. Balfour, "John's use of the Scriptures," 369–70, 374; Bock, *Jesus*, 459–60; Carson, *John*, 323–25; Köstenberger, *John*, 240–41; Morris, *John*, 374–78.

23. Cf. Lindars, *John*, 298.

24. Keener (*John*, 1:728) affirms the possibility that the Evangelist "elsewhere midrashically blends various texts and that he is following that practice here"; cf. Fernando, *Relationship between law and love*, 130.

25. Cf. Beasley-Murray, *John*, 116.

26. Ng, *Water symbolism in John*, 68; cf. Bruce, *John*, 182. In a similar vein, Calvin (*John*, 1:308) remarked that "the perpetuity, as well as the abundance, of the gifts and graces of the Holy Spirit, is here promised to us."

27. Köstenberger (*John*, 241) points to a statement found in Eccl Rab. 1:9 about the "eschatological successor to Moses": "As the former redeemer made a well [of water] to rise [Num 21:17–18], so will the latter Redeemer bring up water [Joel 4:18]." Whitacre (*John*) builds on this thought by noting that "Jesus' words and deeds reveal him to be the expected one."

be true of someone from Galilee (John 7:41). After all, they reasoned, the Old Testament foretold that the Anointed One would be a descendant of David and born in Bethlehem (v. 42). In point of fact, all the messianic prophecies recorded in the Hebrew sacred writings were fulfilled in Jesus as Tanakh. The attendees, of course, did not realize this and remained divided over the Nazarene's true identity (v. 43).[28] While some advocated His arrest, none attempted to do so at that time (v. 44).

The chief priests and Pharisees interrogated the temple guards as to why they failed to arrest Jesus (v. 45). In response, the police explained that they had never heard anyone teach with such profound insight (v. 46).[29] The normal procedure was for the chief priests to take the lead in reprimanding subordinates for failing to comply with their orders; but the Pharisees were so annoyed by what they heard that they mockingly asked whether Jesus had also fooled the temple guards (v. 47).[30] The religious leaders showed utter contempt for the police and the laity when they rhetorically asked whether any members of the ruling council had put their faith in Jesus as the Messiah (v. 48). Then the elitists claimed that the riffraff among the pilgrims were ignorant of the law, foolish for being deceived by the itinerant preacher, and faced damnation for being under God's curse (v. 49; cf. Deut 28:15).[31]

Perhaps to the chagrin of the religious leaders, Nicodemus was one of many among the Jewish hierarchy who had become secret followers

---

28. Meeks (*The prophet-king*, 33) comments that the miraculous signs Jesus performed "invariably produce a division between those who 'believe' and those who become hostile toward Jesus and seek to kill him."

29. Teeple (*Mosaic eschatological prophet*, 22) points to a tradition in Gen Rab. 98:9 that in the coming age, "the Messiah will make clear the words of Torah and give teaching." The idea seems to be that when the Messiah comes, He "will interpret the Torah . . . and also give new teaching." The Evangelist regarded Jesus of Nazareth as the fulfillment of this and other similar Jewish expectations.

30. Cf. Beasley-Murray, *John*, 119; Morris, *John*, 382.

31. Whitacre (*John*) clarifies that the religious leaders' derogatory opinion of the throng "corresponds to the rabbinic view of the '*am ha'arets*," a Hebrew phrase that means "the people of the land." In the period of Second Temple Judaism, the rabbis used the phrase as a shorthand designation "for those who [did] not approach the law in the same way as" the elitists. The latter immersed themselves in the study of the Torah in order to devise "meticulous interpretations for how to fulfill its commandments." Allegedly, those who were ignorant of the written and oral law failed to heed its injunctions, especially the "form of ritual purity promoted by the scribes and Pharisees." In turn, the people of the land were declared to be under "God's curse" (cf. Deut 27:15–26). The Fourth Gospel reveals that Jesus rejected this "understanding of faithfulness to the Torah"; cf. Beyler, *Torah*, 67–68; Stern, *Jewish New Testament commentary*, 176, 180.

Jesus as Torah in John 7–9

of Jesus (cf. John 12:42). Nicodemus also happened to be present in the temple courts where Jesus was teaching (7:50). Nicodemus pointed out that the law required a formal hearing to determine the innocence or guilt of the accused before they were condemned (v. 51; cf. Deut 1:16–17; Exod Rab. 21:3). In short, the elitists, by their statements and actions, had violated one of the most foundational principles of justice in the law they claimed to revere, know, and uphold. Their sarcastic response to Nicodemus further disclosed their ignorance of the Tanakh. Allegedly, no prophet whom God sent ever came from such a contemptible place as Galilee, and certainly not the eschatological Prophet foretold in the Torah (John 7:52). In reality, though, the Lord called Jonah, who was from Gath Hepher in Galilee (cf. 2 Kgs 14:25), and Nahum, who was from Elkosh in the northern kingdom of Israel (cf. Nah 1:1), to prophesy to the people of Nineveh.[32] Also, there was nothing specific in the Old Testament that prohibited God from commissioning other spokespersons from this region to be His duly authorized emissaries (cf. Matt 2:23).[33]

Overcoming an Attempt to Entrap Jesus as Torah (John 7:53—8:11)

The pericope of the woman caught in adultery was most likely an independent or oral tradition that did not originally appear in the Fourth Gospel. In terms of the external evidence, the earliest and best Greek manuscripts omit the narrative. Other manuscripts and early translations locate the pericope elsewhere, specifically, after Luke 21:38, after 24:53, after John 7:36, or after 21:25. With respect to the internal evidence, the setting, grammar, and vocabulary of the pericope differ considerably in style and motif from the rest of the Fourth Gospel (but have some affinities with expressions and constructions found in the Gospel of Luke).[34] These observations notwithstanding, the narrative is possibly an authentic witness of apostolic origin to an episode that might have occurred sometime during Jesus' earthly ministry.[35] It stands as a powerful example of the Messiah's compassion for the lost.

---

32. Cf. Lenski, *St. John's Gospel*, 591; Lindars, *John*, 305; Schnackenburg, *John*, 2:161.

33. According to Harris (*John*), the Babylonian Talmud states, "There was not a tribe in Israel from which there did not come prophets" (Bavli Sukkah 27b).

34. Cf. Barrett, *St. John*, 589–591; Beasley-Murray, *John*, 143–44; Brown, *John*, 335–36; Burge, "A specific problem," 141–48; Köstenberger, *John*, 245–49; Morris, *John*, 778–79; Witherington, *John's wisdom*, 164–65.

35. Cf. Bock, *Jesus*, 461–462; Borchert, John 1–11, 225, 369; Harris, *John;* Tenney, *John*, 138; Tenney, "John," 9:89.

John 7:53 records that when some sort of meeting or encounter involving Jesus had ended, all those who were present went home. The Savior, however, spent the night on the Mount of Olives. This ridge of hills extending about 1.8 miles in a north-south direction is located directly east of Jerusalem and the Kidron Valley. The Mount of Olives is about 2,700 feet above Mediterranean Sea level and overlooks the area where the Herodian temple complex once stood. In ancient times, extensive olive groves covered the gently sloping hills and provided a convenient getaway spot for the residents of Jerusalem. Jesus and His followers would customarily travel through and on occasion meet in the orchards (cf. Luke 22:39). Most notably, on the night Judas Iscariot betrayed Jesus to the Jewish and Roman authorities, the Savior and the rest of the Twelve were in an orchard called Gethsemane (cf. Matt 26:36; Mark 14:32). Perhaps it was sometime during the last week of Jesus' life, before His crucifixion in the spring of AD 30, that the incident involving the adulteress occurred (cf. Luke 21:37–38). If so, it would place the event about six months after Jesus' ministry in the courts of the Jerusalem temple during the Festival of Tabernacles in October, AD 29.

John 8:2 says that it was early the following morning when the Messiah returned to the temple courts. Upon His arrival, a crowd gathered around Him. Then, as was typical of rabbis in that day, Jesus sat down and began to teach the people. While the eternal Tanakh spoke, the experts in the Mosaic law (or scribes) and Pharisees brought a woman whom they had caught in the act of adultery and forced her to stand in front of the crowd (vv. 3–4). Evidently, the religious leaders allowed her male partner to escape. This suggests the authorities intended to use the public shaming of the woman as a pretext for tricking Jesus into saying something His opponents could later use against Him. The religious experts noted that the Mosaic law required adulterers to be stoned for their transgression (v. 5; cf. Lev 20:10; Deut 22:22–24). In reality, the Pentateuch only required stoning when the crime involved a man and a betrothed virgin who alleged to have been sexually violated in the town where she lived. Otherwise, the law left the method of execution unspecified.

The scribes and Pharisees asked Jesus what He thought should be done with the accused. If the Messiah declared the woman should be executed by stoning, this would put Him at odds with the civil authorities, since they did not permit the religious leaders to enact the death penalty (cf. John 18:31). In contrast, if Jesus as Torah had advocated the release of the accused, He would appear to be at odds with the Mosaic law. Either option would enable His opponents to charge Him with advocating an objectionable course of action. The Messiah, however, deftly avoided stepping into their trap. His response involved stooping down and using His fingers to write in the dirt on the ground (8:6).[36] Despite much conjecture, the text does not indicate what Jesus wrote.[37] When the agitators kept demanding Him to answer their question, He stood back up and invited anyone who had never sinned to throw the first stone (v. 7; cf. Lev 24:14; Deut 13:9; 17:7). Then Jesus stooped down again and resumed writing in the dirt (John 8:8). In this way, Jesus affirmed the validity of the Tanakh and neutralized the threat posed by His would-be judges (cf. v. 15). None of these discredited antagonists could claim they were without any sin (cf. Exod 23:1; Jer 17:13).

Perhaps as the episode unfolded, the accusers began to pick up some nearby stones; however, upon hearing the Savior's response, they dropped these objects and began to leave. The oldest members of the group might have been the first to slip away, perhaps feeling frustrated and chagrined. Eventually, only Jesus remained with the woman, who had been left standing (John 8:9). Next, the perfection of the gift of the Torah stood up again and asked the woman where her accusers had gone (v. 10). She affirmed that none of them remained to condemn her for her transgression. Jesus likewise would not do so; instead, He directed her to abandon her life of sin (v. 11). It is not hard to imagine that the forgiven woman was filled with gratitude for the opportunity of a fresh start to live in a virtuous and upright manner, presumably as a follower of the Savior. As a result of this incident, Jesus demonstrated one way in which He is the light of God's redemptive truth that shines in the darkness of human sin (cf. 1:5). Centuries earlier, the prophet Isaiah foretold that the people to whom the Savior ministered would be "walking in darkness" and "living in the land of deep darkness" (Isa 9:2). In all likelihood, this means they would be burdened by sin and suffering from religious and spiritual ignorance; but the Messiah's advent promised that a great light would dawn.

---

36. According to O'Day ("John," 9:629), "In the Mediterranean world of Jesus' time, such an act of writing would have been recognized as an act of refusal and disengagement."

37. Cf. Keener, *John*, 1:737–38; Schnackenburg, *John*, 2:165–66.

Disagreement over the Testimony of Jesus as Torah (John 8:12–20)

In the first century AD, light was regarded as a "symbol for the law"[38] (cf. Pss 43:3; 119:105, 130; Isa 51:4; Wis 7:26; 18:3–4). In October, AD 29, sometime during the Festival of Tabernacles, the Messiah declared Himself to be the Light of the world (John 8:12; cf. 9:5). The implication is that the Son, as "eschatological light and life," is the "realization of what was promised/expected in Torah."[39] This was the second of Jesus' seven "I am" statements recorded in the Fourth Gospel.

On the evening of the first day of Tabernacles, a ceremony called the illumination of the temple took place. During that social occasion, four great candelabra were lit to dispel the darkness. It was claimed that the light from these candelabra was so great that it lit up every courtyard in Jerusalem. Then, all night long the holiest men of Israel would celebrate before a fire and sing psalms while the crowds watched.[40] The emphasis in 8:12 is on deciding to follow Jesus. Motivation for becoming His disciple can be found in the promise that believers will never stumble about in the darkness, for Jesus will be their guiding light. The Savior declared this and other truths while in the temple treasury (v. 20), which was located in the Court of the Women. The treasury was the place where 13 funnel-shaped boxes were set up to receive the people's freewill offerings (cf. 1 Macc 14:49; 2 Macc 3:6, 24, 28, 40; Mark 12:41; Luke 21:1). There the religious leaders argued with Jesus about His claim to be the Tanakh of God and thus the full and final revelation of the Father.

Tragically, while Jesus' opponents, such as the Pharisees, had physical sight, they remained in spiritual darkness (cf. John 9:40–41). In their ignorance, they asserted that the Son was merely testifying about Himself and that what He said was invalid (8:13). In short, the religious leaders considered Jesus' testimony legally unacceptable because they did not think there were any corroborating witnesses.[41] Perhaps the Pharisees also thought Jesus could not prove His claims and that these were baseless exaggerations. Jesus and His critics were operating under completely dif-

---

38. Fernando, *Relationship between law and love*, 133.

39. Casselli, "Jesus as eschatological Torah," 30.

40. Cf. Witherington, *John's wisdom*, 170.

41. Keener (*John*, 1:740) points out that the religious leaders conveyed their "response in legal language, perhaps preparing the sort of argument that could later prove useful in a forensic context." Köstenberger (*John*, 250) adds this corresponding observation: "In a reversal of the Synoptic portrayal of Jesus as on trial before the Romans and the Jews, John shows how it is not Jesus, but ultimately the world (including the Jews), that is on trial."

ferent assumptions, and this shows in His response to them. The Son declared that the claims He made about Himself were legally acceptable and thus valid and true. The reason is that He was clear about His eternal preexistence with the Father and the Spirit and about His eventual return to the other members of the Godhead (v. 14).

The Pharisees, however, were ignorant of where Jesus came from and where He was going. On one level, the religious leaders mistakenly thought Jesus came from Galilee, when in fact He was born in Bethlehem in Judea (cf. 7:52). On another level, the authorities failed to appreciate the heavenly origin of the divine, incarnate Torah. Jesus noted that His critics made snap judgments based on outward appearances, whereas He was not passing judgment on anyone (8:15). This did not mean the Messiah would never judge humanity; it is just that this was reserved for a future time. At the eschatological end of the age, the evaluation He rendered would be accurate and fair in every respect. The Son noted that He was not alone in His assessment, for He and the Father who sent Him rendered their decisions together (v. 16). Jesus as Tanakh directed the Pharisees to the Mosaic law, which they highly prized (and which pointed them to the Messiah).[42] In particular, Deuteronomy 17:6 and 19:15 stated that when two or more legitimate witnesses agreed on a matter, their testimony was to be accepted as valid (John 8:17). Without equivocation, the Son declared that He was one witness and that His Father, who had sent Him to earth, was the second witness (v. 18). The idea is that because Jesus had the witness of God, no other testimony was necessary, for God is always right.[43]

Not surprisingly, the Pharisees—who used human standards to pass judgment on the Messiah—thought the claim He made was a reference to His physical father. Perhaps the religious leaders would have relished the opportunity to challenge Jesus about the true nature of His parentage (for example, by alleging He had been born out of wedlock). The authorities, of course, got it all wrong. The Son was not addressing His miraculous conception through the agency of the Holy Spirit; rather, Jesus was talking about His close relationship with the Father as a member of the Trinity. The Son declared that His critics neither knew Him nor His Father (v.

---

42. Carson (*John*, 340) remarks that Jesus declared Himself "to be the new locus of revelation from the Father such that the law finds fulfillment in him"; cf. Fernando, *Relationship between law and love*, 88–89.

43. According to Keener (*John*, 1:741), when Jesus says, "In your own Law" (John 8:17; cf. 10:34; 15:25), it does not signify a pejorative or derogatory attitude toward the Torah, but rather towards the appeal His antagonists make to it. The religious elite fail to recognize Him as the "embodiment and fulfillment" of the Tanakh; cf. Whitacre, *Johannine polemic*, 65–68; Westcott, *John*, 129.

19). Because they refused to acknowledge Jesus' messiahship, they would remain ignorant of the Father, for it was through the Torah of God that one came to know the Father (cf. 1:18; 14:9). Though Jesus' opponents wanted to have Him arrested and executed, this would not happen until the divinely appointed time (8:20).

Two observations arise from what Jesus declared. First, He had a clear sense of His mission on earth, including His passion or suffering, and He never deviated from His divinely ordained path. Second, the Father remained in full control of all that happened to His Son. Indeed, nothing took the Lord by surprise. It would be incorrect to conclude that Jesus went to the cross with stoic resignation. The Fourth Gospel does not record the Savior's prayers in the Garden of Gethsemane, as the Synoptic Gospels did (cf. Matt 26:36–46; Mark 14:32–42; Luke 22:39–46); but John 12:27 reveals that Jesus was troubled about the Crucifixion even before Gethsemane, and He had already decided that He would not ask the Father to rescue Him from that time of great anguish. Thus, when Jesus said "not my will, but yours be done" (Luke 22:42) the night before His death, it was most likely the conclusion of a long process of dealing with what He knew He had to do.

Disagreement over the Identity of Jesus as Torah (John 8:21–29)

During the Festival of Tabernacles, Jesus announced to all that He was going away to a place where those who rejected His messianic claims could not come (John 8:21). This was a veiled reference to His upcoming death, burial, resurrection, and ascension into heaven. The Jewish authorities failed to understand what the Torah of God meant. They wondered whether He intended to commit suicide (v. 22). In response, Jesus stated that His antagonists would "die in [their] sin" (v. 21). By this the Messiah meant they would eternally perish with their transgressions against the Mosaic law unforgiven. Later, as Peter (along with John) stood before the Sanhedrin, the apostle declared that salvation is found only in the Messiah. In fact, God had decreed that there was "no other name under heaven" (Acts 4:12) that could save anyone.

In John 8:23, Jesus revealed that His critics were from the domain of Satan, which Jesus referred to as "from below" and "of this world." The devil is the ruler of the powers of the unseen world. He is also the evil spirit now at work in the hearts of those who refuse to obey God (Eph 2:2). People who follow Satan's ways have a worldly wisdom that is earthly, unspiritual, and demonic (Jas 3:15). In contrast, Jesus is "from above" (John 8:23), that is, from heaven. Though the Son came to earth as a human being, His priorities, goals, and values were those of the Father, not those of this world. In order for Jesus' hearers to be saved, they needed to accept His claim to be the perfection of the gift of the Tanakh (v. 24). This included believing the truth that He is Yahweh, the eternal, living God revealed in Exodus 3:14 as "I AM WHO I AM" (cf. Isa 41:4; 43:10–13; John 8:58).

The Jewish authorities failed to comprehend Jesus' true identity as the Son of God, so they demanded Him to state who He was. In response, Jesus reiterated His claim, which He made from the start of His public ministry, to be the Messiah (John 8:25). Jesus added that He had many things to pronounce in judgment against His accusers, especially in light of their rejection of Him. Their unbelief, however, did not nullify the testimony of the Father on behalf of the Son, for the Father remained completely truthful in all He said and did. Likewise, the Torah of God declared to the world only what He heard from the Father (v. 26). Thus, to reject the testimony of the Son was to reject the Father, who had sent Him. The religious leaders failed to appreciate the divine origin and truth of the Messiah's teaching.

The religious hierarchy also did not understand that Jesus was talking to them about His Father (v. 27). It was only after the authorities lifted up the Son of Man on a cross (v. 28) that it would be clear they had "crucified the Lord of glory" (1 Cor 2:8).[44] For instance, it was following Jesus' death, that a Roman centurion standing in front of the Cross exclaimed that Jesus is "the Son of God" (Mark 15:39). The same Greek verb rendered "lifted up" (John 8:28) can also mean "to be exalted." The truth is that the Father would glorify His Son through His atoning sacrifice at Calvary (cf. John 12:23, 32; 17:2–5; Phil 2:6–11). Because Jesus as Tanakh has the authority to judge (John 5:27) and the power to grant eternal life (6:27), He is also the one in whom people must believe in order to be saved (9:35). As on other occasions, the Messiah reiterated that He did nothing on His own initiative; instead, He spoke only what His heavenly Father had taught Him (8:28). The implication is that the Son's ministry on earth met with the Father's approval. Indeed, because the Son only did those things that pleased the Father, God was with the Savior and would not abandon Him (v. 29).

44. According to Ratzinger (*Jesus of Nazareth*, 349), what the reader finds in John 8:28 "is not metaphysical speculation, but the self-revelation of God's reality in the midst of history."

Disagreement over the Paternity of Those Critical of Jesus as Torah (John 8:30–47)

After the Messiah had finished speaking, many people in the crowd put their faith in Him (John 8:30). Two slightly different Greek phrases are used in verses 30 and 31 for the act of believing in the Messiah. The Greek text literally says that some believed "in him" (v. 30), while others only "believed him" (v. 31). The phrase "in him" is found elsewhere in the Fourth Gospel in key passages about belief (e.g. 3:16–17). This suggests that those referred to in 8:30 had a heart knowledge of Jesus, while the group described in verse 31 had merely acknowledged Him intellectually.[45] To the latter the Messiah declared that by continuing in His teaching, they showed the genuineness of their decision to become His disciples. Conversely, those who failed to persevere demonstrated the superficiality of their faith.

Abiding in the teachings of Jesus as Tanakh was an eternally serious matter. For instance, those who remained unwavering in their commitment to Him would come to a fuller understanding of and appreciation for the truths He declared. In point of fact, He is the truth (cf. 14:6) and leads His followers (through what He taught) to genuine and lasting freedom from slavery to sin (8:32).[46] In contrast, possessing mere intellectual knowledge can never lead to the same result, regardless of how scintillating that information might seem. Furthermore, there is no spiritual freedom in possessing truth in the abstract philosophical sense. The focus in the Fourth Gospel is on the person and work of the Messiah. Only faith in Him can deliver people from the darkness of sin.

Jesus' listeners bristled at the notion of being set free, for it implied that they were somehow in bondage. They failed to realize that the Messiah was speaking about slavery to sin. His listeners, however, took His remarks concretely and narrowly as a reference to their political and economic status as Jews. The Savior's audience retorted that they were descendants of Abraham and had never been slaves to anyone (v. 33). This overly generalized assertion failed to account for years of bondage to such despotic rulers as the Assyrians and Babylonians. The Jewish people also had to endure occupation by the Persians, Greeks, Syrians, and Romans.[47] In light of

---

45. Cf. Lightfoot, *St. John's Gospel*, 192.

46. Keener (*John*, 1:750) states that "Jewish texts speak of the Torah bringing freedom, whether from worldly cares, from national bondage, or from slavery in the coming world" (cf. Gen Rab. 92:1; Num Rab. 10:8; Pesiq Rab. 15:2). The freedom anticipated in the Torah finds its ultimate fulfillment in the redemptive work of the Messiah.

47. Cf. Tenney, *John*, 148.

this long history of being oppressed, how could Jesus' listeners sincerely claim to never having been anyone's slaves? Perhaps it was because they saw themselves as never having adopted the gods of their captors. A good example was the Jewish revolt against their Greek rulers in 167 BC when a statue of Zeus was erected in the Jerusalem temple and sacrifices were made to it. That act sparked a revolution that forced out the Greeks and gave the Jews political freedom for the next 100 years.

When the Romans eventually succeeded in establishing control over the Jewish people and their homeland, the relationship was unceasingly turbulent. The captors kept an uneasy peace with the Jews by generally giving the people the freedom to worship as they wished and allowing them to handle their own religious matters. That small sense of freedom, however, began to break down when the Roman Emperor Caligula (AD 37–41) threatened to put a statue of himself in the temple to be worshiped. That event helped spark the Jews to an unsuccessful revolt in AD 70. The Romans then destroyed the Jewish temple and later built on the site their own shrine dedicated to Zeus—complete with a statue of the emperor Hadrian on the former spot of the Holy of Holies. These sorts of events ended up reinforcing the tenacity of the Jewish people to hold tightly to their time-honored heritage. This not only included their status as Abraham's descendants, but also their reception of the covenants, the law, the temple liturgy, and a host of divine promises. In addition, the Messiah was a descendant of Abraham (cf. Rom 9:4–5).

This information clarifies why Jesus' listeners took issue with His statement about being set free (John 8:33). In response, the one who fulfills all the types and prophecies recorded in the law explained that He was talking about bondage to sin. This was certainly the case for those whose lifestyle was characterized by incessant wrongdoing (v. 34). The latter included a stubborn refusal to accept Jesus' messianic claims and authority, despite the mountain of confirming evidence. Only God's intervention could bring a change of heart. The Son as Torah was unapologetic about maintaining that even His Jewish listeners needed to be freed from sin, for He knew that all had transgressed and fallen short of God's glory (cf. Eccles 7:20; Isa 59:2; Rom 3:23). This continued to be true regardless of one's physical ancestry. As long as Jesus' critics remained in spiritual bondage to sin, they could never enjoy a permanent status within the family of God. In contrast, by putting their faith in the Messiah, they could be given the never-ending right to become God's children (John 8:35; cf. 1:12). Thus, only by trusting in the Son could His listeners truly be released from their bondage to sin (8:36).

The one who is infinitely greater than Abraham had not overlooked the claims of His Jewish listeners to being descendants of the patriarch (v. 33). The Savior readily admitted this fact, though it did not negate the truth that Abraham's true spiritual descendants were those who put their faith in the Messiah for salvation (cf. Rom 4:9–17; 9:8). Paradoxically, despite the claims of Jesus' critics, they revealed by their actions that they were not Abraham's spiritual descendants.[48] After all, among them were those who sought to bring about Jesus' arrest and execution. This was part of their agenda because the Savior's teaching had found no place in their hearts (John 8:37). Expressed differently, what the Son declared made no headway in their lives due to their unbelief.

Jesus eternally abided in the presence of the Father (1:1). Even the Messiah's incarnation did not change the fact of His status as God (v. 14). Only the Son as Tanakh could make the Father known, for the Anointed One enjoyed a uniquely intimate relationship with the Father (v. 18). In faithfulness to His Father, the Son declared to His audience what He had seen in His Father's presence (8:38). Some Greek manuscripts omit the plural pronoun at the end of the verse. In turn, this results in the TNIV marginal rendering, "Therefore, do what you have heard from the Father" (cf. NRSV, NET, NAB). In other words, Jesus was urging His critics to practice what God had revealed in the Mosaic law. Despite the plausibility of this option, there is strong textual support for the more traditional rendering. The idea, then, is that Jesus' detractors operated according to the dictates of their spiritual "father," which verse 44 reveals was the devil. Because they drank heavily from the cesspool of his toxic doctrines, they refused to accept Jesus as the perfection of the gift of the Torah and acknowledge that He represented the interests of the Father.

Perhaps there was an element of consternation as Jesus' listeners declared Abraham to be their father (v. 39). Members of the Jewish com-

---

48. Köstenberger (*John*) says that within rabbinic Judaism, it was predominantly believed that Abraham "fulfilled the whole Torah, even before it was given" (264). Levenson ("The conversion of Abraham") points to one prevailing view that Abraham had "personal access to an ancient tradition" that became "public at Sinai" (27). For instance, Genesis Rabbah 43:6, in its commentary on Genesis 14:18, asserts that Melchizedek (a king of Salem and a priest of the Most High God) "taught Abraham the laws of priesthood" and made the Torah known to him. Also, Genesis Rabbah 56:11, in its discussion of the omission of Isaac from Genesis 22:19, maintains that Abraham continued the "esoteric tradition" that eventually became the "manifest possession of all Israel at Mount Sinai" centuries after the patriarch's death (28). Ironically, while Abraham was "receptive to the divine revelation and acted in obedience to it" (Köstenberger, *John*, 265), the religious elite of Jesus' day—who claimed to be the patriarch's descendants—failed to follow the moral example he set.

munity in the Second Temple period often referred to Abraham as their father and themselves as his descendants (cf. Exod 4:22; Deut 14:1–2; 4 Macc 6:17, 22; 18:1; Gen Rab. 1:4; Matt 3:9; Gal 3:7).[49] Scripture reveals him to be a person characterized by faith in and obedience to the Lord (cf. Rom 4:1–25; Heb 11:8–12, 17–19; Jas 2:21–23). In contrast, Jesus' audience, while being Abraham's biological descendants, showed by their actions that they were not his spiritual descendants. Otherwise, they would have accepted Jesus' messianic claims and authority. In reality, the religious leaders were searching for a way to arrest and execute the Tanakh of God, because they were outraged by the truth He taught, which came from His Father in heaven. Because Abraham was never guilty of such a murderous intent (John 8:40), it was clear that Jesus' listeners imitated their real spiritual father, the devil. In protest, the audience rejected any accusation of having someone else other than God as their Father. They might have also insinuated that Jesus was born out of wedlock, being the illegitimate son of Joseph (v. 41).[50]

Jesus as Torah did not waver from His claim of originating with God, being sent by Him, and operating under His authority. Thus, if the Messiah's critics truly had God as their Father, they would love, rather than despise, His Son (v. 42). In reality, their hearts were spiritually hardened to the truth concerning the Redeemer, and this prevented them from understanding and accepting His teaching (v. 43). Satan, the god of this age, had blinded their unbelieving minds, making them unable to recognize the light of the glorious gospel about the Messiah, who is the exact likeness of God (cf. 2 Cor 4:4). The murderous intent of the antagonists toward the Son indicated they were the devil's spiritual offspring and sought to do the same sorts of evil things he desired (cf. 1 John 3:8–15). Jesus noted that from the dawn of time, Satan was a murderer, rejected the truth, and was devoid of truth. In keeping with his deceitful character, he not only lied, but also was the father of all lies (John 8:44). It stood to reason that those who followed the devil's wicked ways would spurn, rather than accept, the Messiah and the truth He declared (v. 45).

Despite the opinion of His critics to the contrary, Jesus had an absolutely clear conscience about His message and ministry. Because He knew He was sinlessly perfect (cf. 2 Cor 5:21; Heb 4:15; 7:26; 1 John 3:5), He risked asking His opponents whether any of them could prove Him to be

---

49. Keener (*John*, 1:755) notes that in Jesus' day, "Jewish people" would "seek God's blessings . . . on the basis of his covenant with Abraham" (cf. Exod 32:13; Deut 9:5, 27; 2 Kgs 13:23; Ps 105:8–9, 42–45; Mic 7:18–20; 2 Macc 1:2).

50. Cf. Brown, *John*, 357; Carson, *John*, 352; Köstenberger, *John*, 265.

guilty of committing sin. Of course, the answer was no. Accordingly, since the Son as Torah always did His Father's will, those who also claimed the Lord as their Father should have believed the Messiah and the truth He taught (John 8:46). Jesus explained that if His listeners truly belonged to God, they would hear and heed His message, especially as spoken by His duly authorized emissary; but by rejecting the Anointed One and what He declared, they demonstrated that they did not belong to God (v. 47). The divine, incarnate Tanakh came and granted believers a spiritual understanding that makes knowledge of God possible. All genuine believers abide in the Son, who is truly God and possesses eternal life (cf. 1 John 5:20).

The Eternal Preexistence of Jesus as Torah (John 8:48–59)

The members of Jesus' audience were Jewish residents of Jerusalem and its environs. Since they could not refute His claim to be the sinless Son of God (John 8:46), they diverted attention away from the truth by alleging that Jesus was a "Samaritan" (v. 48) and demon-possessed (cf. Matt 9:34; 12:24, 31; Mark 3:22; Luke 11:15; John 7:20; 8:52; 10:20). The Savior's antagonists might have used the first contemptuous statement to insinuate either that He was a foreigner to the covenant promises (cf. Eph 2:12) or of illegitimate parentage (cf. John 6:41).[51] Another possibility is that the dual remarks alleged Jesus to be not only a heretic but also insane.[52] In any case, the Messiah only responded to the second charge. After denying that He was demon-possessed, the Son declared that He honored His Father and that His opponents dishonored Him (v. 49).[53] Jesus could make the first claim because what He said and did as the perfection of the gift of the Torah represented God's will. In terms of the second claim, Jesus' critics, by slandering Him through their erroneous accusations, were guilty of blasphemy, for He is God the Son. Despite the sarcastic remarks of His antagonists, Jesus' agenda did not include self-promotion. He did not

---

51. Whitacre (*Johannine polemic*) states that Jesus' interlocutors, by alleging Him to be a "Samaritan and demon-possessed," showed the "depth of their alienation from God" (77). The paradox is that, rather than being the "champions of Jewish monotheism," they stood opposed to God the Father and His accredited emissary (78). For the Evangelist, "it is impossible to refuse to confess Jesus and still honor" God (79); cf. Duke, *Irony*, 75; Hoskyns, *The Fourth Gospel*, 345; Lincoln, *John*, 274; Thomas, "Fourth Gospel," 168–169.

52. Cf. Beasley-Murray, *John*, 136; Sanders and Mastin, *John*, 232; Schnackenburg, *John*, 2:218.

53. Köstenberger (*John*, 269) notes that "according to Jewish law, rejection of someone's messenger was tantamount to rejection of the sender as well" (cf. John 5:23).

need to get praise for Himself, for His heavenly Father would glorify Him through His resurrection from the dead (cf. 17:5). The Father in turn would judge those who spoke derisively about His Son (8:50).

Even though many among Jesus' listeners refused to accept His claims about Himself, He knew there were some who would trust in Him for eternal life. Because these believers obeyed His teachings, they would never experience the judicial punishment associated with death (v. 51). Put differently, though they might physically die, they would enjoy eternal life in the presence of the triune God (cf. 5:24; 11:25–26). This truth was a reality even now for those who believed in the Tanakh of God for salvation. Ironically, the Savior's opponents mistook Him to be speaking about avoiding physical death. For that reason, they concluded that He was as deranged as a demon-possessed person. They reasoned that Abraham, their beloved patriarch, as well as the Old Testament prophets, had heeded God's commands and yet had died. How was it possible, then, that those who abided by the teachings of the Lord Jesus would "never taste death" (8:52)? The Son's interlocutors failed to appreciate that He is the realization of the Mosaic law's types, prophecies, and expectations.[54]

As the Savior's listeners wrestled with His claims, they asked whether He thought He was greater than the previously mentioned luminaries. Such a claim must have seemed both preposterous and brazen to the audience (v. 53); but Jesus countered that if He was really trying to glorify Himself, any accolades He obtained from such an endeavor would be worthless. In reality, He was not engaged in self-promotion. His heavenly Father, whom Jesus' listeners claimed to be their God, glorified His Son (v. 54). Ironically, despite the assertions of Jesus' opponents, they showed by their actions that they did not really know the Lord. Furthermore, despite their opinions of Jesus, He could not back away from His claim to know the Father. The Son as Torah declared that asserting anything less would be the same as lying, a sin that He noted His detractors were guilty of committing (v. 55). In this way, they followed the lead of the devil, whom Jesus said was a deceiver and an enemy of the truth (cf. v. 44).

Unlike the the Son's opponents, He knew the Father intimately and personally; and the Tanakh of God demonstrated this by obeying His Father's teachings, especially those revealed in the Old Testament (v. 55). The sacred Hebrew writings have the Messiah as their ultimate focus. Even

---

54. Johnson (*Writings of the New Testament*, 547) explains that the "functions of Torah are totally subsumed by Jesus." As the perfection of the gift of the Tanakh, "he reveals God's will, he judges, he offers the spirit, he gives light, he liberates, he gives life." In short, "what Torah was as text, Jesus is as living Son: God's Word."

Abraham, despite his limited vantage point, could discern that the prophetic trajectory of Scripture pointed to the Savior (cf. 12:41).[55] The patriarch rejoiced in the truth that the Messiah would one day come and set His people free from their spiritual bondage (8:56; cf. Gen 22:13–15; Gal 3:8; Heb 11:17–19).[56] The audience failed to take in the eternal, spiritual aspects of Jesus' comments. They were thinking merely about the temporal realm of human existence when they questioned how Jesus, a person less than 50 years old, could possibly have seen Abraham in a literal sense (John 8:57; cf. Num 4:3). In response, Jesus possibly raised His right hand toward heaven and boldly declared in the precincts of the temple that before the legendary patriarch was ever born, the Son eternally preexisted with the Father and the Spirit (John 8:58).[57]

This is one of the great "I am" statements appearing in the Fourth Gospel and points back to the divine declaration in Exodus 3:14. In response to Moses' question, God said, "I AM WHO I AM" (or "I WILL BE WHAT I WILL BE"). Though the name "I am" may seem odd to the modern ear, Moses apparently understood what God was saying to him. The Hebrew root of this name conveys the idea of God's eternal self-existence. God never came into being at any point in time, for He has always existed. To know God—the "I am"—is to know the eternal one. This knowledge of God's nature and character would be Moses' strength (as well as that of New Testament Christians). John 8:58 makes it clear that the Son as Tanakh claimed to be God (cf. Isa 41:4; 43:13).[58] Because His opponents rejected this assertion, they attempted to stone Him for blasphemy (John 8:59).[59] Such would have been the punishment enjoined in the law (cf.

---

55. Ratzinger (*Jesus of Nazareth*, 350) clarifies that "in Jesus' origin we see the perfect fulfillment of the mystery of Israel, to which the Jews have alluded by moving beyond descent from Abraham to claim descent from God himself." In a similar vein, Köstenberger (*John*, 272) explains that because "Jesus fulfills what is written of and announced in the OT, for the Jews to be true children of Abraham would have meant for them to share in his attitude of joyful expectation" concerning the Messiah; cf. Calvin, *John*, 1:360–61.

56. Whitacre (*Johannine polemic*, 49) notes the rabbinic literature recounting "Abraham having had a vision" of God (cf. Apoc Ab. 9–32; Gen Rab. 44:21–22, 25; 59:6); also, cf. Bruce, *John*, 205; Heschel, *Heavenly Torah*, 290; Morris, *John*, 417–418; Westcott, *John*, 140.

57. Cf. Goldsmith, *Gospel of John*.

58. Cf. Tenney, "John," 9:99.

59. Köstenberger (*John*) clarifies that it was the "temple grounds at large," not "the temple building itself," that was "still under reconstruction" during the time of Jesus (109). Indeed, the "availability of stones in the temple area points to the fact that the temple area . . . was still being renovated" (273; cf. John 2:20).

Lev 24:13–16). Whether through natural or supernatural means, Jesus somehow hid Himself and exited the temple area.[60]

Jesus as Torah Heals a Man Born Blind (John 9:1–41)

The Healing of the Congenitally Blind Man by Jesus as Torah (John 9:1–12)

The sixth sign featured in the Fourth Gospel reveals Jesus as the Light of the world (John 8:12; 9:5). The miracle demonstrated His infinite superiority to all the Old Testament prophets, for none of them ever cured blindness (9:30–33). Giving sight to the blind was a messianic activity foretold in the Old Testament (cf. Exod 4:11; Ps 146:8; Isa 29:18; 35:5; 42:7), and it validated the Son's claim to be the divine, incarnate Torah (John 20:30–31).[61] This healing also illustrated the way Jesus opens spiritual eyes to God's truth. Most likely, the Son performed the miracle while in Jerusalem in the fall of AD 29, not long after the Festival of Tabernacles had ended.[62]

Perhaps as Jesus and His disciples exited out of an open gate of the Jerusalem temple (cf. Acts 3:1–7), they encountered a beggar who had been born blind (John 9:1).[63] In that day, begging was the only means of support for those with a severe physical disability like congenital blindness. It is not hard to imagine him sitting on a straw mat and holding up

---

60. Coloe (*God dwells with us*, 143) thinks Jesus' departure "from the temple grounds" (John 8:59) was a harbinger of divine judgment: "Once before the glory of God's presence departed the Temple and it heralded the forthcoming destruction of the Temple" (cf. Ezek 10:18–19; 11:22–23). Similarly, in the Fourth Gospel, the "departure of the one who . . . so revealed himself as the tabernacling presence of Israel's God (8:12, 58) acts as a judgment on Israel's cult."

61. Lincoln (*Truth on trial*, 99) notes that "trial and judgment" constitute the narrative framework for John 9. The religious leaders are the interrogators and the formerly blind beggar is the chief witness in the lawsuit against Jesus. The "concluding scene" involves a "final dramatic and ironic reversal" in which a "verdict of judgment" is rendered, "this time not by the Pharisees on Jesus but by Jesus on the Pharisees" (cf. vv. 39–41). Also, cf. Asiedu-Peprah, *Johannine sabbath conflicts*, 29–33.

62. Resseguie ("John 9," 122) considers John 9 as a "superb piece of literature" because its "form and content are so carefully woven together." There are "dualistic images, contrasting opinions, opposing movements of plot, and diverse characterisation" operating as a group to "show the reader the interrelationship between light and judgment."

63. Cf. Barrett, *St. John*, 356; Harris, *John*.

a saucer into which sympathetic passersby could drop their coins.[64] Most likely, Peter, as the spokesperson for the Twelve, asked Jesus whether the man's blindness was a result of his own sins or those of his parents (John 9:2; cf. Exod 20:5; 34:7; Ps 109:13–15; Isa 65:6–7). In the first century AD, it was widely believed that sin caused all suffering, especially such a serious condition as blindness. Some of the rabbis of the period speculated that one could sin in the womb before birth, thereby causing one to be born blind. Others suggested that possibly one could sin in a preexistent state and thereby cause an affliction at birth.[65]

Perhaps because the Twelve had been exposed to countless disabled beggars, their compassion for the blind man seemed to be minimal. For them he had been reduced to a theological riddle. They assumed this man's suffering was the result of someone's offense against God, but did not understand how. While sin may be the cause of some affliction, as clearly indicated in Scripture (cf. John 5:14; 1 Cor 11:30), it is not always the case necessarily (Job; Ezek 18; 2 Cor 12:7). Jesus reflected this view in His clear and direct response to the disciples' question. The Tanakh of God stated that the man's blindness was not due to his sin or his parents' sins; rather, he had been born blind so that the Lord's power, as seen in the working of a miracle, could be displayed in the man (John 9:3). Expressed differently, though the Father had not inflicted this man with blindness, the Son promised to eliminate this beggar's disability to demonstrate God's compassion and glory (cf. John 11:4, 40; 1 Pet 4:12–19).

Jesus declared that as long as it was daytime, it was necessary for He and His disciples to perform the deeds of His Father, who sent the Son to earth as His emissary. Once nighttime arrived, no further work could be done (John 9:4). In this verse, daytime metaphorically referred to the bodily presence of the Redeemer, while nighttime denoted the passing of His earthly ministry as a result of His crucifixion. The divinely ordained tasks included giving sight to the blind and revealing God's truth to the lost. Jesus as Torah was the Light that unveiled God's plan of redemption to a dying world. Correspondingly, it was not enough to be theologically correct about the cause of the man's blindness. More importantly, something had to be done about it. Then, Jesus reassured His disciples that while He was still on earth, He was the "light of the world" (v. 5). He did not mean that He somehow ceased being the light once He ascended to heaven. Rather, the Savior meant the light of His presence shone brightly

---

64. Cf. Goldsmith, *Gospel of John*.
65. Cf. Nicol, *Semeia*, 59.

among people when He was on earth doing His Father's will. The Son would prove His claim by giving the blind man the ability to see.

The Fourth Gospel provides no indication that Jesus was asked to heal the man. Evidently, while the Twelve stood by and watched, Jesus took the initiative to spit on the ground, make mud with the saliva, and smooth the mud over the blind man's eyes (v. 6). In that day, many people believed that saliva possessed the power to cure physical ailments. The ancient world thought that the saliva of someone of particular importance was especially effective in the treatment of blindness.[66] While Jesus could have cured the man without such a hands-on procedure, perhaps this outcast needed the Savior's reassuring, personal touch. Jesus also used His spit on two other recorded occasions, to give hearing to a deaf man (Mark 7:33) and sight to another blind man (8:23). Just as God had originally made human beings out of the dust of the ground (cf. Gen 2:7), so too the divine, incarnate Tanakh used clay to create a seeing pair of eyes for the blind man (cf. Job 10:9; Isa 45:9; Jer 18:6; Sir 33:13).[67] Because it was a Sabbath, the religious leaders considered this activity as a form of work that violated their traditions (cf. John 9:14).

The Redeemer told the beggar to go and wash in the Pool of Siloam, in which the latter term means "sent" (v. 7). Just as the Father had sent the Son into the world (cf. 4:34; 5:23, 37; 7:28; 8:16, 18, 26, 29, 42; 10:36; 12:44; 14:24), so now the Son was sending the blind beggar to the pool, which was probably a substantial distance from the temple.[68] This would have called for a degree of faith from the man (cf. 2 Kgs 5:10–14). Hezekiah originally built the reservoir southeast of Jerusalem. An underground tunnel carved out by the king's workers carried water to the pool from the Gihon Spring in the Kidron Valley. During times of siege, having clear access to water was imperative (2 Kgs 20:20; 2 Chr 32:30). In Jesus' day, during the Festival of Tabernacles, worshipers would draw water from the pool and pour it out at the base of the altar in the Jerusalem temple.

Just as Jesus directed, the blind man picked up his belongings, including a walking stick, and gradually made his way to the pool. Perhaps after finding an open spot, he knelt down by the edge of the pool, set his walking stick to one side, cupped some water in his hands, and began

66. Cf. Lightfoot, *St. John's Gospel*, 202; Lindars, *John*, 343; Witherington, *John's wisdom*, 181.

67. Cf. Brown, *John*, 372; Sanders and Mastin, *John*, 238–39.

68. Borchert (*John 1–11*, 315) suggests that the name of the pool is "indicative both of Jesus' mission and his command to those who would receive his blessings and become identified as his followers"; cf. Carson, *John*, 364–65.

rubbing it in his eyes.[69] A growing sense of excitement must have filled the man as he began to see. For the first time in his life, his once useless eyes were now able to gaze upon an array of images, colors, and movements. His neighbors and others who knew him as a blind beggar could not miss the joy he expressed over the miracle that had occurred in his life (John 9:8). Some thought the man was the former blind beggar, while others who did not recognize him thought the completely healed man was someone else. In the midst of the debate, the man kept insisting that he was the same person (v. 9).

When the neighbors and acquaintances of the former blind beggar asked how the miracle occurred (v. 10), he testified to them in a simple and straightforward manner what Jesus had done (v. 11). Then, when asked where Jesus might be, the man said he did not know (v. 12). Evidently, the onlookers wanted to speak to Jesus themselves (as did the neighbors of the Samaritan woman at the well; cf. 4:28–30). As the narrative in John 9 develops, there is a corresponding increase in the cured man's understanding of Jesus' identity and commitment to Him as the Messiah.[70] The former beggar first referred to Jesus as a "man" (v. 11), then as a "prophet" (v. 17), and finally as an emissary from God (v. 33). The healed man also doubted whether Jesus ever sinned (v. 25). Though the onetime beggar was eventually banned from the synagogue by the religious leaders (v. 34),[71] that did not deter him from putting his faith in Jesus as the Son of Man and worshiping Him as Lord (vv. 35–38).

The Interrogation of the Formerly Blind Beggar (John 9:13–34)

Perhaps the man bore witness to Jesus in the precincts of the temple. If so, this caught the attention of the religious authorities, who directed the temple police to bring the former beggar to them for questioning (John 9:13). Undoubtedly, the man felt some anxiety as he was escorted into a large chamber and made to stand before his interrogators. Most of them were likely seated behind a long table with various important documents spread out in front of them. One person would have been assigned the task

---

69. Cf. Goldsmith, *Gospel of John*.

70. Cf. Harstine, *Moses*, 69.

71. According to Whitacre (*John*), later Jewish writings spoke of "different degrees of exclusion that were exercised" by the religious authorities. This ranged "from a week-long exclusion from the congregation, to a thirty-day exclusion, to an unlimited exclusion from the congregation with avoidance of all contact, to an exclusion from the entire community of Israel."

of recording what occurred at this makeshift tribunal, including any decisions involving the healed beggar and Jesus, his benefactor.[72] The previous series of incidents in the temple involving the preacher from Nazareth were fresh in the minds of the Pharisees. Thus, they were keen to investigate this new development, which had taken place on the Sabbath (v. 14).

When the authorities questioned the man about the circumstances surrounding his healing, he gave an even shorter account than he had to his neighbors. He just reported the facts (v. 15). The healed beggar's response confirmed in the minds of some of the Pharisees that despite Jesus' claims, He was not from God. After all, Jesus dared to break their Sabbath traditions (e.g., by kneading together spittle and dirt to make a clay-like paste),[73] which they considered as sacred and binding as the Mosaic law. The implication is that Jesus was "opposed to the basis of Israel's very existence" and thus an "enemy of the Jewish nation."[74] Others, however, wondered how someone whom they concluded was a sinner could perform such an amazing miracle. Bultmann notes the dilemma facing the authorities: "the miracle seems to show that Jesus' actions are divinely accredited."[75] Despite the disagreement among the inquisitors, those antagonistic toward Jesus seemed to be in the majority (v. 16).

Next, when the panel asked the healed beggar for his opinion about the miracle-working Nazarene, the man called Jesus a prophet (v. 17; cf. 2 Kgs 2:19–22; 4:18–44; 5:1–14). One can only imagine the commotion such a statement created among the Pharisees. Despite the evidence, the tribunal refused to believe that Jesus was the Torah of God. They rejected the fact that the Father had sent the Son and empowered Him; but the authorities were perplexed as to how to invalidate the miracle and brand Jesus as a fraud. The religious leaders acted as if they were standing in judgment over the former beggar and the Galilean who had healed him; but ironically the panel's rejection of the Son of God meant they were the ones who stood condemned as sinners before the Father (cf. John 3:36; 5:22–23; 9:39).

The tribunal continued their investigation by summoning the man's parents for questioning (9:18).[76] Perhaps in the interim, the healed beg-

---

72. Cf. Goldsmith, *Gospel of John*.

73. O'Day ("John," 9:654) points out that "kneading was one of the thirty-nine categories of work explicitly forbidden on the sabbath" (e.g. *m. Sabb.* 7:2); cf. Carson, *John*, 367; Thomas, "Fourth Gospel," 173.

74. Umoh, *The plot to kill Jesus*, 185–86.

75. Bultmann, *John*, 334.

76. Köstenberger (*John*, 287) thinks the former blind beggar might have "stayed under

gar was escorted out of the chamber. Once the temple guards brought in the parents, the religious leaders asked them how their son, despite being born blind, was now able to see (v. 19). The couple gave a non-committal response. They affirmed that the man being questioned was their son and that he had been born blind (v. 20); but the parents declined to speculate how he had miraculously overcome his disability. Undoubtedly with a tone of respect, the couple asked the inquisitors to question their son, who was mature enough to give legal testimony for himself (v. 21). The couple responded in this way because they feared being banned for life from attending the synagogue. Since the latter was the heart of their religious and social existence, to be excommunicated meant being cut off from their cultural identity as Jews. The parents had heard this was the penalty for acknowledging Jesus as the Messiah (vv. 22–23).[77]

Most likely, the authorities had the temple guards escort the couple out of the chamber before bringing their son back in for further questioning.[78] Once the healed man was standing before the panel, he was formally placed under oath and directed to promise before God that he would speak the truth (cf. Josh 7:19; 1 Esdr 9:8; *m. Sanh.* 6:2).[79] For the Pharisees this meant declaring the itinerant preacher to be a sinner, for He violated their ban against doing any kind of work on the Sabbath (John 9:24). The former beggar refused to speculate as to whether Jesus was a

---

his parents' roof and spent his days begging in the temple courts."

77. Tenney ("John," 9:106) notes that "excommunication in this passage is not a late reflection of an ecclesiastical practice." In a similar vein, Witherington (*John's wisdom*, 39) observes that the Fourth Gospel was not penned to "address a current social crisis between the synagogue and the Johannine community." He also maintains that there is no basis for seeing in the account of Jesus' healing the blind beggar an "allegory of a past trauma in the Johannine community dealing with the *community's expulsion from the synagogue*. We have no historical evidence that the Johannine community was ever attached to, or an integral part of, or ever met in a diaspora synagogue" (182; italics are his). Hakola (*Identity matters*, 53) expresses a correspondent view by noting that the prevailing scholarly consensus "ignores the lack of any positive evidence for the exclusion of Christians, and it is also based on the wrong presupposition concerning the character and power of the rabbinic movement." Schnelle (*Antidocetic Christology*, 27–31), as a result of his analysis of the Fourth Gospel's relationship to the Second Temple period of Judaism, concludes that the "threat of expulsion from the synagogue reported in John 9:22; 12:42; and 16:2 is not an acute problem for the evangelist; instead, this is a retrospective glance, not a purely literary means for depicting the unbelief of the Jews in its full compass" (31). Also, cf. Carson, *John*, 359–361, 369–372; Keener, *John*, 1:208–214; Lioy, *Search for ultimate reality*, 8–10; Ridderbos, *John*, 341–44; Wilson, *Our father Abraham*, 69–72.

78. Cf. Goldsmith, *Gospel of John*.

79. Cf. Barrett, *St. John*, 362; Beasley-Murray, *John*, 151, 158; Stern, *Jewish New Testament commentary*, 184–85; Westcott, *John*, 148.

sinner. All the man could say, undoubtedly with a deep measure of gratitude, is that whereas before he was congenitally blind, he could now see, and this was due to the miraculous intervention of Jesus (v. 25). Because the tribunal was convinced that the Nazarene was a fraud, they struggled to make sense of the healed man's testimony. When they asked him what Jesus had done (v. 26), the man became exasperated. Instead of rehearsing the facts again, the former beggar asked with biting sarcasm whether they also wanted to become disciples of Jesus (v. 27).[80]

Perhaps by this point it dawned on the healed man that even the risk of being expelled from the synagogue would not stop him from becoming a follower of Jesus. Of course, such a notion infuriated the religious leaders. The panel heaped insults on him by declaring that while he had chosen to follow a charlatan, they were loyal disciples of Moses (v. 28).[81] The authorities were convinced that God had spoken to Moses and that the preacher from Galilee was a fraud (v. 29).[82] Despite the truth Jesus had declared in the synagogue, the miracles He had performed, and the testimony others had given on His behalf, the religious hierarchy still refused to acknowledge Him as the divine, incarnate Torah. Their efforts, however, to intimidate the healed man backfired. Rather than incriminate Jesus of wrongdoing, the man noted that the tribunal's doubt concerning Jesus was remarkable. After all, the Nazarene had given sight to someone who once was congenitally blind (v. 30).

Next, in a display of amazing courage, the former beggar told the panel of Torah experts that the Lord only blessed and empowered the

---

80. Carson (*John*, 373) observes that "the healed man, hitherto polite, now discovers that the professed impartiality of his interlocutors is nothing but a show." Consequently, the formerly blind beggar "begins to deploy a quite marvelous gift of sardonic repartee."

81. O'Day ("John," 9:659) notes that in the literature written during the Second Temple period of Judaism, the phrase "disciple of Moses" (cf. John 9:28) "occasionally appears as a designation for the rabbis" (cf. Evans, *Word and glory*, 151). Meeks (*The prophet-king*, 319) furthers this train of thought by explaining that "Jesus fulfills for the believer those functions elsewhere attributed to Moses." Consequently, "one who had formerly accounted himself a 'disciple of Moses' would now have to decide whether he would become instead a 'disciple of Jesus.'" From the perspective of the Evangelist, refusing to follow Jesus was equivalent to forsaking the "real Moses, for Moses only wrote of Jesus and true belief in Moses led to belief in Jesus."

82. Whitacre (*Johannine polemic*) remarks that the Jewish hierarchy was convinced Jesus stood "condemned by the Law." Thus, it was out of "loyalty to Moses and the Scriptures" that Jesus' interlocutors believed they were duty bound to oppose Him (26). Furthermore, "it becomes evident from their accusations against Jesus that they believe they can judge religious claims because they possess the Torah" (29). Supposedly, their purview included the validity of "messianic claims," especially those Jesus made about Himself (35).

godly, namely, those who were devout in their worship of and obedience to Him. In contrast, He did not grant the request of sinners, namely, those who were impious and violated His commandments (v. 31; cf. Job 27:9; 35:13; Pss 32:15–16; 66:18; 145:19; Prov 15:29; 28:9; Jas 5:16; 1 John 3:21–22). The healed man testified that the evidence substantiated Jesus' claim to be the promised Messiah (cf. Isa 29:18; 35:5; 42:7). In fact, since God created the world, there was no record of anyone else giving sight to someone born blind (John 9:32). Only those who came from God could have the power to perform such a miracle (v. 33). With indignation, the Pharisees declared the cured man to be permeated with sin from birth. Perhaps they insinuated that God had punished him with blindness because of his depraved character, which was evident to them by his contempt for those whom the Lord had put in charge over him. Then they scolded him for having the audacity to lecture them about the things of God. The Pharisees terminated the interrogation by having the man forcibly removed from their presence. In short, they branded him as an outcast among his people (v. 34; cf. 12:42; 16:2). In this way, he served as a convenient proxy (at least temporarily) for what the tribunal intended to do to Jesus.

The Faith of the Formerly Blind Beggar in Jesus as Torah (John 9:35–41)

The old system of temple rituals connected with the law of Moses was like a faint outline of the eternal blessings and realities that found their ultimate fulfillment in Jesus as Tanakh (cf. Heb 10:1).[83] Consequently, while the religious leaders shunned the healed man, the true Shepherd of God's people looked for and found him (e.g. standing in a public place or walking along the streets of Jerusalem; cf. John 10:11, 14).[84] While some ancient authorities read "Son of God" in 9:35 (cf. KJV, NKJV), the better Greek manuscripts record Jesus asking whether the former beggar had faith in "the Son of Man." The Redeemer already knew what was in the man's heart (cf. 2:24–25; 6:64), but He wanted the former beggar to make a personal commitment. Little by little Jesus revealed His eternal nature to the man so that his spiritual eyes could now be opened. The man could

---

83. According to Beasley-Murray (*John*, 142), the "idea of Christ as the fulfillment of Judaism" is not presented in the Fourth Gospel to "destroy Judaism and the Jews, but to carry forward the OT revelation to its conclusion in the revelation and redemption of Christ, issuing in the kingdom of God for all nations, including the Jews."

84. Cf. Goldsmith, *Gospel of John*.

not have recognized Jesus by sight, for the healing occurred after the beggar had left the Savior's presence. The man might have remembered Jesus' voice or was told that this questioner had healed him.

In any case, the cured man readily indicated that he wanted to trust in the Messiah, if Jesus would be kind enough to identify Him (9:36). While some experts in the law were watching (cf. v. 40), the Torah of God revealed to the former beggar that he had not only seen the Anointed One, but also was now speaking with him (v. 37). Immediately, the former beggar proclaimed his belief and honored Jesus by addressing Him as "Lord" (v. 38). Then, the cured man prostrated himself before Jesus and worshiped Him (cf. 20:28), a response that is "due God alone."[85] Perhaps the Pharisees were aghast when they saw Jesus making no effort to stop the man from revering Him as the Messiah. At Jesus' first advent, He came to make salvation available to the lost (cf. Luke 19:10; John 3:17; 12:47; Heb 9:28). Those who reject Him as Redeemer will face Him as Judge at His second advent (cf. John 5:22, 27, 30; Acts 10:42; 17:31; Rom 2:16; 2 Cor 5:10; 2 Tim 4:1; 1 Pet 4:5).

In short, Jesus' coming to earth affected people in one of two ways. There are those like the blind man who could not see but received their spiritual sight when they put their faith in the Son. Then there are those like the religious leaders who claimed to know God but remained in spiritual darkness because they refused to believe in the Anointed One, whom the Father had sent (John 9:39; cf. Isa 6:9–10; 42:19; Mark 4:12; John 12:39–41). The Pharisees with Jesus were shocked that He would suggest they were as spiritually blind as other people (John 9:40). Despite the indignation of Jesus' self-assured interlocutors, the Son as Tanakh did not mince words with them. If they had admitted their inability to understand their own spiritual state, they would have recognized their need for divine healing; but because the religious leaders were convinced that they had no such need, they stood condemned before God as guilty sinners. Regrettably, their spiritual blindness prevented them from being forgiven and reconciled with the Father through faith in the Son (v. 41; cf. Rom 5:1, 9–11; 2 Cor 5:18–21).[86]

---

85. Harris, *John*; cf. Bultmann, *John*, 339.

86. Köstenberger (*John*, 295) notes that "John 9:39–41 serves as a kind of interpretive epilogue, transforming the preceding narrative into an acted parable with a message about sight and blindness in the spiritual realm."

Conclusion

In the previous chapters of the Fourth Gospel, Jesus as Torah revealed Himself to be the Creator of all things and the atoning sacrifice for the sins of humankind. He demonstrated that He was greater than the Jerusalem temple and had authority over all the religious institutions associated with it. As the true Rabbi of Israel, the Son had the seal of the Father's approval on His ministry. He asserted Himself to be the source of new life in the Spirit, more powerful than the elements of nature, and supreme over every famed personality mentioned in the Old Testament (including Moses, Abraham, and Jacob). Jesus showed Himself to be the realization of all that was foreshadowed and typified in the festivals, ceremonies, and rituals observed by the covenant community in Bible times. This even included the Festival of Tabernacles with its ceremonial drawing of water and lighting of lamps.

As the Bread of Life, the Messiah was the divine emissary who provided for the Israelites during their days in Egypt, their time of wandering in the Sinai desert, and their sojourn in the promised land; but He did more than provide abundant harvests for the people of God. The embodiment of the Tanakh, as the essence of the Father's glory and the exact representation of His nature, was the source of spiritual light and life for all who put their faith in the Son. Halfway through the Festival of Tabernacles, while Jesus was in the temple courts, He openly declared these truths; and even though He never received advanced training in a rabbinic school, He outshone all the learned scholars of the day with His profound knowledge, understanding, and wisdom.

As on other occasions, the eternal Torah's words and works sparked sharp disagreement among the religious leaders and common people. There was confusion over the Messiah's identity and what the sacred Hebrew writings actually said about Him. Clergy and laity alike also squabbled over the meaning and significance of Jesus' claims. Despite the bickering and consternation, the Son continued to declare His divine origin and redemptive mission. He invited all to put their faith in Him and receive the abundance of the Spirit's indwelling presence in their regenerate lives. When they did, they would come to regard Jesus of Nazareth to be the eschatological Prophet foretold in the Old Testament, the Bethlehem-born descendant of David, and the messianic King of Israel.

Unlike the religious elite, who claimed to know the Mosaic law, Jesus as Torah was the fulfillment of all the Tanakh's prophecies and types. Also, while the authorities claimed to be the enforcers and arbitrators of the law,

Jesus as Torah in John 7–9

the Son demonstrated His explicit adherence to both the spirit and letter of the same. For instance, though He is God the Son, He did not retaliate when the establishment rejected Him and tried to have Him arrested and executed. Even in the episode of the woman caught in adultery, the eternal Tanakh responded with compassion toward her and restraint toward her accusers. Jesus, of course, knew His antagonists were seeking to trick Him into saying something they could later use against Him; but rather than cower in fear, He held His critics to the same divine moral standard they accused the woman of violating.

Tragically, the elitists remained entrenched in their hypocrisy and unbelief. They refused to leave the darkness of sin and put their faith in the Light of the world. Though they claimed to be descendants of Abraham and to have God as their Father, the opponents of the eternal Torah demonstrated by their words and deeds that the devil was their true spiritual progenitor. Indeed, such was the case for all who remained enslaved to sin. Jesus, with infinite compassion for the lost, invited all to believe in Him, the very one whose advent was anticipated by Abraham. To everyone who had the eyes of faith, it was clear that the Son came from God, operated under His authority, and carried out His will. This included the divine necessity of the Messiah being crucified, buried, resurrected, and exalted to heaven.

The one who is the realization of everything recorded in the Tanakh proved the truthfulness of His claims by healing a man born blind. While the religious experts refused to accept the miracle as validating proof of Jesus' messianic status, the former blind beggar put his faith in the Son of Man. The irony is that those who claimed to exist in the light of God's truth remained in spiritual darkness. Meanwhile, a poor blind beggar received physical and spiritual sight. On the one hand, his inquisitors were mired in guilt, especially for the sin of unbelief. On the other hand, the cured man was set free from his sin through faith in the Son and even worshiped Him as the perfection of the gift of the Tanakh. Consequently, the former beggar became one of the sheep in the spiritual fold of the good Shepherd.

7

Jesus as Torah in John 10–12

Introduction

THE EVENTS recorded in John 10 through 12 took place in the last six months of Jesus' life. It was not long after the Jewish Festival of Tabernacles (around October, AD 29) that Jesus, as the Torah of God, declared Himself to be the good Shepherd. Then, two months later, during the Festival of Dedication (around December, AD 29), the Son claimed to be God. Perhaps not long after that (during the winter of AD 29), Jesus validated His claim to be the resurrection and the life by raising His deceased friend, Lazarus, from the dead. Finally, it was six days before the Passover was about to start (in the spring of AD 30) that the Messiah, as the culmination (that is, the destination, goal, outcome, and fulfillment) of the law for believers, made His triumphal entry into Jerusalem. These various episodes, in their unique ways, help establish that Jesus, especially in the temple of His body, is the reality to which the rites and rituals connected with the shrine in Jerusalem pointed.

Jesus as Torah Reveals Himself to Be the Good Shepherd (John 10:1–21)

It seems that Jesus' continued to address the same Pharisees who had questioned Him about the issue of spiritual blindness (John 9:40–41).[1] The shabby way in which the religious leaders had treated the former beggar called into question their ability to shepherd God's people (cf. vv. 28–29,

---

1. Cf. Barrett, *St. John*, 367; Umoh, *The plot to kill Jesus*, 228–30.

34).[2] Sometime during Ezekiel's ministry[3] (593–571 BC),[4] the prophet censured the religious leaders of his day for the deplorable way in which they cared for the covenant community. Ezekiel declared that in the kingdom age, the sovereign Lord would shepherd His flock in a manner characterized by kindness, sensitivity, and compassion. Indeed, at that time, a ruler like David would ensure that peace, equity, and righteousness prevailed (Ezek 34:1–31; cf. Ps 80:1; Isa 40:10–11; 56:9–12; Zech 10:2; 11:5, 8). Scripture discloses that Jesus, as the realization of the law's types,

---

2. Cf. Harris, *John*; Morris, *John*, 446; Lindars, *John,* 353; Tenney, "John," 9:108–9.

3. Ezekiel, whose name means "God strengthens," was the son of Buzi, a priest of the family of Zadok (Ezek 1:3). What is known about Ezekiel's life comes from the information he gives in his book. Also, his prophecies contain dates more specific than almost any others in the Old Testament. This makes it possible to correlate Ezekiel's declarations with Babylonian records and date many of the prophet's oracles (for example, cf. 1:1–3; 8:1; 20:1; 24:1; 26:1; 29:1, 17; 30:20; 31:1; 32:1, 17; 33:21; 40:1). In 597 BC, when Ezekiel was about 25 years old, the Babylonians took him into exile with Jehoiachin and about 10,000 other Jews (cf. 2 Kings 24:10–17). When Ezekiel was 30 years old and living in the Jewish colony of Tel Aviv on the Kebar River (near the ancient city of Nippur), he heard God's call to be His prophet (Ezek 1:2–3; 3:15; about 593 BC). Apparently, Ezekiel was a person of some stature among the leaders of his people, for the prophet's home became a central meeting place (cf. 3:24; 8:1; 14:1; 20:1). Ezekiel was married; but 10 years into the exile, his wife died suddenly, perhaps of the plague (cf. 24:15–18). The couple was evidently childless. Throughout Ezekiel's ministry, which continued until 571 BC (cf. 29:17), he tried to help his fellow exiles deal with the fact that they were far from their homeland. He taught them that the Lord was close at hand to sustain them during their time of displacement. Ezekiel's oracles, like those of Jeremiah, fall into three major categories: declarations against Israel, especially before the fall of Jerusalem in 586 BC; pronouncements against the nations, such as Egypt and Tyre; and words of consolation for Israel's future, including visions of a restored nation and a new temple (chaps. 33–47). Like Jeremiah, Ezekiel is known for his symbolic acts to convey God's message, such as shaving his head and burning some of his hairs to show God's destruction of Jerusalem (chap. 5).

4. For a discussion of the use of Ezekiel in the Fourth Gospel, cf. Fowler, *Influence of Ezekiel*. The author maintains there are "extremely close ties between the thought of the Fourth Evangelist and the prophet Ezekiel" (3). In fact, an examination of the numerous intertextual links between these two portions of Scripture indicates that the Son is "the fulfillment of expectations inherent in Judaism as a whole, many of which had been generated and encouraged by the prophet Ezekiel" (3–4). Manning (*Echoes of a prophet,* 199) advances the discussion by observing that "most of John's allusions to Ezekiel are intended to show how Ezekiel's restoration oracles, especially those involving the Messiah or the giving of the Spirit, are fulfilled through Jesus to his followers." Consequently, the promises recorded in the Old Testament are "redirected from Israel to the followers of Jesus." Moreover, the allusions the Evangelist makes "strongly focus on Ezekiel's themes of life and the giving of the Spirit." The author postulates that for John, "Ezekiel was a sort of window" on the remainder of the Old Testament. Put another way, the Evangelist occasionally "chose imagery from Ezekiel to communicate themes that can be found" in every part of the Old Testament.

prophecies, and expectations, is the eschatological Shepherd who one day restores the prosperity of the Lord's sheep (cf. Heb 13:20; 1 Pet 5:4; Rev 7:17). In truth, Jesus is the messianic King who brings to pass all that God's spokespersons foretold in the Old Testament (cf. Pss 2:6–12; 89:4, 20, 29; Isa 9:6–7; 11:1; Jer 23:5–6; 30:9; Hos 3:5; Amos 9:1–15; Mic 5:2; Luke 1:31–33).[5]

The Pharisees who conversed with Jesus in Jerusalem in October, AD 29, should have readily understood the implications of His identifying Himself as a shepherd, since many of them would have been familiar with sheep husbandry.[6] They grasped the importance of herding sheep into pens and protecting them from hostile forces. They appreciated the seriousness with which shepherds assumed their role as guardians over their sheep. Thus, when Jesus told His listeners to pay careful attention to His analogy of Himself as a shepherd, He wanted them to understand how He could be a shepherd to them. He wanted them to listen to His voice as the Tanakh of God and follow His leading. Also, He wanted them to know to what length He would go in caring for them and how much they could mean to Him as His sheep.

Sadly, the majority of the religious leaders of the day refused to follow the one who is the culmination of all that was prophesied in the Mosaic law. Consequently, they remained in spiritual blindness and condemned

---

5. Cf. Barrett, "Old Testament in the Fourth Gospel," 163–64; Bruce, *John*, 223–24; Hoskyns, *The Fourth Gospel*, 367; Westcott, *John*, 151.

6. In Jesus' day, the raising and breeding of domestic sheep was a major part of the Palestinian economy. Indeed, wealth was often defined in terms of how large a flock one owned. Local residents used sheep to provide meat, wool, and milk. They made arrowheads, needles, scrapers, and lances from the bones of these animals. They also made curtains, leather, and clothing from sheep hides. Even the horns of sheep were valuable for use as musical instruments and containers for olive oil. City dwellers often kept a small number of animals that they grazed outside the city walls and brought home with them at night or left under guard in protected sheepfolds. In contrast, the flocks of tent dwellers were cared for by family members or by shepherds hired for the job. The necessities of the task meant that shepherds often lived apart from cities and villages. Alone or with a small group of other shepherds, they were people of the outdoors who were responsible for caring for themselves as well as their flocks. Some, such as the part-time hirelings, could be irresponsible in times of threat or danger. The positive biblical pictures of a shepherd focus on those who care for the welfare of their animals. In addition to finding adequate shelter for the sheep, the best shepherds also had to lead them to good pasturelands and ample supplies of water. Knowing that their flocks were easy prey, shepherds spent part of their time warding off attacks from savage animals. If necessary, shepherds were willing to risk their own lives to ensure the safety of the flock. Perhaps these caretakers are the reason why, throughout the ancient world, the concept of "shepherd" was a recognized image or title for a nation's leader.

because of their sin. Their intent was to serve their own interests and to use their positions of leadership to exploit the masses. People became objects to promote the self-serving agendas of the religious leaders. Jesus, fully realizing this, solemnly declared in John 10:1 that not every spiritual leader who claimed to be honest and upright truly was. The Messiah used the analogy of the shepherd and his or her flock to convey His remarks.[7] In that day, there were different kinds of sheepfolds. Evidently, Jesus was referring to a courtyard in front of a house. Such a compound was surrounded by a stone wall, which was often covered with briers for protection. There was usually only one entrance or door to the enclosure. This prevented the sheep from wandering out and also kept predators from entering in.

The Son as Torah warned His listeners against thieves and robbers who were not concerned for the welfare of the sheep, but for their own self-interest. These bandits would try to sneak into the fold through some way other than through the proper entrance, that is, the gate. Who were these thieves and robbers to whom Jesus was referring? Since the Messiah had recently told some experts in the law that they remained guilty of sin, His listeners undoubtedly included these leaders among the thieves. Certainly, the Pharisees had set themselves up as the shepherds of God's people, and many of them attempted to lead the people astray by turning them against Jesus. In 9:39–41, Jesus contrasted the Pharisees with the former blind beggar. Now the Son contrasted them with Himself.

Unlike thieves and robbers, the shepherd entered through the gate (10:2). Only the shepherds who guarded the sheep had the right to enter the fold through this entrance. The gatekeeper knew this, and that is

---

7. Jesus' statements are like an extended parable (cf. John 10:6) that reveal the "true nature of a loving and benevolent God" (Rosenblatt, "Parable," 691). In Bible times, Jewish teachers often told stories called parables to illustrate whatever moral principle they were trying to communicate. These parables might have one central point or include several points of comparison. Sometimes spokespersons for God would tell a parable or a riddle that hearers would understand only if they had the key to the interpretation. Thus, with some parables the details had symbolic significance. This teaching device was a way of encouraging the faithful to consider deeply the spokesperson's words and to separate out the uncommitted. The stories conveyed truth to attentive hearers who were eager to understand. At the same time, the figurative language veiled truth from persons who did not want to believe it, such as the religious elite of Jesus' day (cf. Matt 13:10–17; Mark 4:10–12; Luke 8:9–10). According to Boucher ("The parables"), when a comparison of the "parables in the Gospels" is made "with those in other sources," one is "led to conclude that Jesus was a master of the genre, perhaps its most brilliant author ever." For a discussion of the different types of parables used by Jesus and their role in His teaching, cf. Ellison, et al., *Parables in the eye of the storm*; Jeremias, *Parables of Jesus*; Ratzinger, *Jesus of Nazareth*, 183–217; Schottroff, *Parables of Jesus*; Smith and Williams, *Parables of Jesus*.

why he would open the entryway for the shepherds. Much speculation has been written about who the gatekeeper in this allegory represents. For instance, some believe the individual symbolizes leaders in the church who make sure that no one but the Messiah is guiding their congregations. In fact, however, there may be no specific identity necessarily intended. In any case, the sheep recognize the voice of their shepherd, who calls them by their names (v. 3).

Since a pen often enclosed several herds of sheep, each shepherd had a unique name for calling his or her sheep from among the other animals. The shepherd would not only bring them out of the pen, but also go ahead of them (v. 4). A good shepherd in Palestine never drove his or her sheep from behind, but trained the animals to follow by listening to the shepherd's voice. On the other hand, if a stranger tried to call the sheep, they would panic at the sound of his or her voice (v. 5). Jesus' listeners should have understood His parable, but most of them did not. If they were truly His sheep, they would have recognized His voice and followed Him. Their spiritual deafness prevented them from comprehending what He was trying to teach them (v. 6).

Jesus resumed His discourse with another allegorical statement: "I am the gate for the sheep" (v. 7). This is the third of the Son's "I am" statements recorded in the Fourth Gospel. Some sheep pens did not have a gate, and the shepherd would serve as the door by lying across the opening. This not only kept the sheep inside the fold, but also kept out potential intruders. In addition, a good shepherd inspected his or her sheep at the gate and tended to their needs and wounds. The Tanakh of God was declaring that He constantly looked out for His sheep, checked for injuries, and was ready to heal them. The Savior's primary point was that as the one gate to the fold, He is the person who determines who can enter into God's kingdom. There is no other way into the Father's fold except through faith in the Son (v. 9). Other people who claimed to represent the Father had preceded the Son, but they were thieves and robbers (v. 8). They had distorted the truth and, consciously or unconsciously, tried to take God's people from His fold. Jesus was not talking about the Hebrew prophets of the Old Testament era, but about the aberrant religious hierarchy of His day. Furthermore, thieves have only one thing on their minds—to get what they want regardless of the destruction it causes. With Jesus at the gate, however, not only is the flock protected, but the needs of the sheep are also met (v. 10). Expressed differently, only in the Messiah is the abundant, deeply satisfying life made available.

In verse 11, Jesus declared, "I am the good shepherd." This is the fourth of His "I am" statements recorded in the Fourth Gospel. When the Son as Torah said He was "the good shepherd," He portrayed Himself as the ancient Hebrews viewed God (cf. Gen 48:15; 49:24; Pss 23:1; 28:9; 78:52; Jer 23:1–3; Ezek 34:12, 15). The Messiah was not only identifying Himself as God, but also distinguishing a particular characteristic of Himself as God. As the nobleminded and trustworthy Shepherd, Jesus promised to sacrifice Himself for His sheep. In contrast, hired hands would not risk their lives for the sheep. They fulfilled their duties of caring for the flock, not out of concern for them, but for their own self-interest—that is, the wages they were paid. If a wolf threatened to assault the sheep, the hirelings would not endanger themselves, but would instead abandon the flock and flee for safety (John 10:12). Consequently, the wolf would be able to attack and disperse the sheep (v. 13). Jesus' disapproval of the hired hand's response contrasts with other views of the day. For example, the Mishnah taught that the hired shepherd was required to defend the sheep if only one wolf attacked. If more than one wolf struck, however, the hireling would not be blamed for abandoning the sheep. According to the Mishnah (B.M. 7:9), "Two wolves count as unavoidable accident."[8]

Once more, the perfection of the gift of the Torah said He is "the good shepherd" (v. 14). The knowledge that Jesus has of His sheep and they of Him goes beyond mere recognition. They have an intimate familiarity with each other in the same way the heavenly Father and His Son know each other (v. 15). In fact, the love and concern Jesus has for each one of His sheep is so great that He willingly laid down His life for all of them. Jesus made it clear that His sacrificial act would include not only Jewish believers but Gentile believers as well. His current followers composed His present flock, but later Gentiles would also hear His summons to salvation and become His disciples. When this occurred, there would not be two flocks under one shepherd—that is, a Jewish-Christian church and a Gentile-Christian church—but one united flock shepherded by the Messiah (v. 16; cf. John 3:16–17; 11:52; 17:20–23; 1 Cor 12:13; Gal 3:28; Eph 2:11–22; 3:6; 1 Pet 2:4–5, 9–10).

Since perfect harmony exists between what the Father wills and what the Son does, it is only natural that the Father should love His Son; but Jesus' willingness to sacrifice His life in obedience to God's plan did not cause the Father to love Him, for that love has existed from the beginning. Rather, God's love was an expression of His approval of His Son's laying down His life—only to raise Him up from the dead. Jesus wanted

---

8. Morris, "Atonement," 57.

it understood, however, that His death would not be forced upon Him. He would lay down His life voluntarily (John 10:17). Indeed, the Torah of God had the authority—that is, the power and the right—not only to sacrifice His life but also to take it back again in resurrection. The Father Himself gave this authority to the Son (v. 18; cf. John 13:1; 15:13; Acts 2:23–24; 4:27–28).

Once again, Jesus' discourse divided the religious leaders who heard Him speak (John 10:9). On the one side were those who accused Jesus of being an insane demoniac. They warned the crowd not to pay attention to Him (v. 20). Jesus' assertions seemed so absurd to them that the source for His ridiculous claims could only be the devil. This was not the first time that the Redeemer's enemies had accused Him of being demon-possessed (cf. 7:20; 8:48). Evidently, this accusation against Jesus was popular among His enemies. On the other side were those who refused to dismiss the miracles the Tanakh of God performed, particularly the healing of the blind (10:21). They were thinking about the congenitally blind beggar whom Jesus had cured (cf. 9:1–7). If the itinerant preacher from Nazareth could perform such wonderful miracles, how could He be demon-possessed? In their view, Jesus could not be, nor were His teachings like the utterances of a demoniac (10:21). Throughout the Fourth Gospel, the author repeatedly shows Jesus to be the Son of God. The apostle's presentation of Jesus' miracles, teachings, and experiences point to Him as the Messiah. The Fourth Gospel was intended to convince people to place their trust in the Savior, who died for their sins and is coming again.

Jesus as Torah Declares Himself to Be God (John 10:22–42)

The Fourth Gospel recorded another incident during the Festival of Dedication in the Jerusalem temple in December, AD 29. This eight-day Jewish feast was also known as Hanukkah, the Festival of Lights, and the Festival of Rededication (cf. 1 Macc 1:59; 4:36–59; 2 Macc 1:9, 18; 10:1–8). The Jews celebrate Hanukkah as a memorial to the restoration of the worship of Yahweh at the temple in Jerusalem in 165 BC by Judas Maccabeus. Three years earlier, the Syrians had desecrated the temple when Antiochus IV Epiphanes, their king (part of the Hellenistic Seleucid dynasty), sacrificed an adult female pig to Jupiter on the temple altar. After the Maccabean revolt, the Jews defeated the Syrians and rededicated the temple to God. The Jews still observe this feast for eight days, beginning with the twenty-fifth of Kislev (around mid-December). During the festival, candles are lit to signify the illumination of the temple when the sacred lampstands were restored. In addition, the Jews sing the "Hallel" (psalms of praise to God) during this feast while carrying palm and other branches. Hanukkah is a fitting reminder that Jesus as Torah shines the eternal light of God's truth before a sin-cursed world (cf. John 8:12; 9:5).

The author of the Fourth Gospel noted that it was winter (10:22). Jesus was walking through the section of Herod's Temple known as Solomon's Colonnade (v. 23; cf. Acts 3:11; 5:12). This long porch or portico was covered by a cedar roof supported by a row of tall stone columns. The portico was located on the east side of the Court of the Gentiles in the Jerusalem shrine. Though it was popularly believed that Solomon built the colonnade, Herod was most likely responsible for its construction. Worshipers often congregated in this section of the outer court because the roof of the portico sheltered them from the cold winds blowing off the desert. This would have been especially true during the winter months. Scribes also taught in this part of the temple. It is not surprising, therefore, that Jesus encountered the authorities there, perhaps along with a crowd of bystanders.

Three years earlier, in AD 26, the religious leaders had sent a delegation of priests, Levites, and Pharisees to interrogate John the Baptizer about his identity (cf. John 1:19–28). Now it was Jesus' turn to be encircled and questioned about His identity as the Messiah. Evidently, His words and deeds did not meet the expectations of what the inquisitors thought the Anointed One should say and do. Nonetheless, they could not ignore the miracles He had performed, and so they insisted on receiving a straightforward answer to their question. Perhaps there was an element of consternation as the authorities voiced their demand not to be kept guessing any longer (10:24). Popular misconceptions about the Messiah required that the Tanakh of God first establish with clarity the redemptive nature of His ministry.[9]

The Son noted that He had already spoken plainly about His messianic status and authority, but the religious leaders had refused to believe Him (cf. 1:49–51; 4:25–26; 8:28, 58; 9:35–37). Indeed, the miracles He did in the name of His heavenly Father substantiated His claims, for He could not have performed these signs without being empowered by God (10:25; cf. 5:36; 14:11; 15:24). The problem was not in Jesus' words, but in the hearts of His critics. The reason they refused to put their faith in Him as the final expression of God's Torah is that they did not belong to the new community of the redeemed. Becoming members of that sheep-

---

9. Cf. Carson, *John*, 392; Köstenberger, *John*, 311.

fold was not based on one's ethnic heritage, but rather on faith in the Messiah (10:26).

Jesus' plainly stated that His true followers heard and heeded Him in much the same way that sheep follow the voice of their shepherd (v. 27). In fact, the true test of love for the Son as Torah was a willingness to keep His commands (cf. 14:15; 15:10). Those who obeyed Him were the genuine recipients of the eternal life He offered. Because He is the resurrection and the life (cf. 11:25), His disciples would never perish or be lost, but enjoy unending fellowship with the triune God in heaven. Also, their eternal future was secure in the eschatological Shepherd, who promised that no one could seize them from Him (John 10:28). According to the underlying Greek text of the TNIV, Jesus declared that the Father is all-powerful. Nothing in the entire universe can undermine His ability to safeguard the believers' reception of their eternal inheritance in the Son (v. 29; cf. John 17:11–12; Rom 8:31–39; 1 Pet 1:3–5). A less preferred manuscript tradition attributes this greatness to the ones who are given to the Son. In this case, Jesus was saying that those who have been entrusted to His care are more precious to Him than anything else in the world.

In one of His boldest assertions, the divine, incarnate Tanakh declared, "I and the Father are one" (John 10:30). The gender of the Greek term rendered "one" is neuter (not masculine), which undercuts the notion that all three members of the Godhead are one and the same person; rather, they are one in essence (or nature), while remaining distinct in person (cf. Deut 4:35, 39; 6:4; 1 Kgs 8:60; John 17:21; 1 Cor 8:4, 6; Jas 2:19).[10] In short, the Son demonstrated by His actions that He was in harmony with the Father's redemptive will and purpose.[11] Even more important, the Messiah is God the Son, and as such, co-equal and co-eternal with the Father and the Spirit (cf. Isa 48:16; Matt 3:16–17; 28:19; John 14:16; 1 Cor 12:3–6; 2 Cor 13:14). In John 14:28, the Son said the Father was greater than He. The Torah of God was speaking of His status or rank as a human being compared to the Father. Though equal with the

---

10. Harris (*John*) clarifies that in John 10:30, the "identity of the two persons" of the Godhead "is not being asserted, but essential unity (unity of essence) is"; cf. Carson, *John*, 394–95; Tenney, *John*, 167; Westcott, *John*, 159.

11. Cf. Hurtado, *Lord Jesus Christ*, 374; Tenney, "John," 9:112.

Father, the Son had voluntarily subordinated Himself to the authority of the Father.[12] In this sense, then, the Father was greater than the Son.[13]

Earlier, Jesus' critics had demanded that He plainly state whether He was the Messiah (John 10:24). He ended up declaring Himself to be God (v. 30; cf. 20:17, 30–31), an assertion that outraged His interrogators. Because they believed He was blaspheming the name of God, they picked up nearby rocks to stone Jesus to death (John 10:31; cf. Lev 24:16; John 8:59; 11:8).[14] The Torah of God calmly reminded the religious leaders of His miraculous signs, which His heavenly Father had enabled Him to perform. The Messiah asked His inquisitors to name the good deed for which they were about to stone Him (John 10:32). In essence, it was they, not He, who fell under divine scrutiny and faced eternal condemnation for rejecting the Son's messianic claims and authority. Of course, His antagonists saw things differently. They considered the itinerant preacher to be a mere man, not God (v. 33). Since Jesus did not dispute their charge of claiming to be God, we can presume that He had explicitly affirmed His divine nature.[15]

---

12. Cowan ("The Father and Son," 116) argues that the Son's economic subordination (that is, subordination of role) to the Father is a "major theme" in the Fourth Gospel. Moreover, Carson (*John*, 250–51) points out that the "relationship between the Father and the Son is not reciprocal." Indeed, it would be impossible to imagine the Evangelist suggesting that "the Father does only what he sees the Son doing." Keener (*John*, 1:278) advances the discussion by explaining that while the Evangelist "maintains Jesus' subordination to the Father, he also attributes to him a role normally reserved for God in contemporary Jewish thought." According to Gruenler (*Trinity*, xvii), the subordination between the three members of the Godhead is "voluntarily assumed." It also "flows out of the dynamic and mutual hospitality of the divine Family as a unity." In this regard, "each of the persons of the Trinity willingly, lovingly, and voluntarily seek to serve and please the other." Thus, while the Fourth Gospel emphasizes the "distinctive roles of Father, Son, and Holy Spirit," the Evangelist also highlights "their co-inherence as interacting persons." The subordination, then, is not one in which the Son and the Spirit are reduced to "second- and third-class" status within the Godhead; instead, all three "persons of the Triune Family" remain co-equal and co-eternal with one another.

13. Witherington (*John's wisdom*, 191) explains that "Jesus is God's true and faithful agent, carrying out the Father's designs"; cf. Bock, *Jesus*, 442–43.

14. Whitacre (*John*) clarifies that in later Jewish writings, the "understanding of blasphemy . . . has to do with pronouncing the divine name" (cf. *m. Sanh.* 7:5).

15. Sproston ("Johannine Christology") regards the manner in which the Evangelist portrays Jesus of Nazareth to be a "paradox," in which the Son is shown to be fully divine and fully human. Furthermore, both of these depictions are regarded as indispensable to what the Evangelist "wishes to say about Jesus" (80). Moreover, in declaring the Son to be equal with the Father, the Evangelist is not implying Jesus' independence from God; instead, the emphasis is on Jesus being "the unique revealer of God" (82). The inscrutability of Jesus' identity as the God-man stands as a "challenge to faith" in which the reader of

The Jewish hierarchy based their actions on the Hebrew sacred writings, which on occasion were generally referred to as the "Law" (v. 34; cf. 12:34; 15:25). Accordingly, the one who is the fulfillment of the Tanakh directed His critics' attention to Psalm 82:6, which declares, "I said, 'You are "gods"; you are all sons of the Most High'" (cf. vv. 1, 5).[16] *Elohim* is the Hebrew noun rendered "gods." It can refer to Yahweh, pagan deities, or celestial beings. (The latter, whether angels or demons, exercised authority over principalities and powers in heaven and on earth.) The noun can also denote human rulers who functioned in a judicial capacity as surrogates for Yahweh (cf. Exod 21:6; 22:8; Rom 13:1–7).[17] Most likely, this is the sense in which the noun is used in Psalm 82:1, 5, and 6. Despite the lofty nature of these leaders' juridical responsibility, they were still mortals who were condemned to die (cf. v. 7). Yahweh, before His supreme court of justice, deemed this to be a fitting end for them, since they were guilty of favoring the wicked and exploiting the weak (cf. vv. 2–5). Perhaps Jesus, in quoting verse 6, was indicating that the Lord also censured the religious leaders of the Second Temple period who were unjust in their ways.

More specifically, the argument of John 10:34–36[18] is that since the Lord allowed humans and angels to be called "gods," He permitted His Son to assert His external preexistence as God (cf. Phil 2:6; Col 1:15; 2:9; Heb 1:3).[19] In point of fact, scriptural precedent established the legal basis for Jesus as Torah to declare Himself to be the Son of God (and correspondingly equal with the Father and the Spirit). The Messiah noted that because the revelation Yahweh gave the covenant community was inspired and eternally true, Scripture could never be altered or nullified (cf. Matt 5:17–19).[20] What the Son declared was just as inspired, inerrant, and in-

---

the Fourth Gospel is called to trust in the Messiah for eternal life (86).

16. Borchert (*John 1–11*, 65) observes that Jesus, in "supporting his argument of being the Son of God by a strange reference in the Psalter," demonstrated His ability to "debate with the rabbis on their own terms."

17. Cf. Lioy, *Decalogue in the Sermon on the Mount*, 52–53.

18. O'Day ("John," 9:677–78) clarifies that the argument put forward by Jesus "employs several exegetical techniques common to first- and second-century Jewish exegesis," most notably the "common rabbinic pattern of arguing from the lesser to the greater."

19. Cf. Fernando, *Relationship between law and love*, 90.

20. According to Teeple (*Mosaic eschatological prophet*, 14), within rabbinic Judaism it was widely held that "there would never be any change in the written Torah" (cf. 1 Enoch 99:2; Bar 4:1). Whitacre (*Johannine polemic*, 37) explains that, based on Jesus' statement in John 10:36 about the inviolability of Scripture, the biblical testimony concerning Jesus likewise "can be neither avoided nor negated."

fallible.[21] The veracity of this truth is seen in the fact that the Father chose, commissioned, and sent the Son into the world to fulfill a redemptive mission. In light of this, Jesus honored, rather than dishonored, the Father by claiming to be God's Son (John 10:36). Because the Messiah faithfully executed the saving work given to Him by the Father, Jesus' critics should have put their faith in Him (v. 37). Even in the midst of their doubts, the evidence of Jesus' miraculous signs should have convinced them to trust in Him. Doing so would confirm to the religious leaders once and for all that the Father is one with the Son and the Son is one with the Father. Expressed differently, they existed in loving union with each other and the Spirit as eternal members of the Godhead (v. 38; cf. 14:10–11, 20; 17:21–23).[22]

Despite Jesus' appeal, His critics spurned His messianic claims and authority.[23] Once again, they tried to seize and arrest the Messiah, but He somehow eluded their grasp (10:39). Then He went back to the less populated area of Bethany in Perea, on the east side of the Jordan River, where John the Baptizer had ministered before Herod arrested and executed him (v. 40; cf. Matt 3:1–6; 19:1; Mark 1:2–6; 10:1; Luke 3:3–6). In contrast to the growing hostility that the Savior encountered in Jerusalem, the residents of Perea welcomed Him. Since Perea was in the jurisdiction of Herod Antipas, the religious authorities could not arrest Jesus. As the people flocked to the Messiah, they recalled John's ministry. Though the Baptizer never performed a miraculous sign, he testified to Jesus being the Anointed One (John 10:41). Because John's influence had endured in Perea, many people put their faith in Jesus as the Son of God (v. 42).

---

21. Köstenberger (*Studies on John and gender*, 83) observes that "Jesus' messianic consciousness causes him to read the Old Testament" in reference to himself and issue "rabbinic rulings" that transcend the "wisdom of his contemporaries." As Keener (*John*, 1:830) notes, this tendency is consistent with the "repeated Father-Son imagery" found in the Fourth Gospel. The Evangelist depicts the Son as "the Father's imitator, agent, and image—in short, as divine Wisdom."

22. Cf. Lindars, *John*, 376.

23. Caron ("Johannine Jews," 169) remarked that while the Jewish officials claimed "ownership of the Law, of Moses, of Abraham and even of God," Jesus "systematically rejected every one of these claims." In short, He undercut the basis for their rejection of Him as the Messiah.

Jesus as Torah Declares Himself to Be the Resurrection and the Life (John 11:1–53)

The Death of Lazarus (John 11:1–16)

The short time Jesus had spent in the east and northeast of the Sea of Galilee had already come to end. As the prospect of suffering and death grew closer, the Torah of God returned to the area of Jerusalem. Though the religious establishment spurned Him (cf. John 10:39), His closest followers loved Him. Even rejection and scorn could not dim the glory of the Messiah as displayed through the restoration of Lazarus to life, a miracle that occurred in the winter of AD 29. The record of this incident is important, for it serves as an undisputed sign of the divine authority of the Logos. The episode also set in motion the plot of Jesus' enemies to finally do away with Him. Given the significance of Jesus resurrecting Lazarus, it is intriguing that the Synoptic Gospels omit the account. The strongest argument for affirming the historicity of the event is the contention that Peter was possibly absent when it occurred. Since the Fourth Gospel does not mention Peter between 6:68 and 13:6, and since Peter does not appear in the other Gospels during the same time period, it is likely that Peter had remained in Galilee and joined the group later. Because a sizable portion of the material in the Synoptic Gospels is dependent on Peter's eyewitness testimony, and because those Gospel writers had already included two separate incidents of Jesus' raising someone from the dead (cf. Matt 9:18–19, 23–26; Mark 5:21–24, 35–43; Luke 7:11–17; 8:41–42, 49–56), they may have not seen the need to add another example of the Son's divine power to resurrect.

According to John 11:1, Lazarus lived in Bethany with his sisters, Mary and Martha. The village was located on the east side of the Mount of Olives, along the road leading toward Jericho. Bethany was also about two miles from Jerusalem—close enough for Jesus and His disciples to be in danger, but sufficiently far away to avoid attracting unwelcome attention. John 12:2 says that a feast was held in Jesus' honor in Bethany, a week before His crucifixion. Matthew 26:6 reveals that it was at the home of Simon the Leper, someone else whom Jesus knew in Bethany. Luke 24:50–51 records that Jesus' ascension took place near Bethany as well.

The first mention in the Fourth Gospel of the family of Lazarus, Mary, and Martha is found in John 11:1. The sisters are also mentioned in Luke 10:38–42, and Mary's anointing of Jesus is recorded in John 12:1–8. In fact, in anticipation of the latter event, 11:2 says that Mary was the woman who poured the expensive perfume on the Messiah's feet and wiped them with her hair. Somehow Lazarus became ill, and his condition worsened to the point that Mary and Martha turned to Jesus for help (v. 3). The sisters undoubtedly had seen Him perform many miracles. They were convinced of Jesus' ability to help Lazarus. The message to the Savior most likely took about a day to reach Him. He, in turn, remained in Bethany two more days (v. 6), and it probably took about a day for Jesus and His disciples to reach Bethany. It may be that Lazarus died before the messenger reached Jesus. If so, this explains how Lazarus could have been in the grave for four days (v. 17).

Jesus' disciples also heard the grim news about Lazarus. They knew how much Mary, Martha, and Lazarus meant to Jesus. The Messiah's friendship with Mary and Martha is well documented in the Gospels and was apparently familiar to the Fourth Gospel's first-century readers. John 11:5 emphasizes that Jesus loved each member of the family. Jesus' friendship with Mary, Martha, and Lazarus shows the humanity of the Lord. Although He was the divine, incarnate Tanakh, whom the Father sent to die for humanity's sins, Jesus still experienced the same needs as people do today. Thus, it should not be surprising that Jesus had close friends who were dear to Him. In fact, it is reasonable to expect that He would want such relationships outside His ministry and work. Mary seemed to have a more emotional and devoted relationship with Jesus, as is shown when she fell down at his feet after coming to Him (v. 32). Perhaps the most dramatic example of Mary's devotion to Jesus is found in the record of the dinner party that Martha and Mary prepared for the Savior prior to His final entry into Jerusalem (12:1–8). The encounter was sufficiently well known in the church for John to refer to it before he wrote about it (cf. 11:2).

Most likely, the Torah of God sensed His disciples' concern for Lazarus and for this reason gave them an explanation that both reassured and puzzled them. First, the Messiah sought to allay the fears of the Twelve by noting that the illness would not "end in death" (v. 4). Jesus did not mean that Lazarus would not physically die, but that the end of his condition would be life, not death. Second, Jesus explained that both He and the Father would be glorified in the situation.[24] Third, Jesus did not rush

---

24. Köstenberger (*John*, 327) clarifies that "it is not that the sickness occurred *in order* for God to be glorified, but rather that it constituted an *occasion* for God's glory to be re-

off to Bethany in a panic; instead, He stayed where He was for two more days (v. 6). One reason for this delay is that the Son operated according to the Father's timetable, not that of people. A second reason is that the delay would ensure Lazarus had been dead long enough to prevent others from either misinterpreting the miracle as a fraud or as merely a resuscitation.

Based on evidence from the third century AD, it is possible that some rabbis of the New Testament era superstitiously thought the soul hovered over the body for a few days after a person died. Allegedly, it was possible during these few short days for the body to come back to life. If the person did not revive by the fourth day, then that person was deemed to be irrevocably dead (cf. Gen Rab. 100:7; Lev Rab. 18.1; Eccl Rab. 12:6; *m. Yebam.* 16:3).[25] This belief may have originated from situations where people were thought to be dead, but were only in a coma. Waiting a few days would make it clear whether that person was comatose or dead. Since it normally took a few days for decay to become apparent, there was still a possibility for revival as long as decay was absent; but once decay set in, no revival was possible.[26]

Jesus must have surprised His disciples by announcing that He was setting out for Bethany, which was in the province of Judea (John 11:7). The choice was theirs as to whether they would accompany Him despite the peril that awaited. When the Twelve voiced concern for the Rabbi's safety, Jesus as Tanakh responded with an adage probably common at the time, but that had added meaning coming from Him (v. 8). During the winter season, there were typically 12 hours of daylight. With this in mind, the Redeemer spoke of walking in the light and in the darkness. People who walk in the light do not stumble, because they can see, but people who walk in the darkness stumble because they cannot see. This is not only true with regard to physical conditions, but also true with regard to a person's spiritual journey. As long as the Son operated in the Father's will, no harm would come to Jesus. Similarly, only those who walk with the Messiah, the light of the world, can see and avoid stumbling (vv. 9–10).

Next, Jesus explained that Lazarus had "fallen asleep" (v. 11), which was a euphemistic reference to death (cf. Gen 47:30; Matt 27:52; Mark

---

vealed" (italics are his). Witherington (*John's wisdom*, 202) points out that Lazarus's "illness and the way Jesus handles it will serve to reveal God and God's Son for who they are—the authors of life." Moreover, O'Day ("John," 9:686) explains that the restoration of Lazarus to life initiated a chain of events that resulted in the "glorification of Jesus" through His "death, resurrection, and ascension" (cf. John 12:16, 23, 28; 13:31; 17:1, 4).

25. Cf. Bock, *Jesus*, 479; Bruce, *John*, 243; Evans, *Word and glory*, 167.
26. Cf. Barrett, *St. John*, 401.

5:39; Acts 7:60; 1 Cor 15:51; 1 Thess 4:13). Jesus also stated that He was going to Bethany so that He could wake up Lazarus. The disciples took Jesus to mean that Lazarus was literally sleeping, and so they were confused (John 11:13). In their minds, if Lazarus were sleeping, that meant he would also get better on his own (v. 12). Realizing His disciples' confusion, Jesus stated plainly that Lazarus had died (v. 14). The Torah of God again demonstrated His supernatural power to know things beyond normal human ability. Then He explained that this incident would give His followers another opportunity to believe in Him (v. 15).

If Jesus had been with Lazarus during the final moments of his life and healed him of his sickness, the opportunity for an even greater miracle would have been lost. Jesus intended to use the death of Lazarus as an occasion to demonstrate His power over death to the disciples and others. This was not a trivial desire on the part of the Savior. He knew that His closest followers needed their faith in Him clarified, matured, and strengthened. Consider, for example, the dialogue between Martha and Jesus, which is recorded in verses 17–27. Despite Jesus' statement that Lazarus would rise again, Martha failed to grasp what He was saying; instead, she affirmed a more general theological truth about the resurrection of the righteous. Even when Jesus plainly declared Himself to be "the resurrection and the life" (v. 25), Martha still could not quite understand what this meant for Lazarus. Though Martha affirmed Jesus' messiahship (vv. 26–27), she remained unaware of the fact that Jesus would restore Lazarus to life. Furthermore, Martha's sister, Mary, and their friends remained just as oblivious to the truth of what Jesus said He would do for Lazarus (vv. 28–37).

Verse 16 records the statement made by Thomas, who was also called Didymus. Both names literally mean the "twin" (cf. Matt 10:3; Mark 3:18; Luke 6:15; Acts 1:13). It is not known who this disciple's twin sibling might have been (whether a brother or sister). Thomas was also known as the doubter because he initially refused to accept the testimony of the other disciples concerning the risen Lord (cf. John 20:24–29). In the episode involving Lazarus, Thomas challenged his peers to go with Jesus back to Judea, where death seemed imminent for all of them (v. 16). This is the first time John mentioned Thomas. His comment shows his leadership and courage, even though he struggled with doubts.

The Declaration of Jesus as Torah to Be the Resurrection and the Life (John 11:17–37)

After Jesus and His group arrived in Bethany, they learned that four days earlier the body of Lazarus had been placed in a tomb (John 11:17). Since a dead body decayed quickly in the hot Palestinian climate, the family of Lazarus would have had his body anointed, wrapped, and laid in the family tomb soon after he had expired. The four days is significant in that Jesus would not have reached His friend while he was still alive, even if the Savior had left Perea immediately after hearing about the illness of Lazarus. The delay was to assure, in the minds of the people, that the raising of Lazarus from the dead was truly a miracle. Since Jerusalem was no more than a few miles from Bethany (v. 18), a number of Jews from the city paid their respects to Martha and Mary during their time of grief (v. 19). Evidently, this family had a commanding influence or was popular among the local people. The proximity between Bethany and Jerusalem indicates that news of the miracle would have circulated quickly throughout the holy city.

When the sisters of Lazarus heard that Jesus was approaching their village, Martha went out to greet Him, while Mary remained in the house (v. 20). On the surface, Martha's first words to Jesus appear to be a veiled rebuke (v. 21). After all, she previously scolded Jesus for her sister's apparent idleness. Martha, however, probably knew that Jesus could not come in time to heal her brother of his illness. Thus Martha's comment was more likely an expression of regret that Jesus could not be present, a feeling the sisters probably spoke about quite often during the previous four days. Martha's next remark might be interpreted as a sign of a remarkable faith in Jesus' power to raise people from the dead (v. 22). Later, however, Martha was the one who complained when Jesus ordered the stone to be removed from the entrance to the tomb of Lazarus (cf. v. 39). It is possible that Martha was merely noting that she still had faith in Jesus, for Martha was certain that God granted Jesus whatever request He asked (v. 22).

After the Son as Torah declared to Martha that her brother would rise from the dead (v. 23), Martha showed that she had not thought about Jesus' bringing Lazarus back to life at that time; instead, Martha voiced the view of the Pharisees that God would resurrect the just at the last day (v. 24; cf. Isa 26:19; Dan 12:2; Matt 22:23; Acts 23:7–8). Jesus' statement may have been said to Martha and her sister many times by others to comfort them, and now it may have sounded hollow to her. Jesus' response is incredible. He could have said that He would resurrect Lazarus; instead,

Jesus declared, "I am the resurrection and the life" (John 11:25). His declaration is the fifth of seven "I am" statements that highlight His divinity and messiahship. Jesus, in fact, is the life of the age to come, and all who put their trust in Him will experience the resurrected life (v. 26). When Jesus asked Martha whether she believed what He was saying, He was actually asking her whether she believed in Him. The Messiah wanted her (and all other people) to begin experiencing right now the joys of eternal life. The raising of Lazarus was intended to foster such faith in the Son of God; and the apostle's inclusion of this miracle in the Fourth Gospel was designed to encourage people down through the ages to put their trust in Jesus as the Messiah (cf. 20:30–31).

Regardless of her fretful nature, Martha had amazing faith in Jesus. She not only replied positively, but was also clear about what she believed—that Jesus is the Messiah, God's only divine Son, and the one who came into the world from heaven and became a human being (11:27). Few, if any, could have affirmed the Son any better than Martha. Her confession of faith parallels that voiced by Peter (cf. Matt 16:16). Leaving Jesus outside her village, Martha went back home and told Mary that the Teacher wanted to see her. The Greek article rendered "the" in John 11:28 is important here because it denotes that the sisters regarded the Tanakh of God as having far more authority than other Jewish rabbis. Naturally, Mary took Jesus' request as a command and hurried to the place where Martha had conversed with Him.

Apparently, Mary was in such a rush to comply—and probably was also anxious to see Jesus—that her Jewish comforters (e.g. relatives, friends, and neighbors) took notice and followed her. They assumed that she was going to continue her mourning at her brother's tomb and thought they would join in her grieving (vv. 29–31). Although Mary's words are almost identical to her sister's first words to Jesus, her actions departed dramatically from Martha's. Mary fell at the feet of the Lord Jesus in homage to Him and wept as she spoke (v. 32). She, too, believed He had the power to heal her brother of his illness, but now it was apparently too late.

The Messiah eventually arrived at the tomb where the body of Lazarus had been placed. Verse 33 says that at the sight of the wailing, Jesus was "deeply moved in spirit and troubled." On one level, the phrase suggests Jesus was touched with sympathy at the sight and perhaps indignant at the sorrow caused by death that sin has brought to the human condition.[27] On

---

27. According to Ridderbos (*John*, 403), Jesus, as the Father's emissary, was "moved to resist the demonstration of human impotence in the face of death." By restoring Lazarus to life, the Son would prove that death did not have the "last, decisive word in the world."

another level, though, the Savior seemed agitated by the unbelief of His closest followers.[28] The Messiah had plainly stated that He would restore Lazarus to life. Nonetheless, Martha and Mary, instead of rejoicing over what the Son as Torah was about to do, remained filled with despair over their brother's death. This attitude of unbelief and doubt is reflected in the statement made by some of the onlookers (recorded in v. 37).

So that Jesus could demonstrate His divine power at Lazarus's tomb, He asked where the burial site was located (v. 34). As the sisters directed Jesus to the grave, He showed His grief by crying (v. 35). The Greek word used to describe His tears suggests a quiet mourning, not the loud wailing of the other mourners. In response to Jesus' tears, some of bystanders noted how much He loved His friend (v. 36), while others wondered why He had not healed Lazarus of his sickness. After all, Jesus was able to restore sight to a blind man several months earlier (v. 37; cf. 9:1–7). None of onlookers, however, were anticipating the awesome display of glory that was about to take place in their presence. God's glory often shines brightest when circumstances seem like they could not be more dark.

The Restoration of Lazarus to Life by Jesus as Torah (John 11:38–44)

One can only imagine the emotions the Son felt as He approached the tomb of Lazarus, a cave with a stone rolled across its entrance (John 11:38). In Jesus' day, people used caves carved in the limestone rock of a hillside as tombs. These graves were large enough for people to walk inside, and a tomb could hold several corpses. Martha did not understand why Jesus would want the stone removed from the tomb's entrance. She noted that after four days the smell from the decomposing corpse of Lazarus would be terrible (v. 39). The Messiah as Torah, ever patient in the midst of such confusion, stated once again that if Martha had faith, she would witness the glory of God (for example, in Jesus' restoring Lazarus to life; v. 40). Unlike the Egyptians, the Jews neither tightly wrapped the body of the deceased nor embalmed it. Instead, they loosely wrapped the body in linen cloth and added spices between the layers and folds.[29] The aromatic spices helped to counteract (but not completely eliminate) the objection-

---

28. Nicol (*Semeia*, 61) observed that "Jesus' anger at unbelief is in harmony with the Jewish notion that God's wrath rests on unbelief"; cf. Beasley-Murray, *John*, 193; Bock, *Jesus*, 480; Carson, *John*, 415–16; Lenski, *St. John's Gospel*, 807–9; Lightfoot, *St. John's Gospel*, 229; O'Day, "John," 9:690; Westcott, *John*, 170–71; Witherington, *John's wisdom*, 203–4.

29. Cf. Keener, *John*, 2:848.

able odors resulting from the decomposition of the corpse. One can only imagine the bewilderment and skepticism among the onlookers. Though Jesus' command to remove the stone from the tomb of Lazarus seemed to go against common sense, it was done anyway (v. 41).

The prayer voiced by the Son, which is recorded in verses 41 and 42, is not so much a petition as it is an expression of thanksgiving to the Father. The Anointed One knew in advance that the Father would grant His request, and so the Redeemer gave thanks for this. Jesus declared in the hearing of the onlookers that the Father always answered His requests. Jesus stated this openly, not for His own benefit, but rather for the sake of the bystanders. It was His desire that in seeing the miracle, they would believe His claim to be the Messiah. In restoring Lazarus to life, Jesus would prove that He is the master of death. Ironically, though, this miracle would set in motion a series of events that would lead directly to His arrest and eventual execution; yet even in the Son's crucifixion, both He and the Father would be glorified (17:1, 5).

When the divine, incarnate Tanakh had finished praying, He simply and directly commanded Lazarus to exit from the tomb (11:43). In one sense, this served as a preview of the power of the Son that will be fully displayed in the final resurrection when all who have died will hear His voice and live (cf. 5:25, 28–29). Lazarus, who had been unquestionably dead, came out of the tomb. His hands and feet were still wrapped with strips of burial cloth, and a separate cloth covered his face. Next, Jesus told the people to unwrap the burial clothes and headcloth from Lazarus and let him go (11:44). By doing this, they would know that Lazarus was truly alive and that his appearance was not merely a magic trick.

The Plot to Kill Jesus as Torah
(John 11:45–53)

Many of the bystanders, when they saw the miracle, put their faith in Jesus as the Messiah (John 11:45). In fact, Lazarus became something of a curiosity, for he drew numerous onlookers who wanted to see for themselves the person whom Jesus had brought back to life (cf. 12:9). Other bystanders responded oppositely to the miracle. They went to the Pharisees and reported what Jesus had done (11:46). In turn, they and the chief priests convened an informal meeting of the ruling council to explore their options (v. 47). None of the religious leaders could deny the miraculous signs the Nazarene performed; but rather than accept His messianic claims, the authorities feared what would happen if Jesus was allowed to continue unchecked. The worst possibility was that a riot would ensue as a result of so many people believing in Him. In the process of quelling the revolt, the Roman legions would also destroy the temple, the holy city, and the entire nation (v. 48). Paradoxically, this happened in AD 70 at the hands of Titus, a Roman general and future emperor.[30]

Caiaphas, who was the high priest from AD 18–36, lampooned the idea that such a doomsday scenario was inevitable (v. 49). He noted that it was politically advantageous to eliminate the Galilean in order to keep the entire nation from perishing (v. 50). In the providence of God, Caiaphas, as high priest, unwittingly foretold that the eschatological Lamb would die to make redemption possible for the Jewish people (v. 51; cf. Isa 53:8; Mark 10:45; 1 Pet 1:18–19). The Messiah's atoning sacrifice would also lead to the formation of a worldwide spiritual body of regenerate Jews and Gentiles (John 11:52; cf. Isa 43:5; 49:6; Ezek 34:12; Matt 28:18–20; Luke 24:47; John 1:12–13, 29; 3:16; 4:42; 10:16; 17:20–23; Acts 1:8; Gal 6:16; Jas 1:1; 1 Pet 1:1). Thus, it was after the restoration of Lazarus to life that the religious elite finally determined to put Jesus to death (John 11:46–53). In short, this miracle becomes the "immediate cause of the passion and resurrection of Jesus."[31]

Jesus as Torah Discloses the Reality of His Upcoming Death and Resurrection (John 11:54—12:50)

The Threat to the Life of Jesus as Torah (John 11:54–57)

Because of the increasing levels of hostility Jesus encountered from the religious authorities in Jerusalem, He decided to stop traveling around publicly in the capital and its environs. He and His disciples went out to a town called Ephraim, which was near the wilderness (John 11:54). The identity and location of this village remains uncertain, though it was possibly 12 to 15 miles northeast of Jerusalem. As AD 29 ended and AD 30 started, Jesus began His final trip to the holy city to die on the cross as an atoning sacrifice for the lost (cf. Luke 9:51).[32] The journey leading up to His divinely appointed end involved Him traveling from one town or vil-

---

30. Cf. Köstenberger, *John*, 350.
31. Labahn, "Between tradition and literary art," 180.
32. Cf. Schnackenburg, *John*, 1:15.

lage to the next and teaching the residents about the kingdom of God (cf. 13:22; 17:11; 18:31; 19:28, 41). The Greek of 9:51 literally says that Jesus "set His face" to go to the capital, which is an idiomatic way of indicating the Messiah's steadfast resolve to complete the mission of redemption His Father had given Him (cf. Isa 50:7). In short, the Son as Tanakh came to earth to give His life as a ransom for many, and nothing would deter Him from that end (Matt 20:28).

It was the spring of AD 30, six days before the Passover was to begin, that the Messiah went back to Bethany (cf. John 12:1). It was there He had earlier restored Lazarus to life (cf. 11:38–44). This would be the last Jewish festival to occur before Jesus went to the cross. In the days leading up to the feast, pilgrims from the rural areas around Jerusalem traveled to the capital to prepare themselves ritually (11:55). In order to participate, the religious establishment required that worshipers ceremonially purify themselves. As they congregated in the temple courts, the pilgrims kept looking for Jesus and wondering whether He would come to observe Passover (v. 56). Meanwhile, the ruling council had publicly ordered that anyone who saw the Nazarene should report it at once to the authorities. In this way, the chief priests and Pharisees hoped to bring about Jesus' arrest (v. 57).

The Anointing of Jesus as Torah at Bethany (John 12:1–11)

While Jesus stayed at Bethany (John 12:1), Martha prepared a meal for Him and the rest of the guests (v. 2). Possibly the dinner was given in honor of the Messiah to thank Him for what He had done for Lazarus.[33] Indeed, Lazarus reclined at the table with the Torah of God, no doubt giving Him his undivided attention. In those days, guests in wealthy homes normally did not eat a meal while sitting at a table; instead, they leaned on cushions with their left arm and ate food with their right hand. Their head would be near the table and their feet extended away from it.

At some point during the meal, Mary broke the seal on a jar containing about 12 ounces of pure nard and poured it on Jesus' feet.[34] (The more

---

33. Cf. Keener, *John*, 2:862.

34. Nard is an herb with rose-purple flowers and fibrous roots that give off a pleasant aroma. In Bible times, people dried the roots of this plant and used them to make perfume or ointment. The Romans anointed their heads with the product. Nard can be found throughout western Asia and is also native to the high elevations of the Himalayan Mountains. The perfume made from the nard that is mentioned in the Bible most likely originated in the Himalayas (Song 1:12; 4:13–14; Mark 14:3; John 12:3). Merchants transported the product in carefully sealed alabaster jars. The seal ensured both the preservation

common practice was to anoint a person's head.) After pouring the nard on Jesus' feet, Mary used her hair to wipe His feet. As Mary did this, the sweet smell of the perfume diffused throughout the house (v. 3). In Jesus' day, slaves usually took care of the guests' feet. Thus Mary's actions were a sign of humility. In Jewish culture, most women would not unbind their hair in public; but Mary did not allow this social convention to stop her from showing devotion to the Son as Tanakh. The sacrificial aspect of Mary's action is underscored by the expense of the perfume she used to anoint Jesus' feet.

Judas Iscariot, the imminent traitor of the Messiah, protested against Mary's action (v. 4). Judas noted that the ointment cost 300 denarii, which was about one year's wages for a rural worker. He asked why the perfume had not been sold and the proceeds given to the poor (v. 5). Evidently, the rest of the Twelve shared his view (cf. Matt 26:8–9; Mark 14:4–5). On the surface, the idea advanced by Judas sounded pious; but the author of the Fourth Gospel explained that Judas did not really care about the poor. He was irritated because Mary's action prevented Judas from having more money to pilfer, since he was the group's treasurer and sometimes stole the money (John 12:6). Interestingly, the cost Mary bore to show devotion to the Messiah was several times the amount Judas later accepted to betray Jesus (cf. Matt 26:5). It is also worth noting that the remarks Judas made were inconsiderate of the Redeemer and unnecessarily harsh toward Mary.

Jesus told Judas to leave Mary alone. The Savior explained that Mary had kept the perfume to anoint Him in anticipation of His upcoming burial (John 12:7). In those days, it was a Jewish custom to anoint the body of a deceased loved one with sweet-smelling oil and spices prior to burying the corpse. The Messiah was alluding to the fact that in less than a week, the authorities would arrest, condemn, and crucify Him.[35] The Son as Torah further noted that while it is important to minister to the poor, they would always be present in society; yet He would not always be visibly present among His followers (v. 8). That is why Mary's costly act of devotion was appropriate and commendable. Previously, Jesus had stressed

---

and the conservation of the perfume. The customer would break the seal only when he or she intended to use the ointment. Because merchants shipped nard over great distances, the product was very expensive. In New Testament times, a pint of pure nard cost about a year's wages (cf. Mark 14:3–5). Because of its great expense, the product was used only by the wealthy, and then only for the anointing of special guests.

35. Köstenberger (*John*, 358) states that the account of the anointing at Bethany is a "tale of contrasts." For instance, "Mary's lavish devotion to Jesus is set against the backdrop of the looming prospect of Judas's betrayal of his master." Also, "the man whom Jesus had raised from the dead, Lazarus, takes part in the dinner, while Jesus himself is anointed for burial."

the ongoing need to help the poor (cf. Matt 25:34–36). In the anointing at Bethany, the Redeemer affirmed another important truth, namely, that it is never a waste to give one's best to honor the Lord.

When residents from the rural areas around Jerusalem learned that the Savior was in Bethany, many flocked to see Him. They also wanted to see Lazarus, whom they learned Jesus had restored to life (John 12:9). The miracle involving Lazarus prompted many to reject the religious leaders and put their faith in Jesus as Tanakh. Because this turn of events stoked the fears of the chief priests, they made plans to have both Lazarus and Jesus murdered (vv. 10–11). Judas Iscariot would play a pivotal role in helping the authorities eliminate the itinerant preacher from Galilee. When Judas met with the chief priests, he asked how much they would pay him to help them in their efforts to arrest Jesus. In response, the religious leaders agreed to give the traitor 30 pieces of silver (about how much a rural worker would earn over a two- or three-month period). From then on, Judas began to look for a good opportunity to betray the Savior (cf. Matt 26:14–16).

The Triumphal Entry of Jesus as Torah to Jerusalem (John 12:12–19)

It was Sunday when the Messiah made His triumphal entry into Jerusalem while seated on a young donkey (John 12:12, 14). This was a pivotal event described in all four Gospels. Jesus and His followers were approaching Bethphage, a village whose name in Aramaic means "house of unripe figs." It was somewhere on the eastern slopes of the Mount of Olives, near Bethany. From this town one could perhaps look down upon the Kidron Valley and Jerusalem. The Messiah sent two of His disciples into the nearby village to arrange His transportation into Jerusalem (cf. Matt 21:1; Luke 19:29). He told them that as soon as they entered Bethphage (perhaps just inside the village gate), they would see a female donkey with its colt, both tethered (Matt 21:2). Luke 19:30 reveals that no one had ever ridden the colt. Since the animal was probably unbroken, the Torah of God's success in riding it is evidently an indication of His control over nature.

The disciples were to untie the animals and bring them to Jesus. If His followers were questioned, they were to offer the explanation, "The Lord needs it" (v. 31). Furthermore, they were to assure any challenger that the Lord would return the donkeys soon—right after He was done with them (cf. Matt 21:3). Jesus' purpose in riding a donkey into the capital was to present Himself to Jerusalem as the kingly Messiah promised in Zechariah 9:9. The donkey was so noble an animal to people of that time that a monarch often rode astride one when visiting a region of his kingdom on a peaceful mission (cf. Judg 5:10; 1 Kgs 1:33). Probably the divine, incarnate Tanakh determined to display His own royal nature by entering Jerusalem as the Prince of Peace.[36]

Matthew 21:2 is the only passage that mentions two animals in Jesus' triumphal entry. The other three Gospels refer only to the colt. Zechariah 9:9 says that the Messiah would come riding on a donkey colt, an unbroken "foal," which no person had ever ridden (cf. Mark 11:2). Unused animals were often taken for religious purposes (cf. Num 19:2; 1 Sam 6:7–8). Jesus rode the young colt, but the colt's mother could also have been taken along as a steadying influence, leading the way as the colt followed (cf. Matt 21:7). Therefore, the mention of two animals is more than likely an eyewitness detail from Matthew. The other Gospel writers simply mentioned the actual animal that Jesus rode. Luke 19:32–34 reveals that Jesus' disciples followed His instructions, bringing the donkey and the colt to Him. In fact, everything occurred just as the Torah of God had said. The disciples found the animals; the owners questioned the disciples; and they told about the Lord's need.

Once the disciples had obtained the colt, they brought the animal to Jesus. Then His followers threw their cloaks[37] on the colt and had the Savior mount the animal (John 12:14; cf. Luke 19:35).[38] As the news

---

36. Cf. the theme of Jesus' kingship in the Passion narrative recorded in John 18:28—19:22.

37. In Bible times, most people had very few articles of clothing. Often what people wore was all they owned; however, the one indispensable and most useful piece of clothing was a cloak. For example, the cloak became a kind of knapsack in which loose items could be wrapped and slung over the shoulder for easy transport. As the Israelites left slavery behind in Egypt, they most likely carried their meager belongings in this fashion. Women used their cloaks as infant carriers, while farmers sowed crops with grain carried in a sack made from a cloak and hung around the neck. At night, a cloak served as a pillow or blanket, depending on the time of year. Moreover, when a special guest came to visit, bound by proper etiquette, a good host might cover the dusty ground with a cloak to provide a place to sit.

38. The donkey on which Jesus rode into Jerusalem was much different from its stubborn European counterpart. The donkeys of Palestine were more tame and peaceful animals. They had an easy gait and were surefooted. Most were North African in origin, and their color was reddish brown. People used these animals as beasts of burden, and seldom did the donkeys have riders. When they were ridden, heavy saddles were not placed upon them; instead, a soft woven covering was placed over their backs and attached with a cord. They accepted almost any burden placed over them. In Old Testament times, although the people of Israel considered donkeys as objects of wealth, they saw owning at least one beast of burden as necessary for basic survival. The number of donkeys a person owned was often

of Jesus' arrival quickly spread throughout Jerusalem, a large number of people hurried to meet Him along the route. These were probably Jewish pilgrims on their way to the city of God to celebrate the Passover festival. Most likely, they had heard about Jesus' demonstrations of power. Indeed, they praised Him with palm branches (John 12:13).[39]

In Bible times, the Jews applied religious symbolism to the palm tree. For example, the psalmist described the righteous as flourishing like the palm tree (cf. Ps 92:12). Also, in accordance with the Mosaic law, they celebrated the Feast of Tabernacles with palm branches (cf. Lev 23:40). During the intertestamental period, the covenant community used palm branches in their observance of other feasts as "symbols of national triumph and victory"[40] (cf. 1 Macc 13:51, 2 Macc 10:7; 14:4). Early Christians adopted this appreciation of the palm tree. John himself noted that people in heaven will pay homage to the Messiah with palm branches (Rev 7:9), which became a symbol of His victory over death. In fact, the emblem of the palm leaf frequently accompanied the monogram of the Savior on Christian tombs.

Jesus entered the holy city fully aware that its religious leaders were already planning to kill Him (cf. John 12:10–11); yet He made no attempt to sneak into Jerusalem unnoticed. Indeed, to the acclaim of the masses, Jesus entered the capital as a king and courageously welcomed the people's praise of Him as the Messiah (cf. Luke 19:38). John 12:13 quotes Psalm 118:25 and 26 to emphasize the salvific, regal status of the one who fulfills all the types and prophecies of the Old Testament. The pilgrims' cry of "Hosanna" (John 12:13) is a one-word prayer that means "(O Lord,) give salvation now!" The worshipers joyously acclaimed that the Anointed One, who came in the name of the Lord, was the object of His favor. Indeed, the Father chose, commissioned, and empowered His Son to be the King of Israel.

---

a measure of that person's economic worth. While the Israelites used donkeys for plowing, the law forbade them to yoke a donkey to an ox (cf. Deut 22:10). The law also prohibited them from eating a donkey's flesh. People considered the donkey a royal animal, as kings often rode them in times of peace.

39. From ancient times, people in the Middle East have valued the palm tree for its usefulness and beauty. Its branches and leaves are used as ornaments, while its sap is made into sugar, wax, oil, tannin, and dye. People in the Middle East eat its fruit and grind its seed for their camels. They use its branches in the production of mats, roofs, baskets, and fences. To desert travelers, the shade of a palm tree is a welcome sight.

40. O'Day, "John," 9:707; cf. Lightfoot, *St. John's Gospel,* 250; Witherington, *John's wisdom,* 221.

As the "Prince of Peace" (Isa 9:6), the Messiah will one day bring peace and manifest God's glory throughout creation—even to the heights of heaven (cf. Luke 19:38). This truth mirrors what the shepherds heard on the night of the Savior's birth. They were greeted by a chorus of angels who gave glory to God and announced peace for all who received the Lord's favor (cf. 2:14). John 12:14 quotes Zechariah 9:9 to reinforce the providential way in which Jesus as Torah was the realization of all that the Hebrew sacred writings foretold concerning the divine plan of redemption. John 12:16 notes that at first Jesus' disciples did not grasp the deeper meaning of the incidents connected with the Redeemer's triumphal entry into Jerusalem. Like the exuberant crowd, the disciples thought that Jesus was the Messiah; but also like them, they did not comprehend the true nature of His mission. After Jesus was raised into His glory, however, His disciples came to realize that the Old Testament messianic prophecies were about the Savior. They also began to recognize what they themselves had done for their Lord.

As Jesus rode along, the pilgrims spread their cloaks on the road (cf. Luke 19:36). This was a mark of respect sometimes used in that culture. Those people who had followed Jesus from Bethany mixed with the larger crowd that had come to worship Jesus. They told the others that they had witnessed an incredible miracle. They had seen Jesus call Lazarus from his tomb and return him to life. News of this miracle quickly spread so that people from Jerusalem and the surrounding area came to see the extraordinary healer who had performed this sign (John 12:17–18). When Jesus entered Jerusalem at the Passover season, Israel was celebrating its deliverance from slavery in Egypt. At Passover, the city teemed with possibly hundreds of thousands of Jews who had flocked to it for Israel's patriotic festival. No doubt they were interested in deliverance from the occupying Roman armies.

The Pharisees responded to this fanfare with panic and pessimism. They had attempted to ruin Jesus' popularity among the people, but had utterly failed; instead, it appeared to them that the whole world had become enamored with the teacher from Nazareth, who was becoming more and more of a thorn in their side (12:19). Tradition maintains that the crowd who shouted praises to Jesus on Palm Sunday was the same group that called for His crucifixion on Good Friday; however, the people who acclaimed Him on Sunday were more likely Galilean Jews on the road into town who recognized Jesus' power and desired His ministry. Those at the end of the week who wanted His death probably lived in Jerusalem and the area of Judea. The religious leaders plotting to kill Jesus may have also handpicked that group.

The Suffering and Glorification of Jesus as Torah (John 12:20–36)

At this point in John's narrative, the apostle briefly mentioned "some Greeks" (John 12:20), who were on a pilgrimage to Jerusalem to worship at the Passover feast. The term "Greeks" does not necessarily mean that they were from Greece, nor does it mean that they were Greek-speaking Jews. Instead, they were probably Gentiles who had converted to Judaism.[41] Haenchen notes that for "the Evangelist they represent the Greek world in general, and thus also the pagan world."[42] Since Jesus as Tanakh generated so much excitement, it is not surprising that both Jews and Gentiles eagerly wanted to see Him. Some of these Greeks approached Philip, hoping to gain an audience with the Savior through a member of His inner circle. John did not say why they asked Philip, though the Evangelist noted once more that Philip was from Bethsaida in Galilee (cf. 1:44). The pilgrims might have selected Philip because he had a Greek name and presumably would respond more kindly to their request (12:21).[43] In any case, he told Andrew, and together they delivered this message to Jesus (v. 22).

Jesus' reply must have bewildered the two disciples. He not only seemed to ignore their petition, but He also voiced a series of enigmatic statements.[44] Actually, the interest of the Greeks is significant, for it indicated that the scope of the Redeemer's ministry went beyond the Jews, encompassing the whole world. Now that He was drawing the attention of both Jews and Gentiles, the time would soon be right for Him, as the Son of Man, to lay down His life and then be glorified.[45] It would later become clear to His disciples that their Master did not die just for the Jews, but for Jewish and Gentile believers. Thus the Torah of God did answer their question. Anyone who seeks the Messiah can come to Him in faith (v. 23). Jesus gave the analogy of a grain of wheat to indicate the purpose of His ministry. A wheat kernel is a single seed, but if it is buried in the ground and dies, it will spring up into a plant and produce a multitude of seeds (v. 24). Likewise, after the Son died and was buried, the Father would raise

---

41. Cf. Hoskyns, *The Fourth Gospel*, 423; Schnackenburg, *John*, 2:381.
42. Haenchen, *John 2*, 96.
43. Cf. Barrett, *St. John*, 422.
44. Cf. Bultmann, *John*, 423.
45. Cf. Bultmann, *John*, 425–26.

Him from death to life so that many could be redeemed and live through Him (cf. 1 Enoch 49:1; 62:14; Pss Sol 17–18; 4 Ezra 7:28–29). Obviously, Jesus was speaking about Himself.

Jesus extended the analogy of a wheat kernel by applying it to people in general. Using the expression of love and hate, Jesus did not intend for His words to be taken literally. By loving one's life, Jesus was speaking of serving oneself above all others and making one's own life more important than anything else. When people do this, they fail to preserve their life and instead will lose it. By hating their life, Jesus was speaking of serving others before oneself and submitting one's life to the Lord. When people do this, God will bless them with a life in which they will enjoy eternal fellowship with Him (John 12:25). In short, believers must die to themselves if they expect to bear much fruit for God.[46] The key to the abundant life is being a servant to Jesus, and to be His servant, believers must follow wherever He leads them. In truth, Jesus serves as a model for believers to follow. As the Son served the Father, even to the point of sacrificing His life, believers are to give their lives in sacrificial service to Him (cf. 13:14–16; 15:18—16:4). Furthermore, because of the Father's love for His Son, He will honor all who faithfully serve Jesus and will include them in His Son's glory (12:26).

Despite the adoration being lavished upon Him, Jesus revealed His inner anguish to His close friends. He knew that the cross awaited Him. Unlike everyone else who presumed that the Torah of God would be exalted in a worldly sense, Jesus knew the tide would turn. He was about to suffer intensely, and only His Father could deliver Him from the coming ordeal. Despite His unease, Jesus also knew that it was for this purpose that He came into the world—to die so that others could live (cf. 2 Cor 5:21). Accordingly, He remained firm in His determination to serve God in this way (John 12:27; cf. Ps 6:4). Indeed, the Son would do it in order to glorify His Father (John 12:28). In the garden of Gethsemane, the Messiah displayed a similar unwavering commitment to fulfill the redemptive plan and purpose of God (cf. Matt 26:38–39; Mark 14:34–36; Luke 22:42).

After Jesus as Tanakh concluded His discourse with prayer, the Father acknowledged and affirmed His Son in a voice so that all who were present could hear.[47] The Father declared that His name not only had been

---

46. Keener (*John*, 2:873) thinks that while the idea of fruitfulness in John 12:24–26 "can refer to the produce of a believer's life (15:8)," in the present context it "refers to the harvest of other lives (4:36)."

47. In rabbinic literature, the sound from heaven was called the *bat qol*, which literally means "daughter of the voice," that is, an "echo of a heavenly voice." Köstenberger

glorified (e.g. through the Son's obedience while on earth), but also would be glorified again (e.g. through the Son's death, burial, resurrection, and ascension; John 12:28). God's voice, however, perplexed the people. Some mistook the sound for thunder, while others thought that an angel had spoken (v. 29). In response to their confusion, Jesus noted that God's audible endorsement of Him and His ministry was for their encouragement (v. 30).[48] This is the third recorded occasion in which a heavenly voice was publicly heard concerning Jesus, and the first instance in the Fourth Gospel. The other two events were during Jesus' baptism (cf. Matt 3:17; Mark 1:11; Luke 3:22) and transfiguration (cf. Matt 17:5; Mark 9:7; Luke 9:35). The first was at the beginning of Jesus' public ministry, the second at a crucial turning point in His ministry, and the last toward the end of His ministry.

The eternal Torah explained that the voice from heaven was for the benefit of those listening to Him (John 12:30). Moreover, Jesus noted that the hour had come, not only for Him to be glorified, but also for Satan and the world to be judged (cf. John 14:30; 16:11; 2 Cor 4:4; Eph 2:2; 6:12). When Jesus was raised up in glory, God's enemies would be driven out in defeat and disgrace, and await certain doom at the end of the age (John 12:31; cf. Rev 12:12; 19:11–21; 20:7–15). The Son's crucifixion, burial, and resurrection would draw people from all over the world to Him in saving faith (John 12:32).[49] Jesus described His death in this way to indicate not only how He was about to die, but more importantly, what it would mean (v. 33). As 1:9 reveals, the Messiah's redemptive mission brings the light of divine truth to a sin-cursed world and exposes the spiritual need

---

(*John*, 382) notes the common belief in the Second Temple period of Judaism that the "prophetic office had ceased and would not be renewed until the onset of the messianic age." Allegedly, the *bat qol* was all that God's people could anticipate until then. In contrast with the rabbis, who "thought of the divine voice as a mere echo," the "voice from heaven" (John 12:28)—which endorsed the Son—came from the Father. The idea, then, is that the heavenly voice, along with the testimony of John the Baptizer and the witness of Scripture, helped confirm the divine, messianic identity of Jesus; cf. Carson, *John*, 441; Evans, *Word and glory*, 158; Keener, *John*, 1:458; Stern, *Jewish New Testament commentary*, 193.

48. Keener (*John*, 2:877) puts forward the possibility that the reference to thunder in John 12:29 might be an allusion to the thunder and lightning the Israelites witnessed at Mount Sinai (cf. Exod 19:16; 20:18). If so, then "God's confirmation of Jesus' mission of the cross would constitute the new Sinai revelation."

49. Scannell (*Fulfillment of Johannine signs*) mentions that as a result of Jesus being crucified, "the hold of evil over human beings" was broken, allowing "all people to be drawn to the Son of Man" (107). Also, for the first time, people once blinded by "the power of the devil" were given the ability to "see Jesus and his signs with the eyes of faith," enabling them to trust in Him for salvation (108).

that all people have for salvation. All who encounter the Light can either choose to receive or renounce Him (cf. 3:19–21). It is by putting their faith in Him that believers become truly enlightened.[50]

The crowd listened to the eternal Tanakh, but they did not understand what He meant. They contended that His words were in conflict with the Mosaic law (possibly a general reference to the entire Old Testament; cf. 10:34; 15:25).[51] Furthermore, they alleged that, according to the Hebrew sacred writings, the Messiah would never die, but remain forever (cf. Pss 89:30–37; 110:4; Isa 9:7; Ezek 37:25; Dan 7:14; Mic 5:2).[52] In this case, the people were reading their expectations into the Scriptures. They were so confused about Jesus' teaching concerning the Son of Man that they inquired as to this person's identity (John 12:34). Jesus did not directly answer the question posed to Him. Rather than proclaiming Himself to be the Son of Man and trying to explain His divine mission in that role, Jesus stressed how urgent it was for His hearers to decide and act upon what He declared as the Torah of God. Using the symbols of light and darkness, Jesus warned His audience that He, as the light, would be with them in His earthly presence only a short time longer (v. 35).[53] Now was the time to put their trust in Him, before the darkness came. Those who did not would remain lost in the darkness, but those who entrusted themselves to the Son would become children of light. After Jesus spoke to the crowd, He went away and secluded Himself with His disciples (v. 36). Jesus' public ministry was coming to a close, and He needed to prepare for the rejection and suffering He was about to experience.

The Consequences of Belief and Unbelief in Jesus as Torah (John 12:37–50)

Most of the pilgrims who came to see Jesus refused to put their faith in Him, despite having witnessed the many miracles He had performed

---

50. Lioy, *Search for ultimate reality*, 76.

51. Cf. O'Day, "John," 9:713; Tenney, "John," 9:131.

52. Carson (*John*, 445) states that "the Palestinian Judaism of the time expected the Messiah to be triumphant." Additionally, "most expected him to be eternal" (cf. 1 Enoch 49:1; 62:14; Pss Sol 17:4). Also, cf. Beasley-Murray, *John*, 215; Fernando, *Relationship between law and love*, 91–92.

53. Keener (*John*, 2:882) notes that the "conflict between the forces of light and darkness," which forms the backdrop of Jesus' remarks in John 12:35–36, "fits the language of sectarian Palestinian Judaism, which also spoke of the 'children of light' . . . versus the 'children of darkness'" (cf. Luke 16:8; Eph 5:8; 1 Thess 5:5).

(John 12:37). In fact, the prophet Isaiah[54] had foretold that the people of Jesus' day would reject the suffering Servant of God (v. 38; cf. Isa 53:1). John pointed to the ministry of the prophet Isaiah to explain the people's unbelief. The Lord had commissioned Isaiah to take His message to the people of Judah, while warning him that His words would blind their eyes and deaden their hearts (John 12:39–40; cf. Isa 6:10; 29:10; Matt 13:13–14; Mark 4:12; Luke 8:10; Acts 28:26–27; Rom 11:8). The people would become so obstinate that they could neither see nor understand God's message, and so hardened that they could not repent and be healed of their sins. They were like a child who has misbehaved, and once scolded, becomes even more rebellious. Similarly, the people who heard the Tanakh of God and witnessed His great deeds, refused to repent. In contrast, when Isaiah witnessed the preincarnate glory of the divine Messiah enthroned in His heavenly temple (cf. Isa 6:1–5), the prophet fell down in worship (John 12:41).[55] Jesus' glory included dying as an atoning sacrifice, rising

---

54. Isaiah, whose name means "Yahweh is salvation," was born about 760 BC and reared in Jerusalem during days of prosperity. Evidently, his family was affluent, enabling him to obtain a good education. Jewish tradition holds that Isaiah's father, Amoz, was a brother of King Amaziah (cf. 2 Chron 26:22; Isa 1:1). If so, Isaiah was a grandson of King Joash and a first cousin of King Uzziah. Isaiah was married to a "prophetess" (Isa 8:3). This may only mean she was the wife of a prophet, but it is conceivable she also prophesied, like Huldah (cf. 2 Kings 22:14). Isaiah and his wife had two sons, whose names were filled with symbolic meaning (Isa 7:3; 8:3). Isaiah received his call to ministry in the year of King Uzziah's death, that is, about 740 BC. Isaiah's ministry continued throughout the reign of Hezekiah, who died around 686 BC. Undoubtedly, Isaiah spent much time in the company of royalty. He even gave advice on foreign affairs to King Hezekiah. Throughout Isaiah's long ministry, he preached about the Lord's righteousness, warned about judgment for sin, and proclaimed God's love and forgiveness. Especially enthralling were Isaiah's prophecies about the glory that awaits those who remain faithful to God. According to Jewish and Christian tradition, Isaiah was martyred during the reign of Manasseh (697–642 BC) by being sawed in half inside a hollow log. (Possibly Hebrews 11:37 refers to this event.)

55. For a discussion of the literary function of John 12:41 in the Fourth Gospel, especially with respect to the Old Testament context of the verse, cf. Robar, *Isaiah's vision of glory*. According to the author, "Isaiah understood that God's glory was not dependent on the faith of Israel." Indeed, God could display His glory through the unbelief of Israel, particularly within the context of judgment. Also, "God's glory had a facet incomprehensible to most of Israel, as revealed in the suffering servant." Because this "kind of glory" contradicted "what Israel expected in her Messiah," there were only a few "ever able to perceive its true nature." The Evangelist used the reference to Isaiah's vision of the divine glory to assert that the "unbelief of the Jews is not an obstacle to the gospel." In truth, there are times when God "chooses to manifest his glory against a foil of human spiritual obduracy" (100). The irony is one of "power in powerlessness and glory in seeming lack of glory" (101). Also, cf. Brown, *John*, 487; Carson, John, 449–50; Cook, *The theology of John*, 54; Westcott, *John*, 185.

from the dead, and being exalted to heaven (cf. Isa 52:13—53:12 John 1:1, 14, 18; 14:9; Phil 2:6–11).[56]

John would not want us to think that the entire Jewish population outside of Jesus' closest followers refused to believe in Him. In fact, many of the religious leaders believed (e.g. Nicodemus and Joseph of Arimathea; cf. Mark 15:43–46; Luke 23:50–53; John 3:1–2; 7:50–52; 19:38–40). Sadly, however, they would not publicly acknowledge the messianic claims and authority of the eternal Torah because they were afraid of the Pharisees, who had the desire and the influence to expel Jesus' disciples from the synagogue (John 12:42; cf. 9:22). They preferred to remain comfortable in their social standing while accepting the approval of people rather than the honor of God (12:43).[57]

The eschatological Tanakh concluded His public ministry with one last appeal to the people to put their trust in Him.[58] Believing in Him would be the same as believing in the Father, who had sent Him (v. 44). Indeed, God the Father and His Son are so close that to see one is to see the other (v. 45). As 10:30 reveals, though they are distinct persons within the Godhead, they are one in essence (along with the Holy Spirit). The members of the Trinity alike possess the fullness of the divine nature with all its perfection; in addition, they are united in redemptive purpose.

Not only is Jesus one with God, but He also is the Light that dispels the darkness. Everyone is condemned to spiritual darkness except for those who receive Jesus by faith as the spiritual Light. Jesus urged the people to enter into His light and be delivered from the world's darkness (12:46).[59] The Messiah's purpose for coming into this world was not to judge those who refused to listen and obey His teachings. In fact, they condemn them-

---

56. Cf. Hurtado, *Lord Jesus Christ*, 374–381; Lindars, *John*, 387; Morris, *John*, 538.

57. Scannell (*Fulfillment of Johannine signs*, 128) points out that the "human factors involved in the non-confessing response to Jesus" were "still part of God's universal plan and a fulfillment of the Scriptures" concerning the Messiah.

58. Harris (*John*) points out that John 12 "brings to a close the public ministry of Jesus." In fact, "nothing more is said in the Fourth Gospel of anything spoken by Jesus to the people at large." The remaining chapters primarily record "Jesus' words to his disciples in the Upper Room in preparation for his departure and return to the Father and the account of his arrest, trials, crucifixion, and resurrection."

59. Duke (*Irony*, 114) has surfaced "two major movements" of irony in the Fourth Gospel: "the downward plunge of those who will not receive Jesus; and the upward sweep of Jesus' exaltation, with the associated triumph of those unlikely people who believe in his name." Duke notes that "one is a movement toward tragedy," while the "other is a movement toward a high and holy comedy."

selves by rejecting Jesus as Torah and His words.[60] The Son's purpose for entering the realm of human existence was to save the world—that is, to redeem those who receive Him as their Lord and Savior (vv. 47–48). Jesus did nothing apart from His heavenly Father, who had sent Him into the world to deliver the message of eternal life. Jesus conveyed the divine message exactly as God desired. Since Jesus delivered the message using the precise words and methods His Father instructed, Jesus is rightly described as the divine, incarnate Tanakh (vv. 49–50).[61]

Conclusion

The Torah of God, as the good Shepherd of the sheep, willingly and freely offered Himself as an atoning sacrifice for the sins of humankind. Unlike a hired hand, who abandons the flock of God's people at the first sign of trouble, the eternal Tanakh remained faithful to bring to pass the Father's plan of redemption. Jesus, by allowing Himself to be sacrificed, proved His love for the Father and the new community of the redeemed. Together, the Father and the Son, who are one in purpose and essence, ensure the eternal salvation of those putting their faith in the Messiah. It is all made a reality because of the work of the Logos at Calvary.

Jesus' critics repeatedly accused Him of being a liar and insane; but He remained steadfast in declaring His truthfulness and sanity no matter how life-threatening the opposition became. The divine status and authority the Son maintained for Himself was grounded in a clear and levelheaded understanding of the Hebrew sacred writings. Regrettably, the elitists of the day refused to acknowledge the life-giving connection between the Tanakh and the Messiah. He proved this, of course, by restoring His deceased friend, Lazarus, to life. Some bystanders who witnessed the miracle, believed in Jesus as the resurrection and the life. The religious

---

60. Lincoln (*Truth on trial*, 106) clarifies that in God's cosmic court of justice, there is "outright unbelief in the face of the evidence provided by Jesus' signs." Köstenberger (*John*, 394) adds that it is "the word that Jesus spoke that will condemn the unbeliever on the last day." Along with Jesus' statements recorded in John 5:45 and 7:51, Köstenberger clarifies that the Messiah's statement in 12:46 is "in keeping with instances in Second Temple literature, where the law seems to take a more active part in the process of judging" (cf. 2 Bar 48:47; 2 Esdr 13:30–35; Wis 9:3).

61. Beasley-Murray (*John*, 218) makes the following observation: "While Moses was known as the First Redeemer, Jesus is not simply the Second but the final, eschatological Redeemer, who by his living, dying, exaltation, and sending of the Spirit brings in the kingdom of God and the new covenant for the renewed people of God."

hierarchy, however, refused to do so and instead plotted how to bring about the death of Lazarus and his Galilean benefactor.

In the face of such mounting opposition, the Son as Torah avoided doing anything that would prematurely set in motion a chain of events leading up to His arrest and crucifixion. Everything transpired according to the Father's sovereign plan and timing. So, at first, the Messiah discontinued His public ministry among the people and avoided Jerusalem; but then, six days before the Passover, He returned to Bethany to attend a dinner held in His honor and hosted by the family of Lazarus. It was at this meal that Mary used some expensive nard to anoint the feet of the Savior, an action which He declared anticipated the day of His burial. Not even the forces of darkness, working through a traitor such as Judas Iscariot, could thwart the Redeemer from fulfilling His God-given mission.

The future accomplishments of the suffering Servant were prophesied in the Tanakh. The Old Testament also foretold the Messiah's triumphal entry into Jerusalem to bring the blessings of eternal salvation and the divine kingdom to all humanity. This amazing event occurred at the start of Jesus' last week of life before He died on the cross. He humbly entered Jerusalem on a donkey as the Prince of peace. His regal splendor was neither demonstrative nor exaggerated, but rather reflected the grandeur of His person and the eternal blessings connected with His redemptive work at Calvary. Through the suffering and glorification of the Lamb of God, all people from every walk of life have an opportunity to put their faith in Him and become His regenerate followers.

8

Affirming the Truth of Jesus as Torah

The Profound Truth of Jesus as Torah

THIS STUDY began by introducing two different cultures, one based on entitlement and the other based on merit. At first glance, these two orientations appear as polar opposites, when in reality they might be likened to two sides of the same coin. In both cases, there is an excessive preoccupation with self. Expressed differently, people operating under the credo of entitlement ("it's all about me") or merit ("you only get what you earn") epitomize a religion of self in which the individual is believed to be the measure of all things. Such a narcissistic way of life might feel good and even bring some measure of worldly success, at least for a while; but eventually this man-centered, materialistic approach becomes a disease-wasting cancer of the soul that leads to spiritual slavery and death, both temporal and eternal (cf. John 8:34; Rom 6:23).

The Messiah is the only cure for this malady. The Savior must displace self as the Lord of life and King of the universe (cf. 1 Cor 12:3; Rev 19:16). For believers He becomes the source of their righteousness, holiness, and redemption (1 Cor 1:30). Such an attitude requires jettisoning the hubris of self-worship and replacing it with the lifelong decision to humbly submit to the Anointed One. Because of the Father's undeserved and unrelenting love (cf. John 3:16; Rom 5:5), the Son enables those who put their faith in Him to experience true freedom and abundant new life (cf. John 8:36; 10:10; 20:30–31). Admittedly, there is little incentive in today's world to replace the cultures of entitlement and merit with a culture of grace. In reality, it was just as difficult for others—such as Abraham, John the Baptizer, and Paul (who were discussed in chapter 1)—to do so, especially as they battled the rampant paganism of their respective time periods. The Lord honored their wholehearted devotion by giving them the strength to endure; and He has continued to do so for countless believers down through the centuries.

Jesus of Nazareth, as the Torah of God, is the reason for deciding to live in such a radical manner. Put another way, the Redeemer is the culmination (that is, the destination, goal, outcome, and fulfillment) of the law for believers. All the types, prophecies, and expectations found in the Tanakh are realized in the Son. He is the Creator of the universe and the ultimate reality behind everything that exists.[1] Because of the Savior's atoning work at Calvary, the universal moral absolutes conveyed in the law remain authoritative and applicable for His followers. For them, Jesus as Torah is light and life, fulfillment and joy, in fellowship with the triune God for all eternity. The Son of God is the one to whom all the Old Testament luminaries—such as Abraham, Jacob, Moses, and Isaiah—pointed and in whom their eschatological hopes were realized. The Anointed One is greater than and supreme over all the religious institutions once associated with the Jerusalem tabernacle and temple. Even such Jewish festivals as Tabernacles, Pentecost, Dedication, and Passover find their fulfillment in the Messiah.

An examination of the contemporary religious landscape indicates that worship takes a wide variety of forms. Sadly, much of it is idolatrous in nature. People are eager to placate their false gods in the hope of finding some sort of salvation. This kind of worship rests on the assumption that if one does enough, prays enough, or sacrifices enough, the deity will be pleased. The Fourth Gospel reveals that the Christian faith rests on an entirely different foundation. In fact, the Evangelist stressed that no one can ever do enough to earn salvation. For believers, true worship is the acknowledgment that the Father has done everything necessary through His Son, the eschatological Tanakh. Accordingly, those who truly worship God hammock themselves upon Jesus as their Savior. It should come as no surprise that God will not settle for anything less.

Jesus as Torah in John 1–12

An examination of John 1–12 substantiates the truth that Jesus is the perfection of the gift of the Torah. The Son existed in the beginning with the Father and Spirit as God. The eternal Tanakh created all things and is the source of light and life. No matter how hard the forces of darkness might try, they cannot overcome the real and enduring Light. Not even widespread rejection can deter the Messiah from giving all who believe in Him the right to become spiritually reborn children of God. They are

---

1. Cf. the appendix of this study for a discussion of a God-centered and Christ-centered view of making sense of reality.

living proof that the new birth comes from above by the sovereign work and grace of the Holy Spirit. Along with such a faithful witness as John the Baptizer, they testify that the divine Torah became incarnate, revealed the glory of the Father, and made the fullness of God's grace and truth available to humankind. The Son not only provides salvation, but in so doing, unveils the loving and redeeming heart of the Father for all to see.

An entire lineup of witnesses exist to confirm the exalted status of the Messiah as Tanakh, one of whom was John the Baptizer. Like a voice in the wilderness, he summoned all who would listen to come to the Light of the world. John declared that the Holy Spirit rested on the Son and the Father affirmed Him to be the chosen one of God. The Baptizer urged others to become disciples of the Redeemer, for He is the Lamb of God who has atoned for the sins of humankind. The ancient Hebrew writings also testified to the truth of Jesus as Torah. For instance, the famed lawgiver and leader, Moses, wrote about the Anointed One. Likewise, the revered patriarch, Abraham, rejoiced at the thought of seeing the day of the Messiah's advent. Moreover, Isaiah witnessed the preincarnate glory of the divine Messiah enthroned in His heavenly temple. Jesus of Nazareth was even greater than Jacob, Abraham's grandson. Of all who bore witness, the testimony of the Father concerning His Son was without equal. God's affirmation of Jesus' messianic status and authority was clear, consistent, and final.

From the opening verses of the Fourth Gospel, John—a devoted follower of Jesus and an eyewitness of His miracles—emphasized as one of his major themes, the Savior's mastery over all creation. John's chief means of doing this was to describe in detail the signs that Jesus performed. His turning water into wine revealed the Tanakh of God as the Creator of all things. The healing of the royal official's son showed the Messiah to be the source of new life. The healing of the 38-year-old invalid at the pool of Bethesda revealed Jesus as the master over time. The feeding of over 5,000 showed the Redeemer to be the Bread of Life. Jesus' walking on water and stilling the storm revealed Him as master over nature. The healing of the man blind from birth showed the Messiah to be the Light of the World. Finally, the raising of Lazarus from the dead revealed that the Son has supreme power over death.

Throughout John 1–12, the Messiah is portrayed as the omniscient Torah. This is especially manifest in His supernatural knowledge of all people. For instance, when the Messiah saw Simon, He foretold that the new disciple would one day be called Cephas or Peter, both of which mean "rock" and anticipate the strength of character for which he would be known. Jesus disclosed to Nathaniel that He had supernaturally seen the young man sitting alone under a fig tree before they ever personally met. Even more profound, the Tanakh of God knew all people, especially the motives and priorities of their heart. Thus, later in Jesus' earthly ministry, when His would-be followers took offense at what He said and deserted Him, He was not caught off-guard. Even the betrayal of Judas Iscariot did not take the Savior by surprise. Also, when the Son faced harm from clergy and laity alike, He remained fully aware of everything that took place.

The exalted status of Jesus as Torah is seen in the fact of His divine origin. He not only comes from above, but is also above all things. He discloses to humankind the truths of heaven, including God's wisdom, power, and love. The Son as Tanakh is the Redeemer of the world and the judge of the human race. His gift of eternal life is comparable to a fountain of water that vigorously wells up in believers in an unending and overflowing supply. Likewise, for all who put their faith in the Redeemer, He causes to flow within them the life-giving, life-sustaining presence of the Spirit. The eternal Torah reorients the life of His followers so that they are focused on serving God and their fellow human beings. This especially includes recognizing that the evangelistic fields are ripe and ready to yield an abundant crop of converted souls. In this other-worldly paradigm, those who sow the seed of the gospel and those who reap the harvest of many converts are overjoyed that so many are brought to eternal life.

Over three thousand years ago, the Lord entrusted the Israelites with the Mosaic law (cf. Rom 3:2), a revelation from Him that is holy, righteous, and good (cf. 7:12). Indeed, the Tanakh bears witness to the righteousness of God given through faith in the Messiah (cf. 3:21–22). As the Father used the law to provide moral guidance and instruction for His people, now He does so in a greater and more complete way through His Son as Torah. Given the deplorable manner in which the religious elite of the day spiritually led the covenant community, Jesus' declaration to be the good Shepherd was a welcomed, sharp contrast. He is the messianic ruler greater than David who brings peace, equity, and righteousness to beleaguered saints. As the eschatological Shepherd of God's flock, Jesus of Nazareth enables them to experience God's kindness, sensitivity, and compassion in ways never before realized.

What the Son as Torah declared about Himself was not a radical departure from the law of Moses. In fact, Jesus' teaching served as a needed corrective to the legalistic and reductionistic misinterpretations imposed upon the Tanakh by the religious experts of the day. When questioned by the elitists, the Son boldly asserted that He only declared what His Father had decreed. In contrast to the Son, who was committed to fostering life and upholding righteousness, His detractors sought to kill Him, even though He was innocent. Also, unlike Jesus' critics, who spoke on their own authority and sought the praises of both clergy and laity, the Torah of God was a person of integrity who taught divine, eternal truths.

Despite the negative opinion of His opponents, the divine-human Logos remained active in fulfilling His redemptive mission. In a display of compassion, Jesus fed a multitude of people using common food sources such as inexpensive barley bread and fish. Then, in a display of sovereignty over the elements, He walked on water in the presence of His disciples. These miracles were signs affirming the Son's claim to be the Anointed One of God. Tragically, despite the presence of these and other works of power that Jesus performed, both religious leaders and common people alike refused to put their faith in Him. This did not deter the eternal Tanakh from urging His listeners to find real satisfaction and joy by living in vital union with Him.

The Torah of God was either a liar, a lunatic, or the Lord of life (a trilemma used by scholar and novelist C. S. Lewis, among others). While Jesus of Nazareth stood condemned before the bar of opinion among the religious hierarchy of the day, His messianic status and authority was a settled matter before the supreme court of divine justice. Regrettably, the power brokers of that era refused to believe and consequently stood eternally condemned before almighty God. While various groups accused the Messiah of being demon-possessed, He was completely sane, rational, and courageous to go against Pharisaic tradition by healing a paralytic on the Sabbath. His opponents claimed that His deed of mercy broke the Sabbath law; but the eternal Tanakh disclosed how flawed and inconsistent was their reasoning. He revealed that since a less important deed was permissible on the Sabbath, the more important act of kindness He performed was even more legitimate. He urged His listeners to evaluate what He did and said by the true standard reflected in the Torah, rather than some arbitrarily concocted standard that did not accurately reflect God's will.

To the end of the Messiah's time on earth, He remained faithful to His redemptive mission. The fact of His crucifixion was not an indication of divine failure, but rather victory. Indeed, everything that took place in the last week of Jesus' life on earth, including the unbelief of many elitists and the belief of a few religious leaders, was foretold in the Tanakh. Nothing deterred the perfection of the gift of the Torah from openly and freely offering eternal life to all who would believe in Him. To the very end, He was like a messenger heralding good news in the public square and at the city gate. The Son urged all to accept the salvation He made available. By doing so, they would leave the darkness of sin and enter the light of redemption. They would be freed from the certainty of judgment and unending condemnation. With all their iniquities pardoned, they would enjoy unending fellowship with the triune God for time and eternity.

Jesus as Torah in John 13–21

Jesus as the embodiment and fulfillment of the Torah is evident in the second half of the Fourth Gospel. Whereas in John 1–12, the emphasis is on the signs performed by the Tanakh of God, in chapters 13–21, the principal focus is on the salvation He provides. It was noted in chapter 1 that the intent of this section is to discuss selected portions of chapters 13–21 in light of the recurrent theme of Jesus as Torah. The following observations are stated in a concise, non-technical manner to round out the preceding discussion.

Observations from John 13

Chapter 13 reveals that Jesus knew the time had come for His departure from the world. The cross had always been on the horizon for Him, but now He was fully aware of its imminence. This was the time appointed by the Father for His Son's saving work to be completed. Throughout Jesus' earthly ministry, He loved those entrusted to His care. His compassion for the disciples was not superficial; instead, it was unselfish, unconditional, and unbounded. The eternal Tanakh demonstrated His love completely and to the very end of His life. He knew that after His crucifixion and burial, He would be resurrected from the dead and exalted to the right hand of the Father (v. 1).

The chain of events leading to Calvary were set in motion prior to the start of Jesus' farewell meal with His disciples. Satan had put it into the mind of Judas Iscariot to betray his loyalty to the Savior (v. 2). It is unlikely that the Messiah as Torah felt any personal sense of defeat about this, for He was aware that the Father had given Him authority over everything. Jesus also knew that nothing could happen to Him apart from the will of God, from whom He had come and to whom He was returning (vv. 3, 11). The Savior predicted this act of betrayal before it ever happened so that when it occurred, His disciples would believe that He is the Messiah (v. 19). The Greek is literally rendered "that I am." As in other portions of the Fourth Gospel, the Redeemer as Tanakh was making a reference to

Exodus 3:14, and in so doing, declaring Himself to be the all-powerful, ever-living God.

In an amazing display of humility, the embodiment of the Word washed the feet of His disciples. Then He stood up, put on His outer garment, and returned to His place at the table. Once Jesus was seated, He took the opportunity to explain the significance of His actions. He asked His followers whether they grasped the importance of the foot-washing incident (v. 12). Jesus referred to the typical terms with which His disciples respectfully addressed Him. The Son as Torah fully approved of being recognized as their "Teacher" (v. 13; which is equivalent to "Rabbi") and "Lord"; yet even though they rightfully submitted to His authority and instruction, He was willing to humbly and unselfishly serve them. If the Tanakh of God ministered to His subjects in this most unassuming and sacrificial way, what should be their response?

The Redeemer said the disciples were obligated to follow His example (v. 14). He had given them a demonstration of humility by washing their feet. The foot-washing episode also points to the Lamb of God's atoning sacrifice at Calvary. Those who accept the Son's act of humiliation likewise embrace by faith His redemptive work on the cross. The Anointed One, by example as well as by precept, introduced to His disciples the principle of servanthood toward one another. Therefore, He is the believers' model of unselfish service. Those who willingly, consistently, and wholeheartedly follow His example are promised eternal blessings (v. 17). Thus, the only way for believers to be truly fulfilled and satisfied in their relationship with the Son is for them to accept and perform the role of a servant.

As well, a generous and sacrificial attitude should characterize Jesus' followers in their relationships with each other (v. 15). Moreover, because the foot-washing symbolized the spiritual cleansing that comes through the Redeemer's blood (which He was about to shed on the cross), He was urging His disciples to be willing to lay down their lives for one another, if necessary, as an act of sacrificial love (cf. 15:13). If any of those who put their faith in the Tanakh of God thought they were too good to stoop to any menial task of serving others, they did so only by placing themselves above their Lord. He was the suffering Servant, who had come to minister to others and give His life as a ransom for the sins of the world (cf. Mark 10:45). Jesus as Torah solemnly assured His disciples (and all who trust in Him for eternal life) that slaves are not greater than their master. Likewise, messengers are not greater than the person who sends them (John 13:16). Jesus' use of the word "sent" reminded His followers that He came to them from the Father. In turn, the divine, incarnate Tanakh was sending

His followers out to serve others, beginning with the proclamation of the gospel (cf. 20:21–23).

During the remainder of Jesus' final meal with His closest disciples, the eternal Torah spoke at length about the purpose of His earthly ministry and their responsibilities as His chosen apostles. The Son of Man was about to be glorified through the offering of Himself on the cross for humankind, and in this way the Father would also be glorified. The Messiah's completion of His redemptive mission was an expression of unconditional love for His disciples. As well, they would demonstrate their commitment to Him by loving one another in a sacrificial, wholehearted manner. Furthermore, Jesus warned that one of their number would betray Him and said that He was about to depart from them. In particular, the all-knowing Torah mentioned Peter's denials, which probably further disturbed the disciples. Although they had proclaimed their faithfulness to Jesus, He knew that they would falter during His darkest hour. After the Messiah's resurrection and ascension to heaven, they would need some comforting words to look back on (13:31–38).

Observations from John 14

The Tanakh of God encouraged His distressed followers to put their trust in the Father as well as in the Son. John's use of the Greek verb rendered "trust" (14:1) can be interpreted in many ways. It would not be surprising if the apostle intended multiple meanings to enrich Jesus' exhortation. Here are possible renderings of verse 1b: two commands—"Believe in God, believe also in me"; two statements—"You believe in God, you also believe in me"; a statement followed by a command—"You believe in God, believe also in me"; a command followed by a statement—"Believe in God, you also believe in me"; a question followed by a command—"Do you believe in God? Believe also in me"; and a statement followed by a question—"You believe in God. Do you also believe in me?" In any case, it is remarkable that the good Shepherd focused on comforting His followers rather than dealing with His own needs. The treachery of Judas and the fickleness of the other disciples did not prevent Jesus as Torah from maintaining a calm presence among them. In that moment, He showed Himself to be the Prince of peace.

The eternal Tanakh spoke about heaven, perhaps to further ease the minds of His followers. He referred to the celestial abode as a large house, belonging to His Father and having plenty of room. Though Jesus was leaving the disciples, He was going there to prepare a place for them. The

Affirming the Truth of Jesus as Torah

Redeemer told the disciples that if this were not so, He would not have made this promise to them (v. 2). The pledge, however, was true; and so the disciples could count on the Son one day returning to bring them back with Him to heaven (v. 3). This promise of being reunited with Him would be fulfilled no matter what happened to Him or to them. Throughout the Torah of God's public ministry, He taught His disciples what it meant to follow Him. Now He told them that they should know the way to the place He was going. As they followed that way, they would end up there with Him (v. 4).

Thomas openly expressed his confusion. He was probably speaking for the other disciples as well. They did not know where Jesus was going, and they did not know the way (v. 5). The Savior's reply to Thomas is the most profound "I am" declaration in John's Gospel. The divine, incarnate Tanakh not only identified who He was, but made it clear that He is the only possible path to God (v. 6). When Thomas asked Jesus the way, the Messiah did not hand him a road map and give him directions. Jesus told all of them that He Himself is the way to God. In a few hours some of His followers would see the Lamb of God hanging on a cross and would wonder how this could be true; but after His resurrection, they would understand that as the atoning sacrifice for their sins, the suffering Servant is the only link between God and repentant sinners.

Previously, Jesus' disciples had not fully known Him. They had seen glimpses of His true identity and had a partial understanding of who He was—but they had not fully experienced Him. If they had, they would have known that they were seeing what God the Father is like by seeing the Messiah as the realization of the Torah. In the coming days, however, they would know the Son and thus they would know the Father (v. 7). When Philip asked Jesus to show the Father to them, the everlasting Tanakh was disappointed. After all, the disciples had spent over three years with the Son. There was no need for Philip or any of them to ask Him to show them the Father. If they truly knew the Messiah, they would have known that to see Him was to see the Father's divine nature (v. 9).

The Torah of God continued to describe His unity with the Father (and the Spirit) by asking the disciples whether they believed their Teacher was in the Father and the Father was in Him. Jesus was urging His disciples to consider what would have been outrageous to the Jewish mind—that the Logos could be one in essence with Yahweh (the Lord)—while expecting them to believe it. In fact, the divine, incarnate Tanakh's words and works were a revelation of the triune Godhead, for the Father gave the Son the message He spoke and performed through Jesus the miracles He did

(v. 10). Once more, Jesus exhorted His disciples to believe that He is in the Father and the Father is in Him. After living with Jesus and experiencing the life He lived, they should have taken Him at His word; but even if they could not at this point, they could at least base their belief on the miraculous signs they had witnessed (v. 11).

Jesus as Torah revealed to the disciples that those who believed in Him would do even greater things than He had done (v. 12). Jesus certainly was not saying that they would possess greater powers than Him, nor that they would perform greater miracles. Evidently, the Tanakh of God was talking about the mighty works of conversion. Whereas the Redeemer's ministry was primarily confined to Galilee and Judea, they would take the gospel to distant lands; yet they could do none of this unless the Son first returned to the Father. The Savior knew His followers could not serve Him effectively in their own power; they would need supernatural assistance. In particular, they would need the gift promised by the Father—the Holy Spirit. When the Spirit came, the disciples would be filled with courage and the ability to witness about Jesus. Their testimony would not be confined to Jerusalem. They would take the message to the surrounding regions of Judea and Samaria, and even to the ends of the earth (cf. Acts 1:8). They could do this knowing that the Father had given the divine, incarnate Torah all authority in heaven and on earth (cf. Matt 28:18).

As was noted in chapter 2 of this study, morality for the ancient Hebrews was not an abstract concept disconnected from the present; rather, it signified ethical imperatives concerning how people of faith should live. Accordingly, the Messiah as Tanakh stated that those who genuinely loved Him also kept His commands (John 14:15). As an encouragement to those who would love and obey Him, the Torah of God promised that His disciples would have the indwelling of the Holy Spirit. The third person of the Trinity would come and make His home in believers so that their love could be clearly defined and their obedience could be carefully directed. The Son, referring to the Spirit as "another advocate" (v. 16), indicated that the latter is the same kind of counselor, intercessor, and comforter as the Messiah Himself was to the disciples. Expressed differently, the Spirit comes to the believers' aid to help them meet every challenge to their faith. As the Spirit of truth, He reveals the truth about God, shows what is true, and leads believers into all truth (v. 17). In these ways, the Spirit remains ever present to help believers understand, accept, and apply what the eternal Tanakh commanded.

Jesus as Torah assured His disciples that He would not leave them as orphans (v. 18). In fact, after His death and resurrection, He would appear

Affirming the Truth of Jesus as Torah

to them several times before His ascension into heaven. These appearances would be only for believers, in order to strengthen their faith and persuade them that He would never leave them alone in this world (v. 19). After seeing the resurrected Lord, they would learn that the power that raised Him from the dead would be living in them. Since the everliving Tanakh conquered death, they too would be victorious over death through faith in Him. At that time, they would realize that the Son is indeed in the Father and that there is a mutual indwelling of the Son and believers (v. 20). Moreover, this enduring, close-knit fellowship implies that it is not enough for believers simply to have affection for the Redeemer in their hearts. True love for Jesus as Torah is demonstrated when they keep His commandments in their daily lives. Indeed, when they demonstrate this kind of love for the Tanakh of God, they also enjoy three specific blessings: the love of the Father, the love of the Son, and a deeper knowledge of the Son (v. 21).

As the Logos did in verse 15, He once again referred to the relationship between love and obedience. The Son taught that the Father loves those who truly love Him. In addition, both the Father and the Son come to believers and make their home with them (v. 23). Those who do not obey the teaching of the one who is the embodiment of the Torah show that they really do not love Him. Jesus reminded His followers that His words were not just His own. The message He proclaimed came from the Father, who had sent the Son (v. 24). Thus, to accept the eschatological Tanakh is to accept God. Likewise, to reject the former is to reject the latter. There is no middle ground. The disciples might not have understood all that the Savior revealed to them at that time, but everything would become clear with the arrival of the Spirit (v. 25). The indwelling Spirit would guide the conscience of believers and be their teacher. The words and life of the Son would be the basis for the instruction the Spirit provided (v. 26).

Observations from John 15

Once Jesus as Torah expressed His devotion to His followers and His Father, the Messiah summoned the disciples to prepare to leave the upper room (14:31). It is not hard to imagine the eternal Logos gesturing toward a nearby plant as He referred to Himself as the "true vine" (15:1). This is the last of the seven great "I am" statements, all of which in some way point to the Savior's divinity (cf. 6:35, 48; 8:12; 9:5; 10:7, 9; 10:11, 14; 11:25; 14:6). Jesus' disciples would have been familiar with the use of the vine as a symbol. Not only was agriculture a dominant feature of

Palestinian life, but also the Old Testament writers had often referred to Israel as a vine (cf. Ps 80:8–16; Isa 5:1–7; Jer 2:21; Ezek 15; 19:10; Hos 10:1). In the same way a gardener prunes a grapevine in order for the plant to yield the maximum number of grapes, the Father in heaven removed and discarded deadwood and trimmed productive branches within the household of faith. The Father was vitally concerned with His children's fruitfulness and carefully clipped away anything that drained their spiritual resources (John 15:2).

Those who remain vitally connected by faith to the Torah of God are already spiritually clean; yet the Lord continues to work in their lives, cutting away sin and empowering them to be like the Son (v. 3). As believers remain in Him, His life flows through them, and they continue to bear fruit. Apart from the life-giving resources of the vine, no branch can bear fruit of itself. In the same way, believers are wholly dependent upon the Messiah when it comes to being productive (vv. 4–5). If a branch is not attached to the vine, it is thrown away. Like a severed branch, those who are not in Jesus as Tanakh will be cast into the fire and burned. This is a reference to judgment by the Lord (v. 6). One possibility is that the Messiah was talking about leading many people to Him in faith, while a second option is that He was referring to the moral virtues and characteristics of a godly life. Probably Jesus had both ideas in mind when He talked about being spiritually fruitful.

The concept of fruitful and unfruitful branches can be illustrated by two of the Savior's disciples. The all-knowing Torah chose Judas as a follower. Possibly because of the latter's ability as a businessperson, he was given the job as treasurer for the group (cf. 12:6; 13:29); but due to his greed, the fiduciary inclination of Judas helped lead to his downfall. Though Judas was associated with the Messiah, heard His teaching, and witnessed His works, Judas did not have an abiding spiritual union with the Son; rather than bearing fruit, the life of Judas ended in destruction. The Tanakh of God also chose Peter to be one of His disciples. Jesus taught him the same truths and gave him the same sorts of opportunities to witness that He had given Judas. Peter did not begin his life as a disciple with great success, but after some pruning (such as his denial of the Son and later reinstatement), Peter bore much fruit. He found the key to a productive life in a living relationship with the Savior.

In 15:7–8, Jesus emphasized the importance of prayer and pledged to give the believer whatever is asked. There are, however, certain conditions. First, believers must abide in Him. When they live in oneness with the divine, incarnate Torah, their desires are in line with the will of God.

Second, believers must remain obedient to the Son's teachings. When they are faithful in these ways, they pray for the things God wants, and He grants the petitions of His children. Moreover, when believers show that they are followers of the Son by bearing fruit, they bring glory to the Father. Since fruitfulness is evidence that God is at work in the Messiah's disciples, the abundance of that fruit brings honor to God. Because the Father is the gardener, that fruit is His property—it does not belong to the branches.

The Tanakh of God shared important truths with His friends because He loved them deeply. In fact, the Son's love for His disciples is as great as the Father's love for Him (v. 9). The quintessential Teacher of Israel urged His friends to continue in His love by keeping His commands. In the same way, the Son has stayed in the Father's love by remaining obedient to His will (v. 10). Obeying the embodiment of the Torah is not a burden; in fact, heeding His teaching is the only way to experience lasting joy (v. 11). Jesus was not talking here about a life of pleasure or one filled with unending happy moments. The joy the Savior provides is independent of circumstances because it stems from a dynamic, ever-growing relationship with the Lord—something that can never be taken away from believers. Jesus summed up His teachings with one commandment: His followers are to love one another as He has loved them (v. 12). This kind of love is demonstrated by a willingness to lay down one's life for a friend (v. 13). Indeed, the Redeemer as Tanakh did this very thing for humankind when He willingly subjected Himself to death, even death on the cross. Jesus set the example of the type of sacrificial love believers should demonstrate toward one another.

The Savior, in calling His followers His "friends," implied the presence of fondness, affection, and intimacy between Himself and them. The one who is the culmination of the Torah is the believers' friend in the truest sense, for His friendship is in deed as well as in word. His disciples show the genuineness of their devotion to the Messiah by doing whatever He commands (v. 14). Those who refuse to submit to the teaching and will of the Tanakh of God show they are His enemies. In this type of relationship, believers obey the Son out of love rather than compulsion. Jesus' followers are not to relate to Him as "servants" (v. 15), or slaves, for the nature of their association with Him has fundamentally changed. A master would normally relate to his slaves in a formal and detached manner. The slaves did not usually understand their master's thoughts and plans, for they were simply expected to obey his directives. It is true that believers are the Messiah's servants and expected to heed His commands;

yet they are more than mere servants, for their relationship with the Savior is intimate and tender.

In Bible times, pupils would select a popular instructor or rabbi. The disciples of the eternal Torah, however, did not choose Him. In unconditional love, He chose them to be in an intimate relationship with Him. He also placed them in the world to bear spiritual fruit that would endure forever. Because the Son enabled His disciples to be fruitful in their work for Him, the Father heard whatever they asked for in the Son's name (v. 16). By this Jesus meant that His followers were to pray in harmony with all that He taught, accomplished, and willed. Then the Father would carry out their requests. Since Jesus was about to leave His disciples, He again stressed the need for His followers to love one another (v. 17). The presence of Christlike love among the disciples would be the best evidence that they were abiding in the perfection of the gift of the Tanakh and obeying His will.

There is a striking contrast between the love of believers and the hatred of non-believers (v. 18). The world loves those who either renounce the Messiah as Torah or are indifferent to His commands. Resistance to the Son or apathy toward Him is an indication of allegiance to the world. Those who follow the Savior do not belong to the world, for Jesus has chosen them and set them apart from the world. The world hates those whom the omniscient Tanakh has chosen because the world has lost its power over them and can no longer control them (v. 19). Jesus told His disciples that allegiance to Him brings persecution and peace—never just one or the other. The eschatological Logos further explained that those who identified with Him would suffer because their persecutors did not know God (v. 21).

If the oppressors had known the Father, they would have recognized the Son, because the Father sent Him. Ignorance, however, is no excuse. The revelation of God was given to them through the appearance and teachings of the divine, incarnate Tanakh. Because they rejected that revelation, the guilt of their sins remained (v. 22). Despite the miracles Jesus had performed before His enemies, they still refused to believe in Him. In fact, they despised Him. By hating the Son, they were expressing a deeply felt hatred for the Father (vv. 23–24). Though Jesus' enemies contended that they were upholding God's law by opposing and persecuting the Son, they were actually breaking the very law that bore witness to the Messiah as Torah. Jesus quoted from the Tanakh to expose the hypocrisy and treachery of those religious rulers who were hostile to Him (v. 25; cf.

Pss 35:19; 69:4; 109:3). The words of the psalmist found their ultimate fulfillment in the persecution of the Messiah.

The Old Testament is not alone in testifying about the Torah of God. Jesus promised that He would send the Holy Spirit to bear witness to Him as well. Jesus referred to the Spirit as the Advocate who comes from the Father to impart truth. An essential function of the Holy Spirit is to continue to present Jesus as the Messiah to the world (John 15:26). Along with the Spirit, Jesus' disciples also are to testify about Him. This specific command was intended for those who were with Him at the Last Supper, for they had been with Him from the beginning of His public ministry (v. 27). The principle behind this command is applicable to all believers. As followers of Jesus, the one who fulfills all the types and prophecies recorded in the Tanakh, believers seek to cooperate with the Holy Spirit in testifying to the world about the Son of God.

Observations from John 16

This chapter is one the Bible's chief passages describing the Holy Spirit and His work. Jesus as Torah revealed that the Spirit of God, like a legal counselor, would act as a prosecutor to bring about the world's conviction. He does not merely accuse the world of wrongdoing, but also presents indisputable evidence to prove the world's sinfulness. The Spirit would establish the case of the Father and Son against nonbelievers by presenting evidence in three different areas: sin, righteousness, and judgment (v. 8). In terms of the first area, the Spirit convicts the world of sin because people do not believe in the Tanakh of God (v. 9). Jesus might have meant that the classic sin was unbelief, or that sin remains because of unbelief, or both. In any case, the Holy Spirit convicts people of sin because they reject and repudiate the Redeemer's message.

With respect to the second area, the righteousness of God was manifested in the life and character of His Son as Torah. The Messiah's return to the Father vindicated His character and established Him as the standard of all righteousness; but when the Son returned to the Father, He was no longer visible to His disciples and the world (v. 10). It was now the Holy Spirit's responsibility to convict the world according to the standard of righteousness set by the eternal Tanakh. In connection with the third area, the Son told His disciples that the Father has already condemned Satan, the prince of this world. In fact, the Messiah's crucifixion and resurrection sealed the defeat of the evil one. Since the world has followed the prince of darkness, the world stands condemned with him (v. 11).

The purpose for the Spirit's advent was not only to convict the world of its guilt, but also to guide the disciples into all truth. The divine-human Logos wanted to share these truths with His friends, but He knew that what the Holy Spirit would later convey to them would be too much for them to presently bear (v. 12). Jesus might have meant that this knowledge was too difficult for them to understand, or too difficult to emotionally absorb, or perhaps both. In any case, the Spirit would help them understand these truths in the future and give them the ability to incorporate them into their lives. The Spirit never works independently from the Father and the Son. The Spirit would pass along to Jesus' followers whatever is given to Him (v. 13). Just as the Son as Torah glorified His heavenly Father during His earthly ministry, the primary function of the Holy Spirit's ministry is to glorify the Son. The Spirit does this by taking the teachings of the eternal Tanakh and making them known to believers (v. 14). Anything the Messiah conveys to the Spirit was given to the Son by His Father (v. 15). This verse describes the intimate communion, concert, and cooperation among the three persons of the Godhead.

Observations from John 17

After the Torah of God delivered His final discourse to His disciples before His arrest, He lifted His eyes toward heaven and prayed aloud to His Father. This is the Savior's longest recorded prayer. In it He prayed for Himself (vv. 1–5), the disciples who were with Him (vv. 6–19), and everyone who would come to believe in Him after His ascension (vv. 20–26). The petition made by the embodiment of the Tanakh is often referred to as His High Priestly Prayer. In the Old Testament, the high priest had a special role in representing God's people. Once a year, on the day of Atonement, the high priest entered the Most Holy Place in the temple to make atonement for the sins of the nation (cf. Lev 16:5–17); but the blood of bulls and goats was only a forerunning substitute for the spotless Lamb of God, who offered Himself as the perfect, once-for-all sacrifice of atonement for humanity's sins (cf. Heb 7:27; 1 Pet 3:18).

The Son began His prayer by declaring that the moment had arrived for Him to die on the cross. Previously, the author of the Fourth Gospel noted several instances in which Jesus' time had not yet come. At the beginning of the Messiah's public ministry, He told His mother that His time had not yet come when she informed Him that the wine was gone at the wedding in Cana (cf. John 2:4). Later, after Jesus' brothers urged Him to perform His miracles in Judea, Jesus said His time had not yet come (cf.

Affirming the Truth of Jesus as Torah

7:6, 8). Then, when Jesus' enemies failed to seize Him, John mentioned that Jesus' time had not yet come (cf. 7:30; 8:20). Now hours before the Redeemer's crucifixion, the time had finally come for Him to be glorified through His atoning sacrifice on Calvary. The all-knowing Tanakh was aware that He was about to die on the cross and He knew the cross would be the consummation of His earthly ministry. Ironically, the cross meant something considerably different to Jesus than it did to the people of His day. From their perspective the cross was a symbol of shame, but to Jesus it meant glory.

The time had come for the heavenly Father to glorify His Son as Jesus glorified the Father on the cross. The religious hierarchy in Jerusalem thought they had authority over the Lamb of God. His humiliating death on the cross would seem to be proof of their supremacy. In truth, however, the Father had given the Son authority over all humanity. His gift of eternal life to believers exemplified that authority. Though Jesus seemed to hang helplessly on the cross, through this act He was able to grant eternal life to those whom the Father had given to Him (17:2). The Son defined eternal life as enjoying a personal relationship with the Father based on knowing Him as the one true God. Furthermore, it is only possible to truly know the Father through faith in the divine, incarnate Tanakh, whom the Father had sent to reveal Himself (v. 3). In short, eternal life is a growing relationship with the triune God that begins, not just when the believer dies, but at the moment of conversion.

The Messiah's decision to go to the cross was irrevocable. Though He had the choice not to place His life in the hands of His enemies, Jesus as Torah was firm in His resolve to finish the task His Father had assigned Him. The Son always performed His duties on earth with the intent of glorifying His Father in heaven. Even now, as the Redeemer prayed in the shadow of the cross, He was confident that the completion of His work on earth would bring honor to His Father (v. 4). Then, the Son asked His Father to glorify Him. The eternal Tanakh asked for the same glory He had enjoyed with the Father before the creation of the world, and the Son asked that it be done in His Father's presence (v. 5). Jesus' petition reveals two significant attributes of His deity. First, He is not a created being, but has always existed. Second, He is equal with the Father and the Spirit in that all three share the same glory. In essence, Jesus was saying what He had publicly acknowledged before: "I and the Father are one" (10:30).

The omniscient Logos knew that His followers were about to face the worst crisis in their lives. His death and their abandonment would rock their wobbly faith. Thus, the Son reserved the major portion of His prayer to commit the disciples into the hands of His Father. Even before the Torah of God had revealed the Father to the disciples, they had belonged to the Father. In fact, the Father had taken them from the world and given them to His Son. Jesus praised them for having kept the Father's word. Despite their impending but brief lapse into questioning, they had been and would be obedient to the truth revealed in the divine, incarnate Tanakh (17:6). Not only Jesus' followers but also everything that belonged to the Son came from the Father (v. 7). The Savior's disciples finally understood that all they knew about the embodiment of the Torah had God as its source. The disciples' comprehension was based on their receiving and believing the message Jesus imparted to them. Though their understanding was not yet complete, they were convinced that Jesus came from heaven and that the Father sent the Son to earth to proclaim divine words of truth. The all-knowing Tanakh understood that His disciples had much more to learn and that their faith needed to be strengthened, but He also realized that He could count on their devotion. His Father had given them to Him and they truly believed in Him for salvation (v. 8).

The Torah of God made it clear that He was praying for His disciples and not for the world (v. 9). This did not imply a lack of concern for the world or other people. Jesus wanted His immediate followers to know about His specific concern for them, they who would be the first to take the gospel into the world. These disciples belonged to the Father, and the Father had specifically given them to the Son. As the Father had released them into His Son's care, now the Son was giving them back into His Father's care. Jesus as Tanakh could do this, for He knew that all that is the Father's also belongs to the Son. A mere mortal could not legitimately make such a claim, so here the Redeemer was clearly asserting His equality with the Father and the Spirit. Furthermore, the disciples heard their Lord and Teacher express His confidence in them by stating that glory had come to Him through them (v. 10).

The Son as Torah indicated that He was not going to be with His disciples much longer, but that He was returning to His Father in heaven. For a short period of time, they would be left alone in the world. Without the Messiah they would need protection from those things that could cause disunity among them. They would also need protection from their human and supernatural enemies who would vigorously and violently attempt to oppose their efforts to declare the good news of salvation. Consequently, the Tanakh of God petitioned His Father to guard the disciples by the power of His name (vv. 11–14). Though Jesus' disciples did not belong to the world, the Son did not ask the Father to deliver them out of the world.

Affirming the Truth of Jesus as Torah

They had a mission to fulfill, and they could not do it if they were taken out of the world. Nevertheless, Jesus did pray for their protection from Satan. The omnipotent Tanakh did not ask that His disciples be freed from hardship and persecution (for these things certainly came to all of them), but that they would not fall under Satan's control as a result of these difficult circumstances (v. 15).

Once more, Jesus as Torah emphasized in His prayer that He and His disciples were not of the world. While they listened, they could not miss the implication of their Teacher's statement. They had come to learn that He truly was not of the world. Now they were beginning to understand that in the same way, they did not belong to the world and so were in no way obligated to follow its Satan-inspired path (v. 16). The Son, having called His Father holy (v. 11), now asked Him to make the disciples holy. The Tanakh of righteousness asked that God use His truth—that is, His Word—to separate the disciples from evil and consecrate them for a life of service (v. 17). In fact, just as the Father had commissioned the Son to perform His earthly ministry, Jesus charged the disciples to herald His message of redemption to the far corners of the earth; but they could not serve the Messiah without first being sanctified in Him (v. 18). When Jesus said, "I sanctify myself" (v. 19), this was most likely a reference to the cross. The Redeemer as Torah did not mean that He had to make Himself holy; instead, He was affirming His dedication to finish the Father's plan of salvation so that believers could be sanctified.

The scope of the Messiah's prayer broadened as He prayed specifically for those who would believe the message of the disciples (v. 20). Previously, the Tanakh of God had spoken about the message He had given to His followers, but now He noted the message they would proclaim to others. Thus, Jesus' petitions from that point forward were for all believers, starting with the desire for them to be unified in their faith. The Son prayed that the unity of His disciples be like the oneness that He has with His heavenly Father. The divine, incarnate Logos was not calling for all believers to be the same in every way, just as the Father and the Son are not identical; instead, Jesus was praying that all believers would bond together in mutual love while preserving their distinctiveness. Furthermore, the Son prayed that as the world sees believers dependent upon the Father, many would come to believe that He did in fact send the Son into the world to die for their sins. They would recognize that the Father loves them just as much as He loves His Son (v. 21).

Next, Jesus spoke about the glory that He had given His disciples and that the Father had given the Son (v. 22). The Messiah as Torah was referring to His earthly mission, which would eventually lead to His death on the cross. The path of the cross leads not to worldly honor, but to the eternal glory that only God can give. The Son gave this glory to His disciples so they would be unified in the same way He and His Father are one. In fact, the Son indwells believers even as the Father indwelled the Son. Unity among believers shows the world that the Son was from the Father and that the Father loves His Son and His followers (v. 23). The fact that the Father loved the Son before the creation of the world demonstrates that Jesus was not a created being (v. 24).

Jesus was not merely human, nor was He an angel. He was equal to the other members of the Godhead and present with them before the creation of the world. In addition, the intimacy between the Father and the Son (along with the Holy Spirit) demonstrates the love of the triune God, even before anything was created. The Son's prayer was that those who loved Him would one day be with Him in heaven to enjoy the Father's glory. In another unique reference to God, the Son called the Father "Righteous" (v. 25). Although the world remains ignorant of this upright and powerful God, the omniscient Tanakh knows Him intimately. Finally, the Son noted that He had made the Father's name known to the disciples and would tell them more about what He is like (v. 26). Jesus mentioned two reasons for this. First, the Son wanted believers to have the love the Father had for the Son. Second, the Son wanted to indwell believers.

Observations from John 18

Chapters 13 through 17 record the farewell meal Jesus as Torah ate with His disciples and the speech He made to them. Most of these final moments took place in a large, furnished upper room somewhere in Jerusalem (cf. Mark 14:13–15; Luke 17:10–12). It is also possible that a portion of Jesus' closing remarks were delivered after the group left the upper room, crossed the Kidron Valley, and made their way to an orchard called Gethsemane (John 18:1; cf. Matt 26:36; Mark 14:32). Like the three Synoptic Gospels, the Fourth Gospel identifies Judas as the disciple who betrayed the Tanakh of God. Because the Savior regularly spent time with the Twelve in the olive grove, Judas knew he could find Jesus and His followers there that evening (John 18:2). The chief priests and Pharisees had given Judas a detachment of Roman soldiers and temple guards to accompany the betrayer to Jesus. Most likely, Pilate (the Roman governor) authorized them to assist the Sanhedrin in apprehending the Nazarene. The squad arrived at the orchard carrying blazing torches, lanterns, and weapons such as clubs (v. 3).

Some might mistakenly think that Jesus was caught off guard by the dire turn of events; but according to verse 4, the omniscient Torah fully knew everything that was going to happen to Him. With the arrival of Judas, along with the squad of Roman soldiers and temple guards, the nighttime silence was shattered. In turn, the commotion must have awakened Jesus' disciples and caused their adrenaline to flow. At this point, Jesus stepped forward and asked the squad whom it was they wanted. While verse 4 does not specify, it is possible that either the commander of the Roman soldiers or one of the lead officials of the Jewish authorities responded, "Jesus of Nazareth" (v. 5); and to this Jesus replied, "I am he." The author of the Fourth Gospel noted that "Judas the traitor" was standing there with the Roman and Jewish authorities. According to verse 6, when the Messiah identified Himself, the squad at once backed away and "fell to the ground." This unexpected occurrence suggests that all those present were overwhelmed by the majesty of the eternal Tanakh. From a theological standpoint, they were encountering the God of Exodus 3:14 (cf. John 6:35; 8:24, 28, 58). Before the presence of the Creator of the universe (cf. 1:2), even Judas the betrayer fell prostrate to his knees in submission.

Perhaps after the contingent returned to their feet, Jesus again asked whom they wanted, to which they replied "Jesus of Nazareth" (18:7). The Lamb of God noted that He had already identified Himself to the squad. Since He was the person whom they wanted to apprehend, He asked that His followers be allowed to leave the scene unharmed (v. 8). Despite the fact that Jesus was about to be arrested, beaten, and crucified, He showed unwavering concern for His disciples. Indeed, He intentionally watched out for them, ensuring that none of them was lost (except for Judas the traitor; cf. 17:12). Jesus had previously declared that none of those whom the Father had given the Son would be lost (cf. 6:39). According to 18:9, this statement was fulfilled in the unfolding events connected with Jesus' arrest.

Earlier, during Jesus' farewell speech to His disciples, Peter asserted, "I will lay down my life for you" (13:37). In response, the all-knowing Torah revealed that His headstrong and impetuous disciple would say three times that he did not even know the Savior (v. 38). Later, after Jesus had identified Himself to the squad sent to arrest Him, Peter pulled out a short sword or dagger attached to his side and used the weapon in a bungled attempt to defend Jesus; but all Peter succeeded in doing was slashing off the right ear of one of the high priest's slaves named Malchus (18:10). The righteous Tanakh, however, would have none of this; and so

He commanded Peter to put his sword back into its sheath. After all, it was the will of the Father for the Son to drink from the cup of suffering and wrath the Father had given to Him (v. 11; cf. Matt 26:39; Mark 14:36; Luke 22:42). In an act of compassion, Jesus touched the ear of Malchus and healed him (cf. Luke 22:51).

Even after living closely with the Lamb of God for three years, Peter held a view of Jesus that was limited by the culture of the day. Peter did not want to consider Jesus as a suffering and dying Messiah. Like other Jews, Peter held fast to God's promise of one who would sit on the throne of David. For much of their history, the Jews had been under the rule of one Gentile kingdom after another, but the promise of a future anointed ruler—a Messiah—never faded from their hope. Their eschatological vision anticipated a political ruler who would free them from foreign military powers. Jesus of Nazareth, a miracle worker, one who claimed divine authority, looked like that Messiah. His followers stubbornly interpreted Him in light of what they expected the Messiah to be. While the divine, incarnate Torah repeatedly told His followers that His mission meant rejection, humiliation, and death, it was not until after His resurrection that they comprehended what He said.

Nothing now stood in the way of the Messiah's arrest. Thus the squad of Roman soldiers, their commanding officer, and the temple guards seized Jesus and tied Him up (John 18:12). The latter action was possibly standard procedure in that day. The contingent first escorted the eschatological Torah to Annas, the father-in-law of Caiaphas, who was the high priest at that time (v. 13). The latter was the same individual who previously had advised the religious leaders that it was to their advantage for "one man [to die] for the people" (v. 14). This is a reference to 11:49–50. Throughout the entire ordeal that unfolded before Jesus, He faced His enemies' hostility with God-inspired boldness and courage because He had prayed (18:19–24). The good Shepherd had given Himself to the will of the Father; and now Jesus surrendered to the tide that would sweep Him directly to the cross. He had no hesitation to offer Himself freely as a sacrifice for the sins of humankind (cf. 1:29).

Jesus had two trials—one Jewish and one Roman. Each of these trials had three parts. The Jewish trial began with a preliminary hearing before Annas, a former high priest (18:12–14, 19–23). Next, the Sanhedrin tried Jesus in the quarters of the current high priest, Caiaphas (Mark 14:53–65). This trial ended with an official condemnation of Jesus at daybreak (15:1). The Jewish authorities took Jesus over to the Roman governor of Judea, Pontius Pilate, who questioned the Nazarene (vss. 2–5; cf. John 18:28–40).

Affirming the Truth of Jesus as Torah

Then Pilate sent Jesus to be examined by Herod, the ruler of Jesus' home territory of Galilee (Luke 23:6–12). Finally, Pilate rendered a judgment against Jesus, which opened the way for His crucifixion (Mark 15:6–15).

Jesus must have seemed like an unusual prisoner to Pilate. The governor would have been accustomed to defendants shouting their innocence; but the Tanakh of God acted differently. It was as though He intended to die and would do nothing to interfere with His destiny. For instance, when Pilate asked whether Jesus was "the king of the Jews" (John 18:33), the accused countered with a question (v. 34). Pilate's response underscored the frustration he felt at the Lamb of God's vague answer (35). In interrogating Jesus, Pilate was trying to uncover the facts. The governor wanted to know whether the charge of sedition was true and thus whether Jesus was guilty of treason. As verses 33–35 indicate, Pilate had some doubt about the veracity of the accusations and did not immediately abandon his efforts, despite Jesus' vague response.

Though the governor could have immediately granted the request of the Jewish leaders, he did not do so, perhaps because he did not see Jesus as a danger to the empire. This impression is reinforced by Pilate's dialogue with Jesus, which is recorded in verses 36–37. The prisoner claimed to be a heavenly king, not an earthly ruler. He also asserted that His goal was to bring truth to the world, not stage a revolt against Rome. Instead of talking further with the one who is "the way and the truth and the life" (14:6), the governor cut off the conversation with a cynical retort, "What is truth?" (18:38). Then he set in motion the divinely preordained chain of events that led to the Redeemer's crucifixion (vv. 39–40).

Observations from John 19

When the crowd outside the Praetorium insisted on Barabbas's release, Pilate ordered his soldiers to flog the Son of Man. After pressing a crown of thorns on Jesus' head and wrapping a purple robe around Him, they mocked Him by repeatedly saying in derision, "Hail, king of the Jews!" Then they smacked Him in the face (vv. 1–3). Perhaps the governor thought this harsh treatment of Jesus would elicit the crowd's sympathy for Him. No such compassion was demonstrated, however. After Pilate told the crowd once more that he found Jesus innocent of any charge, and after parading Him before them in ridiculous attire, Pilate presented the Lamb of God to them, saying, "Here is the man!" (vv. 4–5).

Next, Pilate told the religious officials to crucify the one who is the embodiment of the Torah; yet they persisted, arguing that the Mosaic law required that He be executed since He professed to be the Son of God (v. 6). Learning about Jesus' divine claim frightened Pilate, who was evidently superstitious due to his pagan background. Furthermore, his wife had warned him about a troubling dream she had about Jesus (cf. Matt 27:19). Since Pilate did not want to offend the gods, he withdrew once more and asked the Nazarene to reveal His origin. Jesus, however, did not respond, perhaps because the truth was beyond Pilate's grasp. The Redeemer's silence agitated Pilate, who reminded the Galilean itinerant preacher that as governor he possessed the authority to free Jesus or sentence Him to die on the cross (John 19:10). In response, the King of the universe told Pilate that whatever authority he had was granted by God. While Pilate had the power to sentence Jesus to death, Caiaphas had delivered Him to the Roman governor. Jesus maintained that Caiaphas was guilty of a worse sin (v. 11).

When Pilate sought some way of releasing the embodiment of the Tanakh, the religious hierarchy warned him loudly that such an act would be treason to Tiberius Caesar. Veiled in their outcry was the threat of notifying the Roman emperor that Pilate had freed someone who claimed to be a king. Since Tiberius was noted for being suspicious of rivals to his throne, he would have interpreted Pilate's ruling as an act of disloyalty, and likely would have ended Pilate's career—or his life (v. 12). Faced with this implied threat, Pilate ordered Jesus to stand before His accusers while the governor sat on the judgment seat, which was located on the "Stone Pavement," or, in Aramaic, "Gabbatha" (v. 13). This word means "ridge" or "height." It was Friday morning of the Passover week when Pilate pointed to Jesus and contemptuously said to the crowd, "Here is your king" (v. 14). The people had turned into a mob thirsty for blood. They repeatedly yelled for the eschatological Shepherd to be crucified. Pilate asked them whether they really wanted him to do this. Ironically, the religious leaders, who had condemned Jesus for blasphemy, proclaimed Caesar to be their only king (v. 15). Thus, having exhausted all attempts to free the Son of God, Pilate finally yielded to their demands and commanded his soldiers to take Jesus away to be crucified (v. 16).

Before Jesus was executed, a group of Roman soldiers took Him inside the Praetorium, which was the governor's official residence. The soldiers well knew that Jesus had been convicted for calling Himself the King of the Jews. So they decided to treat Him derisively like a monarch, or like Caesar. In mockery of the purple robe worn by a king, the soldiers put a scarlet robe—possibly the short red cloak worn by a Roman military official—on Jesus (Matt 27:28). In mockery of the wreaths worn by emperors, the soldiers made a crown of thorns and pressed it down on Jesus' head. In mockery of the scepter held by a king, the soldiers placed a staff in Jesus' right hand (v. 29). In mockery of the greeting "Hail, Caesar!" given to the emperor, the soldiers knelt before Jesus and cried out, "Hail, king of the Jews!" In mockery of the kiss of homage given to a king, the soldiers spat on Jesus. Then they beat Him with the staff (v. 30).

After Jesus' flogging, the soldiers who were responsible for His crucifixion took charge of Him (Mark 15:16). This execution squad, which normally consisted of four legionnaires and a centurion, led Jesus away "to be crucified" (John 19:16). Crucifixion as a means of torture and execution was invented in the East and adopted by the Roman authorities, who used it for slaves and lower-class individuals. As was customary practice in a Roman crucifixion, the Son of Man was made to carry His own cross (v. 17). Most likely, this was only the crossbeam, since the upright beam usually remained in the ground at the place of execution. This excursion was typically a humiliating procession through crowded city streets, with the victim stripped naked and enduring the crowd's taunts.

Hebrews 13:11 refers to the Day of Atonement ritual in which the high priest carried the blood of a bull and a ram into the holiest part of the tabernacle to sprinkle it on and in front of the ark of the covenant (cf. Lev 16:11–16a). The bodies of the animals that were sacrificed for this ritual were to be burned outside the camp. They had been associated with sin, and therefore were considered unclean (v. 27). The author of Hebrews saw a parallel between these practices and the way the Lamb of God was sacrificed for people's sins outside the walls of Jerusalem (cf. Heb 13:11–12). In order to offer sinners grace, Jesus underwent great disgrace (v. 13). Isaiah had prophesied that the Messiah would be "numbered with the transgressors" (Isa 53:12) in His suffering. In fulfillment of this, two thieves were crucified with Jesus (John 19:18). What an additional agony it must have caused the sinless Son of God to be publicly identified with criminals!

It was common practice for the execution squad to erect a sign stating the crime for which the victim was being crucified. This sign was either hung around the victim's neck or nailed above his head. The message and public execution were designed to deter others from committing crimes. In Jesus' case, Pilate directed that the placard read, "Jesus of Nazareth, the King of the Jews" (v. 19). This statement was written in "Aramaic, Latin and Greek" (v. 20) so that many residents of Jerusalem could read it. The religious leaders complained to Pilate about the wording of the tablet (v. 21); nevertheless, the governor refused to change it (v. 22).

It was accepted Roman practice for the soldiers who performed a crucifixion to divide among themselves the possessions of the person being executed. Thus, the Son of God's execution squad divided His outer garments into "four shares" (v. 23) so that each of them could get their own piece. The soldiers did not do this, though, with Jesus' tunic, namely, the long garment He wore under the cloak next to His skin. This item was seamless, being woven in one piece "from top to bottom." Because of this garment's value, the executioners decided to cast lots for it (v. 24). These lots probably were marked pebbles or broken pieces of pottery that were tossed like dice. By throwing the marked objects (on which were possibly written their names), the soldiers determined the winner of Jesus' tunic. In so doing, they unwittingly fulfilled the prophetic words of Psalm 22:18.

A number of women who had accompanied Jesus during His earthly ministry stood near the cross (John 19:25). Upon spotting His mother, Mary, and the disciple He loved (probably the apostle John), the one who is the fulfillment of the Tanakh said to Mary, "Woman, here is your son" (v. 26). This was Jesus' normal, polite way of addressing women. The Savior then said to John, "Here is your mother" (v. 27). From then on, John took Mary "into his home." Someone would soon need to provide for Mary, since Jesus, her oldest son, would no longer be there. Perhaps the eternal Logos was distancing Himself from Mary so that John could take Jesus' place as Mary's earthly son. If so, the Redeemer probably used the term "woman" (v. 26) to help establish Mary and John in a new "mother-son" relationship.

By now, the omniscient Torah realized that everything concerning His earthly life had been accomplished; also by now, He was severely dehydrated. So that "Scripture would be fulfilled" (v. 28), the Messiah said, "I am thirsty." John saw this statement as fulfilling the description of a godly sufferer given in Psalm 69:21 (also, cf. 22:15). The Savior's thirst was met with a sponge soaked in "wine vinegar" (John 19:29). This refers to a cheap beverage diluted heavily with water. It was the drink of slaves and soldiers, and offered to those being crucified as a momentary relief from agony. One soldier used the stalk of a hyssop, probably three feet in length, to extend the sponge to Jesus' mouth. The plant was a small aromatic bush whose exact identification is uncertain. Based on Matthew 27:48 and Mark 15:36, the hyssop may have been a form of reed. A standing soldier could easily reach Jesus' mouth with the hyssop stalk, for the vertical crossbeam was generally never raised above 10 feet high. John's mention of the hyssop is significant, as it recalled the blood of lambs placed with hyssop stalks on Jewish doorposts at Passover so the angel of death would pass over the homes (cf. Exod 12:22). Now the Paschal lamb was about to finish His suffering; and, through His death, He would give saving protection to those marked with His blood through faith.

Jesus died with a prayer on His lips, a quotation from Psalm 31:5 (cf. Luke 23:46). It was a prayer of trust and confidence in God during a storm or some adversity. While carrying the world's sins, the Tanakh of righteousness faced the darkest moments of His life. He faced death alone, deserted by His followers and abandoned by His Father (cf. Mark 15:34); but even at this low point, the Son kept His confidence and trust in the Father. The Redeemer committed His spirit into the hands of the Father. The circumstances of Jesus' death and the way He died made an impression on many who witnessed the Crucifixion. The Roman centurion in charge admitted, "Surely this was a righteous man" (Luke 23:47). Also, others went away pounding their chests, an expression of deep remorse or grief (v. 48). Among the eyewitnesses were some of Jesus' followers—mostly women from Galilee (v. 49). They watched from a distance, either out of fear or to protect Jesus' privacy.

Crucifixion was the Roman government's method of humiliating and defeating those who opposed their rule; but the cross on which the all-powerful Torah died, did not defeat Him. He triumphed over every evil it represented on Golgotha. Thus, when Jesus declared, "It is finished" (John 19:30), He meant His work of redemption was now completed. The Greek verb rendered "finished" was often used in the first and second centuries AD for paying, or "fulfilling," a debt; and it appeared as such on receipts. This fact helps to explain why "It is finished" can literally be rendered "paid in full." From a theological standpoint, the Lamb of God paid humankind's debt of sin to the Father in full when the Son became "sin [or a sin offering] for us" (2 Cor 5:21). To know the Son is to securely bank on the sufficiency of His finished work at the cross for a right standing before a holy God. The cross was not where Jesus was victimized. It was where He was victorious over all that separates people from God.

According to the law of Moses, God forbade the Israelites to leave an executed person hanging on a tree overnight lest the dead body desecrate the land (John 19:31; cf. Deut 21:22–23). To allow the body to remain on a cross during the Sabbath was especially disturbing to the Jews. It was even more offensive if the Sabbath was special (that is, associated with one of the major feasts—in this case, the Passover Festival). Since Jesus and the two criminals were crucified on the day of preparation for Passover, the religious officials petitioned the governor to order the legs of the three men broken and their bodies removed from their crosses. By pushing up with their legs, the crucified were able to continue breathing; and so when their legs were broken, death was hastened. Though the Romans normally left bodies to hang on crosses as a warning not to violate any of their laws, Pilate yielded to the petition. The soldiers broke the legs of the two men who were crucified with Jesus (John 19:32), but when they came to the eschatological Shepherd, they discovered that He had already died. So they did not fracture His legs (v. 33).

One of the soldiers was evidently not convinced of Jesus' death, or perhaps the soldier was just a brutal person, for he pierced the Redeemer's side with his spear. Blood and water instantly poured from the wound, which the author of the Fourth Gospel personally observed (v. 34). John insisted on the reliability of the one who testified to this event—most likely himself—in order that those who read this account would put their faith in the Torah of God (v. 35). What happened to the embodiment of the Tanakh after His death was another fulfillment of Scripture (v. 36). That Jesus' bones were not broken could pertain to Exodus 12:46 and Numbers 9:12, in which God commanded that the bones of the Passover lamb not be broken. Another possibility is that this protection alluded to Psalm 34:20, which speaks of God protecting the bones of the righteous man. The quote about piercing in John 19:37 is taken from Zechariah 12:10, which culminated the scriptural prophecy relating to the Messiah as the suffering Servant. Joseph of Arimathea, a member of the Sanhedrin, asked for permission to take Jesus' body. Another member of the council, Nicodemus, helped Joseph. Together they prepared Jesus' body for burial and placed the body in Joseph's unused tomb. After the burial, some of the women went home to prepare additional spices and embalming perfumes that would finish what Nicodemus and Joseph had begun (Luke 23:50–56; John 19:38–42).

Observations from John 20

Like the other Gospel writers, John concluded his account of the divine, incarnate Torah with His resurrection; yet John's presentation provides some unique glimpses into this astonishing event, especially in regard to the reactions of some of the people who were close to the Redeemer, including Mary of Magdala and Thomas. The Fourth Gospel reveals that the Son's resurrection not only was a decisive affirmation of His divinity and messiahship, but it also left an enduring impression on the people who loved Him and put their faith in Him. John began his version of the Resurrection by focusing on one woman, Mary of Magdala, not on the several women who had also visited the empty tomb, as described in the Synoptic Gospels. The Fourth Gospel's exclusive focus on Mary was probably because she was the one who informed John of the empty tomb, and Mary had the distinction of being the first person to encounter the risen Lord.

Once the Passover Sabbath had ended, Mary hurried to the Lamb of God's tomb early Sunday morning, apparently to complete the burial anointing of His body (20:1). Mary and the other women with her wondered how they would be able to move the massive stone away from the entrance. Their concern vanished when they discovered that the rock had already been removed. Though it was still early, they were able to see that the tomb was empty. Mary dashed to Peter and the "other disciple" (v. 2), who most likely was John. Mary frantically told them that people had transferred the body of the Lord to a place she and the other women did not know. Mary probably thought that Jesus' enemies had stolen His body, and Mary had not considered the possibility that the Father raised the Son from the dead. Alarmed by Mary's news, Peter and John ran to the tomb to see for themselves whether the body was missing (v. 3). John outran his peer and thus arrived first at the sepulcher (v. 4).

In ancient times, the entrance to such burial chambers was often less than three feet high; thus an adult would have to bend down to look inside. John did this and saw the strips of linen that had been used to cover the Savior's body; but John decided not to go into the tomb (v. 5). When Peter arrived, he immediately entered the sepulcher (v. 6). The apostle saw both the strips of linen and the face cloth that had been placed around the head of the Tanakh of God. The cloth was rolled up in a spot by itself (v. 7). These details indicate that thieves had not stolen the Son's body, for it is unlikely that anyone who had come to remove the corpse would have bothered to unwrap it before removing it. When John went inside the tomb, he saw the evidence and believed that Messiah had risen from the dead (v. 8). John's awareness, however, was incomplete, for neither he nor the rest of the disciples understood the Scripture concerning the Resurrection (v. 9). Once Peter and John were done examining the scene, they went back to their homes (v. 10).

Evidently, Mary Magdalene returned to the tomb with Peter and John. At this point, Mary did not understand that the eternal Torah had risen from the dead. Mary still thought bandits had stolen the Teacher's body, and this possibility so traumatized Mary that she "stood outside the tomb crying" (v. 11). At some point, Mary decided to look into the tomb, and when she did, she saw two white-robed angels sitting at the head and foot of the place where the body of Jesus had been lying (v. 12).

Even while Mary was reexamining the tomb, she continued to weep. This prompted the angels to ask her, "Woman, why are you crying?" (v. 13). Mary explained that she was grieved over the fact that the body of the Lord had somehow been stolen. Mary still did not realize that the omnipotent Tanakh had risen from the dead. When Mary glanced over her shoulder, she saw someone standing behind her. Though she did not recognize Him, the person was Jesus (v. 14). The Savior, with undeniable compassion, asked Mary why she was weeping and whom she was trying to find (v. 15). Mary, while still in a state of shock, mistakenly thought that Jesus was the local gardener. The reason for Mary's inability to recognize Jesus is uncertain. Perhaps it is because Mary's tears blurred her eyes, or possibly the memories of Jesus' bruised and battered body were still etched in Mary's mind. Another option is that the Lord supernaturally prevented Mary from recognizing Him until He chose for her to do so.

In any case, it took a direct statement from Jesus to Mary to get her to see that she was talking to the Savior (v. 16). On that first Easter morning, tears, defeat, and despair clouded Mary's heart and mind. She was loving and brave, but she needed a special word from the good Shepherd to grasp the reality of His resurrection. Suddenly, Mary's sorrow turned to joy, and she exclaimed, "Rabboni!" Mary had spoken in Aramaic, which was the language the people of Palestine commonly used in Jesus' day. The author of the Fourth Gospel explained to his readers that this term meant "Teacher." Excitedly, Mary tried to hold the Son of God, but He stopped her (v. 17). It was not that Jesus forbade Mary to touch Him at all; rather, the phrase "Do not hold on to me" conveys the idea of "stop clinging to me." Mary wanted to cling to the Lord she thought she had lost, but He had an ascension for Himself and an assignment for her. Mary was to return to the disciples with the great news of the Redeemer's victory over death. Mary could not run fast enough to tell them (v. 18).

For centuries, skeptics have considered the Gospel writers' resurrection accounts as myth or legend. In this regard, it is significant that after the resurrection of the everliving Tanakh, He first appeared to Mary Magdalene and then assigned to her the responsibility of informing His disciples of His return to the Father. In ancient Judaism, the witness of women mattered very little judicially and socially. Thus, no ancient Jewish author would have made up such a story with a woman being the first witness to this important event. Further undermining Mary's testimony was her being from Magdala, a city Jewish rabbis condemned for its wickedness. Also, she had a history of demon possession (cf. Luke 8:2). Thus even if she seemed cured, her testimony would have been questioned.

Consequently, the Fourth Gospel's account fortifies the historical fact of the Son's resurrection.

Many of Jesus' disciples, which included most of the apostles, had secretly convened to discuss the strange yet marvelous reports that their Lord had risen from the dead. Nevertheless, since they still feared the religious authorities, they bolted the doors (John 20:19). As the disciples talked that Sunday evening, the Torah of God suddenly stood among them. The author did not explain how Jesus could have entered the house when the doors were locked. On the one hand, the Savior's resurrection body clearly had powers and capabilities that did not exist in an earthly body. On the other hand, John demonstrated shortly afterward that Jesus' body had substance when He showed His pierced hands and side (v. 20). Luke 24:39 adds that the Messiah told His disciples to touch Him to see that He had flesh and bones and was not a spirit or ghost. Jesus addressed His friends by exclaiming, "Peace be with you!" (John 20:19). Although this phrase was a common Hebrew greeting, the good Shepherd probably said it to allay their fears at His sudden and unexpected appearance. Luke mentioned that the Savior's appearance had frightened His followers (cf. Luke 24:37–38). Once convinced of Jesus' identity and presence, the disciples were overcome with joy (John 20:20). They traveled from the depths of despair to the pinnacle of happiness in a matter of seconds.

Once again, the divine, incarnate Tanakh exclaimed, "Peace be with you!" (v. 21). This time, however, the Redeemer wanted to strengthen the resolve of His disciples to obey His commission and proclaim the message of salvation. In the same way the Father had sent the Son into the world to fulfill His earthly mission, the Son was sending His followers into the world to continue His ministry. This commission and the peace of the Messiah are also given to believers today (cf. Matt 28:18–20; Mark 16:15; Luke 24:46–49; Acts 1:8). Jesus not only charged His disciples with a commission to preach the gospel, but also empowered them with the Holy Spirit to do so. John said that the eternal Torah breathed on His followers, and they received the Holy Spirit. This endowment of the Spirit was made complete 40 days later on Pentecost (John 20:22; cf. Acts 2:1–4). Furthermore, the Messiah addressed the heart of His commission to His disciples. He spoke about forgiveness (John 20:23). He did not imply that certain believers, or even the church, possessed the power to determine the salvation of people. What the Logos of God meant when He talked about forgiving and not forgiving sins, was that being pardoned is at the heart of the gospel message. The disciples were to herald the good news about the Father's love and forgiveness in the Son. Those who received it could be declared forgiven by the Messiah's followers, while those who rejected it could be declared unforgiven.

For some reason, Thomas was absent when the others saw the risen Lord, and so they told Thomas about it (v. 24). This disciple, however, was obstinate. Whether it was an expression of his grief or his faith beginning to wane toward skepticism, Thomas demanded proof. He refused to believe the good news, no matter how many times his peers repeated it to him, unless he could touch the wounds inflicted on the Lamb of God by the Roman soldiers (v. 25). The disbelief shown by Thomas is one proof that the resurrection appearances were not just visions arising from the wishful thinking of the disciples. A week later, while Thomas and the other disciples were assembled in the same place, he got his opportunity. The everliving Tanakh again came through locked doors and issued a greeting of peace (v. 26). Then He directly challenged Thomas' doubting. If the disciple needed to touch the wounds of the suffering Servant to believe, now was the time to do so (v. 27).

Thomas immediately addressed Jesus as his Lord and God (v. 28). This is the first recorded instance in which anyone revered the divine, incarnate Torah in this way. It is remarkable that a Jew would have uttered such a phrase, for Hebrew law harshly condemned anyone who elevated a human being to the status of deity; yet when Thomas came to believe that the Messiah rose from the dead, he also came to realize that the Logos is God. Thomas was privileged to see and talk with the risen Lord. Few have had such a marvelous privilege. Because Thomas saw, he believed. The eschatological Shepherd commended the believers who had not seen Him, yet still placed their faith in Him (v. 29). In this statement, Jesus was praising future Christians as well. We love Him, even though we have not seen Him—yet. The author made it clear why he wrote the Fourth Gospel. He could have described many other miracles that he witnessed, which are not contained in his account of the Redeemer's public ministry (v. 30). What John did write, however, was sufficient to convince readers that Jesus of Nazareth is "the Messiah and the Son of God" (v. 31), and that by believing in Him they might have eternal life.

Observations from John 21

Sometime after Jesus' first two post-resurrection appearances to His followers, He appeared to them a third time by the Sea of Tiberius (or Galilee) while they were fishing (21:1). Perhaps at this time, the disciples were loading gear into a boat on the shoreline (v. 2). Undoubtedly, as Peter helped, he reflected on the recent events, especially how he had acted when the authorities arrested the Torah of God. The memory of denying the Lord three times must have haunted Peter. At some point, the disciple announced he was going fishing and removed his outer garment to begin the task. In turn, the rest followed his lead; however, despite their efforts, they failed to catch any fish all night (a favored time to fish in the ancient Mediterranean world; v. 3). At dawn the next day, the risen Lord was standing on the shore of the lake, though His disciples did not realize it was Him (v. 4). Jesus, addressing them as "friends" (literally, "children"; v. 5), asked whether they had caught anything. In turn, they shouted back "No."

Next, the all-knowing Tanakh directed the group to let their net down on the right-hand side of the boat, and He assured them that by doing so they would make a worthwhile catch. When they did as He said, their net became so full of fish that they could not drag the net up into the boat (v. 6). Then John suddenly realized that it was the Lord standing on the shoreline. As soon as John told Peter, he put on his tunic. He evidently did so because he felt he was inadequately dressed to greet the Savior (v. 7). The disciple then plunged into the water and vigorously swam the short distance from the boat to the shore (about a hundred yards). Meanwhile, the rest of the group stayed in the boat and towed the loaded net to shore (v. 8). After the disciples got out of the boat, they spotted a charcoal fire with fish on it, along with some loaves of unleavened bread (v. 9).

When the Messiah invited the group to bring some of the fish they had just caught (v. 10), Peter climbed back into the boat and led the effort to drag the net the rest of the way to shore. This was quite a job, given that the net held a large number of fish, 153 in all. Despite the amount, the net did not rip from the strain (v. 11). As soon as Jesus' disciples returned with some fish, He invited them to eat breakfast with Him. No one in the group, however, dared to ask about Jesus' identity, for they knew He was the risen Lord (v. 12). Perhaps once the group was seated on the sand around the charcoal fire, the Logos of God took some of the flat loaves of bread, broke them into smaller pieces, and gave the food to His disciples. Then, Jesus did the same thing with the fish (v. 13). Undoubtedly, the group was moved by this gracious gesture of fellowship and service on the part of the Lord. Verse 14 states that this was the third instance recorded in the Fourth Gospel in which Jesus appeared to a group of His followers after He had risen from the dead. Every detail of the episode indicates that what John wrote accurately reflected his eyewitness account of his encounter with the Redeemer.

The good Shepherd's reinstatement of Peter to a position of leadership in the church is the focal point of verses 15–17. There is some debate about the significance of the use of two different Greek words for "love"—*agapaō* and *phileō*—in these verses. Some think a distinction in meaning is intended, while others maintain the variations in wording are only for stylistic reasons. Regardless of which view is preferred, it is clear that the Messiah had a place of service in the church for Peter (as well as for all believers). There are also two Greek words rendered "know" in these verses. In Peter's first two responses, he only used the term *oida*, which denotes an intellectual understanding of a fact; but in the apostle's third response, he also used the term *ginōskō*, which signifies awareness obtained from experience. In this way, Peter seemed to strengthen his affirmation of his devotion to Jesus.

Jesus' reinstatement of Peter took place after the group had finished eating breakfast. Verse 15 says that the eternal Tanakh asked Peter about the true nature of his love for the Lord, a question that can be understood in at least three ways: (1) "Do you love me more than these other disciples love me?" (2) "Do you love me more than you love these other disciples?" (3) "Do you love me more than these things (namely, the boats, nets, and fishing gear nearby)?" Regardless of which option is preferred, it is clear that Peter had denied the Lord three times and that Jesus asked the disciple three times whether he truly loved the Savior. On each occasion, Peter affirmed his love for and commitment to Jesus. By the third round of questioning, Peter was distressed and grieved. Nonetheless, he affirmed the Torah of God's knowledge of everything, including Peter's love for Him (v. 17).

The risen Lord, in turn, took Peter at his word. Because the disciple was wholeheartedly committed to the Savior, Peter was now ready to serve Him. In this way, the Messiah renewed the apostle's commission to serve as His witness to the lost. The good Shepherd also directed Peter to minister to the needs of his fellow believers. In particular, the apostle was to ensure that they were spiritually fed, guided, and protected from harm. The Redeemer's commands to Peter contain subtle distinctions. In verses 15 and 17, Jesus directed Peter to feed (or pasture) His flock; but in verse 16, Jesus told Peter to take care of (shepherd) His flock. The idea is that Peter was to do more than spiritually feed God's people. The apostle was also to watch over them, just as a shepherd would stand guard over the vulnerable sheep.

In Jesus' meeting with Peter (and the rest of the disciples present that morning), the omniscient Tanakh foretold that Peter's reinstatement to service would involve dying for his Lord. Jesus noted that when Peter was younger, he had the freedom to dress himself and go wherever he desired. In contrast, when Peter was an elderly man, he would be ordered to stretch out his hands so that others could dress him and take him where he did not want to go (v. 18). The early church understood the risen Lord's statement as a prophecy of Peter's eventual death by crucifixion (v. 19). In 2 Peter 1:13, the apostle referred to his approaching death. He knew that he would soon be done with the tent of his body. The Greek word translated "soon" (v. 14) suggests a swift and sudden end, not a lingering death as with illness. Peter might have been thinking about the Messiah's words to him regarding the kind of death by which the apostle would glorify God (John 21:18–19). Peter's metaphorical reference to "the tent of this body" (2 Pet 1:13) carries the idea of one's physical body being a temporary dwelling. While Peter was on earth, he would use the "tent" of his body in obedience to God's will. Death was simply putting aside the physical tent so that the soul could depart to be with God. That "tent" would be raised again on the day of resurrection.

Jesus as Torah commanded His newly reinstated disciple to follow Him (John 21:19). Peter then turned around and noticed John following behind them (v. 20). This is the same disciple who, during the Lamb of God's final meal with His followers, leaned over to the Messiah and asked who would betray Him (cf. 13:23–25). Peter, perhaps in an attempt to deflect some of the attention away from himself, asked the risen Lord what the future held for John (21:21). Would he also be martyred for the faith? In response, Jesus questioned the legitimacy and sincerity of Peter's concern for John. Even if it was the Lord's will for John to remain alive until the Messiah's second advent, that still did not eliminate the imperative for Peter (as well as for all believers) to follow the Tanakh of God, regardless of the personal cost (v. 22).

Jesus' statement fueled a rumor in the early church that the Savior would return before His beloved disciple experienced death. John, however, explained that this rumor was false (v. 23). Revelation 1:9 discloses that even though John lived until old age, he did not escape suffering for the Lord. Because of the apostle's witness for the exalted Messiah, the Roman authorities imprisoned John for a time in a penal colony on the small, rocky island called Patmos, which is located in the Aegean Sea. He is the same disciple who authored the Fourth Gospel. John 21:24 reflects the testimony of the early church that the apostle's account of what took place during the three years of the Son's earthly ministry is accurate, reliable, and true. Accordingly, it rightfully deserves to be studied and heeded by all believers.

Conclusion

This work has sought to be more than an academic treatise on the Fourth Gospel; instead, the writer shares the unabashed goal of the apostle John, namely, to encourage initial and enduring faith in Jesus of Nazareth as the Messiah, the Son of God. As this study has maintained, He is the perfection of the gift of the Torah, the one who eternally preexisted with the Father and Spirit and became incarnate. Jesus, as the embodiment and fulfillment of the Tanakh, revealed God's light and life to others through much teaching and many miracles. Both clergy and laity alike were graced by the presence of the Redeemer and offered the gift of the new birth. While some gladly received by faith the one who is the way, the truth, and the life, others spurned His offer of salvation. Even today, those who reject the Messiah as Torah remain enslaved to sin and condemned before God. In contrast, those who trust in the Son have their sins pardoned and are declared to be God's children.

As the Fourth Gospel reveals, not even the grave could hold the all-powerful, everliving Logos. Though He died on the cross and was buried in a tomb, Jesus of Nazareth rose from the dead and now lives forevermore. His victory through the Resurrection enables Him to control the keys of death and Hades (the place of the dead). In ancient times, keys were symbols of authority. Also, death and Hades were considered places where people were bound and held captive. The Son wants His followers to know that He alone has the power and the authority to free them from the shackles of death and give them eternal life (cf. Rev 1:18). Moreover, the good Shepherd encourages them not to let their hearts be troubled, for He is in heaven right now preparing a place with plenty of room for them to dwell (cf. John 14:1–3).

Some six decades after Jesus' resurrection and ascension, the apostle John found himself in the presence of the Torah of God; but now John's closest friend was exalted, honored, and glorified. As he stood before the risen Tanakh, the apostle dropped to his knees as though he were dead (cf. Rev 1:17). Isaiah, Ezekiel, and Daniel had similar responses when suddenly exposed to the glorified presence of God (cf. Isa 6:5; Ezek 1:28; Dan 8:17). This was not the same experience John had when he leaned toward the Messiah at the Last Supper. The Savior touched John, perhaps both to strengthen him physically and comfort him emotionally. The Son as

Torah encouraged the apostle not to be afraid, for He is the first and the last (cf. Rev 1:17). This is a divine title that appears elsewhere in Scripture in reference to the Lord (cf. Isa 41:4; 44:6; 48:12). It means essentially the same thing as the title "the Alpha and Omega" (Rev 1:8).

At the time John wrote the Fourth Gospel and the Book of Revelation, the Roman government was pressuring believers to renounce the Messiah and declare the emperor to be their lord. Jesus' words to John underscored why it was wrong to do so. All human authorities are mortal and limited, whereas the Redeemer is immortal and infinite in power. The gods created and venerated by people are lifeless, whereas Jesus as Tanakh is the one who lives forevermore (cf. v. 18). This means that His essential nature is characterized by life. The good news is that the eschatological Torah will one day return. With John let all believers affirm the certainty of this promise by declaring, "Amen. Come, Lord Jesus" (Rev 22:20).

Appendix

Making Sense of Reality: A God-Centered and Christ-Centered View

Seeking to Define Reality

IN THE first chapter of this study, it was noted that when people insist they are complete within themselves, it leads to a rejection of virtually every truth claim about God and His existence. At the heart of this issue is the ongoing struggle to define reality. Part of the debate centers around how the term "reality" should be understood; and surprisingly, there does not seem to be any consensus favoring a single, clear definition. Theoretical physicist and Anglican priest, John Polkinghorne, considers reality to be multilayered and multidimensional.[1] Likewise, he regards the world in which we live to be "intricate and interrelated."[2] Others say reality is the sum total of events and entities that genuinely exist. Those favoring this view see a distinction between the state of things as they actually are versus an imaginary or idealistic concept of reality.[3]

There are some experts who consider reality to be an ever-present state of affairs. An eighteenth-century empiricist named David Hume was a proponent of this view. He linked reality to each person's conscious awareness of moment-by-moment events they were experiencing. There are other experts who claim that reality is anything that exists independently of other beings. A seventeenth-century rationalist named Spinoza advocated one version of this view. In this paradigm, reality (whether God, nature, the cosmos, and so on) is neither derived from nor dependent upon anyone or anything for its continued existence; rather, it is absolute, self-sufficient, and objective.[4]

---

1. Polkinghorne, *Exploring reality*, ix–x.
2. Polkinghorne, *Science and theology*, 132.
3. Mish, "Reality."
4. Adler, "Idealism."

Appendix

Striving to Fathom Reality

For some, the desire to fathom the true nature of reality has become a "holy grail," that is, a quest to be earnestly pursued at all costs. Boa and Bowman, in their discussion about the evidence of reality, point to a blockbuster movie called *The Matrix* as a noteworthy fictional example of this search. The main character, Neo, discovers that the world in which he lives is a "virtual reality" manufactured by "alien machines," which control the planet. Neo becomes relentless in his efforts to uncover the truth about the real world. In doing so, he hopes to free humankind from its enslavement to a horde of computerized monsters terrorizing the planet.[5]

A similar kind of zeal is evident among specialists across a variety of disciplines who invest large amounts of time, energy, and resources to shed light on the inner workings of reality, whether at the micro-level of the atom or the macro-level of the universe. Some are enthralled by the possibility of conceptualizing a new theory that will unlock one or more of life's mysteries. Others are enticed by the challenge of being the first to solve a riddle of nature or an enigma of science. Many, after devoting their entire careers to probe the unknown, end up feeling disappointed and disillusioned. They realize that, despite their herculean efforts, they have not achieved their ambitious goals.

String theory is one example of this undertaking by those exploring the realm of fundamental physics. The hypothesis, which began to surface in the late 1960s, attempts to describe the nature of all elemental particles and how they interact. The primary components of reality are said to be exceedingly tiny, vibrating loops called "strings" that are 10^{-33} cm across. One of the more popular versions of the theory speculates that the physical universe, rather than being a fixed, three-dimensional expanse, could have as many as 11 dimensions. The allure of this hypothesis is centered in the possibility of conceiving a "theory of everything," in other words, a model of physics that will explain all the basic aspects of existence. The goal is to precisely describe the forces and particles that make up the universe at the quantum level.[6]

Despite decades of research, many of the predictions put forward by string theory remain scientifically unverifiable. In some cases, the technology does not exist to conduct experiments on claims made by the theory. In other cases, foundational aspects of the hypothesis are either debated or not fully understood. This has led some experts to question whether

---

5. Boa and Bowman, *Compelling evidences*, 13–14.
6. Greene, *Elegant universe*.

Appendix

string theory warrants being regarded as a scientific hypothesis. According to Richard Sloan, "science depends completely upon the capacity to measure phenomena. If something can't be measured, it can't be studied scientifically."[7] Because string theory cannot be proved or disproved by means of quantifiable, measurable, and repeatable experimentation, detractors say it is a metaphysical construct of reality that rests more on faith than on fact.[8]

Failing to Make Sense of Reality

From a Christian perspective, all direct and indirect endeavors to make sense of reality point to humankind's ongoing attempt to fulfill the creation mandate. Genesis 1:26 and 27 state that at the dawn of time, God made human beings in His own image. Admittedly, scholars continue to debate the precise meaning of this passage. Nonetheless, we see from verse 28 that a primary focus is on rulership. In particular, God has authorized humanity to govern the world as His benevolent vice-regents. Doing so, in turn, is a reflection of His image in them (cf. Gen 9:2; Ps 8:5–8; Heb 2:5–9). This includes attempts to answer the opening question of this essay—what is reality?[9]

As I have noted elsewhere, scientists, philosophers, and theologians down through the centuries have sought to decipher ultimate reality.[10] Nonetheless, when the existence of God is left out of the picture, all such efforts to apprehend existence go awry. Just when one generation appears to be on the verge of a breakthrough in fathoming the mysteries of

---

7. Sloan, "Trivializing the Transcendent."

8. According to Flatow ("String theory"), some scientists claim the hypothesis is "sloppy and founded on unwarranted assumptions"; cf. Polkinghorne, *Exploring Reality*, pp. 14, 34–36, 91–92.

9. The Foundational Questions Institute (FQXi) is a noteworthy organization devoted to exploring issues connected with the question asked at the beginning of this essay. According to their mission statement, they seek "to catalyze, support, and disseminate research on questions at the foundations of physics and cosmology, particularly new frontiers and innovative ideas integral to a deep understanding of reality but unlikely to be supported by conventional funding sources." FQXi maintains that there are unanswered questions that "lie at the frontier of science and at the foundation of our understanding of the universe." Also, such unresolved queries "intimately connect with and inform not just scientific fields, but also philosophy, theology and religious belief systems." The Institute notes that "answers to these questions will have profound intellectual, practical, and spiritual implications for anyone with deep curiosity about the world's true nature" (Tegmark, "Mission, scope, and emphasis").

10. Lioy, *Search for ultimate reality*, 1.

the universe, the occurrence of death prevents them making any further progress. A new generation of researchers, explorers, and thinkers might continue where others left off; yet, the brevity of life also shunts their ability to resolve the enigmas of life, regardless of whether it involves science, philosophy, or religion.

Ecclesiastes 3:11 comments on the attempts of individuals to press beyond the confines of the here and now. The sage declared that God has "set eternity in the human heart." The idea is that people have a divinely-given sense of the past and the future. They are aware that the extent and flow of history encompasses vast stretches of time. Their curiosity, along with their desire to understand reality, motivates them to explore the intricacies of the world and figure out everything God does "from beginning to end." The task, however, is seemingly infinite, while people are finite.

In a previous essay dealing with Ecclesiastes 1 (particularly vv. 13–18), I commented at length on the limitations of what people can accomplish.[11] This includes attempts to make sense of reality. On the one hand, "there is some value to human endeavors, including enjoyment, satisfaction, and security." Yet, on the other hand, "the gains represented by such achievements are checkmated by death." The sage admitted that this truth also applied to him. Even his repeated attempts to "fathom the mysteries of life were ultimately crushed by the sheer enormity of the task." Indeed, despite his best efforts, he was "unable to explain the enigmas of life, right its wrongs, and remedy its deficiencies." He was forced to admit that the ways of God surpass human understanding.

The Bible reveals that God has inherent characteristics or qualities that distinguish Him from His creation. One of His attributes is called *omniscience*, a term that literally refers to "all knowledge." Scripture teaches that God has unlimited awareness, understanding, and insight; in other words, His knowledge and grasp of all things is universal and complete. His comprehension is also instantaneous, exhaustive, and absolutely correct. Even though all things are eternally present in God's view, He still recognizes them as successive, finite events in time. The Lord is aware of every thought people have and every action they perform (1 Chron 28:9). He can objectively and fairly evaluate the actions of people because He knows everything (1 Sam 2:3). All wisdom and counsel reside with Him (Job 12:13), and His understanding has no limit (Ps 147:5). There is nothing in the entire universe that is hidden from God's sight (Dan 2:20–22). Everything is exposed by His penetrating gaze (Heb 4:13).

---

11. Lioy, "Checkmating the human drive for life."

Appendix

Believers of all ages have understood that God knows the least detail about them. In Psalm 139, David acknowledged that the Lord routinely looked deep within the king's heart and was intimately familiar with everything about him, including when he sat down to rest and when he got up to work. Additionally, even though God made His abode in heaven, this did not hinder His ability to perceive David's thoughts and understand his motives. The Lord knew what David would say before he uttered it. In fact, God did not miss a single one of the psalmist's thoughts. In short, God knew everything the psalmist desired and imagined. Also, regardless of whether David was traveling or pausing from his journey, the Lord carefully observed everything the poet did. The realization that God knows all and still loves each person filled the psalmist with awe (vv. 1–6).

In Isaiah 40:12–14, the prophet pointed to the unfathomable depths of God's knowledge and greatness, especially as seen in the work of Creation. He alone measured the ocean and stretched out the sky. Also, only He carefully weighed the soil of the earth, including its mountains and hills. Not even the most learned academic or astute scientist is able to advise the Lord or tell Him something He does not already know. Moreover, there is no esteemed cleric or world-renowned ethicist who can instruct Him in the ways of justice. A similar emphasis can be found in Romans 11:33–36. This passage contains Paul's doxology of praise to God, with verse 34 quoting Isaiah 40:13. The apostle was awed by how God's plan of salvation for all people—Jew and Gentile—demonstrated His infinite wisdom and knowledge. Paul declared that God's judgments are unsearchable and His paths beyond tracing out.

In 1 Corinthians 13:12, Paul used an analogy involving a mirror to emphasize the limitations of our present knowledge. In that day, mirrors were made of polished metal and provided a poor, distorted image of what they were reflecting. The glimpse of the Lord that we get as He is reflected in our spiritual gifts is like looking in such an imperfect mirror. In a future era, however, our awareness of the Lord will not be mediated by our spiritual gifts, for we will see Him face-to-face. The apostle switched from the language of sight to that of knowledge when he noted that he, like all believers in the present era, knew God only partially; but Paul looked forward to a time when he would know God fully. Of course, the apostle was not suggesting that human beings will ever have knowledge equaling that of God. Moreover, the Lord is not limited, as people are, by conditions of the present era. He already knows all people fully, completely, and perfectly.

Appendix

Affirming the Existence of God

In an interview with *Newsweek* correspondent Jon Meacham, the elderly evangelist, Billy Graham, said that he thought "God's ways and means are veiled from human eyes and wrapped in mystery."[12] Given that we live in a universe that defies comprehension, affirming the existence of God is the starting point for making sense of reality. According to Hebrews 11:6, it is imperative for people to believe that God exists and that He will honor the faith of those who seek Him earnestly. When He is at the center of our worldview, He looks with favor upon the sincere efforts of believers to explore and learn more about the cosmos He has created. They affirm by their life pursuits that everything comes from God, exists by His power, and is intended for His glory (Rom 11:36). As Boa observes, "all beauty, goodness, and truth flow out of the infinite-personal Lord of all creation."[13]

In contrast, the imprudent operate under the premise that God does not exist (Ps 14:1). Society might regard such morally deficient people as intellectual geniuses; but by trivializing or ignoring the centrality of God to all of life, they remain ignorant of the true nature of reality. At every turn, such practical atheists intentionally discount the invisible attributes of God evident throughout the world. Regardless of whether they are examining subatomic particles or investigating the intricacies of the human psyche, an objective analysis of the data ultimately points to God's "eternal power and divine nature" (Rom 1:20). Indeed, affirming God's existence is crucial in discerning "where we come from (origin), why are we here (purpose), and where are we going (destiny)."[14]

Making Sense of Reality by Trusting in the Son

Many world religions affirm the existence of God. In some eastern traditions, the divine is understood to be a "superhuman being or spirit" who is worshiped as "having power over nature or human fortunes." In monotheistic traditions (such as Judaism, Christianity, and Islam), He is said to be the Creator and Ruler of the universe and the source of all moral authority.[15] Only Christianity, however, affirms the triune existence of God, declares the Son to be the foundation of existence, and insists

---

12. Meacham, "Pilgrim's progress."
13. Boa, "Logo."
14. Boa, "Logo."
15. Simpson, Weiner, and Berg, "God."

Appendix

that trusting in Him is the only way to make sense of reality. The Messiah, then, is the starting point for fathoming the mysteries of life. As was noted in chapter 2 of this study, He is the meta-narrative of life, whether temporal or eternal in nature.[16] Indeed, for our benefit, the Father has made the Son to be the quintessential essence of wisdom (1 Cor 1:30). In union with the Lord Jesus, we find the spiritual discernment and insight we need to grow in our knowledge of God and the world He created through the Messiah (Eph 1:17).

The introductory chapter of Genesis reveals that God created all things. Polkinghorne aptly noted that the Lord is the "Ground of being and the Source of the order and fruitfulness of the universe."[17] He not only formed and filled the cosmos, but also made the entire world His sanctuary. In a corresponding fashion, the introductory chapter of John's Gospel discloses that the "divine, omnipotent Word" brought all things into existence. By taking on flesh, or becoming incarnate, the "transcendent Creator" identified and interacted with "humankind in a profound manner." The involvement of the Logos with humanity is "characterized by love, intentionality, and commitment."[18]

The Son is also at the center of the Father's covenantal relationship with humankind. As I have noted elsewhere, it is through the Lord Jesus that the covenant "links God's various affirmations of His creative and salvific purposes toward humanity."[19] This is especially so with respect to God's new and everlasting covenant (Isa 54:10; Jer 31:31–34; Ezek 34:25; Heb 8:7–13). Through the Son's shed blood, He "establishes the new

---

16. Webber and Kenyon ("An Ancient Evangelical Future") observe that "today, as in the ancient era, the Church is confronted by a host of master narratives that contradict and compete with the gospel." They summon evangelicals "to recover the truth of God's word as *the* story of the world, and to make *it* the centerpiece of Evangelical life." Miller ("Who do your books say that I am?") reflects a similar viewpoint in his analysis of the numerous "soaring meta-narratives" offered in our "post-Christian, postmodern" world. He concludes that despite all the flowery, spiritualized rhetoric, "we're left with . . . the highly particular, often idiosyncratic, mainly muddled world of everyday human experience." The result of contemporary society moving "farther away from our Christian identity and framework" is that people have an "intensified longing for viva vox, the living voice." As this study on the Fourth Gospel has maintained, the divine-human Logos is the only one who can pierce through "our misery and darkness" and "our pluralizing cacophony" to shine the light of God's truth on us.

17. Polkinghorne, *Exploring reality*, 132.
18. Lioy, *Search for ultimate reality*, 90.
19. Lioy, "Progressive covenantalism."

Appendix

covenant," perfectly keeps its conditions, and acts as its Mediator. When people trust in Him, their sins are pardoned and they receive eternal life.[20]

Hebrews 1:2, in saying that the Son "made the universe," used a Greek term that denotes the temporal ages and includes the spatial realm. The Lord Jesus not only created the vast number of galaxies, but also holds them together by His powerful word. Put another way, it is through His sustaining royal decree that He prevents the cosmos from destruction. Colossians 1:16 makes a similar declaration concerning the One who is at the heart of all that is real. Every entity that exists, whether they dwell in heaven or inhabit the earth, whether we can see them or they are imperceptible to our eyes, is dependent on the Son for life. In fact, if He were to abandon His creation, utter chaos would result. These passages reveal that the ultimate purpose of creation is Jesus Christ Himself. Accordingly, those who seek to make sense of reality must recognize that God designed the world in such a way that it can have real meaning only in Christ.

These same truths are affirmed in the Book of Revelation. Indeed, it "begins and ends with Christ" (cf. 1:1; 22:21). Most would agree that the Apocalypse is "filled with magnificent visions and symbols" that are often "difficult to understand." Regardless of the debates about how to interpret this final portion of Scripture, all can affirm that Revelation keeps the spotlight of attention on the Messiah, especially "His character, His mission, and His final goal of bringing all things into subjection to His Father's perfect will" (cf. 1:5-8).[21] In the concluding portion of John's unfolding vision, he saw the new Jerusalem "coming down out of heaven from God" (21:2). The apostle noted that "the Holy City" did not have a temple, for "the almighty Lord and the Lamb were its sanctuary" (cf. v. 22). In this description of the final state, "God and the Lamb are joint owners of the throne." Moreover, the "imperial rule of the Father and the Son has become a functional unity." The conclusion is that none other than the Lord Jesus is fully divine and absolutely equal to the Father and Spirit.[22]

Because of the Son's central role as Creator, Redeemer, and Lord, it is prudent for all who want to make sense of existence to do so by first putting their trust in Him. He both "created all things and is a new (spiritual) beginning for all who believe in Him."[23] Only He "reigns in regal splendor

---

20. Lioy, "Progressive covenantalism."
21. Lioy, *Book of revelation*, 1.
22. Lioy, *Book of revelation*, 154–55.
23. Lioy, *Search for ultimate reality*, 11.

over the cosmos" and He "alone deserves to be worshiped by humankind."[24] Without question, then, ultimate reality is found through faith in the Son. Only when this God-centered and Christ-centered view is adopted will the efforts of researchers to fathom the enigmas of the universe prove to be eternally fruitful and relevant. In contrast, when the Son of God is removed from consideration, all attempts to make sense of reality will be "filled with anxiety and frustration." Even the work of the brightest, most gifted scientists, philosophers, and theologians will amount to nothing when they divorce themselves and their research "from their Creator." In the end, "all they have is what they work for now, and soon every aspect of it will pass away."[25]

The good news is that there can be meaning and purpose to scientific inquiry when the Lord Jesus is on the throne of all such endeavors. In fact, when the goal of doing all forms of research is to bring glory to the Son, it is never a wasted effort, for in Him, the regenerate "bear eternal fruit and reap a heavenly reward." It is reasonable to conclude that "only in Christ" can attempts to fathom existence "be enjoyable, beneficial, and fulfilling for people of faith."[26]

---

24. Lioy, *Search for ultimate reality*, 91.
25. Lioy, "Checkmating the human drive for life."
26. Lioy, "Checkmating the human drive for life."

Bibliography

Adeyemi, F. *The new covenant Torah in Jeremiah and the law of Christ in Paul*. New York: Peter Lang, 2006.

Adkisson, R. L. *An examination of the concept of believing as a dominant motif in the Gospel of John*. Ph.D. diss. New Orleans: New Orleans Baptist Theological Seminary, 1990.

Adler, J. "The new naysayers." *Newsweek*, September 11, 2006. Online: http://www.msnbc.msn.com/id/14638243/site/newsweek/.

Adler, M. "Idealism." In *Encyclopædia Britannica*. Chicago: Encyclopedia Britannica, 2006. Online: http://www.britannica.com/.

Anderson, D. "Changing a culture of entitlement into a culture of merit." *The CPA Journal*, November 2002. Online: http://www.nysscpa.org/cpajournal/2002/1102/nv/nv8.htm.

Anderson, P. N. "The having-sent-me Father: aspects of agency, encounter, and irony in the Johannine Father-Son relationship. *Semeia*. 85 (1999) 33–57.

Asiedu-Peprah, M. *Johannine sabbath conflicts as juridical controversy*. Tübingen: Mohr Siebeck, 2001.

Badenas, R. *Christ the end of the law: Romans 10:4 in Pauline perspective*. Sheffield: Journal for the Study of the New Testament Press, 1985.

Balfour, G. "The Jewishness of John's use of the Scriptures in John 6:31 and 7:37–38." *Tyndale Bulletin*. 46:2 (1995) 357–380.

Balmer, R. *Encyclopedia of evangelicalism*. Revised and expanded edition. Waco, TX: Baylor University Press, 2004.

Bammel, E. "Jesus und der Paraklet in Johannes 16." In *Christ and Spirit in the New Testament*. Edited by B. Lindars, et al., 199–217. Cambridge: Cambridge University Press, 1973.

Bandstra, A. J. *The law and the elements of the world: an exegetical study in aspects of Paul's teaching*. Kampen: J. H. Kok, 1964.

Banks, R. *Jesus and the law in the Synoptic tradition*. Cambridge: Cambridge University Press, 1975.

Barrett, C. K. "The Old Testament in the Fourth Gospel." *Journal of theological studies*. 48 (1947) 155–169.

———. *The Gospel according to St. John*. Second edition. Philadelphia: The Westminster Press, 1978.

Barth, G. "Matthew's understanding of the law." In *Tradition and Interpretation in Matthew*. Edited by G. Bornkamm, et al., translated by P. Scott, 58–164. Philadelphia: The Westminster Press, 1976.

Beasley-Murray, G. R. *Gospel of life: theology in the Fourth Gospel*. Peabody, MA: Hendrickson Publishers, 1991.

———. *John*. Second edition. Thomas Nelson, 1999.

Bennema, C. "The giving of the Spirit in John's Gospel—a new proposal?" *Evangel Quarterly*. 74:3 (2002) 195–213.

Bibliography

Beutler, J. "The use of 'scripture' in the Gospel of John." In *Exploring the Gospel of John: in honor of D. Moody Smith.* Edited by R. A. Culpepper, et al., 147–162. Louisville, KY: Westminster John Knox Press, 1996.

Beyler, C. V. *Torah in the Fourth Gospel.* Ph.D. diss. Louisville, KY: Southern Baptist Theological Seminary, 1957.

Bible. *Zondervan TNIV Study Bible.* Edited by K. L. Barker, et al. Grand Rapids: Zondervan, 2006.

Bird, M. F. "When the dust finally settles: coming to a post new-perspective perspective." *Criswell Theological Review.* 2:2 (2005) 57–69.

Blasi, A. J. "Definition of Religion." In *Encyclopedia of religion and society.* Edited by W. H. Swatos. Walnut Creek, CA: AltaMira Press, 1998. Online: http://hirr.hartsem.edu/ency/defreligion.htm.

Bloesch, D. G. *Jesus Christ: Savior and Lord.* Downers Grove, IL: InterVarsity, 1997.

Blomberg, C. L. *The historical reliability of John's Gospel: issues and commentary.* Downers Grove, IL: InterVarsity, 2001.

Blunt, S. H. "Marginalized again: Evangelicals protest mandatory Christian curriculum in Israel." *Christianity Today*, November 17, 2006. Online: http://www.christianitytoday.com/39321.

Boa, K. D. "Logo." Atlanta: Reflections Ministries, 2006. Online: http://www.kenboa.org/logo.

Boa, K. D. and Bowman R. M. *20 Compelling evidences that God exists.* Second Edition. Colorado Springs, CO: Victor Books, 2006.

Bock, D. L. *Jesus according to Scripture: restoring the portrait from the Gospels.* Grand Rapids: Baker, 2002.

Boismard. M. É. *Moses or Jesus: an essay in Johannine Christology.* Translated by B. T. Viviano. Minneapolis: Fortress Press, 1993.

Bolton, S. *The true bounds of Christian freedom.* Carlisle, PA: The Banner of Truth Trust, 1978.

Borchert, G. L. *John 1–11.* Nashville: Broadman & Holman Publishers, 1996.

Borgen, P. "God's agent in the Fourth Gospel." In *Religions in antiquity: essays in memory of Erwin Ramsdell Goodenough,* 137–148. Leiden: E. J. Brill, 1970.

———. *Bread from heaven: an exegetical study of the concept of manna in the Gospel of John and the writings of Philo.* Leiden: E. J. Brill, 1981.

———. "John 6: tradition, interpretation and composition." In *From Jesus to John: essays on Jesus and New Testament Christology in honour of Marinus de Jonge.* Edited by M. C. De Boer, 268–291. Sheffield: Sheffield Academic Press, 1993.

Boucher, M. I. "The parables." In *The parables.* Wilmington, DE: Michael Glazier, Inc., 1980. Online: http://www.pbs.org/wgbh/pages/frontline/shows/religion/jesus/parables.html.

Branscomb, B. H. *Jesus and the law of Moses.* New York: Richard R. Smith, Inc., 1930.

Bray, G. L. "God," In *New dictionary of biblical theology.* Edited by T. D. Alexander, et al., 511–521. Downers Grove, IL: InterVarsity, 2000.

Brown, R. E. *The Gospel according to John (i–xii).* New York: Doubleday, 1966.

———. *An introduction to the New Testament.* New York: Doubleday, 1997.

———. *An introduction to the Gospel of John.* Edited by F. J. Moloney. New York: Doubleday, 2003.

Brown, T. G. *Spirit in the writings of John: Johannine pneumatology in social-scientific perspective.* Edinburgh: T.&T. Clark, 2003.

Bruce, F. F. *The gospel of John.* Grand Rapids: Eerdmans, 1983.

Bibliography

Bube, R. H. "Science and Christianity." In *The international standard Bible encyclopedia*. Edited by G. W. Bromiley, 4:351–356. Grand Rapids: Eerdmans, 1988.

Bultmann, R. *The Gospel of John: a commentary*. Translated by G. R. Beasley-Murray, et al. Philadelphia: The Westminster Press, 1976.

Burge, G. M. "A specific problem in the New Testament text and canon: the woman caught in adultery (John 7:53—8:11)." *Journal of the Evangelical Theological Society*. 27:2 (1984) 141–148.

———. *The anointed community: the Holy Spirit in the Johannine tradition*. Grand Rapids: Eerdmans, 1987.

———. *John: The NIV application commentary*. Grand Rapids: Zondervan, 2000.

Busenitz, I. A. "The Reformer's understanding of Paul and the law." *The Master's Seminary Journal*. 16:2 (2005) 245–259.

Byassee, J. "Be happy: the health and wealth gospel." *The Christian Century*. 122:14 (2005) 20–23.

Cahill, J. P. "Johannine Logos as center." *Catholic Biblical Quarterly*. 38:1 (1976) 54–72.

Calvin, J. *Commentary on the holy gospel of Jesus Christ according to John*. Volumes one and two. Translated by W. Pringle. Grand Rapids: Baker, 1999.

Caron, G. "Exploring a religious dimension: the Johannine Jews." *Studies in Religion*. 24:2 (1995) 159–171.

Carson, D. A. *The Gospel according to John*. Grand Rapids: Eerdmans, 1991.

———. "Summaries and conclusions." In *Justification and variegated nomism. Volume 1: the complexities of Second Temple Judaism*. Edited by D. A. Carson, et al., 1:505–548. Grand Rapids: Baker, 2001.

Casselli, S. J. "Jesus as eschatological Torah." *Trinity Journal*. 18:1 (1997) 15–41.

Chalker, W. H. *Science and faith: understanding meaning, method, and truth*. Louisville, KY: Westminster John Knox Press, 2006.

Chancey, M. A. "Paul and the law: E P Sander's retrieval of Judaism." *The Christian century*. 123:12 (2006) 20–23.

Clowney, E. P. *How Jesus transformed the ten commandments*. Phillipsburg, NJ: P&R Publishing, 2007.

Coloe, M. L. *God dwells with us: temple symbolism in the Fourth Gospel*. Collegeville, MN: The Liturgical Press, 2001.

Cook, W. R. *The theology of John*. Chicago: Moody Press, 1979.

Corbett, J. "The Pharisaic revolution and Jesus as embodied Torah." *Studies in religion*. 15:3 (1986) 375–391.

Cowan, C. "The Father and Son in the Fourth Gospel: Johannine subordination revisited." *Journal of the Evangelical Theological Society* 49:1 (2006) 115–135.

Cude, W. *The Ph.D. trap revisited*. Toronto: The Dundurn Group, 2001.

Culpepper, R. A. *John, the son of Zebedee: the life of a legend*. Minneapolis: Fortress Press, 2000.

Danker, F. W. *A Greek-English lexicon of the New Testament and other early Christian literature*. Third edition. Chicago: The University of Chicago Press, 2000.

Das, A. A. *Paul, the law, and the covenant*. Peabody, MA: Hendrickson Publishers, 2001.

———. *Paul and the Jews*. Peabody, MA: Hendrickson Publishers, 2003.

Daube, D. *The New Testament and rabbinic Judaism*. Peabody, MA: Hendrickson Publishers, 1956.

Davids, P. H. "James and Paul." In *Dictionary of Paul and his letters*. Edited by G. F. Hawthorne, et al., 457–461. Downers Grove, IL: InterVarsity, 1993.

Bibliography

Davies, G. H. "Glory." In *The Interpreter's Dictionary of the Bible*. Edited by G. A. Buttrick, et al., 2:401–403. Nashville: Abingdon Press, 1962.

Davies, W. D. *Torah in the messianic age and/or age to come*. Atlanta: Society of Biblical Literature, 1952.

———. *Christian origins and Judaism*. Philadelphia: The Westminster Press, 1962.

De Jonge, M. "Jewish expectations about the 'Messiah' according to the Fourth Gospel." *New Testament Studies*. 19 (1972) 246–270.

———. "Jesus as prophet and king in the Fourth Gospel." *Ephemerides theologicae Lovanienses: commentarii de re theologica et canonica*. 49:1 (1973) 160–177.

DeSilva, D. A. *An introduction to the New Testament: contexts, methods, and ministry formation*. Downers Grove, IL: InterVarsity, 2004.

Dodd, C. H. *The interpretation of the Fourth Gospel*. Cambridge: Cambridge University Press, 1953.

Domeris, W. R. "The confession of Peter according to John 6:69." *Tyndale Bulletin*. 44:1 (1993) 155–167.

Duke, P. D. *Irony in the Fourth Gospel*. Louisville, KY: John Knox Press, 1985.

Edersheim, A. *Sketches of Jewish social life in the days of Christ*. Grand Rapids: Eerdmans, 1979.

———. *The life and times of Jesus the Messiah*. Grand Rapids: Eerdmans, 1980.

Ellis, P. F. *The genius of John: a composition-critical commentary on the Fourth Gospel*. Collegeville, MN: The Liturgical Press, 1984.

Ellison, S., Bailey, M. (Foreword), and Lioy, D. (Epilogue). *Parables in the eye of the storm: Christ's response in the face of conflict*. Grand Rapids: Kregel, 2001.

Epp, J. E. "Wisdom, Torah, Word: the Johannine prologue and the purpose of the Fourth Gospel." In *Current Issues in Biblical and Patristic Interpretation. Studies in honor of Merrill C. Tenney presented by his former students*. Edited by G. G. F. Hawthorne, 128–146. Grand Rapids: Eerdmans, 1975.

Evans, C. A. *Word and glory: on the exegetical and theological background of John's Prologue*. Sheffield: Sheffield Academic Press, 1993.

Fairbairn, P. *The revelation of law in Scripture*. Grand Rapids: Zondervan, 1957.

Fanning, B. M. "A theology of Hebrews." In *A biblical theology of the New Testament*. Edited by R. B. Zuck, et al., 369–415. Chicago: Moody Press, 1994.

———. "A theology of James." In *A biblical theology of the New Testament*. Edited by R. B. Zuck, et al., 417–435. Chicago: Moody Press, 1994.

Farnell, F. D. "The new perspective on Paul: its basic tenets, history, and presuppositions." *The Master's Seminary Journal*. 16:2 (2005) 189–243.

Fernando, G. C. A. *The relationship between law and love in the Gospel of John*. New York: Peter Lang, 2004.

Flatow, I. "String theory." *Science Friday*, August 18, 2006. Online: http://www.sciencefriday.com/pages/2006/Aug/hour2_081806.html.

Fowler, W. G. *The influence of Ezekiel in the Fourth Gospel: intertextuality and interpretation*. PhD diss. Mill Valley, CA: Golden Gate Baptist Theological Seminary, 1995.

Freed, E. D. *Old Testament quotations in the Gospel of John*. Leiden: E. J. Brill, 1965.

Gaffin, R. "A reformed critique of the new perspective." *Modern Reformation*, 2002. Online: http://www.modernreformation.org/rg02newp.htm.

Gager, J. G. *Reinventing Paul*. Oxford: Oxford University Press, 2000.

Geisler, N. L. *Christian ethics: options and issues*. Grand Rapids: Baker, 1989.

Bibliography

Gieschen, C. A. "Paul and the law: was Luther right?" In *The law in holy Scripture: essays from the Concordia Theological Seminary symposium on exegetical theology*. Edited by C. A. Gieschen, 113–147. Concordia Publishing House, 2004.

Glasson, T. F. *Moses in the Fourth Gospel*. London: SCM Press, 1963.

Goldsmith, J. *The visual Bible: Gospel of John*. Burbank, CA: Visual Bible International, Inc., 2003.

Greene, B. *The elegant universe*. Boston: WGBH Educational Foundation, 2003. Online: http://www.pbs.org/wgbh/nova/elegant/.

Gruenler, R. G. *The Trinity in the gospel of John: a thematic commentary on the Fourth Gospel*. Eugene, OR: Wipf and Stock, 1986.

Guilding, A. *The Fourth Gospel and Jewish worship: a study of the relation of St. John's Gospel to the ancient Jewish lectionary system*. Oxford: Oxford University Press, 1960.

Guthrie, D. *New Testament theology*. Downers Grove, IL: InterVarsity, 1981.

Haenchen, E. *John 1*. Translated by R. W. Funk. Minneapolis: Fortress Press, 1984.

———. *John 2*. Translated by R. W. Funk. Minneapolis: Fortress Press, 1984.

Hafemann, S. J. "Paul and his interpreters." In *Dictionary of Paul and his letters*. Edited by G. F. Hawthorne, et al., 666–679. Downers Grove, IL: InterVarsity, 1993.

Hakola, R. *Identity matters: John, the Jews and Jewishness*. Leiden: E. J. Brill, 2003.

Hanson, A. T. *The prophetic Gospel: a study of John and the Old Testament*. Edinburgh: T.&T. Clark, 1991.

———. "John's use of Scripture." In *The Gospels and the Scriptures of Israel*. Edited by C. A. Evans, et al., 358–379. Sheffield: Sheffield Academic Press, 1994.

Harris, W. H. *The Gospel of John: introduction and commentary*. Richardson, TX: Biblical Studies Press, 2001. Online: http://www.bible.org/series.php?series_id=72.

Harrison, E. F. "Glory." In *The International Standard Bible Encyclopedia*. Edited by G. F. Bromiley, et al., 2:477–483. Grand Rapids: Eerdmans, 1982.

Harstine, S. *Moses as a character in the Fourth Gospel: a study of ancient reading techniques*. Sheffield: Sheffield Academic Press, 2002.

Harvey, A. E. *Jesus on trial: a study in the Fourth Gospel*. Louisville, KY: John Knox Press, 1976.

Hawthorne, G. F. "The Concept of Faith in the Fourth Gospel." *Bibliotheca Sacra*. 116:462 (1959) 117–126.

Henry, C. F. *Christian personal ethics*. Grand Rapids: Baker, 1957.

Heschel, A. J. *Heavenly Torah as refracted through the generations*. Edited and translated by G. Tucker, et al. London: Continuum, 2005.

Hoppe, L. J. "Judaism." In *The Collegeville pastoral dictionary of biblical theology*. Edited by C. Stuhlmueller, et al., 501–503. Collegeville, MN: The Liturgical Press, 1996.

Horsley, R. A. and Hanson, J. S. *Bandits, prophets, and messiahs: popular movements in the time of Jesus*. Harrisburg, PA: Trinity Press International, 1999.

Horton, M. "Déjà vu all over again." *Modern Reformation*. 13:4 (2004). Online: http://www.modernreformation.org/mh04dejavu.htm.

Hoskins, P. M. *Jesus as the replacement of the temple in the Gospel of John*. Ph.D. diss. Deerfield, IL: Trinity Evangelical Divinity School, 2002.

Hoskyns, E. C. *The Fourth Gospel*. Edited by F. N. Davey. London: Faber and Faber Limited, 1947.

Hughes, J. "The new perspective's view of Paul and the law." *The Master's Seminary Journal*. 16:2 (2005) 261–276.

Hurtado, L. W. *Lord Jesus Christ: devotion to Jesus in earliest Christianity*. Grand Rapids: Eerdmans, 2003.

Bibliography

Huttar, D. K. "Glory." In *Evangelical Dictionary of Biblical Theology*. Edited by W. A. Elwell, 287–288. Grand Rapids: Baker, 1996.

Irvine, M. "Young workers want it all, now." *The Associated Press*, June 27, 2005. Online: http://seattlepi.nwsource.com/business/230177_entitlement27.html.

Jaffee, M. "Torah." In *Encyclopedia of Religion*. Second edition. Edited by L. Jones. 13:9230–9241. New York: Macmillan Reference, 2005.

Jeremias, J. *New Testament theology: the proclamation of Jesus*. Translated by J. Bowden. New York: Charles Scribner's Sons, 1971.

———. *The parables of Jesus*. Revised third edition. Translated by S. H. Hooke. London: S.C.M. Press, 2003.

Johns, L. L. "The signs as witnesses in the Fourth Gospel: reexamining the evidence." *Catholic Biblical Quarterly*. 56:3 (1994) 519–535.

Johnson, L. T. *The writings of the New Testament: an interpretation*. Revised edition. Minneapolis: Fortress Press, 1999.

Johnson, P. "A defense of the old perspective on Paul: what did St. Paul really say?" *The Threshold*. Monergism, January 10, 2004. Online: http://www.monergism.com/thethreshold/articles/onsite/new_p.html.

Johnston, G. *The Spirit-Paraclete in the Gospel of John*. Cambridge: Cambridge University Press, 1970.

Jones, D. C. *Biblical Christian ethics*. Grand Rapids: Baker, 1994.

Julian, P. *Jesus and Nicodemus: a literary and narrative exegesis of Jn. 2,23—3,36*. New York: Peter Lang, 2000.

Kaiser, W. C. "The law as God's gracious guidance for the promotion of holiness." In *The law, the gospel, and the modern Christian: five views*. Edited by W. G. Strickland, 177–209. Grand Rapids: Zondervan, 1993.

Keener, C. S. *The gospel of John: a commentary*. Volumes One and Two. Peabody, MA: Hendrickson Publishers, 2003.

Kellstedt L., et al. "Evangelicalism." In *Encyclopedia of religion and society*. Edited by W. H. Swatos. Walnut Creek, CA: AltaMira Press, 1998. Online: http://hirr.hartsem.edu/ency/evan.htm.

Kerr, A. R. *The temple of Jesus' body: the temple theme in the Gospel of John*. Sheffield: Sheffield Academic Press, 2002.

Kierspel, L. *The Jews and the world in the Fourth Gospel: parallelism, function, and context*. Tübingen: Mohr Siebeck, 2006.

Kim, S. *Paul and the new perspective: second thoughts on the origin of Paul's gospel*. Grand Rapids: Eerdmans, 2002.

Kim, S. S. *The relationship of the seven sign-miracles of Jesus in the Fourth Gospel to the Old Testament*. Ph.D. diss. Dallas: Dallas Theological Seminary, 2001.

Kinnaman, D. "A new generation of adults bends moral and sexual rules to their liking." *Barna Updates*. Ventura, CA: The Barna Group, October 31, 2006. Online: www.barna.org.

Kohler, K. and Blau, L. "Shekinah." In *Jewish Encyclopedia*. Edited by I. Singer, et al. Philadelphia: The Kopelman Foundation, 2002. Online: http://www.jewishencyclopedia.com.

Köstenberger, A. J. *Studies on John and gender: a decade of scholarship*. New York: Peter Lang, 2001.

———. *John*. Grand Rapids: Baker, 2004.

Kruse, C. G. *Paul, the law, and justification*. Peabody, MA: Hendrickson Publishers, 1996.

Bibliography

Kümmel, W. G. *The theology of the New Testament according to its major witnesses: Jesus—Paul—John.* Translated by J. E. Steely. Nashville: Abingdon Press, 1973.

Kysar, R. "John, the Gospel of." In *The Anchor Bible Dictionary.* Edited by D. N. Freedman, et al., 3:912–931. New York: Doubleday, 1992.

Labahn, M. "Between tradition and literary art: the miracle tradition in the fourth Gospel." *Biblica* 80 (1999) 178–203. Online: http://www.bsw.org/project/biblica/bibl80/Comm06.htm.

Ladd, G. E. *A theology of the New Testament.* Revised edition. Grand Rapids: Eerdmans, 1997.

Laato, A. "Paul's theology of 'righteousness through faith' in the context of Tanak and Jewish interpretive traditions." In *Ancient Israel, Judaism, and Christianity in Contemporary Perspective: essays in memory of Karl-Johan Illman.* Edited by J. Neusner, et al., 195–224. Lanham, MD: University Press of America, 2006.

Lea, T. D. "The reliability of history in John's Gospel." *Journal of the Evangelical Theological Society.* 38:3 (1995) 387–402.

Lee, B. J. *The Galilean Jewishness of Jesus: retrieving the Jewish origins of Christianity.* Mahwah, NJ: Paulist Press, 1988.

Lee, D. A. "The symbol of divine fatherhood." *Semeia.* 85 (1999) 177–187.

Lenski, R. C. H. *The interpretation of St. John's Gospel.* Minneapolis, MN: Augsburg Publishing House, 1961.

Levenson, J. D. "The conversion of Abraham to Judaism, Christianity, and Islam." In *The idea of biblical interpretation: essays in honor of James L. Kugel.* Edited by H. Najman, et al., 3–40. Leiden: E. J. Brill, 2004.

Levine A. "How the church divorces Jesus from Judaism: misusing Jesus." *The Christian Century.* 123:26 (2006) 20–25.

Lewis, G. R. "God, attributes of." In *Evangelical dictionary of theology.* Edited by W. A. Elwell, 492–500. Second edition. Grand Rapids: Baker, 2001.

———. "The attributes of God," In *The portable seminary.* Edited by D. Horton, et al., 98–117. Minneapolis, MN: Bethany House, 2006.

Lichtenberger, H. "The understanding of the Torah in the Judaism of Paul's day." In *Paul and the Mosaic law.* Edited by J. D. G. Dunn, 7–23. Grand Rapids: Eerdmans, 2001.

Lierman, J. *The New Testament Moses: Christian perceptions of Moses and Israel in the setting of Jewish religion.* Tübingen: Mohr Siebeck, 2004.

———. "The Mosaic pattern of John's Christology." In *Challenging perspectives on the Gospel of John.* Edited by J. Lierman, 210–234. Tübingen: Mohr Siebeck, 2006.

Lightfoot, R. H. *St. John's Gospel: a commentary.* Edited by C. F. Evans. Oxford: Oxford University Press, 1983.

Lincoln, A. T. *Truth on trial: the lawsuit motif in the Fourth Gospel.* Peabody, MA: Hendrickson Publishers, 2000.

———. *The Gospel according to Saint John.* Peabody, MA: Hendrickson Publishers, 2005.

Lindars, B. *The Gospel of John.* Grand Rapids, Eerdmans, 1986.

Lioy, D. "Spiritual care in a medical setting: do we need it?" *Global Journal of Classical Theology.* 3:2 (2002). Online: http://www.trinitysem.edu/journal/lioyv3n2.htm.

———. *The book of Revelation in Christological focus.* New York: Peter Lang, 2003.

———. *The Decalogue in the Sermon on the Mount.* New York: Peter Lang, 2004.

———. *The search for ultimate reality: intertextuality between the Genesis and Johannine prologues.* New York: Peter Lang, 2005.

Bibliography

———. "Progressive covenantalism as an integrative motif of Scripture." *Conspectus* 1 (2006). Online: http://www.theological-research.org/conspectus.php.

———. "Checkmating the human drive for life: A biblical-theological examination of Genesis 5, Ecclesiastes 1, and 1 Corinthians 15:50-58." *Conspectus*. 2 (2006). Online: http://www.theological-research.org/conspectus.php.

———. "The moral law in Christ-centered perspective: a canonical and integrative approach." *Conspectus*. 3 (2007). Online: http://www.theological-research.org/conspectus.php.

———. "The unique status of Jesus as the divine Messiah: an exegetical and theological analysis of Mark 1:1, 9–13." *Conspectus*. 3 (2007). Online: http://www.theological-research.org/conspectus.php.

———. "Jesus as Torah in John 2:1–22." *Conspectus*. 4 (2007). Online: http://www.theological-research.org/conspectus.php.

Loader, W. R. G. *Jesus' attitude towards the law: a study of the Gospels*. Grand Rapids, Eerdmans, 2002.

Lowery, D. K. "A theology of Matthew." In *A biblical theology of the New Testament*. Edited by R. B. Zuck, et al., 19–63. Chicago: Moody Press, 1994.

Macleod, D. *The person of Christ*. Downers Grove, IL: InterVarsity, 1998.

MacRae, G. W. "Theology and irony in the Fourth Gospel." In *The word in the world: essays in honor of Frederick L. Moriarty*. Edited by R. J. Clifford, et al., 83–96. Cambridge, MA: Weston College Press, 1973.

Manning, G. T. *Echoes of a prophet: the use of Ezekiel in the Gospel of John and in literature of the second temple period*. Edinburgh: T.&T. Clark, 2004.

Markus, A. *Beyond finitude: God's transcendence and the meaning of life*. New York: Peter Lang, 2004.

Marshall, I. H. "Johannine theology." In *The international standard Bible encyclopedia*. Edited by G. W. Bromiley, et al., 2:1081–1091. Grand Rapids: Eerdmans, 1982.

———. *New Testament theology*. Downers Grove, IL: InterVarsity, 2004.

Martin, B. L. *Christ and the law in Paul*. Eugene, OR: Wipf and Stock, 2001.

Mattison, M. M. "A summary on the new perspective on Paul." *The Paul Page*. Jewish Christian Webring, 2006. Online: http://www.thepaulpage.com/Summary.html.

McGee, M. *Self-help, inc.: makeover culture in American life*. Oxford: Oxford University Press, 2005.

McGrath, A. E. "Justification." In *Dictionary of Paul and his letters*. Edited by G. F. Hawthorne, et al., 517–523. Downers Grove, IL: InterVarsity, 1993.

———. *The foundations of dialogue in science and religion*. Boston: Blackwell Publishing, 1998.

———. *Science and religion: an introduction*. Boston: Blackwell Publishing, 1999.

McGrath, J. F. *John's apologetic Christology: legitimation and development in Johannine Christology*. Cambridge: Cambridge University Press, 2001.

McQuilkin, R. *Biblical ethics: an introduction*. Second edition. Wheaton, IL: Tyndale House Publishers, 1995.

Meacham, J. "Pilgrim's progress." In *Newsweek*, August 14, 2006. Online: http://www.msnbc.msn.com/id/14204483.

Meeks, W. A. *The prophet-king: Moses traditions in the Johannine christology*. Leiden: E. J. Brill, 1967.

———. "Moses as God and King." In *Religions in antiquity: essays in memory of Erwin Ramsdell Goodenough*, 354–371. Leiden: E. J. Brill, 1970.

Bibliography

Meier, J. P. *Law and history in Matthew's Gospel: a redactional study of Mt. 5:17–48*. Rome: Biblical Institute Press, 1976.

———. "The historical Jesus and the historical law: some problems within the problem." *Catholic Biblical Quarterly.* 65 (2003) 52–79.

Menninger, R. E. *Israel and the church in the Gospel of Matthew.* New York: Peter Lang, 1994.

Meyer, P. W. "'The Father': the presentation of God in the Fourth Gospel." In *Exploring the Gospel of John: essays in honor of D. Moody Smith.* Edited by R. A. Culpepper, et al., 255–273. Louisville, KY: Westminster John Knox Press, 1996.

———. *The Word in this world: essays in New Testament exegesis and theology.* Edited by J. T. Carroll. Louisville, KY: Westminster John Knox Press, 2004.

Miller, E. "Who do your books say that I am? New volumes tell much about our Lord—and our cultural movement." *Christianity Today*, June 25, 2007. Online: http://www.christianitytoday.com/ct/2007/june/24.38.html.

Mish, F. C. "Humanism." In *Merriam-Webster OnLine*. Springfield, MA: Merriam-Webster, Inc., 2006. Online: http://www.m-w.com.

———. "Meritocracy." In *Merriam-Webster OnLine*. Springfield, MA: Merriam-Webster, Inc., 2006. Online: http://www.m-w.com.

———. "Reality." In *Merriam-Webster OnLine*. Springfield, MA: Merriam-Webster, Inc., 2006. Online: http://www.m-w.com.

Mitchell, N. B. "Works righteousness and the synagogue of Satan: rethinking Christian caricatures of 1st century Judaism." Paper presented to the First Joint Australian & New Zealand Religious Studies Conference, Lincoln University, Canterbury. International Council of Christians and Jews, July 4–7, 1996. Online: http://www.jcrelations.net/en/?id=770.

Mlakuzhyil, G. *The Christocentric literary structure of the fourth Gospel.* Rome: Editrice Pontificio Istituto Biblico, 1987.

Moo, D. J. "Law." In *Dictionary of Jesus and the* Gospels. Edited by J. B. Green, et al., 450–461. Downers Grove, IL: InterVarsity, 1992.

———. "The law of Christ as the fulfillment of the law of Moses: a modified Lutheran view." In *The law, the gospel, and the modern Christian: five* views. Edited by W. G. Strickland, 319–376. Grand Rapids: Zondervan, 1993.

———. "Israel and the law in Romans 5– 11: *the paradoxes of Paul.* Edited by D. A. Carson, et al., 2:185–216. Grand Rapids: Baker, 2004.

Moreland, J. P. "Science and theology." In *Evangelical dictionary of theology.* Edited by W. A. Elwell, 1071–1075. Grand Rapids: Baker, 2001.

Morris, L. *The Gospel according to John.* Revised edition. Grand Rapids: Eerdmans, 1995.

———. "The atonement in John's Gospel." *Criswell Theological Review.* 3:1 (1988) 49–64.

———. *New Testament theology.* Grand Rapids: Zondervan, 1990.

———. "What do we mean by 'evangelical'?" Richmond, BC: World Evangelical Alliance, July 11, 2001. Online: http://www.worldevangelicalalliance.com/wea/evangelical.htm.

Motyer, A. *Look to the Rock: an Old Testament background to our understanding of Christ.* Grand Rapids: Kregel, 1996.

Murray, J. *Principles of conduct: aspects of biblical ethics.* Grand Rapids: Eerdmans, 1957.

Neyrey, J. H. "Jacob traditions and the interpretation of John 4:10–26." *Catholic biblical quarterly.* 41 (1979) 419–437.

———. "Jesus the judge: forensic process in John 8:21–59." *Biblica.* 68 (1987) 509–541.

Ng, W. *Water symbolism in John: an eschatological interpretation.* New York: Peter Lang, 2001.
Nicol, W. *The semeia in the Fourth Gospel: tradition and redaction.* Leiden: E. J. Brill, 1972.
Neusner, J. "Pharisaic law in New Testament times." *Union Seminary quarterly review.* 26:4 (1971) 331–340.
———. *The perfect Torah.* Leiden: E. J. Brill, 2003.
———. *Rabbinic literature and the New Testament: what we cannot show, we do not know.* Eugene, OR: Wipf and Stock, 2004.
———. "Rabbinic Judaism in Late Antiquity." In *Encyclopedia of Religion.* Second edition. Edited by L. Jones. 11:7583–7590. New York: Macmillan Reference, 2005.
O'Brien, P. T. "Was Paul a covenantal nomist?" In *Justification and variegated nomism. Volume II: the paradoxes of Paul.* Edited by D. A. Carson, et al., 2:249–296. Grand Rapids: Baker, 2004.
O'Collins, G. *Christology: a biblical, historical, and systematic study of Jesus.* Oxford: Oxford University Press, 1995.
O'Day, G.R. "The Gospel of John." In *The new interpreter's Bible.* Edited by L. E. Keck, et al., 9:493–865. Nashville: Abingdon Press, 1995.
Olson, G. A. "The importance of protocol." *ChronicleCareers.* Washington, D.C.: The Chronicle of Higher Education, 2006. Online: http://chronicle.com/jobs/news/2006/10/2006103101c/careers.html.
Packer, J. I. "God," In *New dictionary of theology.* Edited by S. B. Ferguson, et al., 274–77. Downers Grove, IL: InterVarsity, 1988.
Page, R. M. "Science in the Bible." In *The Zondervan Pictorial Encyclopedia of the Bible.* Edited by M. C. Tenney, 5:294–296. Grand Rapids: Zondervan, 1976.
Painter, J. "Eschatological faith in the Gospel of John." In *Reconciliation and hope: New Testament essays on atonement and eschatology presented to L. L. Morris on his 60th birthday.* Edited by R. Banks, 36–52. Grand Rapids: Eerdmans, 1974.
Pancaro, S. *The law in the fourth Gospel: the Torah and the Gospel, Moses and Jesus, Judaism and Christianity according to John.* Leiden: E. J. Brill, 1975.
Park, C. H. *Transcendence and spatiality of the triune creator.* New York: Peter Lang, 2005.
Paroschi, W. *Incarnation and covenant in the prologue to the Fourth Gospel (John 1:1–18).* New York: Peter Lang, 2006.
Pate, C. M. *The reverse of the curse: Paul, wisdom, and the law.* Tübingen: Mohr Siebeck, 2000.
Pelikan, J. "Jesus as Rabbi." In *The illustrated Jesus through the centuries,* 9–23. New Haven, CT: Yale University Press, 1997. Online: http://www.pbs.org/wgbh/pages/frontline/shows/religion/jesus/rabbi.html.
Pierard, R. V., and W. A. Elwell. "Evangelicalism." In *Evangelical dictionary of theology.* Edited by W. A. Elwell, 405–410. Second edition. Grand Rapids: Baker, 2001.
Polkinghorne, J. *Quarks, chaos, and Christianity: questions to science and religion.* New York: Crossroad, 1997.
———. *Science and theology: an introduction.* Minneapolis: Fortress Press, 1998.
———. *Exploring reality: the intertwining of science and religion.* New Haven, CT: Yale University Press, 2005.
Pond, E. W. *The theological dependencies of John's Gospel on Isaiah.* Th.M. thesis. Dallas: Dallas Theological Seminary, 1985.
Portalatín, A. *Temporal oppositions as hermeneutical categories in the Epistle to the Hebrews.* New York: Peter Lang, 2006.

Bibliography

Ráisánen, H. *Paul and the law*. Minneapolis: Fortress Press, 1986.

Ratzinger, J. (Pope Benedict XVI). *Jesus of Nazareth: from the baptism in the Jordan to the transfiguration*. Translated by A. J. Walker. New York: Doubleday, 2007.

Reed, D. A. "How Semitic was John? Rethinking the Hellenistic background to John 1:1." *Anglican Theological Review*. 85:4 (2003) 709–726.

Reinhartz, A. "Jesus as prophet: predictive prolepses in the Fourth Gospel." *Journal for the Study of the New Testament*. 36 (1989) 3–16.

Resseguie, J. L. "John 9: a literary-critical analysis." In *The Gospel of John as literature: an anthology of twentieth-century perspectives*. Edited by M. W. G. Stibbe, 115–122. Leiden: E.J. Brill, 1993.

Rhee, V. *Faith in Hebrews: analysis within the context of Christology, eschatology, and ethics*. New York: Peter Lang, 2001.

Rhyne, C. T. *Faith establishes the law*. Chico, CA: Scholars Press, 1981.

———. "*Nomos dikiaosynes* and the meaning of Romans 10:4." *Catholic biblical quarterly*. 47:3 (1985) 486–499.

Ridderbos, H. *Paul: an outline of his theology*. J. R. De Witt, trans. Grand Rapids: Eerdmans, 1975.

———. *The Gospel according to John: a theological commentary*. Translated by J. Vriend. Grand Rapids: Eerdmans, 1997.

Riddlebarger, K. "Reformed confessionalism and the new perspective on Paul: a new challenge to a fundamental article of faith." *Modern Reformation*, 1996. Online: http://www.modernreformation.org/krnpp.htm.

Robar, E. J. *Isaiah's vision of glory in John: a literary and biblical-theological study of John 12:41*. M.A. Thesis. South Hamilton, MA: Gordon-Conwell Theological Seminary, 2004.

Rosenblatt, M. E. "Parable." In *The Collegeville pastoral dictionary of biblical theology*. Edited by C. Stuhlmueller, et al., 698–692. Collegeville, MN: The Liturgical Press, 1996.

Rule, A. K. "Religion, religious." In *Evangelical dictionary of theology*. Edited by W. A. Elwell, 1006–1007. Second edition. Grand Rapids: Baker, 2001.

Russell, W. "The Holy Spirit's ministry in the Fourth Gospel." *Grace Theological Journal*. 8:2 (1987) 227–239.

Salerno, S. *Sham: how the self-help movement made America helpless*. New York: Crown Publishers, 2005.

Sanders, E. P. "Torah and Christ." *Interpretation*. 29:1 (1975) 372–390.

———. *Paul, the law, and the Jewish people*. Minneapolis: Fortress Press, 1983.

———. *Jesus and Judaism*. Minneapolis: Fortress Press, 1985.

———. *Jewish law from Jesus to Mishnah*. Philadelphia: Trinity Press International, 1990.

Sanders, J. N. and Mastin, B. A. *A commentary on the Gospel according to St. John*. Peabody, MA: Hendrickson, 1988.

Saucy, R. L. "God, doctrine of." In *Evangelical dictionary of theology*. Edited by W. A. Elwell, 500–504. Second edition. Grand Rapids: Baker, 2001.

———. "The biblical concept of God," In *The portable seminary*. Edited by D. Horton, et al., 86–97. Minneapolis, MN: Bethany House, 2006.

Scannell, T. J. *Fulfillment of Johannine signs: a study of John 12:37–50*. Ph.D. diss. New York: Fordham University, 1998.

Schnackenburg, R. *The Gospel according to St John*. Vols. 1–3. Translated by K. Smyth. New York: Crossroad, 1987.

Bibliography

Schnelle, U. *Antidocetic Christology in the Gospel of John: an investigation of the place of the Fourth Gospel in the Johannine school*. Translated by L. M. Maloney. Minneapolis: Fortress Press, 1992.
Schoneveld, J. "The Torah in the flesh: A new reading of the prologue of the Gospel of John as a contribution to a Christology without anti-semitism." In *The New Testament and Christian-Jewish Dialogue: Studies in Honor of David Flusser*. Edited by M. Lowe. Jerusalem: Ecumenical Theological Research Fraternity in Israel, 1990.
Schottroff, L. *The parables of Jesus*. Minneapolis : Fortress Press, 2006.
Schreiner, T. R. "Law of Christ." In *Dictionary of Paul and his* letters. Edited by G. F. Hawthorne, et al., 542–544. Downers Grove, IL: InterVarsity, 1993.
———. "Paul's view of the law in Romans 10:4–5." *Westminster Theological Journal*. 55 (1993) 113–155.
———. "Works of the law." In *Dictionary of Paul and his* letters. Edited by G. F. Hawthorne, et al., 975–979. Downers Grove, IL: InterVarsity, 1993.
———. "Law." In *Dictionary of the later New Testament and its developments*. Edited by R. P. Martin, et al., 644–649. Downers Grove, IL: InterVarsity, 1997.
Schwarz, H. *Christology*. Grand Rapids: Eerdmans, 1998.
Seifrid, M. A. "The narrative of Scripture and justification by faith: a still fresher reading of Paul." *Symposia*. Fort Wayne, IN: Concordia Theological Seminary, 2006. Online: http://www.ctsfw.edu/events/symposia/papers/sym2006seifrid.pdf.
Sidebottom, E. M. *The Christ of the Fourth Gospel in light of first-century thought*. London: SPCK, 1961.
Silva, M. "Approaching the Fourth Gospel." *Criswell Theological Review* 3:1 (1988) 17–29
Simpson, J. A., Weiner, E. S. C., and Berg, D. L. "God." In *Compact Oxford English dictionary*. Oxford: Oxford University Press, 2006. Online: http://www.askoxford.com/dictionaries.
Sloan, R. P. "Trivializing the transcendent. What can science really tell us about faith?" In *Christianity Today Magazine*. August 1, 2006. Online: http://www.christianitytoday.com/ct/2006/008/22.42.html.
Sloyan, G. S. *Is Christ the end of the law?* Philadelphia: The Westminster Press, 1978.
Smith, D. E. and Williams, M. E. *The parables of Jesus*. Nashville: Abingdon Press, 2006.
Smith, D. M. *The theology of the Gospel of John*. Cambridge: Cambridge University Press, 1995.
Smith, R. H. "Exodus typology in the Fourth Gospel." *Journal of Biblical Literature*. 81 (1962) 329–342.
Suggs, M. J. *Wisdom, christology, and law in Matthew's gospel*. Cambridge, MA: Harvard University Press, 1970.
Spencer, A. B. "Father-ruler: the meaning of the metaphor 'father' for God in the Bible." *Journal of the Evangelical Theological Society*. 39:3 (1996) 433–442.
Sprinkle, J. M. *Biblical law and its relevance: a Christian understanding and ethical application for today of the Mosaic regulations*. Lanham, MD: University Press of America, 2006.
Sproston, W. E. "'Is this not Jesus, the son of Joseph . . . ?' (John 6:42). Johannine Christology as a challenge to faith." *Journal for the Study of the New Testament*. 24 (1985) 77–97.
Stanton, G. N. "The law of Moses and the law of Christ." In *Paul and the Mosaic law*. Edited by J. D. G. Dunn, 99–116. Grand Rapids: Eerdmans, 2001.
———. *Jesus and the Gospel*. Cambridge: Cambridge University Press, 2004.
Stern, D. H. *Jewish New Testament commentary*. Clarksville, MD: Jewish New Testament Publications, 1992.

Bibliography

Strickland, W. G. "The inauguration of the law of Christ with the gospel of Christ: a dispensational view." In *The law, the gospel, and the modern Christian: five views.* Edited by W. G. Strickland, 229–279. Grand Rapids: Zondervan, 1993.

Teeple, H. M. *The Mosaic eschatological prophet.* Atlanta: Society of Biblical Literature, 1957.

Tegmark, M. "Mission, scope, and emphasis." The Foundational Questions Institute (FQXi), 2006. Online: http://www.fqxi.org/about.html.

Tenney, M. C. *John: the Gospel of belief.* Grand Rapids: Eerdmans, 1987.

———. "The Gospel of John." In *The expositor's Bible commentary,* Edited by F. E. Gaebelein, et al., 9:3–203. Grand Rapids: Zondervan, 1981.

Tew, G. T. *The pneumatology of John as seen in the Fourth Gospel.* PhD diss. New Orleans, LA: New Orleans Baptist Theological Seminary, 1993.

Thielman, F. "Law." In *Dictionary of Paul and his letters.* Edited by G. F. Hawthorne, et al., 529–542. Downers Grove, IL: InterVarsity, 1993.

———. *Paul and the law: a contextual approach.* Downers Grove, IL: InterVarsity, 1994.

———. *Theology of the New Testament: a canonical and synthetic approach.* Grand Rapids: Zondervan, 2005.

Thomas, J. C. "The Fourth Gospel and rabbinic Judaism." *Zeitschrift für die neutestamentliche Wissenschaft und die Kunde des Urchristentums.* 82:3–4 (1991) 159–182.

Thomas, R. L. "Hermeneutics of the new perspective on Paul." *The Master's Seminary Journal.* 16:2 (2005) 293–316.

Thompson, M. M. "John, Gospel of." In *Dictionary of Jesus and the Gospels.* Edited by J. B. Green, et al., 368–383. Downers Grove, IL: InterVarsity, 1992.

———. "The living Father." *Semeia* 85 (1999) 19–31.

———. *The God of the Gospel of John.* Grand Rapids, Eerdmans, 2001.

Tolmie, D. F. "The characterization of God in the Fourth Gospel." *Journal for the Study of the New Testament.* 20:69 (1998) 57–95.

Tolson, J. "The new unbelievers." *U.S. News and World Report,* November 5, 2006. Online: http://www.usnews.com/usnews/news/articles/061105/13atheism.htm.

Trites, A. A. *The New Testament concept of witness.* Cambridge: Cambridge University Press, 1977.

Trueman, C. "A man more sinned against than sinning? The portrait of Martin Luther in contemporary New Testament scholarship: some casual observations of a mere historian." Paper delivered at the Tyndale Fellowship in Cambridge. Westminster Theological Seminary, 2000. Online: http://www.crcchico.com/covenant/trueman.html.

Turek, M. M. *Towards a theology of God the Father: Hans Urs von Balthasar's theodramatic approach.* New York: Peter Lang, 2001.

Twenge, J. M. *Generation me: why today's young Americans are more confident, assertive, entitled—and more miserable than ever before.* New York: Free Press, 2006.

Umoh, C. *The plot to kill Jesus: a contextual study of John 11.47–53.* New York: Peter Lang, 2000.

Unterman, A., et al. " Shekhinah." In *Encyclopaedia Judaica.* Second Edition. Edited by M. Berenbaum, et. al., 18:440–444. Detroit: Macmillan Reference.

Van Belle, G. *The signs source in the Fourth Gospel: historical survey and critical evaluation of the semeia hypothesis.* Leuven: Leuven University Press, 1994.

Van Biema, D. "God vs. science." *Time Magazine.* 168:20 (2006). Online: http://www.time.com/time/magazine/article/0,9171,1555132,00.html.

Bibliography

Vander Zee, L. J. 2004. *Christ's baptism and the Lord's Supper: recovering the sacraments for evangelical worship.* Downers Grove, IL: InterVarsity, 2004.

VanDrunen, D. M., ed. *Report on justification presented to the seventy-third general assembly of the Orthodox Presbyterian Church.* Orthodox Presbyterian Church, 2006. Online: http://www.opc.org/GA/justification.pdf.

VanGemeren, W. A. "The law as the perfection of righteousness in Jesus Christ: a Reformed perspective." In *The law, the gospel, and the modern Christian: five views.* Edited by W. G. Strickland, 13–58. Grand Rapids: Zondervan, 1993.

Venema, C. P. "Evaluating the new perspective on Paul: Scripture, confession, and historical reconstruction." Glenside, PA: World Reformed Fellowship, March 2003. Online: http://www.wrfnet.org/articles/article.asp?id=733.

Vermes, G. *Jesus and the world of Judaism.* Minneapolis: Fortress Press, 1984.

Waters, G. P. *Justification and the new perspectives on Paul: a review and response.* Phillipsburg, NJ: P&R Publishing, 2004.

Watson, F. "Not the new perspective." A paper delivered at the British New Testament Conference in Manchester. University of Aberdeen, September 2001. Online: http://www.abdn.ac.uk/divinity/staff/watsonart.shtml.

Wead, D. W. *The literary devices in John's Gospel.* Basel: Friedrich Reinhardt Kommissionsverlag, 1970.

Webber, R. E. *The younger evangelicals: facing the challenges of the new world.* Grand Rapids: Baker, 2002.

Webber, R. E. and Kenyon, P. "A call to an ancient Evangelical future." Lombard, IL: Northern Seminary, 2006. Online: http://www.ancientfutureworship.com/afw_wkshps.html.

Wenham, D. *Paul: follower of Jesus or founder of Christianity?* Grand Rapids: Eerdmans, 1995.

Westcott, B. F. *The Gospel according to St. John.* Grand Rapids: Eerdmans, 1981.

Westerholm, S. "Justification by faith is the answer: what is the question?" *Symposia.* Fort Wayne, IN: Concordia Theological Seminary, 2006. Online: http://www.ctsfw.edu/events/symposia/papers/sym2006westerholm.pdf.

Whitacre, R. A. *Johannine polemic: the role of tradition and theology.* Chico, CA: Scholars Press, 1982.

———. *John.* Downers Grove, IL: InterVarsity, 1999. Online: http://www.biblegateway.com/resources/commentaries/index.php

Williams, C. H. *I am he: the interpretation of 'anî hû' in Jewish and early Christian Literature.* Tübingen: Mohr Siebeck, 2000.

———. "The testimony of Isaiah and Johannine christology." In *"As those who are taught": the interpretation of Isaiah from the LXX to the SBL.* Edited by C. M. McGinnis, et al., 107–124. Atlanta: Society of Biblical Literature, 2006.

Wilson, M. R. *Our father Abraham: Jewish roots of the Christian faith.* Grand Rapids: Eerdmans, 1991.

Witherington, B. *John's wisdom: a commentary on the Fourth Gospel.* Louisville, KY: Westminster John Knox Press, 1995.

Wright, C. J. *Jesus the revelation of God: his mission and message according to St. John.* London: Hodder and Stoughton, 1950.

Wright, N. T. *The climax of the covenant: Christ and the law in Pauline theology.* Minneapolis: Fortress Press, 1991.

Wucherpfennig, A. "Torah, gospel, and John's prologue." *Theology Digest.* 50:3 (2003) 211–216.

Subject Index

Abraham 4–5, 11, 28, 30, 39, 45–47, 55 n. 12, 64, 100, 154–156, 156 n. 48, 157, 157 n. 49, 159–160, 160 n. 55, 160 n. 56, 170–171, 209, 210, 211

agent, divine/heavenly 8 n. 23, 52 n. 5, 69 n. 52, 75–76 n. 3, 87 n. 40, 114, 114–115 n. 18, 115, 117, 119, 121, 127 n. 47, 129, 129 n. 55, 132, 133, 134 n. 67, 135 n. 70, 140, 143, 153, 158, 158 n. 51, 158 n. 53, 163, 164, 182 n. 13, 182–183 n. 15, 184, 184 n. 21, 190 n. 27, 205 n. 59, 206, 217–218, 226, 239

aion (temporal ages, universe) 38

aletheia (truth) 28

'*am ha'arets* (the people of the land) 146 n. 31

angels 11, 39, 238

amnos (lamb) 63

anothen (again, from above) 90, 90 n. 54

anthropon (everyone) 51

agapao (love) 242

arche (beginning) 26

ascension/exaltation 27, 28, 61 n. 34, 79, 84 n. 33, 93, 101, 135 n. 70, 138 n. 4, 143, 145, 152, 202, 205, 214, 218, 219, 226

baptism 4, 16 n. 50, 55–56, 58, 58 n. 22, 62, 91, 95, 202

bat qol (daughter of the voice) 201–202 n. 47

belief, faith, trust 6, 31, 33, 39, 43, 44–47, 52, 52 n. 5, 70, 73, 75, 81, 81 n. 23, 81 n. 24, 88, 93, 94, 99 n. 76, 104, 106, 112, 115, 115–116 n. 21, 116, 118, 121, 122, 127, 127 n. 47, 128, 129–133, 134, 143, 145, 146, 146 n. 28, 153, 154, 155, 156, 163, 164, 169, 177, 179, 181, 182–183 n. 15, 184, 188, 189, 190, 191, 192, 196, 200, 202, 202 n. 49, 203, 204, 205, 205 n. 59, 209, 212, 213–214, 216, 218, 225, 236, 237, 240, 244, 252–255

Bethany 185, 186, 187, 188, 189, 194, 195 n. 35, 196, 199, 226

Bethlehem 142, 142 n. 15, 146, 151

Bread of Life 11, 130–133

Cana 68, 70, 72, 76–77, 81, 105, 106, 107, 224

canonical exegesis 13 n. 36

Capernaum 81–82, 106, 125, 126, 130–131, 134, 137

charakter (exact representation) 38

charin anti charito (grace upon grace) 28

charis (grace) 28

christological titles 11

circumcision 34, 58 n. 22, 96, 141–142

cloak 197 n. 37

cross/crucifixion 27, 28, 29 n. 15, 32, 35 n. 36, 38–39, 61 n. 34, 63, 70, 73, 78, 79, 80–81, 83, 83 n. 32, 84 n. 33, 85, 85–86 n. 37, 93, 101, 103, 107, 113, 132, 134, 138 n. 4, 143, 145, 148, 152, 153, 178–179, 188, 192, 193–194, 195, 196, 200–201, 202, 202 n. 48, 202 n. 49, 204, 213, 214, 215, 217, 221, 223, 224, 225, 228, 232–236

culture of entitlement 1–4, 12, 209

culture of merit 1–4, 12, 209

darkness 12, 50 n. 2, 51, 73, 94, 150, 162, 169, 169 n. 86, 187, 203, 203 n. 53, 205, 210, 214

Subject Index

David 55 n. 12, 60 n. 31, 76 n. 6, 76 n. 8, 84 n. 32, 98–99, 102 n. 86, 142, 146, 174, 212, 230, 251

diabolos (devil) 135

disciples, discipleship 62, 65, 66–67 n. 45, 66–68, 81, 95, 104, 124, 125–126, 134–135, 136, 137, 146–147, 150, 154, 161–163, 163 n. 68, 167, 181, 187–188, 196–198, 201, 211–212, 214–215, 216–217, 219–224, 225–229, 239–244

donkey 197–198 n. 38

doxa (glory) 27

Elijah 29 n. 15, 57, 57–58 n. 20, 61, 62, 73, 118, 123 n. 40

Elisha 123, 123 n. 40

elohim 183

'emet (faithfulness) 28

Ephesus 16

erchomenon (was coming) 51

eucharistic language 132 n. 63

evangelical 13–14

exegeomai (to expound) 30

exodus traditions/typology 120–121, 121 n. 34, 130 n. 56

Ezekiel (the prophet) 174, 174 n. 3, 174 n. 4

Fourth Gospel, authorship 15 n. 47, 16

Fourth Gospel, historicity 15–16 n. 50, 82 n. 26, 90 n. 53, 121 n. 36, 185, 236, 238–239, 243–244

ginomai (accomplished) 25

ginosko (know) 242

glory/glorification 12, 27 n. 10, 27 n. 11, 29, 29 n. 15, 38, 49, 50 n. 2, 53, 53 n. 6, 53 n. 9, 54, 61 n. 34, 81, 81 n. 25, 100 n. 77, 102 n. 85, 119 n. 26, 138 n. 4, 153, 161 n. 60, 162, 186, 186–187 n. 24, 191, 192, 199, 200, 201, 202, 204, 204 n. 54, 204 n. 55, 211, 216, 225, 226, 227–228, 243

God the Father 6, 52 n. 5, 53–54, 60, 85, 85–86 n. 37, 86, 93–94, 96, 100–102, 100 n. 77, 101 n. 81, 101 n. 82, 102 n. 85, 103, 108, 113–114, 114 n. 15, 114–115 n. 18, 115, 116, 116 n. 23, 117, 118–119, 127 n. 47, 127 n. 48, 129–130, 131, 133, 133 n. 64, 134, 140, 143, 151, 153, 156, 158–159, 178–179, 180, 181–182, 182 n. 12, 182 n. 13, 182–183 n. 15, 184, 184 n. 21, 186–187 n. 24, 192, 201–202, 201–202 n. 47, 205, 206, 210–211, 214, 216–222, 224–228, 235, 239, 254

Good Shepherd 11, 39, 113 n. 12, 122, 129, 168, 173–179, 212, 242

Hanukkah 109 n. 2, 173, 179–180, 210

hesed (enduring love) 28

holiness 4, 20, 34 n. 35, 41, 50 n. 2, 227

Holy One of God 135, 135 n. 70, 136

Holy Spirit 6, 62, 65, 65 n. 40, 73, 88, 90–92, 101 n. 82, 134, 145, 145 n. 26, 206 n. 61, 211, 212, 218, 219, 223–224, 239

hosanna (Jewish liturgical term) 198

humanism 3

humility 3–6, 62–63, 215

I Am 11, 128, 128 n. 54, 129, 150, 153, 160–161, 177, 178, 190, 214, 217, 219

idolatry 22

Iesous (Jesus) 88

incarnation 10 n. 28, 27, 29, 38, 49, 51, 53 n. 6, 94 n. 61, 127 n. 47, 129, 132, 132 n. 63, 135 n. 70, 156, 190, 253

Ioudaioi (Jews) 86–87, 86–87 n. 39, 87 n. 40

Isaiah (the prophet) 28, 61 n. 34, 98, 204 n. 54, 210, 211

Jacob 11, 71, 71 n. 62, 72, 72 n. 66, 96, 98, 98 n. 73, 98 n. 74, 107, 210, 211

Jericho 55, 55–56 n. 14

Jerusalem 16 n. 50, 27 n. 11, 55, 55 n. 12, 58, 61 n. 34, 83, 84 n. 32, 85, 96, 100, 100 n. 77, 105, 109 n. 2, 111, 118, 120, 121, 122, 138, 139, 142, 148, 150, 158, 161, 163, 173, 175,

Subject Index

184, 185, 189, 193, 196–197, 197 n. 38, 198, 199, 200, 218, 228, 233

Jesus as Torah 6–12, 26–30, 81, 97–98 n. 71, 107, 111 n. 8, 114 n. 16, 119 n. 29, 124 n. 42, 128 n. 52, 132, 150, 151 n. 43, 159 n. 54, 168 n. 83, 170–171, 184 n. 21, 184 n. 23, 206, 206 n. 61, 207, 209–214, 244–245, 253 n. 16

John the Baptizer 4–5, 16 n. 50, 28, 50–68, 91, 94–95 n. 64, 95, 104, 117, 118, 121, 124, 180, 184, 202 n. 47, 209, 211

Joseph (legal father of Jesus) 70, 70 n. 57, 76, 76 n. 8, 130, 157

Judaism, Jewish life/customs 7 n. 19, 8 n. 23, 9–10 n. 26, 15 n. 50, 33–34, 40–41, 51, 51 n. 3, 52, 52 n. 3, 53 n. 7, 56 n. 15, 58 n. 22, 59 n. 24, 60 n. 31, 63, 63 n. 37, 64, 68, 69 n. 52, 69 n. 53, 71, 76, 76 n. 8, 77–78 n. 11, 78, 79–80, 80 n. 18, 82, 82 n. 26, 83 n. 31, 83–84 n. 32, 84–85, 85 n. 34, 87, 87 n. 41, 89 n. 51, 95–96, 98 n. 74, 99–100, 100 n. 77, 101, 103, 104, 109, 109 n. 1, 109 n. 2, 110, 114–115 n. 18, 117–118 n. 25, 120 n. 31, 122–123 n. 37, 123, 123 n. 39, 124, 124 n. 41, 125, 131 n. 58, 131 n. 60, 133, 136, 137–138, 139, 139 n. 5, 139–140 n. 6, 141 n. 10, 143 n. 17, 144, 146 n. 31, 150, 156, 156 n. 48, 157, 157 n. 49, 161–162, 163, 165, 165 n. 73, 166, 166 n. 77, 167 n. 81, 168 n. 83, 175 n. 6, 176–177, 179–180, 182 n. 14, 187, 189, 191, 191 n. 28, 194, 194–195 n. 34, 195, 196, 197 n. 37, 197–198 n. 38, 198, 198 n. 39, 199, 203 n. 52, 203 n. 53, 219–220, 222, 230, 233, 237, 238–239, 240

Judas Iscariot 134, 134 n. 66, 135, 148, 195, 195 n. 35, 196, 212, 214, 220, 228–229

Judea/Israel/Palestine 4, 55 n. 13, 58, 95–96, 105, 105 n. 89, 120, 121, 137, 218, 224

judgment 12, 32, 44, 56, 57 n. 19, 61 n. 34, 83, 83–84 n. 32, 85, 87 n. 40, 93, 94, 96, 107, 113, 115–117, 120, 130, 135 n. 70, 136, 151, 152, 153, 159 n. 60, 161 n. 61, 165, 169, 182, 183, 202, 204 n. 54, 204 n. 55, 205–206, 212, 213–214, 220, 223

katharismos (purged) 38

katalyo (abolish) 23

kingdom of God 3

kolpos (bosom) 29

kosmos (world) 50 n. 1, 86, 86–87 n. 39, 222–224, 226–227

Lamb of God 11, 32, 54 n. 11, 63–64, 66, 73, 85–86 n. 37, 100 n. 77, 132, 193, 211, 224, 233, 234–236, 254

law (moral) 19–48, 49

law (Mosaic) 12, 23, 29, 30–36, 39, 40, 51, 53 n. 8, 57 n. 17, 57 n. 18, 57 n. 19, 58 n. 22, 60, 63, 63 n. 37, 71, 75, 79, 80 n. 18, 90, 92, 93 n. 60, 100 n. 77, 110–111, 111 n. 7, 111 n. 8, 113, 114, 119, 119 n. 29, 133, 136, 139, 139–140 n. 6, 140 n. 8, 140 n. 9, 141, 141 n. 10, 146 n. 31, 147, 148–149, 150, 151, 151 n. 42, 151 n. 43, 152, 154 n. 46, 155, 156, 156 n. 48, 165, 168, 173, 175, 183, 198, 198 n. 38, 203, 210, 212, 222–223, 235

lawsuit/trial motif 59, 59 n. 27, 59 n. 28, 60, 75 n. 1, 86–87, 87 n. 40, 94, 113–114, 117–120, 120 n. 30, 120 n. 31, 137, 137 n. 1, 143 n. 17, 147, 150–152, 150 n. 41, 153, 161 n. 61, 164–168, 206 n. 60, 213, 223–224, 230–232

Levites 56 n. 15, 56 n. 16, 59, 85 n. 34, 118, 143, 180

life (eternal) 11

light 11, 50, 50 n. 2, 51, 73, 94, 136, 149, 150, 161, 162–163, 168–169, 169 n. 86, 180, 187, 202–203, 203 n. 53, 205, 210, 214, 253 n. 16

logos (Word) 9 n. 24, 9 n. 25, 10 n. 28, 10 n. 29, 11, 26, 27, 80, 129

Subject Index

manna 120, 120 n. 32, 121, 121 n. 34, 122, 125, 127–128, 128 n. 51, 128 n. 52, 132, 133

Mary (mother of Jesus) 70 n. 57, 76, 76 n. 6, 76 n. 8, 77–79, 81, 98, 130, 224, 234

messiah 60, 60 n. 30, 60 n. 31, 62, 67–68, 75. 84 n. 32, 88, 96, 102, 102 n. 86, 102–103 n. 87, 103, 113, 114 n. 17, 122, 124, 124 n. 43, 127, 127 n. 49, 128 n. 51, 138, 142, 142 n. 14, 142–143 n. 16, 147, 169, 180, 184 n. 21, 184 n. 23, 190, 198, 203, 203 n. 52, 230, 240, 244

miracle(s) 60, 72, 75, 75 n. 1, 75 n. 2, 75–76 n. 3, 76, 78, 79, 80, 80 n. 19, 81, 81 n. 24, 87–88, 89, 105, 106, 107, 108, 112, 114–115, 117, 118–119, 120–121, 122, 123 n. 40, 124 n. 43, 124–126, 125 n. 45, 127, 134 n. 67, 135–136, 137, 138, 141, 142, 143, 146 n. 28, 161, 162–164, 165, 166, 167, 168, 179, 180, 184, 185, 186, 187, 190, 191, 192, 196, 199, 203–204, 206 n. 60, 211, 213, 217–218, 224, 240

monogenes (one and only) 27–28, 29

Moses, Moses traditions/typology 8 n. 21, 8 n. 23, 9 n. 25, 10 n. 26, 11, 12, 28, 29, 29 n. 15, 39, 40, 52 n. 5, 53, 53 n. 7, 54 n. 10, 59 n. 28, 60, 69, 69 n. 52, 70, 74, 75, 75 n. 3, 80 n. 19, 92 n. 59, 92–93, 93 n. 60, 100, 100 n. 77, 105, 106, 110, 111, 117, 119 n. 29, 120, 120 n. 31, 120 n. 32, 122, 124, 124 n. 43, 125 n. 45, 127, 127 n. 49, 128, 128 n. 51, 128 n. 52, 131, 135–136, 140, 140 n. 8, 140 n. 9, 141–142, 145, 145 n. 27, 160, 167, 167 n. 81, 206 n. 61, 210, 211

Mount of Olives 148

nard 194, 194–195 n. 34

natsar (to guard, to watch) 70 n. 57

netser (sprout, branch, shoot) 70 n. 57

Nazareth 68, 70, 70–71 n. 57, 71, 76 n. 8, 77, 105, 130, 139 n. 6, 143

new perspective on Paul (NPP) 2, 33–35

Nicodemus 4, 88–93, 95, 97 n. 68, 104–105, 107, 146–147, 205, 236

nomos (law) 9 n. 25, 10 n. 29, 20, 28, 32, 69 n. 53

oida (know) 242

Old Testament quotations in John 61 n. 34, 63 n. 37, 120 n. 33, 145 n. 24, 174 n. 4, 175, 184 n. 21

omniscience (all knowledge) 250

palm branches/trees 198, 198 n. 39

parables 176, 176 n. 7

Passover 55 n. 12, 63, 82, 82 n. 26, 83, 84, 84 n. 33, 88, 89, 105, 109 n. 2, 110, 120, 121, 122, 123 n. 39, 124, 194, 198, 199, 200, 210, 232, 234–236, 237

Paul 2, 4–5, 209

Pentecost 82, 82 n. 27, 110, 119, 135–136, 210

Peter 15, 16, 29 n. 15, 66, 67–68, 73, 135, 135 n. 70, 136, 162, 185, 211–212, 216, 220, 229–230, 237, 240–244

Pharisees 2, 25, 57, 57 n. 17, 57 n. 18, 57 n. 19, 59, 62, 62 n. 35, 89, 90, 95, 111, 118, 124, 143, 146, 146 n. 31, 148–149, 150–152, 161 n. 61, 165, 168, 169, 173, 175, 176, 180, 189, 192, 194, 199, 205, 228

phileo (love) 242

phos (light) 51

Pilate 60, 87 n. 40, 228, 230–232, 233–234, 235–236

pleroo (fulfill) 24

pneuma/ruah (spirit/wind) 91

priests/priesthood 39–40, 56 n. 15, 56 n. 16, 57, 57 n. 19, 59, 72, 74, 85 n. 34, 118, 143, 146, 156 n. 48, 180, 194, 196, 228, 229, 230, 232, 233

prosperity gospel 1–2

prophet 99, 99 n. 76, 105

rabbi 67, 67 n. 47, 67 n. 48, 71, 89, 92 n. 57, 103, 107, 140, 187

Subject Index

rabbinic literature/rabbinicism 7 n. 20, 33–34, 40, 69 n. 52, 69 n. 53, 92 n. 59, 109 n. 1, 111 n. 7, 111 n. 8, 112, 114–115 n. 18, 115 n. 19, 119 n. 26, 119 n. 27, 124 n. 41, 127 n. 49, 131 n. 59, 132 n. 62, 136, 139 n. 5, 140 n. 7, 141, 141 n. 12, 142 n. 14, 142–143 n. 16, 144 n. 21, 146 n. 31, 154 n. 46, 156 n. 48, 158 n. 53, 162, 164 n. 71, 165 n. 73, 166 n. 77, 167 n. 81, 178, 182 n. 14, 183 n. 18, 183 n. 20, 187, 201–202 n. 47, 206 n. 60, 213

reality 247–255

regeneration/new birth 52–53, 65, 90–93, 93 n. 60, 107, 109 n. 1, 118, 134, 210–211

repentance 56, 58, 58 n. 22, 65, 73, 91, 204

resurrection 27, 27 n. 11, 57 n. 19, 70, 73, 79, 83 n. 32, 84 n. 33, 85–86, 87, 88, 101, 115, 130, 132, 133, 134, 136, 138 n. 4, 143, 145, 152, 159, 173, 179, 185, 189–192, 200–201, 202, 205, 214, 223, 236–240, 243, 244

righteousness/justification 2, 4, 20, 24, 30–31, 32, 33, 34, 34 n. 35, 35, 35 n. 36, 41–42, 43, 44–47, 50 n. 2, 90, 212, 223, 228

Sabbath 12, 34, 51, 109 n. 2, 110–111, 112, 113, 114, 114 n. 15, 131 n. 58, 135, 136, 141–142, 163, 165, 166, 213, 235, 237

Sadducees 57, 57 n. 19, 59, 143

Samaritans 95–96, 99–102, 102–103 n. 87, 104, 104 n. 88, 105, 120 n. 31, 158

Sanhedrin 40, 57 n. 18, 59, 83, 89, 95, 143, 152, 192, 194, 228, 230, 236

Satan/the devil 50 n. 2, 64, 94, 135, 136, 152–153, 156, 157, 159, 202, 202 n. 49, 214, 223, 227

scribes 57, 57 n. 17, 95, 146 n. 31, 148–149, 180

Sea of Galilee 66, 66 n. 43, 68, 82, 121, 125–126, 185, 240–241

Sermon on the Mount 20

sheep husbandry 175, 175 n. 6, 176–177

shekinah (glorious presence of God) 27 n. 11, 29 n. 15

skenoo (tabernacled) 27

Sodom and Gomorrah 4

Son of God 37–39, 52 n. 5, 52–53 n. 6, 59 n. 27, 60 n. 30, 65–66, 69 n. 52, 71, 74, 75, 126, 153, 168, 183, 183 n. 16, 190, 232, 240, 244

Son of Man 60 n. 30, 72, 73, 74, 92, 93, 93 n. 60, 116, 126, 127 n. 47, 132, 134, 153, 164, 168, 200, 202 n. 49, 203, 216, 231

Suffering Servant 64, 73, 204, 204 n. 55, 217, 236

synagogue 58 n. 22, 129, 131, 131 n. 58, 131 n. 59, 137, 139 n. 6, 164, 164 n. 71, 166, 166 n. 77, 167, 205

tabernacle, temple 12, 27, 27 n. 11, 39, 40, 55 n. 12, 56 n. 16, 57 n. 19, 72, 81–88, 83–84 n. 31, 84 n. 33, 85 n. 34, 85 n. 36, 89, 99–100, 100 n. 77, 107, 108, 109 n. 1, 111, 112, 113, 114, 122, 123 n. 37, 131 n. 58, 139, 143, 147, 148, 150, 155, 160 n. 59, 161 n. 60, 163, 165–166 n. 76, 168, 173, 179–180, 193, 194, 204, 210, 211, 224, 233, 254

Tabernacles (Jewish festival) 82, 84 n. 33, 109 n. 2, 110, 137–139, 144, 148, 150, 152, 161, 163, 164–168, 173, 198, 210

Taheb 102 n. 86

Tanakh 11 n. 33

telos (end) 35

Ten Commandments 9 n. 25, 20, 36

theos (God) 26, 29

threskos (religious) 42

Torah/*tora* 8 n. 21, 8 n. 23, 19–20, 80 n. 18, 131 n. 60, 140 n. 9, 146 n. 29, 151 n. 43

transfiguration 27, 29 n. 15, 57 n. 20, 202

Subject Index

Trinity 6, 26, 28, 38, 65, 92, 92 n. 58, 101 n. 82, 181, 181. n. 10, 182, 182 n. 12, 182 n. 13, 184, 205, 224, 225, 228, 254
triumphal entry 83, 196–200
wedding ceremony 5, 76–78, 77–78 n. 11, 79–80
wisdom, divine 3, 9 n. 24, 10 n. 29, 11, 12
wisdom, worldly 3, 12, 152–153

Reference Index

Old Testament

Genesis

1:1—2:3	58 n. 23
1:26–27	249
1:28	249
2:2–3	114
2:7	4, 163
3:1–7	21
8:8, 10	65
9:2	249
11:4	72
14:18	55 n. 12, 156 n. 48
15:5	46
15:6	46
17:1–14	141
18:16–33	4
18:27	4
21:4	141
22:1–19	46
22:8	64
22:12	46
22:13–15	160
22:19	156 n. 48
24:11	97
27:34–36	71
27:35	71 n. 62
28:10–17	71
28:12	72
32:28	71
33:18–19	96
35:6–7	71
38:11	42
47:30	187
48:3–4	71
48:15	178
48:21–22	96
49:11	76
49:24	178

Exodus

3:13–15	128
3:14	153, 160, 215, 229
4:1–9, 28–31	75 n. 3
4:11	161
4:22	157
7:1–7	75 n. 3
10:1–2	75 n. 3
12:1–11	64
12:1–30	82
12:12–13	75 n. 3
12:5	64
12:21	63
12:22	235
12:44, 48	141
12:46	236
15:24	130 n. 56
16:2, 7, 12	130 n. 56
16:4, 15	127
16:7	27 n. 10
16:10	27 n. 10
16:27	110
17:6	144
19:16	202 n. 48
20:1–17	20, 26
20:3–6	119
20:4	22
20:5	162

20:13	141	24:13–16	160–161
20:18	202 n. 48	24:14	149
21:6	183	24:16	182
22:8	183		
22:22–23	42	**Numbers**	
23:1	149	4:3	160
24:3	9 n. 25	6:12, 14	63
24:15–18	81	9:1–14	82
25:8	27	9:12	236
29:43	72	11:1	130 n. 56
30:13–16	85	11:13	122
32:13	157 n. 49	12:8	119
32:30–34	120	14:2, 27	130 n. 56
33:13	28	14:11	106
33:18	27 n. 10, 53	19:2	197
33:18–19	28	20:2–13	144
33:19-23	53	20:7–11	144
33:20	29, 131	21:5	92
33:23	53	21:6	93
34:6–7	28	21:8	93
34:7	162	21:17–18	145 n. 27
34:28	9 n. 25	23:36	144
34:29–35	81	28:16	82
35:1	9 n. 25	29:12–39	138
40:34–35	27	35:30	117
40:34–38	81		
		Deuteronomy	
Leviticus		1:1	9 n. 25
7:26–27	133	1:16–17	147
12:3	141	4:12, 15	119
14:10–25	63	4:35, 39	181
16:5–17	224	5:6–21	20, 36
16:11–16	233	5:7–10	119
16:27	233	5:8	22
17:10–14	133	5:17	141
19:18	21, 36, 43	5:24	27 n. 10
20:10	148	5:24–27	119
22:17–25	64	6:4	45, 101 n. 82, 181
23:5	82	6:4–5	119
23:33–43	138	6:4–9	131 n. 58
23:40	198	6:5	21

8:3	128	**Ruth**	
9:5, 27	157 n. 49	1:8	42
10:4	9 n. 25		
10:18	42	**1 Samuel**	
11:3	75	2:3	250
12:23–24	133	2:6	115
13:9	149	6:7–8	197
14:1–2	157	16:7	88
16:1–7	82	20:6	142
16:13	139, 144		
16:13–17	138	**2 Samuel**	
16:18–19	142	7:16	98
17:6	59, 117, 151	7:8–16	60 n. 31
17:7	149	7:12–16	142
18:15, 18	28, 60 n. 31, 61, 117, 124, 145	**1 Kings**	
18:15–22	52 n. 5	1:33	197
19:15	59, 117, 151	4:25	71
21:22–23	235	8:10–11	27
22:10	198 n. 38	8:39	88
22:22–24	148	8:60	181
27:12–13	96	17:1	57 n. 20
27:15–26	146 n. 31	18:41–46	57 n. 20
28:15	146	19:16–21	123 n. 40
29:2	75		
32:39	115	**2 Kings**	
32:47	9 n. 25	1:8	57, 57 n. 20
34:10	54 n. 10	2:11–12	58 n. 20
		2:19–22	165
Joshua		2:19–25	123 n. 40
2:1–21	47	4:18–44	165
7:19	166	4:9	123 n. 40
8:33–35	96	4:42–44	123
15:25	134 n. 66	5:1–14	165
24	40	5:7	115
24:32	96	5:10–14	163
11:2	66 n. 43	13:23	157 n. 49
		14:25	147
Judges		17:9	70 n. 57
5:10	197	18:8	70 n. 57

20:20	163	22:15	234
22:14	204 n. 54	22:18	234
24:10–17	174 n. 3	23:1	178
24:15	60 n. 31	28:9	178
25:27–29	60 n. 31	28:16	28
		29:3–4, 10–11	125

1 Chronicles

28:9	250	31:5	235
29:10–13	123 n. 39	32:2	71
		32:15–16	168

2 Chronicles

20:7	46	33:1	41
26:22	204 n. 54	34:14	41
32:30	163	34:20	236
		35:19	223
		36:9	98

Nehemiah

3:1, 32	111	37:17	41
9	40	37:25	41
9:15	127, 144	43:1	115
12:39	111	43:3	150
13:15	112	55:22	41
		60:3	81

Job

9:8	125	65:5–7	125
10:9	163	66:18	168
12:13	250	69:4	223
27:9	168	69:9	86
30:19	4	69:21	234
35:13	168	75:8	81
38:8–11	125	77:19	125
42:6	4	78:15–16, 20	144
		78:24–25	127

Psalms

		78:52	178
		80:1	174
		80:8–16	220
2:1–2	28	82:1, 2–7	183
2:6–7	71	89:3–4	142
2:6–12	175	89:4, 20, 29	175
5:12	41	89:9	125
6:4	201	89:30–37	203
8:5–8	249	92:12	198
19:13	31	103:7	141
22	28	105:8–9, 42–45	157 n. 49

105:24–25	130 n. 56	1:15	65
105:40	127	2:14	65
105:40–41	144	4:13–14	194 n. 34
106:23	120		
107:23–32	125	**Isaiah**	
109	115	1:1	204 n. 54
109:3	223	1:10	9 n. 25
109:13–15	162	1:17	42
110:4	203	2:3	9 n. 25
118:22	28	5:1–7	220
118:25–26	198	5:24	9 n. 25
119:105	9 n. 25, 50 n. 2, 150	6:1–5	204
		6:5	244
119:130	150	6:9–10	169
132:17	118	6:10	204
139:1–6	251	7:3	204 n. 54
140:13	41	7:14	70, 98
141:1	252	8:3	204 n. 54
145:19	168	9:2	149
146:8	161	9:6	199
147:5	250	9:6–7	98, 175
		9:7	203
Proverbs		11:1	175
3:11–12	86	11:3–4	142
8:35	135 n. 70	12:3	98, 145
10:28	41	20:1–4	75 n. 3
10:29	41	25:6	76, 80
11:8	41	25:6–9	84
14:32	41	26:19	115, 189
15:29	168	29:10	204
28:9	168	29:18	161, 168
		32:15	91, 145
Ecclesiastes		35:5	151, 168
3:1	138 n. 3	35:5–6	107
3:11	250	40—55	87 n. 40
3:13–18	250	40:3	56, 61
7:20	155	40:5	27 n. 10
12:7	47	40:10–11	174
		40:12–14	251
Song of Songs		41:4	153, 160, 245
1:12	194 n. 34	41:8	4

41:14	135	17:13	98, 149
42:1	61 n. 34, 65	17:21–27	112
42:7	161, 168	18:6	163
42:19	169	23:1–3	178
43—48	59	23:5–6	175
43:2, 16	125	25:15–16	81
43:3	135	30:9	175
43:5	193	31:5	76
43:10–13	153	31:31-34	33, 65, 84, 125, 253
43:13	160	31:33	92
44:3	98, 145	36:30	60 n. 31
44:3–5	91		
44:6	245		
45:9	163		

Ezekiel

47:4	135	1:1–3	174 n. 3
48:12	245	1:2–3	174 n. 3
48:16	101 n. 82, 181	1:3	174 n. 3
49:6	193	1:28	244
50:7	194	3:15	174 n. 3
51:4	150	3:24	174 n. 3
52:13—53:12	28, 73, 205	4:1–4	75 n. 3
53:1	204	5	174 n. 3
53:7	64	8:1	174 n. 3
53:8	142, 193	10:18–19	161 n. 60
53:12	233	11:22–23	161 n. 60
54:10	253	12:8–16	75 n. 3
54:13	131	14:1	174 n. 3
55:1	98, 145	15	220
56:7	84	18	162
56:9–12	174	18:31	91
58:11	145	19:10	220
59:2	155	20:1	174 n. 3
65:6–7	162	24:1	174 n. 3
		24:15–18	174 n. 3

Jeremiah

		26:1	174 n. 3
2:13	98	29:1, 17	174 n. 3
2:21	220	30:20	174 n. 3
6:19	9 n. 25	31:1	174 n. 3
8:17	93	32:1, 17	174 n. 3
9:24	4	33:21	174 n. 3
11:19	64	34:1–31	174

34:12	193	**Micah**	
34:12, 15	178	4:2	9 n. 25
34:25	253	4:4	71
36:25–27	91, 145	5:1–5	142 n. 16
37:3–12	115	5:2	175, 203
37:9–10	91	5:2, 4	142
37:24–25	60 n. 31	7:18–20	157 n. 49
37:25	203		
39:29	145	**Nahum**	
40:1	174 n. 3	1:1	147
40—44	84 n. 32		
47:1–12	145	**Zechariah**	
		3:10	71
Daniel		6:12	70 n. 57
2:20–22	250	7:9	141
7:13–14	73	9:9	197, 199
7:14	203	10:2	174
8:17	244	11:5, 8	174
9:1–19	40	12:10	236
12:2	115, 189	13:1	145
		14:8	98, 145
Hosea		14:21	85
2:22	76		
3:5	175	**Malachi**	
10:1	220	3:1	56, 142
		3:1–4	86
Joel		3:18	41
2:19, 24	80	4:5–6	57, 61
2:28–32	65, 145		
3:18	76, 80		
4:18	145 n. 27	*New Testament*	
Amos		**Matthew**	
9:1–15	175	1:1–16	76 n. 6
9:11	60 n. 31	1:19	76 n. 8
9:13	76, 125	1:21	88
9:13–15	80	1:23	70
		1:24	76 n. 8
Jonah		1:24–25	70, 81
1:17	88	2:1	105
2:9	54 n. 11		

2:5–6	142	12:1–14	142
2:14, 21	76 n. 8	12:8	112
2:22–23	105	12:12	112
2:23	70 n. 57, 147	12:24, 31	158
3:1–6	184	12:24–32	141
3:6	55	12:38–41	88
3:7	59	12:46	81
3:9	157	13:10–17	176 n. 7
3:11	62	13:13–14	204
3:16	65, 101 n. 82, 181	13:55	76 n. 8
3:17	65, 101 n. 82, 181, 202	13:57	105
		13:58	112
4:1–11	135	14:3–12	118
4:13	82	14:9	105
4:18	66	14:13	121, 122
5:17	23, 24, 35, 49, 140 n. 6	14:14	122
		14:17	122
5:17–18	21	14:22	125
5:17–19	183	14:23	125
5:17–20	19, 23–25	14:24	125
5:18	24, 25	14:25	125
5:19	25	14:26	125
5:20	25	14:27	126
5:20, 38	21	14:28–31	126
5:21–48	21, 23	14:32	126
5—7	20	14:33	126
6:1–18	2	15:1–9	21
7:28–29	21, 139	15:28	78
9:18–19, 23–36	185	16:1–4	88
9:22	112	16:16	135, 190
9:34	158	16:17	68
9:37–38	104	16:23	135
10:1	95	17:1–8	29 n. 15
10:2–4	68	17:1–13	27
10:3	188	17:2	27 n. 10
11:2	118	17:3	57 n. 20
11:5	107	17:5	202
11:11	66	17:10–13	61
11:14	61	19:1	184
11:23–24	126	20:2	122
11:30	47	20:28	194

Reference Index

21:1	196	1:11	65, 202
21:2	196, 197	1:13	135
21:3	196	1:14	118
21:7	197	1:16–18	66
21:12–17	83	1:21	82
21:42	28	1:22	139–140
22:23	189	1:24	135
22:34–40	36	1:27	135 n. 70
22:36–38	119	2:1	82
22:37–40	21	2:23—3:6	142
23:1–36	21	2:27	112
25:34–36	196	2:28	112
26:5	195	3:1–19	68
26:6	185	3:14	95
26:8–9	195	3:18	188
26:14–16	134 n. 66, 196	3:21	81
26:17	82	3:22	158
26:36	148, 228	3:22–30	141
26:38–39	201	4:10–12	176 n. 7
26:39	230	4:12	169, 204
26:26–46	152	5:21–24, 35–43	185
26:61	83	5:39	187–188
27:19	232	6:3	81, 139 n. 6
27:28	233	6:4	105
27:29	233	6:5–6	112
27:30	233	6:14	61, 105
27:40	83	6:17–29	118
27:48	234	6:34	122
27:52	187	6:38	122
28:18	218	6:40	123
28:18–20	193, 239	6:45	125
28:19	101 n. 82, 181	6:46	125
		6:47	125

Mark

		6:48	125
1:2–6	184	6:49–50	125
1:4	55	6:51	126
1:5	55, 57	7:1–23	21
1:6	57	7:9	111
1:7	62	7:19	24
1:8	62	7:33	163
1:10	65	8:23	163

8:27	135	1:5	57
8:31	60 n. 31	1:5–45	54
8:33	135	1:8–10	85 n. 36
9:2–8	29 n. 15	1:17	61, 118
9:2–13	27	1:27	70
9:4	57 n. 209	1:31	88
9:7	202	1:31–33	175
9:31	60 n. 31	1:32	76 n. 6, 98, 99
10:1	184	1:33	99
10:33–44	60 n. 31	1:36	64
10:45	193, 215	2:1–7	142
11:2	197	2:4	105
11:12–18	83	2:14	199
12:28–30	119	2:19, 51	76 n. 6
12:29	45, 101 n. 82	2:21–23	21
12:41	150	2:25–38	85 n. 36
14:3	194 n. 34	2:37	105
14:3–5	195 n. 34	2:39, 51	105
14:4–5	195	2:39–40, 51–52	76 n. 8
14:10–11	134 n. 66	2:40	139 n. 6
14:12–26	82	2:42–48	76 n. 8
14:13–15	228	2:47	139
14:32	148, 228	2:49	85
14:32–42	152	2:52	139 n. 6
14:34–36	201	3:3–6	184
14:36	230	3:15	60
14:53–65	230	3:16	62
14:58	83	3:22	65, 202
15:1	230	4:1–13	135
15:2–5	230	4:14–15	76 n. 8
15:6–15	231	4:16	21, 105
15:16	233	4:16–21	131 n. 58
15:29	83	4:16–30	70 n. 57, 105
15:34	235	4:24	105
15:36	234	4:34	135
15:39	153	5:1	66 n. 43
15:43–46	205	6:1–11	142
16:15	239	6:5	112
		6:14–16	66
Luke		6:15	188
1:2	76 n. 6	7:11–17	185

7:22	107	19:45–46	83
7:24–28	61	21:1	150
8:2	239	21:37–38	148
8:9–10	176 n. 7	21:38	147
8:10	204	22:3–6	134 n. 66
8:19	81	22:39	148
8:41–42, 49–56	185	22:39–46	152
9:9	118	22:42	152, 201, 230
9:10	121	23:6–12	231
9:11	122	23:46	235
9:13	122	23:47	235
9:14	123	23:48	235
9:20	135	23:49	235
9:28–36	27, 29 n. 15	23:50–53	205
9:30–31	57 n. 20	23:50–56	236
9:35	202	22:51	230
9:51	193, 194	24:25–27, 44–47	28, 119
10:2	104	24:25–27, 44–49	70
10:15	126	24:37–38	239
10:37	97	24:39	239
10:38–42	186	24:44	37
11:15	158	24:45–46	60 n. 31
11:16, 29–32	88	24:45–47	70
13:12	78	24:46–49	239
13:22	194	24:47	193
13:34	16 n. 50	24:50–51	185
16:8	203 n. 53	24:53	147
16:31	119		
17:10–12	228	**John**	
17:11	194	1—4	109
18:9–14	2	1—12	210–214
18:31	194	1:1	6, 9 n. 25, 10 n. 28, 11, 26, 156
19:10	169	1:1–2	128
19:28, 41	194	1:1, 14	53 n. 6, 115 n. 20, 129
19:29	196	1:1, 14, 18	205
19:30	196	1:1, 14, 16–18	26–30, 49
19:31	196	1:1–13	11
19:32–34	197	1:1–14	49, 129
19:35	197		
19:36	199		
19:38	198, 199		

Reference Index

1:1–18	8, 16, 71 n. 58
1:2	229
1:2–5, 9	94
1:3	80
1:5	149
1:6, 8–15	12
1:6–8	50
1:9	50 n. 1, 51, 202
1:10	50 n. 1, 51
1:11	50 n. 1, 62, 105
1:12	26, 52, 155
1:12–13	12
1:12–13, 29	193
1:13	53, 134
1:14	6, 9 n. 25, 10 n. 28, 11, 26, 27, 27 n. 11, 84 n. 33, 141, 156
1:14–18	54
1:15	28, 54
1:16	28
1:17	10 n. 26, 11, 12, 28, 69 n. 53, 141
1:18	11, 29, 54 n. 10, 129
1:17–18	6, 119 n. 29
1:18	29, 53 n. 6, 101, 119, 151, 156
1:19	59, 118
1:19–28	5 n. 16, 50–63, 180
1:19–42	50–68
1:19—2:11	58
1:20	60, 124
1:21	61, 124
1:22	61
1:23	61, 61 n. 34
1:24	59, 62, 62 n. 35, 118
1:26	62
1:27	62
1:28	58, 66
1:29	11, 22, 32, 54 n. 11, 63, 64, 78, 230
1:29–34	63–66
1:30	5, 64
1:31	65
1:31–36	5–6
1:32–33	65
1:33	62
1:34	11, 61 n. 34, 65–65
1:35	6, 66
1:35–37	16 n. 50
1:35–42	66–68
1:35–51	81
1:36	6, 11, 54 n. 11, 66
1:37	66
1:38	67
1:39	67
1:40	66
1:41	11, 67
1:42	65, 68
1:43–51	68–73
1:43	68
1:44	66, 68, 122, 200
1:45	10 n. 26, 12, 68, 69, 70 n. 57
1:46	70, 105
1:47	71, 76
1:48	71
1:49	11, 66, 67, 71
1:49–51	180
1:50	72
1:51	8 n. 23, 11, 72, 73, 84 n. 33, 92, 116
2:1	68, 76
2:1–2	76
2:1–11	76–81, 105
2:1–12	109 n. 1
2:3	77
2:4	78, 81, 224

Reference Index

2:6–7	79
2:8	79
2:9	80
2:10	80
2:11	75, 78, 79, 81
2:12–22	81–88
2:13	82, 88
2:13–22	84 n. 32
2:13–25	109 n. 1
2:14	85
2:15	85
2:16	85
2:17	15 n. 47, 85–86 n. 37, 86
2:17–22	84 n. 33
2:18	86–87
2:18–21	12
2:18–22	84 n. 33
2:19	83
2:20	160 n. 59
2:22	10 n. 26, 15 n. 47
2:23	82, 88, 106
2:23–25	89
2:23—3:21	88–94
2:24	71, 88, 126, 168
2:25	88, 165
3	97 n. 68, 109 n. 1
3:1	89
3:1–2	205
3:1–21	89
3:2	11, 67, 89, 92 n. 57
3:3	90, 90 n. 54
3:3, 5–8	134
3:3–5	90 n. 53
3:4	90, 128
3:5	90
3:6	91
3:7	91
3:8	65 n. 40, 91
3:9	92
3:10	89, 92, 92 n. 57
3:11	92
3:12	92
3:13	92
3:14	12, 93
3:15	93
3:16	11, 50 n. 1, 87 n. 39, 93, 97, 193, 209
3:16–17	154, 178
3:16–21	93
3:17	11, 94, 169
3:18	11, 66, 94
3:19	87 n. 39, 94
3:19–21	51, 203
3:20	94
3:21	94
3:22	16 n. 50
3:22–35	4–6
3:22–36	94–95 n. 64, 95
3:31	90, 92
3:33	141
3:34	11
3:36	11, 165
4	109 n. 1
4:1–26	95–103
4:1–42	95–107
4:1	95
4:2	95
4:3	105
4:3–4	95
4:4–5	96
4:6	97
4:7	97
4:8	97
4:9	97
4:10	97
4:10–12, 32–38	90 n. 53
4:10–14	65 n. 40
4:11	98
4:11–12	11, 97
4:12	72 n. 66, 98, 98 n. 74

Reference Index

4:13	99	4:50	106
4:14	99	4:51	106
4:15	99, 128	4:52	106
4:16	99	4:53	106
4:17–18	99	4:54	106
4:19	11, 99, 99 n. 76	5	109, 109 n. 2
4:20	96, 99	5—6	135
4:20–24	84 n. 33	5:1	82, 110, 119
4:21	78, 100	5:1–15	110–113, 141
4:22	101	5:1–47	110–120
4:23	101	5:2	111
4:24	53, 101	5:3	111
4:25	102	5:4	111
4:25–26	180	5:5	112
4:26	103	5:6	112
4:27	103	5:7	112
4:27–42	103–105	5:8	12, 112, 122
4:28	103	5:9	112, 122
4:28–30	164	5:9, 16	110
4:29	11, 103	5:10	112
4:30	103, 104	5:11	112, 113 n. 12
4:31	67, 103	5:12	113
4:32	103	5:13	113, 113 n. 12
4:33	103	5:14	113, 113 n. 12, 162
4:34	6, 103, 114, 163	5:15	113 n. 12
4:35	104	5:16, 18	113
4:36	104	5:16–30	113–117
4:37–38	104	5:17	114
4:39	104	5:18	26, 114
4:40	104	5:19	114
4:41	104	5:19–27	11
4:42	87 n. 39, 87 n. 40, 193	5:20	72, 114
		5:21	115
4:43	105	5:22	115, 165, 169
4:43–54	105–107	5:23	114 n. 18, 115, 158 n. 53, 163, 165
4:44	105		
4:45	105, 106	5:24	116, 159
4:46	76, 105	5:25	66, 116
4:47	106	5:25, 28–29	192
4:48	105, 106	5:26	116, 116 n. 23
4:49	106	5:27	116, 153, 169

Reference Index

5:28	117	6:11	123, 123 n. 39
5:28–30	115	6:12	124
5:29	117	6:13	124, 127 n. 47
5:30	11, 117, 169	6:14	11, 51, 124, 124 n. 43
5:31	117	6:14–15	60 n. 31, 88
5:31–47	60, 117–120	6:14–21	124–126
5:32	117, 117–118 n. 25	6:15	11, 113, 125
5:33	117, 118	6:16–17	125
5:34	118	6:18	125
5:35	118	6:19	125
5:35–37	129	6:20	126
5:36	117, 118, 180	6:21	126
5:37	119, 163	6:22	126
5:38	12, 119	6:22–59	126–133
5:39	8 n. 23, 10 n. 26, 117, 119 n. 27	6:23	126
5:38–39	10 n. 28	6:24	126
5:39–40	119	6:25	67, 126
5:41	119	6:26	126
5:42	119	6:27	127, 153
5:43	119	6:28	127, 134
5:44	119	6:29	127, 134
5:45	120, 206 n. 60	6:30	126, 127
5:45–46	110	6:31	127
5:45–47	6, 10 n. 26, 12, 70, 120 n. 32	6:32	10 n. 26, 128
5:46	28, 117	6:33	128
5:46–47	120	6:34	128
6	109 n. 2, 120, 120 n. 32	6:35	123 n. 39, 128, 219, 229
6:1	66 n. 43, 121	6:36	129
6:1–13	120–124	6:37	129
6:1–47	120–135	6:38	114 n. 18, 129
6:2	122	6:39	130, 229
6:3	122	6:40	130
6:4	82, 121, 124	6:41	130, 130 n. 56, 158
6:4–51	90 n. 53	6:41–42	92
6:5	122	6:42	130, 130 n. 57
6:6	122	6:43	130
6:7	122	6:44	131
6:10	123	6:45	61 n. 34, 131
		6:45–51	6

Reference	Pages
6:46	29, 131
6:47	131
6:48	132, 219
6:49	132
6:49–51	11
6:50	132
6:51	132, 132 n. 62
6:52	132, 132 n. 63
6:53	132
6:54	133
6:55	133
6:56	133
6:57	133, 133 n. 64
6:58	133
6:59	131
6:60	134
6:60–66	88
6:60–71	134–135
6:61	134
6:62	134
6:63	65 n. 40, 134
6:64	134, 168
6:65	134
6:67	135
6:68	11, 135, 135 n. 70, 185
6:69	11, 135, 135 n. 70
6:70	135
6:71	134 n. 66
7	110
7—8	109 n. 2
7—9	137–169
7:1	95, 137
7:1–13	137–139
7:1—8:59	137–161
7:2	137
7:3	138
7:4	138
7:5	138
7:6	138, 225
7:7	50 n. 1, 138
7:8	139, 225
7:9	139
7:10	139
7:11	139
7:12	139
7:13	139
7:14	139
7:14–24	139–142
7:15	139, 140
7:16	140
7:16–18	11
7:16–19	6
7:17	140
7:18	140
7:19	12, 70, 141
7:19, 22–28	10 n. 26
7:20	141, 158, 179
7:21	141
7:21–23	12
7:22	141
7:23	141
7:24	112, 142
7:25	142
7:25–36	142–144
7:26	142
7:27	142
7:28	141, 143, 163
7:29	143
7:30	143, 225
7:31	143
7:32	143
7:33	143
7:34	143–144
7:35	144
7:36	144, 147
7:37	144
7:37–38	65 n. 40, 144
7:37–52	144–147
7:38	145
7:39	27, 145
7:40	11 145

7:41	142, 146	8:20	150, 151, 225
7:42	105, 142, 146	8:21	152
7:43	146	8:21–29	152–153
7:44	146	8:22	152
7:45	144, 146	8:23	152, 153
7:46	146	8:24	11, 153, 229
7:47	146	8:25	153
7:48	146	8:26	141, 153, 163
7:49	146	8:27	153
7:50	147	8:28	11, 93, 114, 153, 153 n. 44, 180, 229
7:50–52	205	8:28–29	78
7:51	89, 147, 206 n. 60	8:29	114 n. 18, 153, 163
7:52	70, 105, 141, 147, 151	8:30	154
7:53	148	8:30–47	154–158
7:53—8:11	147–149	8:31	154
8:1–11	12	8:32	154
8:2	148	8:32–58	90 n. 53
8:3	27, 148	8:33	154, 155, 156
8:4	148	8:34	44, 155, 209
8:5	148	8:35	155
8:6	149	8:36	155, 209
8:7	149	8:37	156
8:8	149	8:38	156
8:9	149	8:39	156
8:10	78, 149	8:40	157
8:11	149	8:41	157
8:12	12, 144, 150, 161, 180, 219	8:42	157, 163
8:12, 58	161 n. 60	8:43	157
8:12–20	150–152	8:44	156, 157, 159
8:13	117, 150	8:45	157
8:14	151	8:46	158
8:14–17, 31–32, 54–58	6	8:47	158
8:15	149, 151	8:48	97, 158, 179
8:16	151, 163	8:48–52	141
8:17	10 n. 26, 151, 151 n. 43	8:48–59	158–161
8:17–18	60	8:49	158
8:18	151, 163	8:50	159
8:19	151–152	8:52	158, 159
		8:53	98, 159
		8:54	159

Reference Index

8:55	159
8:56	28, 160
8:56–58	11
8:57	160
8:58	11, 26, 128, 153, 160, 180, 229
8:59	113, 160, 161 n. 60, 182
9	113 n. 12, 161 n. 61, 161 n. 62, 164
9:1	161
9:1–3	113
9:1–7	191
9:1–7, 30–32	128
9:1–12	161–164
9:1–41	161–169
9:2	67, 162
9:3	162
9:4	162
9:5	12, 150, 161, 162, 180, 219
9:6	163
9:7	163
9:8	164
9:9	164
9:10	164
9:11	164
9:12	164
9:13	164
9:13–34	164–168
9:14	163, 169
9:14–33	12
9:15	165
9:16	165
9:17	11, 164, 165
9:18	165
9:19	166
9:20	166
9:21	166
9:22	129, 166, 166 n. 77, 205
9:23	166
9:24	166
9:25	71 n. 58, 164, 167
9:26	167
9:27	167
9:28	167, 167 n. 81
9:28–29	10 n. 26, 12, 70, 173
9:29	167
9:30	167
9:30–33	161
9:31	168
9:32	168
9:33	164, 168
9:34	164, 168, 174
9:35	113 n. 12, 153, 168
9:35–37	180
9:35–38	164
9:35–41	168–169
9:36	169
9:37	169
9:38	169
9:39	51, 165, 169
9:39–41	161 n. 61, 169 n. 86, 176
9:40	169
9:40–41	150, 173
9:41	169
10	109 n. 2
10—12	173–206
10:1	176
10:1–21	173–179
10:2	176
10:3	177
10:4	71 n. 58, 177
10:5	177
10:6	176 n. 7, 177
10:7	177, 219
10:8	177
10:9	177, 179, 219
10:10	99, 177, 209

Reference Index

10:11	129, 168, 178, 219	11:1	58, 185, 186
10:12	178	11:1–44	128
10:13	178	11:1–53	185–193
10:14	168, 178, 219	11:1–16	175–188
10:15	178	11:2	186
10:16	178, 193	11:3	186
10:17	179	11:4	66, 162, 186
10:17–18	79	11:5	186
10:18	179	11:6	186, 187
10:19–21	141	11:7	187
10:20	158, 179	11:8	67, 182, 187
10:21	179	11:9–10	187
10:22	180	11:11	187
10:22–42	179–184	11:12	188
10:23	180	11:13	188
10:24	180, 182	11:14	188
10:25	118, 180	11:11–15	90 n. 53
10:25–30, 34–38	6	11:15	188
10:26	181	11:16	188
10:27	181	11:17	186, 189
10:28	181	11:17–27	188
10:29	114 n. 18, 181	11:17–37	189–191
10:30	26, 114 n. 18, 181, 181. n. 10, 182, 205, 225	11:18	58, 189
		11:19	189
		11:20	189
10:31	182	11:21	189
10:32	182	11:22	189
10:33	182	11:23	189
10:34	11 n. 33, 151 n. 43, 183, 203	11:24	189
		11:25	11, 115, 181, 188, 190, 219
10:35	10 n. 28	11:25–26	159
10:34–35	10 n. 26	11:26	190
10:34–36	183	11:26–27	188
10:36	11, 66, 163, 183 n. 20, 184	11:27	11, 51, 66, 190
		11:28	190
10:37	184	11:28–37	188
10:38	114 n. 18, 184	11:29–31	190
10:39	113, 184, 185	11:32	186, 190
10:40	184	11:33	190
10:41	184	11:34	191
10:42	184		

11:35	191	12:12, 14	196
11:36	191	12:12–19	196–200
11:37	191	12:13	11, 198
11:38	191	12:14	197, 199
11:38–44	191–192, 194	12:16	15 n. 47, 187 n. 24, 199
11:38–53	115	12:17–18	199
11:39	189, 191	12:19	199
11:40	162, 191	12:19–20	87 n. 39
11:41	192	12:20	200
11:42	192	12:20–22	87 n. 40
11:43	192	12:20–36	200–203
11:44	192	12:21	66, 200
11:45	192	12:22	200
11:45–53	192–193	12:23	27, 79, 153, 187 n. 24, 200
11:46	192	12:24	200
11:46–53	193	12:24–26	201 n. 46
11:47	192	12:25	201
11:48	193	12:26	201
11:49	193, 230	12:27	152, 201
11:50	193, 230	12:28	27, 201, 202, 202 n. 47
11:51	193	12:29	202, 202 n. 48
11:52	178, 193	12:30	202
11:54	193	12:31	202
11:54–57	193–194	12:32	93, 153, 202
11:54—12:50	193–206	12:33	202
11:55	82, 194	12:34	10 n. 26, 11 n. 33, 69 n. 53, 93, 183, 203
11:56	194	12:35	203
11:57	194	12:35–36	11, 203 n. 53
12	205 n. 58	12:36	113, 203
12:1	58, 82, 194	12:37	204
12:1–8	186	12:37–50	203–206
12:1–11	194–196	12:38	61 n. 34, 204
12:2	185, 194	12:39–40	204
12:3	194 n. 34, 195	12:39–41	169
12:4	195	12:40	61 n. 34
12:5	195	12:41	28, 160, 204, 204 n. 55
12:6	195, 220		
12:7	195		
12:8	195		
12:9	192, 196		
12:10–11	196, 198		

Reference Index

12:42	147, 166 n. 77, 168, 205
12:43	205
12:44	163, 205
12:45	114 n. 18, 205
12:46	12, 51, 205, 206 n. 60
12:47	169, 206
12:48	12, 206
12:49	140, 206
12:50	114, 206
13	214–216
13—17	228
13—21	214–244
13:1	79, 81, 82, 179, 214
13:2	214
13:2, 27	135
13:2, 36	134 n. 66
13:3, 11	214
13:5	62
13:6	185
13:12	215
13:13	215
13:13–14	21
13:14	215
13:14–16	201
13:15	215
13:16	114 n. 18, 215
13:17	215
13:18	10 n. 26
13:19	214
13:23	15
13:23–25	243
13:29	220
13:31	187 n. 24
13:31–32	27
13:31–38	216
13:37	229
13:38	229
14	216–219
14:1	216
14:1–3	244
14:2	217
14:3	217
14:4	217
14:4	217
14:5	217
14:6	11, 28, 72, 116, 141, 154, 217, 219, 231
14:6–7, 9–11	6
14:7, 9	54
14:7	217
14:8	54
14:9	30, 54 n. 11, 114 n. 18, 119, 151, 205, 217
14:10	218
14:10–11, 20	184
14:11	180, 218
14:12	72, 218
14:15	20, 181, 218, 219
14:16	11, 65 n. 40, 181, 218
14:17	65 n. 40, 141, 218
14:18	218
14:19	219
14:20	219
14:21	219
14:23	219
14:24	163, 219
14:25	219
14:26	65 n. 40, 88, 219
14:28	181
14:30	202
14:31	219
15	210–223
15:1	219
15:1–10	11
15:2	220
15:3	220
14:4	220
15:5	133, 220

Reference	Pages
15:6	220
15:7	220
15:8	201 n. 46, 220
15:8, 16	133
15:9	221
15:10	114, 181, 221
15:11	221
15:12	221
15:13	179, 215, 221
15:14	221
15:15	221
15:16	222
15:17	222
15:18	222
15:18–19	50 n. 1, 138
15:19	222
15:18–25	94
15:18—16:4	201
15:21	222
15:22	222
15:23	114 n. 18, 222
15:24	180, 222
15:25	10 n. 26, 10 n. 28, 11 n. 33, 151 n. 43, 183, 203, 222
15:26	65 n. 40, 141, 223
15:27	223
16	223–224
16:2	166 n. 77, 168
16:7	65 n. 40
16:8	65 n. 40, 223
16:9	223
16:10	223
16:11	202, 223
16:12	224
16:13	141, 223
16:13–14	65 n. 40
16:14	224
16:15	224
16:28	51
17	224–228
17:1	79, 187 n. 24
17:1, 4–5	27
17:1, 5	192
17:1–5	224
17:2	225
17:2–5	153
17:3	11, 141, 225
17:4	187 n. 24, 225
17:5	159, 225
17:6	226
17:6–19	224
17:7	226
17:8	226
17:9	226
17:10	226
17:11	26, 227
17:11–12	181
17:11–14	226
17:12	10 n. 26, 229
17:15	227
17:16	227
17:17	227
17:18	114 n. 18, 227
17:19	227
17:20	227
17:20–23	178, 193
17:20–26	224
17:21	181, 224
17:21–23	184
17:22	227
17:23	228
17:24	228
17:25	228
17:26	228
18	228–231
18:1	228
18:1–2	134 n. 66
18:2	228
18:3	229
18:4	229
18:5	229

Reference	Page
18:6	229
18:7	229
18:8	229
18:9	229
18:10	229
18:11	81, 230
18:12	230
18:12–14, 19–23	230
18:13	230
18:14	230
18:19–24	230
18:28	82
18:28–40	231
18:28—19:22	197 n. 36
18:31	148
18:33	231
18:33–37	11, 60 n. 31
18:34	231
18:35	231
18:36–37	125, 231
18:37	141
18:38	231
18:39	82, 231
18:40	231
19	231–236
19:1–3	231
19:4	231
19:5	11, 231
19:6	231
19:7	66
19:10	232
19:11	90, 232
19:12	232
19:13	232
19:14	82, 232
19:15	232
19:16	232, 233
19:17	233
19:18	233
19:19	233
19:19–22	11
19:20	233
19:21	234
19:22	234
19:23	234
19:24	234
19:24, 28, 36–37	10 n. 26
19:25	234
19:26	15, 78, 234
19:27	234
19:28	234
19:29	234
19:30	103, 235
19:31	235
19:32	236
19:33	236
19:34	236
19:35	15, 236
19:36	236
19:37	236
19:38–40	205
19:38–42	236
19:39–42	89
20	236–240
20:1	237
20:2	15, 237
20:3	237
20:4	237
20:5	237
20:6	237
20:7	237
20:8	237
20:9	10 n. 26, 15 n. 47, 237
20:10	237
20:11	237
20:12	238
20:13	238
20:14	238
20:15	78, 238
20:16	11, 67, 238

20:17, 30–31	182, 238	21:23	243
20:18	11, 238	21:24	15, 243
20:19	239	21:25	106, 147
20:20	239		
20:21	115 n. 18, 239	**Acts**	
20:21–23	216	1:5	65
20:22	65 n. 40, 239	1:6	60 n. 31, 125
20:23	239	1:8	193, 218, 239
20:24	240	1:13	68–69, 188
20:24–29	188	1:14	138
20:25	240	2:1–4	65, 145, 239
20:26	240	2:16–21	65
20:27	240	2:23–24	179
20:28	11, 169, 240	2:27	135
20:29	240	2:29–32	70
20:30–31	75, 161, 190, 209, 240	2:36	117
20:31	17, 66	2:38	65
21	240–244	3:1–7	161
21:1	241	3:11	180
21:2	76, 241	3:18, 21, 24	70
21:3	241	3:22	117, 145
21:4	241	4:11, 25–26	28
21:5	241	4:12	152
21:6	241	4:27–28	179
21:7	11, 15, 241	5:12	180
21:8	241	7:32–36	40
21:9	241	7:37	117
21:10	241	7:37–43	40
21:11	241	7:44–53	41
21:12	241	7:52	41
21:13	241	7:52–53	70
21:14	241	7:60	188
21:15	242	7:54–60	41
21:16	242	8:30–35	70
21:17	242	10:2, 44–48	106
21:18	243	10:15	24
21:19	243	10:42	169
21:20	15, 243	10:43	119
21:21	243	11:14	106
21:22	243	11:15–16	65
		15:11	33

15:29	133	5:12	21
16:15, 31–34	106	5:13	21
17:31	115, 169	6:1–7	22
18:8	106	6:1–14	31
23:7–8	189	6:6	30–36
26:22–23	70	6:14	30–36
28:23	70	6:15–18	31, 209
28:26–27	204	7:5	31
		7:5–6	30–36

Romans

		7:6	31, 33
1:2	30, 37, 119	7:7–11	21
1:3	87	7:7–25	25, 40
1:17	31	7:10	8 n. 23
1:20	252	7:12	22, 29, 212
1:32	94	7:21–23	32
2:16	169	8:1	22, 32
2:17–29	141	8:2	32
3:2	141, 212	8:1–4	30–36
3:3–4	118	8:3	32
3:9	32	8:4	22, 32
3:9–18	43, 138	8:31–39	181
3:20	20, 21	9:4	92, 141
3:21	30–36, 37, 119, 212	9:4–5	155
3:22	31, 212	9:5	26
3:23	21, 22, 43, 155	9:8	156
3:24	43	9:30–32	30–36
3:25–26	46	9:30–33	24
3:27	32	9:31	2
3:28	30–36, 45, 46	10:2–3	2
3:31	30–36	10:3	33
4:1–25	157	10:3–4	30–36
4:3	46	10:4	19, 35, 49, 119
4:9–17	156	11:8	204
4:15	21	11:33–36	251
5:1	72	11:36	252
5:1, 9–11	169	12:1–2	90
5:1–11	32	13:1–7	183
5:2	27 n. 11	13:8	36
5:5	209	13:8–10	30–36, 49
5:6	32	13:9	36
5:10	32	13:10	36

14:7	125	3:2	65
15:3	86	3:7	157
		3:8	30, 160

1 Corinthians

		3:6	46
1:22	87	3:11	46
1:23–24	134	3:19–24	21
1:26–30	3	3:21	8 n. 23
1:29	3–4	3:24	36
1:30	4, 209, 253	3:28	178
1:31	4	4:4	21
2:8	153	5:13–14	20
3:5–9	104	5:14	36
5:7	64, 82	5:22	36
5:21	140 n. 6, 235	6:2	8 n. 22, 20, 36
8:4, 6	181	6:10	36
8:4–6	101 n. 82	6:16	193
9:21	8 n. 22, 20		

Ephesians

10:3	28	1:17	253
10:4	144	2:2	94, 152, 202
11:30	162	2:8	28
12:3	209	2:8–9	45, 127
12:3–6	181	2:11–22	178
12:13	65, 178	2:12	158
13:12	251	3:6	178
15:7	138	4:22–24	90
15:35–57	27 n. 11	5:8	203 n. 53
15:51	188	5:9	50 n. 2
		5:11	50 n. 2

2 Corinthians

		5:25	97
4:4	50 n. 2, 157, 202	6:12	202
5:10	169		
5:17	80, 90 n. 54		

Philippians

5:18–21	169	2:6	26, 29, 54, 183
5:21	157, 201	2:6–8	27
12:7	162	2:6–11	153, 205
12:11	4	3:3	134
13:14	101 n. 82, 181	3:5–6	2
		3:20–21	27 n. 11

Galatians

2:16	33, 46
2:20	97

Colossians

1:15	30, 53, 54, 183
1:16	254
1:19	27
2:9	26, 27, 30, 54, 183
3:9–10	90

1 Thessalonians

4:13	188
5:5	203 n. 53

1 Timothy

2:5	39, 54 n. 11, 72, 120
4:4	22
6:16	27 n. 10, 29

2 Timothy

4:1	169

Titus

2:11–12	31
2:11–14	45
3:5	91, 127
3:5–7	90
3:16–17	140

Hebrews

1:1	28, 29, 37
1:1–3	39
1:1–4	36–41, 49
1:2	28, 29, 37, 38, 254
1:3	26, 27, 28, 30, 38, 53 n. 6, 54, 129, 183
1:4–14	39
2:5	39
2:5–9	249
2:10	39
3:1–6	39
3:1–7	29
4:5	27
4:6–11	39
4:13	250
4:14–16	72
4:15	140 n. 6, 157
5:1–10	39
6:4–8	94, 120
6:20—7:25	39
7:1–10	39
7:26	27, 54 n. 11, 140 n. 6
7:26–28	22
7:26—8:2	39
7:27	224
8:1–5	39
8:3–6	39
8:6	39
8:7	39
8:7–13	39, 253
8:8	40
8:8–13	36–41, 49
8:13	22, 25, 40
9:1, 9–10, 23–27	22
9:14	39
9:1–28	39
9:28	169
10:1	29, 168
10:1–14	39
10:11	39
10:22	39
11:6	252
11:6, 31	47
11:8–12, 17–19	157
11:17–19	46, 160
11:28	82
11:37	204 n. 54
12:2	39
12:5–6	86
12:18–24	39
12:18–29	23
13:8	128
13:11	233

Reference Index

13:12	233
13:13	233
13:20	39, 175

James

1:1	193
1:3	122
1:19–20, 22-27	41–47, 49
1:19	41
1:20	41
1:22	42
1:23–24	42
1:25	42, 44
1:26	42
1:27	42–43
2:1–7	43
2:8	43, 49
2:8–27	41–47, 49
2:9	43
2:10	25, 43
2:11	43
2:12	44
2:13	44
2:14	45
2:14–27	44
2:16–17	45
2:18	45
2:19	45, 181
2:20	45
2:21	46
2:21–23	157
2:22	46
2:23	46
2:24	46
2:25	47
2:26	47
3:14	3
3:15	3, 153
3:16	3
4:5	86

4:17	42
5:7	57 n. 20
5:16	168

1 Peter

1:1	193
1:3	90
1:3–5	181
1:7	122
1:10–12	28
1:18–19	54 n. 11, 193
1:19	64
2:4–5	178
2:7–8	120
2:8	94
2:9–10	178
2:24	64
3:3	50 n. 1
3:18	224
4:5	169
4:12–19	162
5:4	175

2 Peter

1:1	26
1:13	243
1:14	243
1:20–21	140

1 John

1:1–4	15
2:2	32, 63
3:5	157
3:8–15	157
3:16–18	36
3:18	47
3:21–22	168
4:12	29
4:14	104
4:17	44
5:2–3	20

5:3	47	21:2	100 n. 77, 254
5:9	118	21:3	100 n. 77
5:9–12	70	21:22	84, 100 n. 77, 254
5:10	118	21:23	100 n. 77
5:10–12	94	22:3	100 n. 77
5:11	118	22:4	100 n. 77
5:12	118	22:20	245
5:19	138	22:21	254
5:20	158		
5:21	22		

2 John

1	16

3 John

1	16

Revelation

1:1	254
1:4, 8	128
1:5	64
1:5–8	254
1:8	244, 245
1:9	243
1:16	27 n. 10
1:17	244, 245
1:18	245
4:8	128
5:6	64
5:9	64
7:9	198
7:14	64
7:17	175
11:17	128
12:11	64
12:12	202
16:5	128
19:11–21	202
19:16	209
20:7–15	202
21:1	100 n. 77

Old Testament Apocrypha

Baruch

3:29—4:1	9 n. 24
3:37—4:1	135 n. 70
4:1	183 n. 20
4:1–2	118

1 Esdras

9:8	166

2 Esdras

13:30–35	206 n. 60

1 Maccabees

1:59	179
4:36–59	179
9:39	5
13:51	198
14:49	150

2 Maccabees

1:2	157 n. 49
1:9, 18	179
2:21	7 n. 19
3:6, 24, 28, 40	150
4:13	7 n. 19
8:1	7 n. 19
10:1–8	179
10:7	198

14:4	198	48:47	206 n. 60
14:38	7 n. 19		

1 Enoch

10:19	80
42:1–3	135 n. 70
48:1	97
48:6	142 n. 14
48:6–7	143
49:1	97, 201, 203 n. 52
62:14	125, 201, 203 n. 52
89:45	64
90:6, 9–19, 37–38	64
90:28–36	84 n. 32
99:2	183 n. 20

4 Maccabees

1:16–17	9 n. 24
6:17, 22	157
18:1	157

Sirach

15:1	9 n. 24
15:1–3	121
19:20	9 n. 24
24:1, 23–24	9 n. 24
24:20–23	121
24:21	128
33:13	163
34:8	9 n. 24
39:1	9 n. 24
45:5	8 n. 23
48:1	118

2 Enoch

3:8	9 n. 24

4 Ezra

7:28	143
7:28–29	201
13:51–52	142 n. 14, 143

Tobit

13:2	115

Psalms of Solomon

17—18	201
17:4	203 n. 52
17:30	84 n. 32

Wisdom of Solomon

7:26	150
9:1–2	9 n. 24
9:3	206 n. 60
16:13	115
16:26	121
18:3–4	150
18:15	9 n. 24

Testament of Benjamin

3:8	64

Testament of Joseph

19:8–11	64

Old Testament Pseudepigrapha

2 Baruch

29:3	143
29:5	80
29:8	127

Rabbinic Works

Apocalypse of Abraham

9–32	160 n. 56

Baba Mesia

7:9	178

Bavli Sukkah

27b	147 n. 33

Genesis Rabbah

1:4	157
17:5	9 n. 24
31:5	9 n. 24
39:11	90 n. 54
43:6	156 n. 48
44:17	9 n. 24
44:21–22, 25	160 n. 56
56:11	156 n. 48
59:6	160
70:5	121
92:1	154 n. 46
98:9	146 n. 29
100:7	187

Exodus Rabbah

18:3	120 n. 31
21:3	147
43	120 n. 31

Leviticus Rabbah

11:3	9 n. 24
18:1	187
19:1	9 n. 24

Numbers Rabbah

10:8	154 n. 46

Ecclesiastes Rabbah

1:9	145 n. 27
3:1	138 n. 3
12:6	187

Pesiq Rabbah

15:2	154 n. 46

Mishnah Sabbath

7:2	165 n. 73

Mishnah Sanhedrin

6:2	166
7:5	182 n. 14
97a	142 n. 14

Mishnah Sukkah

4:1	144

Mishnah Yebamoth

16:3	187

Targum Moses

12:6	120 n. 31

Targum Psalms

68:19	92 n. 59